Marx's Inferno

❖❖❖

Marx's Inferno

❖❖❖

THE POLITICAL THEORY OF *CAPITAL*

William Clare Roberts

PRINCETON UNIVERSITY PRESS

PRINCETON AND OXFORD

Copyright © 2017 by Princeton University Press

Published by Princeton University Press, 41 William Street, Princeton, New Jersey 08540

In the United Kingdom: Princeton University Press, 6 Oxford Street, Woodstock, Oxfordshire OX20 1TR

press.princeton.edu

Jacket art: William Blake, *The Demons Tormenting Ceampolo*, from the illustrated *Divine Comedy*, Canto XXII, 1824. Lebrecht Music and Arts Photo Library / Alamy.

Library of Congress Cataloging-in-Publication Data

Names: Roberts, William Clare, 1974– author.
Title: Marx's Inferno : the political theory of Capital / William Clare Roberts.
Description: Princeton : Princeton University Press, [2017] | Includes bibliographical
    references and index.
Identifiers: LCCN 2016012489 | ISBN 9780691172903 (hardcover : alk. paper)
Subjects: LCSH: Marx, Karl, 1818–1883. Kapital. | Dante Alighieri, 1265–1321.
    Inferno. | Capitalism—Political aspects.
Classification: LCC HB501.M37 R595 2017 | DDC 335.4/12—dc23
LC record available at https://lccn.loc.gov/2016012489

British Library Cataloging-in-Publication Data is available

This book has been composed in Sabon LT Std

Printed on acid-free paper. ∞

Printed in the United States of America

1 3 5 7 9 10 8 6 4 2

Dedicated to H., my ever-present future,
and to the memory of my father, Joe,
who should have lived to see this.

Contents

Acknowledgments

I am not so much the parent of these thoughts and arguments as I am their child. And I have had many midwives, who have, through their engagement, criticism, conspiracy, and nourishment, assisted in my birth.

I first noticed and began to ask questions about Marx's Dante citations in a reading group led by Dan Conway and made incredibly stimulating by the participation of Hasana Sharp and Mike Schleeter. My mentor, Dan, always emboldened my outlandish thoughts. He also put me into contact with Terrell Carver and John Seery, whose attention to the political, rhetorical, and literary complications of Marx's texts pointed me in the right direction, and who have continued to provoke, support, and sustain my research ever since.

My colleagues at McGill University, in both the Department of Political Science and the Research Group on Constitutional Studies, have created an ideal environment for working on this book. They are generous with their time and interest, open and curious interlocutors, and perceptive and always-helpful readers and commenters. My argument and scholarship are much stronger for their inspiration, example, and support. In particular, I would thank Arash Abizadeh, Phil Buckley, Jacob Levy, Catherine Lu, Hudson Meadwell, Victor Muñiz-Fraticelli, Hasana Sharp, Christina Tarnopolsky, Tim Waligore, and Yves Winter.

Numerous students have participated, in one way or another, in the writing of this book. Without downplaying the contributions of others, I would single out several for special mention: Kristin Li, Tara Myketiak, Cameron Fleming, Cameron Cotton-O'Brien, and Chris Brzovic have all discussed the book project with me at length. The students from my first seminar on republicanism and my topics course on Marx and Proudhon listened patiently to my crazy ramblings and offered a wealth of questions and comments. Three students have provided me especially valuable research assistance. Lola Duffort was particularly helpful when I was wrestling with Proudhon, and she generously corrected my French. Jake Bleiberg helped immensely with the initial research, bringing much-needed interest, skepticism, and curiosity to the project. Kyle Jacques was indefatigable and, frankly, invaluable; without his intelligent and apt assistance, the research and writing would have taken twice as long and been half as good. In addition, Eric Tweel and Nicholas Dunn helped in the final stages of manuscript preparation.

Much of my research was undertaken with the support of a grant from the Fonds de recherché du Quebec—Societé et culture. Much of the writing was done while I was a visiting research fellow at CRÉUM, the Centre de recherche en éthique de l'Université de Montréal. I must thank especially Christine Tappolet, Peter Dietsch, and—above all— Valéry Giroux for making my time there so productive. Lawrence & Wishart have generously allowed me to reproduce extracts from their fifty-volume edition of the collected works of Marx and Engels (London: Lawrence & Wishart, 1970–2005).

Early versions of several chapters were delivered as talks at the American Political Science Association, the Association for Political Theory, the Groupe de recherche interuniversitaire en philosophie politique, the University of Alberta, and the Centre de recherche en éthique de l'Université de Montréal. Many thanks to those who listened and questioned.

Several people read the entire manuscript and offered their intelligent and well-informed criticism, challenges, commentary, and advice, without which this would be a far-inferior book, if it were a book at all. Gregory Claeys, John Seery, Peter Dietsch, Pablo Gilabert, and Gavin Walker contributed to an all-day workshop on the manuscript, which tempered and sharpened every aspect of the argument. Jacob Levy, Yves Winter, Arash Abizadeh, Hasana Sharp, Catherine Lu, and Victor Muñiz-Fraticelli all took time out of their schedules to attend the workshop and offer their comments, as well. I am forever in their debt. Thanks also to Bruno Leipold, Ethan Sawyer, and Niko Block for their comments and suggestions. Sam Chambers read an early version of the manuscript and gave copious and perceptive feedback, as well as much-needed encouragement and advice.

Special thanks are due to Jacob Levy, who has championed me and my work since 2007. He has been an invaluable mentor and senior colleague, and he is, perhaps, the most fair-minded person I have ever known. We may be on opposing sides, politically and theoretically, but he is the sort of opponent everyone ought to wish for, the sort whose intelligence and virtue compel one to become better in order not to concede defeat.

I also owe an especially profound debt to four people who read not only the whole manuscript, but multiple drafts of individual chapters, providing ongoing, intelligent, and well-informed conversation about the argument of my book, the texts of Marx, and the larger issues broached by both. Yves Winter has often disagreed, but has always pushed me to clarify and extend my argument, and has been a real friend and fabulous colleague throughout this writing process. Alex Gourevitch, whose own work on labor republicanism in the American context was a revelation to me, has been, for two and a half years, a rich source of provocation, inspiration, and reassurance. Gavin Walker has been a constant comrade in every sense of the word; he has offered incisive criticism, historical and political reality checks, a peerless knowledge of Marx's texts, and countless hours of beer-fueled conversation, commiseration, and debate. Hasana Sharp has been there from before the beginning, full of curiosity, skepticism, interest, insight, and exemplary judgment; I have not always taken her advice, but I have usually regretted such foolishness sooner or later.

My experience with Princeton University Press has been so uniformly pleasant as to seem a bit unreal. This is due, no doubt, to the expertise of my editor, Rob Tempio, and the team assisting him (I should mention, especially, Nathan Carr, Ryan Mulligan, and my copyeditor, Dawn Hall). My thanks go, also, to the two referees who recommended my manuscript for publication. One of these has subsequently revealed himself to be Corey Robin; his enthusiasm and commentary have been a godsend.

Finally, and most crucially, I owe enduring gratitude to Hasana Sharp, who has, above and beyond the intellectual and professional assistance detailed above, also sustained me with love and care throughout this whole process, spending her sabbatical attending to our children and household so that I might devote myself to writing this book. Without you, Hasana, none of this would have been possible.

A Note on References and Translations
❖❖❖

Wherever possible and appropriate, I have provided references to both an English translation and an original language source, preferably from a scholarly edition. All translations from German and French have been checked and modified by myself.

Marx's Inferno

❖❖❖

CHAPTER 1

Introduction: Rereading *Capital*

When word of his death reached New York City, "representatives of the various trades, labor, social, and other organizations" issued a public statement proclaiming that "now it is the duty of all true lovers of liberty to honor the name of Karl Marx."[1] This call has become, over the course of the twentieth century, nigh unintelligible. "Liberty" has become the shibboleth of antisocialism and anticommunism. That Marx was ever taken to be a devoted advocate of "the liberation of all downtrodden people," as these laborers and socialists claimed, seems, not antiquated, but bizarre. Justice, certainly. Progress. Science. Equality. Universal solidarity. But liberty? What has Marx to offer "all true lovers of liberty"?

If this book is to accomplish one thing, it ought to make this eulogy seem not only intelligible but also sensible and reasonable. Marx's critical theory of capitalism diagnosed the rule of capital as a complex and world-spanning system of domination. He sought, in *Capital*, to analyze the mechanisms of this system and to reconstruct a notion of freedom adequate to its abolition. In order to be properly appreciated, Marx's *Capital* must be recovered as a work of political theory, written in a specific political context, but seeking also to say something of lasting importance about the challenges to—and possibilities for—freedom in the modern world.

My argument is twofold. First, I contend that, in *Capital*, Marx had a grand aspiration, to write the definitive analysis of what's wrong with the rule of capital, and that he hung this aspiration on a suitably grand literary framework: rewriting Dante's *Inferno* as a descent into the modern "social Hell" of the capitalist mode of production. Dante, of course, staged his own, individual, salvation story, telling us how his encounter with the evil of the world prepared his soul for its journey to blessedness. But his pilgrim was also supposed to be an Everyman, whose descent into damnation and resurrection into grace might be reiterated by all of the faithful. Marx, on the other hand, cast himself as a Virgil for the proletariat, guiding his readers through the lower recesses of the capitalist economic order in order that they might learn not only how this

---

[1] "Reported Death of Karl Marx," *New York Times*, March 16, 1883.

"infernal machine" works,[2] but also what traps to avoid in their efforts to construct a new world.

Second, I argue that in order to understand Marx's attempt to realize this grand aspiration, *Capital* is best read as a critical reconstruction of and rejoinder to the other versions of socialism and popular radicalism that predominated in France and England in the 1860s and 1870s, when Marx was composing his magnum opus. These competing discourses—the remnants of Owenism, Fourierism, and Saint-Simonianism,[3] the social republicanism of James Bronterre O'Brien,[4] and, most crucially, the mutualism of Pierre-Joseph Proudhon[5]—were at the forefront of Marx's concern when he was writing *Capital*. The foundation of the International Working Men's Association (IWMA) in 1864,[6] and Marx's conviction that the group held the seeds of a renewal of revolutionary politics, spurred him to get his thousands of pages of manuscripts and notes into publishable form. He hoped that the book would provide the theoretical guideposts for the resurgent movement. In order for it to achieve this status, *Capital* had to either co-opt, undermine, or openly confront the existing theoretical commonplaces of the rival camps, which dominated the political landscape that Marx hoped his own outlook would come to occupy. Hence, in the process and for the sake of unfolding Marx's critique of capitalism,[7] my book examines Marx's borrowings from and arguments against the other socialists, many of which remain sub rosa to those unfamiliar with the writers in question.

Marx's grand ambitions and his internecine struggles are not separable from one another, either, but are thoroughly intertwined. The notion that modernity is a "social Hell" was originally suggested by Charles Fourier and his protégé Victor Considérant, and had already been developed in the works of Pierre-Joseph Proudhon into a metaphorical history of humanity's descent into and escape from the underworld. The moral

[2] Jameson, *Representing "Capital,"* 146.

[3] Booth, *Saint-Simon and Saint-Simonism*; Iggers, *The Cult of Authority: The Political Philosophy of the Saint-Simonians*; Harrison, *Robert Owen and the Owenites in Britain and America*; Garnett, *Co-Operation and the Owenite Socialist Communities in Britain, 1825–45*; Claeys, *Machinery, Money, and the Millennium*; Claeys, *Citizens and Saints*; Pilbeam, *French Socialists before Marx*; Pilbeam, *Saint-Simonians in Nineteenth-Century France*.

[4] Plummer, *Bronterre*; Claeys, *Citizens and Saints*, pt. III.

[5] Puech, *Le Proudhonisme dans l'Association internationale des travailleurs*; Hoffman, *Revolutionary Justice*; Prichard, *Justice, Order, and Anarchy*; Vincent, *Proudhon and the Rise of French Republican Socialism*.

[6] Collins and Abramsky, *Karl Marx and the British Labour Movement*; Braunthal, *History of the International*; Stekloff, *History of the First International*.

[7] Throughout, I will use "capitalism" as an umbrella term for those "societies in which the capitalist mode of production reigns" (Marx, *Capital*, 1:125; *MEGA*, II.6:17; *MEGA*, II.7:19).

categories that structure Dante's Hell—incontinence, force, fraud, and treachery—were common terms in the moral discourse of early socialism. Indeed, much of early socialism, as it emerged from Christian and civic republican discourses, consisted in the application of these moral categories to the social question, and this was a crucial point of contention between Marx and his more moralistic predecessors and contemporaries. Marx's distinctiveness comes to the fore in that his opponents want either to avoid political economy, or else, like Proudhon, to remain within it. Only Marx, following Dante, sees the necessity of going *through* political economy in order to get *beyond* it. And, as in the case of Dante's pilgrim, this transit is transformative. But Marx's journey, unlike Dante's, is supposed to de-personalize and de-moralize. Marx recapitulates Dante's descent through incontinence, force, fraud, and treachery in order to show that it is capital, as a system of all-around domination, that is responsible for these evils, not the individuals dominated by capital.

Thus my book is only able to trace either of these two threads by tracing both. By considering together Marx's context and his designs, this study shows how Marx's fights with other socialist theorists in the early years of the IWMA were transmuted by him into *Capital*, and reveals the ambition of *Capital* to lay bare, for the first time, the inner workings of the capitalist mode of production and the political economy that analyzes it, as a Hell into which the proletariat must descend in order to free themselves and the world.

READING *CAPITAL* AS POLITICAL *THEORY*

My argument takes its orientation from some of the literary aspects of Marx's book—its use of tropes and metaphors, its allusions and citations. For all that, however, I do not treat *Capital* as a work of literature. Rather, I treat it as a work of political theory. Its tropes, metaphors, allusions, and citations are approached as signs to be interpreted, as the linguistic traces of intuitions that can be fleshed out in theoretical terms. When socialists and communists, including Marx, call capital a vampire, they do so because the metaphor seems to them an apt one. And the aptitude of the metaphor can be discussed and articulated in language that is not itself merely an elaboration of the metaphor. The sense that capital is parasitical upon something—labor—that is both more primary to human existence and more natural and lively than is capital can be spelled out. These intuitions have their own implicit presuppositions, and these can be made explicit. The judgment against capital implied by the vampire metaphor can, by this process, come to be considered independently of the metaphor itself, and can be assessed as more or less cogent.

The metaphors, tropes, and formulas circulated within a discourse are the anchors of its common sensibility, the moments that give to an utterance an immediate plausibility or attractiveness within a certain community of writers and readers, speakers and listeners, and an immediate outlandishness to members of other communities. Political speech is often an exercise in recollecting, rehearsing, burnishing, and deploying such familiarities, for the sake of signaling one's allegiances and rallying one's allies. It recalls people to their prior commitments and to the shared narratives that make sense of their world by orienting them in it.

In the South Dakota of my youth, for example, it was de rigueur for political speeches and ads to refer to at least one of two scenes: a rancher riding and surveying his range, or a handful of farmers exchanging news and gathering supplies on the Main Street of a small town. The figure of the rancher bespoke the assumption that the land ought to be controlled and supervised by independent men, who could be trusted and expected to take care of things themselves. The tableau of the farming town was to remind the audience of the trust and mutual reliance that exists among neighbors, who know one another for what they are. Whether spoken, written, or depicted by actors on TV, these political tropes signaled adherence to a common sense of what political life was about—its parameters and stakes—in a sparsely populated prairie state, where the native population had been subjugated and confined to reservations and poverty, and where the upsurge of political Christianism had yet to make significant inroads. Every discursive community has such anchoring homilies.

By contrast with the mere reiteration of these metaphors and tropes, however, the attempt to articulate a nonmetaphorical discourse around them is the playing out of a rope that gives a speaker or writer some measure of mobility among communities. Rather than simply stringing together immediately plausible turns of phrase, the watchwords and catchphrases of one's closest circle of interlocutors, a writer might try to make those watchwords and catchphrases understandable to a wider circle of readers, to explicate the sense of them, to motivate them by appeal to experiences and arguments drawn from other communities or common to many communities. By this effort, the anchoring homilies of one's local political dialect are maintained, but are also rendered less parochial. They enter into relations with previously alien metaphors and tropes. The discourse anchored in them attains a more or less limited independence from them, a flexibility and mobility and adaptability that it otherwise would have lacked.

Political theory is, according to this way of thinking, the effort to escape being sunk by one's own anchors. Hence, to read *Capital* as political theory is to show how Marx tried therein to give a more cosmopolitan sense to particular metaphors and tropes that were, in their origins, provincial to the socialism and popular radicalism of the nineteenth century.[8] Such a project requires acknowledging where Marx's linguistic materials came from, and what associations his words would likely have called to mind in the context of their utterance. But it also insists that Marx's work cannot be dispersed into that context. The single-minded internalism that seeks to reconstruct an author's work on the sole basis of what that author wrote is prone to anachronism, to reading works of the past as if they were addressing the reader's present-day concerns and preoccupations. As Gregory Claeys has noted, "Marx and Engels were relative latecomers to a debate [over socialism] that was thirty years old before they began to consider seriously its central issues." In their efforts to include themselves in and influence the direction of that debate, "they incorporated into their own thought many hidden assumptions and even covert first principles which occasionally emerged to the discursive surface, but as often as not remained half-disclosed if not well buried."[9] These half-disclosed references to earlier writers and controversies will not reveal themselves to someone who does not look beyond the various editions of Marx and Engels's collected works to the writings of the other socialists they read and argued with.[10]

On the other hand, as helpful as a familiarity with the context is for grounding the study of works of political theory, and as important as contextual considerations are for the argument of this book, context is not everything. If a work of political theory gains much of its sense and comprehensibility from remaining within "the parameters of a given

---

[8]Instead of seeing political theory in this way—as "party ideas" raised to the level of theory—some will insist that political theory is "always in one way or another constitutional theory; it always necessarily turns on the framing of a constitution" (Jameson, *Representing "Capital,"* 139). On this basis, they will conclude that *Capital* "has no political conclusions" (ibid.). I will argue in chapter 7 that even on this understanding of political theory, *Capital* implies more about the future constitution of communism than is often allowed.

[9]Claeys, *Citizens and Saints*, 9.

[10]The ongoing publication of the second *Marx-Engels Gesamtausgabe* (MEGA) has been a boon for scholars, but scholarly editions of Marx and Engels's works will not push the study of their thought onto the wider terrain of its context. Luckily, I have been able to draw upon the work of a number of historians of political thought who have mapped some of this background, including: Iggers, *The Cult of Authority: The Political Philosophy of the Saint-Simonians*; Loubère, *Louis Blanc: His Life and His Contribution to the Rise of French Jacobin-Socialism*; Harrison, *Robert Owen and the Owenites in Britain and America*; Garnett, *Co-Operation and the Owenite Socialist Communities in Britain, 1825–45*; Goodwin, *Social Science and Utopia*; Taylor, *The Political Ideas of the Utopian Socialists*; Vincent, *Pierre-Joseph Proudhon and the Rise of French Republican Socialism*; Thompson, *The People's Science*; Thompson, *The Market and Its Critics*; Claeys, *Machinery, Money, and the Millennium*; Claeys, *Citizens and Saints*; Pilbeam, *French Socialists before Marx*; Lattek, *Revolutionary Refugees*; Pilbeam, *Saint-Simonians in Nineteenth-Century France*.

political language or . . . certain linguistic conventions,"[11] its cogency or power tends to come more from its idiosyncrasies: its exceptional formal coherence, scope, or rigor. Contextual scholarship has immensely enriched our understanding of British political thought, has resuscitated the tradition of republicanism, and has brought new attention to neglected figures like James Harrington. It has not, however, diminished the stature of Hobbes's *Leviathan* or Locke's *Treatises*. Nor should it. If the "great books" lose a vital quotient of their sense when they are ripped from their contexts and pitted against one another on the barren plain of "the history of the West," approaching them in the settings from which they emerged does not entail denying their greatness.

I am convinced that Marx's *Capital* is one of the great works of political theory. It identifies and analyzes an interrelated set of political problems that are either invisible to or wished away by virtually every other book in the canon of great works, no matter how one might expand that canon in other directions. It does so by taking seriously the experiences and complaints of wage laborers, but also by subjecting those experiences and complaints to a sort of immanent criticism. For this reason, I think the greatness of *Capital*, as well as much of the sense of its argument, emerges only or best when it is read against the background of the socialisms with which Marx was contending, socialisms that grew much more directly out of the everyday political discourse of the workers' movement. Reading *Capital* against the backdrop of this political language of workers requires some reconstruction of the context in which it was written and the audience to whom it was addressed. But discussion of this context, and of the political languages that comprise it, is a means to an end, not an end in itself. Hence, this book lacks the historical and documentary scope of a full-blooded contextual history of Marx's political thought.[12] It makes up for this lack, hopefully, by the depth of attention it gives to the text and argument of *Capital*, and by the reconstruction of certain strands of argument—regarding money, exploitation, exchange relations, and such—central to the non-Marxian socialisms of Marx's day.

---

[11] Claeys, *Citizens and Saints*, 17.

[12] Although it is rather limited in its exploration of context, especially in its second volume, the most sensitive, thorough, and accurate account of Marx as a political thinker remains Richard Hunt's *The Political Ideas of Marx and Engels*, 2 vols. (1974, 1984). Christine Lattek's recent book, *Revolutionary Refugees*, goes much deeper into the context of Hunt's first volume, but this does not displace Hunt's theses about Marx, but rather confirms them in the main. The general shortcoming of works that examine Marx's relationship with other socialists is that of blind partisanship. The Marxists tend not to go beyond *what Marx says* about other socialists (e.g., Draper, *Karl Marx's Theory of Revolution*). Those who look at the other socialists tend to be defenders of those socialists against Marx's criticisms (e.g., Hoffman, *Revolutionary Justice*; Menuelle, *Marx, Lecteur de Proudhon*).

This question of context is closely related to another. One of the difficulties faced in trying to read *Capital* as political theory is that Marx's texts have become anchors for many who write about him or who try to continue his project. That is, Marx's writings acquired, over the course of the century after his death, the opacity and immediacy of metaphors and formulas, self-explanatory or self-refuting, depending upon the party to which one belonged. In order to show that Marx was doing political theory, therefore, it is also necessary to do political theory with Marx. In other words, one must embed his concepts in other discourses, translating his claims into languages not his own. This carries risks, of course. In trying to clarify and bring out the force of Marx's assertions and arguments, for example, I have drawn significantly on the reconstructions of republicanism offered by Quentin Skinner and Philip Pettit.[13] I think their explication of republican freedom as non-domination tracks much more closely the range and types of Marx's concerns than does the more traditional attribution to Marx of a positive conception of freedom as collective self-realization or collective self-mastery. This use of contemporary neo-republican arguments exposes me, however, to the very anachronism that I have tried to ward off by means of contextualizing Marx's arguments. It is one thing, after all, to argue that Marx and Engels were "more indebted to their socialist predecessors than has usually been conceded," and that a central element of this debt consists in the transmission, via the early socialists, of elements of eighteenth-century republicanism into Marxism.[14] It is another thing altogether to claim that freedom as non-domination was one of Marx's central political ideals. Such a claim seems to imply a teleology according to which nineteenth-century socialists, including Marx, knew not what they said; their words implied concepts that would not be developed and properly clarified until the present generation of academic political theorists roused the sense slumbering in the dusty chambers of nineteenth-century books.

However, this misperceives the role played by contemporary republican political theory in the reconstruction of the past (or, at least, forecloses roles that it might play). The rise of neo-republican political theory stems directly from research on the history of political thought. That research, however, did not really cross "the great divide into the nineteenth century."[15] The republicanism that has been reconstructed as neo-republicanism is an aristocratic republicanism, which predated the great emancipation movements of the nineteenth century. There is a significant

---

[13] The literature on republican political thought and neo-republicanism is vast. The leading edge of republicanism's revival in its contemporary form includes: Skinner, "The Idea of Negative Liberty"; Skinner, *Liberty before Liberalism*; Pettit, *Republicanism*.

[14] Claeys, *Citizens and Saints*, 51.

[15] Ibid., 6.

literature devoted to arguing that the historical and social circumscription of the original has bequeathed conceptual limitations to the revival.[16] As Alex Gourevitch has noted, however,

> The best chance republicanism had of "transcending" its aristocratic origins and of developing an egalitarian critique of enslavement and subjection was when someone other than society's dominant elite used republican language to articulate their concerns. This is precisely what happened when nineteenth-century artisans and wage-laborers appropriated the inherited concepts of independence and virtue and applied them to the world of labor relations. The attempt to universalize the language of republican liberty, and the conceptual innovations that took place in the process, were their contribution to this political tradition.[17]

By pursuing the republican tradition into the nineteenth century, and into the writings of plebeian radicals and socialists, one might, therefore, find that traditional republican concerns with freedom, status, and virtue are capable of far-reaching and surprising extensions and transformations. This, in turn, throws into relief the limits of neo-republicanism as a representative of the republican tradition. Hence, the juxtaposition of nineteenth-century radical and socialist deployments of republican terminology with neo-republican understandings of the scope and meaning of republican liberty need not imply that the latter are the destiny of the former. This juxtaposition can just as well serve to highlight the blind spots and narrowness of the contemporary reconstruction of republicanism.

By pursuing these republican themes further, through Marx's immanent criticism of socialism, I hope to portray Marx as delineating an alternative republicanism, one that has a family resemblance to the neo-republicanism presently on the table, but that departs from an analysis of the social form of modern life, rather than holding fast to the purely political constitution of the public sphere. This reconstruction of the political theory of Marx's *Capital* will inevitably flatten somewhat both the historical diversity of socialist and republican political languages from which Marx departed and the complexity of the neo-republicanism that

---

[16] Criticisms along these lines can be found in: Ghosh, "From Republican to Liberal Liberty"; Kapust, "Skinner, Pettit and Livy: The Conflict of the Orders and the Ambiguity of Republican Liberty"; Krause, "Beyond Non-Domination: Agency, Inequality, and the Meaning of Freedom"; Maddox, "The Limits of Neo-Roman Liberty"; Markell, "The Insufficiency of Non-Domination"; McCormick, "Machiavelli against Republicanism: On the Cambridge School's 'Guiccardian Moments'"; Wood, "Why It Matters." Crucial for my own thinking on this matter is Alex's Gourevitch's articulation of what he calls the paradox of slavery and freedom (*From Slavery to the Cooperative Commonwealth*, chap. 1).

[17] Gourevitch, *From Slavery to the Cooperative Commonwealth*, 14.

claims to develop and clarify those languages. If I am able to bring out the specificity and force of Marx's project in *Capital*, these trade-offs are acceptable to me.

READING *CAPITAL* AS *POLITICAL* THEORY

Because political theory is a certain sort of political speech, and political speech is essentially an intervention on one side or another of some political question, the rhetoric, form, and address of a work of political theory are *internal* to the content of its argument. Rather than being read as a work of political theory, however, *Capital* is generally approached either as a treatise of socialist economics or as a work of social theory. If *Capital* is to be regarded as a work of social or economic theory, then its audience is thereby cast in the role of the student. The text is supposed to be fundamentally *didactic*, and its rhetoric and form are reduced to matters of style, external to the real content of the book, which might be formalized without any substantive loss.

Within Marxological literature, therefore, considerations of the structure of *Capital* are generally posed in the guise of questions about "the method of presentation." This picks up on Marx's distinction, in the afterword to the second German edition, between "the method of presentation [*Darstellungsweise*] [and] the method of research [*Forschungsweise*]."[18] Marx draws that distinction in the midst of differentiating his method of inquiry from the "Hegelian sophistry" of which his German reviewers had accused him. Marx denies that his method is Hegelian, writing that research

> has to appropriate the material in detail, to analyze its different forms of development, and to track down their inner connection. Only after this work has been done can the real movement be appropriately presented. If this is done successfully, if the life of the material is now reflected ideally, then it may appear as if we are dealing with an *a priori* construction.[19]

Marx is pretty clearly associating a priori constructions with Hegel here, or assuming that whatever appears to be an a priori construction will, for this reason, appear to be a "Hegelian sophistry."

Nonetheless, at least since Lenin first read Hegel's *Logic*, readers of Marx have been trying to understand the argument and form of *Capital* as some sort of application or modification or instantiation or performance

---

[18] *Capital*, 1:102; *MEGA*, II.6:709. Marx himself takes the distinction over from the review of *Capital* by I. I. Kaufman in the *European Messenger* (*Capital*, 1:100; *MEGA*, II.6:707).

[19] *Capital*, 1:102; *MEGA*, II.6:709.

of Hegelian dialectics.[20] An older manner of doing so, taking its cues from some of Engels's remarks,[21] understood Marx's presentation to be a sort of dialectical history of the development of capitalism, more or less "corrected" for the sake of logical clarity.[22] This approach has largely fallen out of favor, in part because it seemed to require the imputation of a "secular theodicy" to Marx,[23] in part because the textual evidence for some of its central claims evaporated upon publication of scholarly editions of Marx's works—for example, the era of "simple commodity production," supposedly discussed in part one of *Capital*, was in fact wholly the invention of Engels.[24] This dialectical historicism has been supplanted by an approach that is often called "systematic dialectics."[25] Marx's argument in *Capital* is supposed to be systematic because the object of his research, capital, "is a totality where every part has to be complemented by others to be what it is," and which "cannot be comprehended immediately." Marx's "methodological problem," therefore,

> is a matter of how to articulate a complex concept that cannot be grasped by some sort of immediate intuition. In doing so [he has] to make a start with some aspect of it. But the exposition can reconstruct the whole from a particular starting point because we can move logically from one element to another along a chain of internal relations; in strict logic if the very meaning of an element is at issue . . . or with a fair degree of confidence if material conditions of existence are involved. [26]

[20] Lenin's famous "aphorism" is that "It is impossible completely to understand Marx's *Capital*, and especially its first chapter, without having thoroughly studied and understood the whole of Hegel's *Logic*. Consequently, half a century later none of the Marxists understood Marx!!" (*Collected Works*, 38:180).

[21] See Engels's review, for *Das Volk*, of Marx's *Contribution to the Critique of Political Economy* (MECW, 16:475).

[22] A relatively sophisticated representative of this approach would be Ronald Meek, *Studies in the Labour Theory of Value*.

[23] Elster, "Marxism, Functionalism and Game Theory," 206.

[24] For details, see Arthur, "Engels as Interpreter of Marx's Economics."

[25] There are far too many works that might be justifiably included under this heading to list them all here. A representative sample might include the following: Albritton and Simoulidis, *New Dialectics and Political Economy*; Albritton, *Dialectics and Deconstruction in Political Economy*; Arthur, *Dialectics of Labour*; Elson, *Value: The Representation of Labour in Capitalism*; Roth and Eldred, *Guide to Marx's "Capital"*; Hunt, *Analytical and Dialectical Marxism*; Lebowitz, *Following Marx*; Lebowitz, *Beyond Capital*; McCarney, *Hegel on History*; Murray, *Marx's Theory of Scientific Knowledge*; Norman and Sayers, *Hegel, Marx, and Dialectic*; Postone, *Time, Labor, and Social Domination*; Reuten, "The Interconnection of Systematic Dialectics and Historical Materialism"; Bell, *Capitalism and the Dialectic*; Williams, *Value, Social Form and the State*. See also the bibliography in Arthur, *The New Dialectic and Marx's* Capital. Much of the work done in the wake of Backhaus's *Marx und die Marxistische Orthodoxie* might also be included; see, for example, the statement on method in Heinrich, *Introduction to the Three Volumes of Karl Marx's* Capital, 30–32.

[26] Arthur, *The New Dialectic and Marx's* Capital, 24–25.

This logical movement along a chain of internal relations is dialectics. Since this dialectic is only supposed to articulate the systematic nature of capital, the systematic dialectics of Marx's method of presentation has no bearing on the course of history. Any secular theodicy is avoided, and the reader can honor Marx's own programmatic statements, such as his claim that he is "only out to present the internal organization of the capitalist mode of production, its ideal average, as it were."[27]

Whatever merits this approach might have as an effort to make sense of and continue Marx's substantive research program, it does, however, encounter certain difficulties whenever it is confronted with the book Marx actually wrote. If it is claimed, for instance, that "Marx has modeled *Capital* on Hegel's *Logic*,"[28] then this modeling seems to have excluded large swaths of the text, including chapters ten, thirteen through fifteen, and twenty-six through thirty-three, together composing over 40 percent of the book. These chapters, as everyone notes, are historical, not logical. And, indeed, scholars inclined toward systematic dialectics seem impelled to segregate these chapters, setting them aside as a "complement" to Marx's theoretical account;[29] or as "strictly illustrative" and "by no means necessary";[30] or as asides "interrupting the systematic progression of categories";[31] or as excurses, "tangential to Marx's principle line of theoretical development";[32] or as "Marx turning away temporarily from the logical unfolding of the categories . . . to make a lengthy digression."[33] The end of *Capital* seems to be especially embarrassing in this regard. Part eight, on primitive accumulation, is, considered from the point of view of any Hegelian dialectical structure, "tacked on," and "could be omitted without loss."[34] And yet Marx chose to end the book with this, and even to highlight it by elevating it, in the French edition, to a separate part of eight chapters.

A survey of this established literature reveals, therefore, that looking to Hegel for the key to the structure of volume one of *Capital* has so far unlocked only an ideal, counterfactual *Capital*.[35] This has been

---

[27] *Capital*, 3:970; *MEGA*, II.15:806.

[28] Wendling, *Karl Marx on Technology and Alienation*, 99.

[29] Heinrich, *Introduction to the Three Volumes of Karl Marx's* Capital, 32.

[30] Arthur, *The New Dialectic and Marx's* Capital, 75.

[31] Smith, *The Logic of Marx's* Capital, 134.

[32] Shortall, *The Incomplete Marx*, 296.

[33] Ibid., 178.

[34] Arthur and White, "Debate," 130; see also Murray, "Reply to Geert Reuten," 161.

[35] Another sign of this is the stress that many of these authors place on the notion that Marx's conceptualization of capital "requires the whole three volumes of *Capital*" (Arthur, *The New Dialectic and Marx's* Capital, 34). By way of contrast, I will focus exclusively on the first volume. This difference in focus follows naturally from my emphasis on Marx's published text—his speech act—over and against these authors' emphasis upon Marx's research project. Despite the fact that volumes two and three were published well after volume one,

extremely stimulating for certain purposes. The authors of this tendency are quite insightful on Marx's discussion of value, for example, and there is no doubt that they have, collectively, reinvigorated Marx's critique of political economy as an agenda for ongoing research. Nonetheless, all of the most sophisticated practitioners of this approach must admit that the dialectic of concepts does not explain why *Capital* has precisely the order of exposition that it does. Hence, without impugning these authors' real achievements, or downplaying Hegel's influence on Marx, we can recognize that another principle of order must be found if we are to understand why *Capital* takes the form it does. While it would be foolish to argue that it is Dante, *not* Hegel, who provides the key to the structure of Marx's book, Hegel cannot claim our complete attention. There is room to investigate other influences upon Marx's "method of presentation."

If scholarship on the Marx-Hegel relationship has generally shifted from the question of dialectical history to the question of the dialectical systematicity of capital, the scholarship on Marx's relationship to classical political economy has seen an even greater transformation. In 1941, Henryk Grossman could write that "the dominant opinion sees in Marx only a student of, follower of, or successor to the classical economists," and then cite everyone from Pareto to Labriola, Schumpeter to Hilferding and Dobb.[36] While one can still find this old "dominant opinion" circulating widely in more recent discussions—especially by non-Marxian economists and analytical Marxists[37]—there has been a sea change within Marxological scholarship. What is emphasized in most recent works is

---

they—and especially three—were by and large written before it, and have the appearance of volumes, instead of being rough manuscripts like the *Grundrisse*, only because of Engels's intensive editorial work (Krätke, "'Hier bricht das Manuskript sb.' (Engels): Hat *Das Kapital* einen Schluss?"). One does not have to go so far as Cole, who claimed that "Marx stopped thinking fundamentally about the development of capitalism when he had finished writing Volume I of *Das Kapital*" (*History of Socialist Thought*, 2:300). Nonetheless, it is undeniable that "Marx did extraordinarily little work on [volumes two and three] in the period [after 1872]. The material used in volumes II and III comes overwhelmingly from the 1850s and 1860s. Sources from the 1870s are exceedingly sparse and of little consequence" (Collins and Abramsky, *Karl Marx and the British Labour Movement*, 296). The first volume is the only part of *Capital* that Marx finished, and it has to be taken as his last word on most issues. More importantly for my purposes, it has to be taken as Marx's premier act of political speech, his major public statement to the workers' movement on most matters.

[36] Grossman, *Marx, Die Klassische Nationalökonomie und das Problem der Dynamik*, 7.

[37] See, for instance, Howard and King, who claim that "Marx built his political economy upon a critique of his classical predecessors, especially Smith and Ricardo. He refashioned their concepts, corrected what he considered to be their logical defects, reinterpreted results and extended the analysis" (*The Political Economy of Marx*, 40). See also Cohen, *History, Labour and Freedom*, chap. 11, which presupposes that Marx subscribed to a Ricardian labor theory of value.

the extent to which Marx's critique of political economy was intended to "break down the *theoretical field* (meaning the self-evident views and spontaneously arising notions) to which the categories of political economy owe their apparent plausibility."[38] To some extent, this development springs from the influence of the Frankfurt School of critical theory, within which Marx's "critique of political economy is taken to be an attempt to analyze critically the cultural forms and social structures of capitalist civilization."[39] To some extent it is the lone lasting victory of Althusser on the field of Marxological contest, since he insisted that Marx had engaged in a "symptomatic reading" of classical political economy,[40] not in order to complete it by supplying what it omitted, but in order to overturn it, and to displace inquiry onto a new terrain, or direct it to a new object.[41] Whatever the etiology, the effect has been to shift discussion decisively away from the Ptolemaic addition of epicycles to Ricardo's labor theory of value, and toward a metaeconomic discussion of why something like the labor theory of value would have suggested itself to anyone trying to understand the rise of the capitalist economy.[42]

Nonetheless, this new emphasis on the *critique* in Marx's critique of political economy retains, to a great extent, the old focus on the classical authors. Even if Marx's text is no longer plumbed for the rudiments of a socialist political economy, his critique of political economy is still treated like a rejoinder to Smith, Ricardo, Say, and Malthus. Implicitly, the old notion of a debate between the great minds lingers, as if Marx were primarily addressing himself, across the years, to the bourgeois economists who came before.[43] Like the focus on Hegel, this preoccupation with restaging Marx's *Auseinandersetzung* with the classics has both a long pedigree and a motivating impulse in the desire of most Marxologists not merely to study Marx but also to continue his work.[44] But this is not

[38] Heinrich, *Introduction to the Three Volumes of Karl Marx's* Capital, 35.

[39] Postone, *Time, Labor, and Social Domination*, 16. The originating event, here, was quite specific: the debates that emerged from the 1967 conference at Frankfurt honoring the one-hundredth anniversary of the first edition of *Capital*. The papers from this conference are collected in Euchner and Schmidt, *Kritik der politischen Ökonomie heute: 100 Jahre "Kapital."*

[40] Althusser and Balibar, *Reading* Capital, 28.

[41] Ibid., 83–90. Crucial here is the work and influence of Althusser's student, Jacques Bidet; see, especially, his *Exploring Marx's* Capital.

[42] It was John Roemer who declared the errors in the labor theory of value to be Ptolemaic ("Should Marxists Be Interested in Exploitation?," 65).

[43] Even the supposedly contextualist historian, Jonathan Sperber, treats Marx's economic writings as a "backward look" at the authors and problems of the early nineteenth century (*Karl Marx*, 454).

[44] It was 1913 when Lenin identified the "three sources and three component parts of Marxism" as "German philosophy, English political economy and French socialism" (*Collected Works*, 19:23–24).

my project.[45] Rather than attending primarily to Marx's explicit arguments against and references to the classics, for the sake of clarifying and extending those arguments, I am interested instead in asking: For whom, and for what purpose, was Marx performing this *Auseinandersetzung*? This question directs me to his contemporaries, and to his fellow socialists, and that is where I begin.[46]

Two other decisions that have shaped this project should be mentioned and given some preliminary defense, especially since they might seem to run counter to the argument that Marx ought to be read within the context of the socialist and workers' movements. First, mine is an interpretation of *Capital*, not of Marx, and so it pays scant attention to Marx's writings prior to his attempts to compose *Capital*. Second, it is an interpretation of volume one and leaves aside volumes two and three, as well as the notebooks on "Theories of Surplus-Value." These decisions are motivated by the same set of considerations. First and foremost, volume one of *Capital* was prepared by Marx for publication. It is a polished literary work, and a considered piece of political speech. This differentiates it from the immense mass of Marx's writings—the Paris notebooks, the so-called *German Ideology*, the *Grundrisse*, the "Theories of Surplus-Value," volumes two and three of *Capital*, and so on—which were notebooks, or rough drafts, or attempts at self-clarification, or all three. In the unpublished writings, it is hard to say which claims and arguments represent Marx's considered views and which are attempts with which he became unsatisfied. It can be hard, even, to tell which claims

[45]This is not to say that I have no interest in Marx except a scholarly one. I think Marx's criticism of capitalist society is cogent and compelling, and I think it has living import for the contemporary world. But these convictions emerge, in part, from my sense that Marx's political and theoretical engagements have a wider set of reference points than the traditional commentary would suggest. These other points of reference—popular political economy, the cooperative movement, mutualist and associationist tendencies, and traditions of republican political thought—have more potent and varied contemporary analogues than does the classical political economy against which Marx is usually projected.

[46]I confess up front that my argument sets aside one group of Marx's socialist contemporaries: the Germans. Marx's relationship to Ferdinand Lassalle, to Johann Karl Rodbertus, and to the "socialists of the chair" in the German academy is a story yet to be told. To an important extent, it parallels the story of his relationship to French and British socialists. Certainly Rodbertus and Lassalle are doctrinally similar to Proudhon and the Owenites on many crucial points. Indeed, Paul Thomas has convincingly argued that Marx so far assimilated Lassalle to Proudhon that his criticisms of the French mutualist in an "obituary" published in the Lassallean *Sozial-Demokrat* (January 1865) ought to be read as a veiled attack on the German socialist (*Karl Marx and the Anarchists*, 233–38). However, Marx's efforts to win influence among German workers and socialists—and in the German academy—deserves an independent treatment, even if Marx's distance from Germany, and the paucity of German involvement in the IWMA, justify prioritizing the investigation of his more immediate context.

are in his own voice.[47] He is writing for himself, not for the public, and it seems strange to hold him responsible for claims or arguments for which he never took responsibility. Because I am interested in reading Marx against the background of the movements he sought to influence, I am understandably inclined to pay closest attention to his public writings.

Marx also changed his mind on many issues over the years without necessarily declaring that fact. His disagreements with his younger selves, when he does remark upon them, are often registered as criticisms of *others*, writers with whom he agreed earlier in his life, but with whom he had parted ways. Many commentators have noticed this fact of Marx's biography. They sometimes treat it a as character flaw.[48] I will not defend Marx on this point, but I will note as a mitigating circumstance that Marx was not so well known in his life that most of his readers would care that he had changed his mind. It is important to realize that, at least until the 1870s, Marx always labored to make his name against other, better-known contemporaries. He was ever slaying Goliaths. Hence, it seems prudent to establish what Marx thought in a period of his life by reference to what he wrote during that period, rather than using earlier or later texts as the key for deciphering the one at hand.

Additionally, Marx undoubtedly thought of *Capital* as his chef d'oeuvre. Throughout the twentieth century it was relatively neglected, for it was supposed to be the seat of the Marx we already knew from the proclamations of the Marxist parties. Hence, people who were attracted to Marx but repelled by the parties went looking for one "unknown Marx" or another, as new manuscripts became available. This process has certainly enriched our knowledge of Marx's thought, but it has also produced the rather perverse situation in which Marx is better known for his unpublished jottings than for his major public intervention. Ironically, we never actually knew the Marx of *Capital* very well. It is a long and difficult book, lacking the programmatic clarity and generality of Engels's late works. Consequently, as Terrell Carver has argued, "while socialists, communists and even self-declared Marxists paid lip-service to the power of *Capital*," it was the *Anti-Dühring* and *Ludwig Feuerbach and the End of Classical German Philosophy* "that were most widely read, and whose tenets were passed on in lectures, primers and handbooks."[49] It was the Marxism of Engels that people sought to complicate, escape, or counter with the Paris notebooks, the *Grundrisse*, and the rough drafts of the early 1860s. Volume one of *Capital*—Marx's

---

[47] For an illustrative example of this difficulty, see Terrell Carver's discussion of a famous passage from the *German Ideology* manuscripts (*Postmodern Marx*, 98–107).

[48] As, for example, in Sperber, *Karl Marx*.

[49] Carver, *Marx and Engels*, 96–97.

only fully elaborated and published work of theory—ended up being largely neglected. And, so, I think it is important to go back to it, to read it carefully from beginning to end, and to do so without presuming that we know what we will find.

If volume one was Marx's only polished and published statement on most issues, it was also his last major writing project of any sort. Aside from correspondence and some excerpt notebooks—most notably those on mathematics and on the ethnology of primitive societies—Marx wrote very little in the last years of his life. Most crucially for our purposes, he did very little work on volumes two and three of *Capital* after the publication of the last installment of the French edition of volume one in 1875. We might wish that it were otherwise, for one reason or another, but volume one of *Capital* must be taken as Marx's last testament.[50] Finally, while volumes two and three may deepen our understanding of *how*, according to Marx, *capitalism works*, they do not deepen our understanding of *what*, according to Marx, *is wrong with capitalism*. They do not add significantly to Marx's political theory, or to his political intervention in the socialist politics of his day.

For all these reasons, this book maintains a focus on volume one, and I will refer to it simply as *Capital*. I will draw upon Marx's correspondence, his drafts and notebooks, and his other—especially contemporaneous— writings and speeches, but I do so with an eye to explaining what Marx is trying to do in *Capital*. Where what he wrote elsewhere seems to buttress or clarify what he wrote in *Capital*, I will often say so. Where what he wrote elsewhere seems to contradict what he wrote in *Capital*, I will often try to explain the discrepancy. However, I make no claim to exhaustively pursue either sort of comparison. Marx could not reasonably have expected the reader of *Capital* to be familiar with his other works, much less with his unpublished writings. My presumption, therefore, is that the argument of *Capital* is supposed to be intelligible on its own—once, that is, one takes into account the discursive field into which it is meant to intervene.

---

[50]There is a prominent tradition of Marxology according to which volume one is only one-sixth (or less) of Marx's unfinished project. Basing themselves upon the outlines Marx produced in the late 1850s, these interpreters claim that volume one of *Capital* constitutes only the first part of the first book of a massive unwritten theory, which would have included a full treatment of many issues barely touched upon in the published version (see Wilbrandt, *Karl Marx: Versuch Einer Würdigung*; Rubel, *Rubel on Karl Marx: Five Essays*; McLellan, "Introduction," in *Marx's Grundrisse*; Lebowitz, *Beyond "Capital": Marx's Political Economy of the Working Class*). As salutary as this proposition may have been in the face of a Stalinist party that insisted that all theoretical questions were already definitively settled, it now serves as a stumbling block to research into what Marx actually wrote, since it precludes taking as final any of his published claims.

OUTLINE OF THE ARGUMENT

In chapter 2, I motivate and explain my claim that Marx composed *Capital* as a modern, secular *Inferno*. I review, briefly, Marx's knowledge of Dante and his propensity for using literary models to organize his works. I examine the history of socialists comparing modern society to a "social Hell," and show how Proudhon developed this trope in two texts with which Marx was well acquainted. I survey the textual clues that indicate, prima facie, that Marx appropriated this trope for his own critique of political economy, and that he simultaneously transformed its sense. These different forms of evidence set the stage for the rest of the book. They also bring Proudhon to the fore as Marx's primary opponent and clarify the main lines of their opposition. Proudhon articulates a moral criticism of existing economic institutions, informed to some extent by classical political economy. Marx wants to demonstrate, on the contrary, that political economy is nothing but the self-consciousness of novel institutions of domination, and that, therefore, if the laboring classes want to free themselves from this domination, they must get to the bottom of political economy itself, and destroy the social basis of its existence as a scientific discourse.

Chapter 3 begins the analysis of *Capital*, examining part one, where Marx considers capitalism as a market society. I argue that here he brings together the notion of the social Hell with the sense, common to many socialists, that the newly commercial society in which they lived was anarchic or out of control. In the first circles of Dante's Hell, those who lack self-control are tortured by their runaway desires; in Marx's sphere of circulation, producers are tormented by their uncontrollable products, which cannot guarantee a stable living. Furthering a line of thinking begun by Owenites in Britain, Marx teases apart the experience of commercial anarchy and the explanation for this experience, the impersonal domination of the market, which undermines all efforts at self-control. Because they are dependent upon the market, as slaves are dependent upon their masters, commodity producers must keep a "weather eye" out for changing market conditions. Since these are, at bottom, only the desires and choices of their customers and competitors, producers are subject to a novel form of domination. Marx's recognition and analysis of this "objective dependence" supports and explains both his analysis of the fetish character of commodities and his controversial methodological claim to treat individuals only as the personifications of economic relations.

Chapter 4 examines parts two and three of *Capital*, where Marx claims to reveal "the secret of modern society," the capitalist exploitation of labor power, and which corresponds to Dante's circles of force. Socialists before Marx had explained the abstraction of the laborers' product by appealing to the conquest of land and the extortion this allowed the landed to exact upon the poor producer. Hence, the use of force precedes and distorts exchange. Marx, I argue, turned this socialist diagnosis on its head. Because he understood commerce to realize the exchange of equivalent values, he could not explain capitalists' power of self-enrichment by past acts giving them unfair bargaining power. For Marx, on the contrary, exchange precedes and licenses the use of force. The workplace relation between capitalists and wage laborers is one of force because it is one in which the boss directly controls and uses the laborers in order to generate a surplus excessive of the aim of labor itself. Overwork is inherent in this capitalist mode of exploitation. Hence, Marx condemns capitalist exploitation in old-fashioned, Aristotelian terms, as an unnatural use of labor power, even as he takes seriously its novelty and its irreducibility to previous modes of extortion and plunder.

Chapter 5 enters into the longest and most internally complex section of *Capital*—parts four through seven—where Marx, rewriting Dante's long passage through the Malebolge, argues that the capitalist mode of production is a fraud, promising good and delivering evil. The development of the collective forces of production does not redound to the laborers' benefit but subjects them to despotic command within the factory. It also renders them ever more dependent upon capital, destroying as it does their independent capacity to make goods. To add insult to injury, the form of wages makes the laborers' slavery seem like freedom. Finally, the accumulation of wealth as capital requires and creates a dependent population in excess of the demand for labor power. This "relative surplus population"—the jobless adjunct of the labor market—is a field of social impoverishment that expands in time with the fortification of social wealth as capital. The essential condition of capital's fraud is the attractiveness of exchanges and mutually voluntary contracts as a form of social mediation, an attractiveness that other socialists found hard to resist.

Chapter 6 wraps up the analysis of *Capital* with Marx's treatment, in part eight, of "primitive accumulation." Marx's examination of capitalism's origins has been a sticking point for many commentators, since it seems to break with Marx's methodology in the earlier parts of *Capital*. I argue, however, that part eight is the culmination of Marx's argument with Proudhon, and the linchpin of his methodological quarrel with the French mutualist over the status of political economy within socialist theory. Marx tries, in the first place, to substantiate his conviction that there is a sharp break between the feudal world and the capitalist world. Second, Marx's account of the creation of the preconditions of capitalism is supposed to foreclose the separatism of the cooperative and mutualist movements. Worker separatism imagines that workers can build a new world by escaping from capital, either by establishing their own colonies and workshops, or by homesteading in the colonies of the mother country. Built into this desire for separation is a faith in the powers of relatively small-scale production to secure self-subsistence and independence for workers. In the final three chapters of *Capital*, Marx tries to undermine this faith by showing how the modern state has come to be dependent upon capital accumulation, and, therefore, to be the primary agent of primitive accumulation. Only the defeat of this servile and violent state can establish the conditions of emancipation.

Chapter 7 concludes the argument by weaving threads from the earlier chapters into an account of the positive political theory of *Capital*. The terms in which Marx criticizes capitalism reveal the principles according to which communist institutions would have to be constructed and judged. Although Marx is widely read as a proponent of collective self-mastery or autonomy, his diagnoses of capitalism's evils consistently point out forms of domination, not heteronomy. Hence, I read Marx as radicalizing the republican tradition for which freedom as non-domination is the highest virtue of institutions. Since Marx identifies novel forms of domination, his republic of labor looks unlike the republics advocated by others. However, Marx's republic is supposed by him to be the laboring classes' own discovery and creation of the federation of communist republics advocated by Robert Owen's late works. I argue, therefore, that Marx should be appreciated both as a radical republican and an Owenite communist.

CHAPTER 2

Taenarus: The Road to Hell

Descend, so that you may ascend
—Augustine, *Confessions*, IV.xii

The close of the feudal Middle Ages, and the opening of the modern
capitalist era are marked by a colossal figure: an Italian, Dante, both
the last poet of the Middle Ages and the first poet of modern times.
Today, as in 1300, a new historical era is approaching. Will Italy give
us the new Dante, who will mark the hour of birth of this new, proletarian era?
—Friedrich Engels, introduction to the 1893 Italian edition of
The Manifesto of the Communist Party

This book argues that the structure of the first volume of *Capital* was
inspired by Dante's *Inferno*, and that attending to this structure helps
to reveal Marx's argument both in its detail and in its overall scope and
import. Attention to the literary form of *Capital* aids in discerning its
argument, in part, because the structure of Dante's *Inferno* is not only an
imaginative plot but also a rigorously constructed poetic embodiment of
a moral ontology with both Christian and classical, Aristotelian, roots.
This moral ontology—a systematic typology of possible wrongs, which
reflects, negatively, the structure of being itself and humanity's place in
that structure—did not disappear with the Middle Ages. It persisted as
one current of European discourse through Marx's day and even into our
own, helping to form, among other things, the popular moral economy
that has always been a counterpoint and stumbling block to what Marx
called *bourgeois political economy*. In the form of this popular moral
economy, the moral ontology systematized by Dante formed one of the
crucial funds of ideas and intuitions out of which socialism developed in
the nineteenth century.

R. H. Tawney once quipped that, "The last of the Schoolmen was Karl
Marx."[1] As many commentators, friendly and critical alike, have argued,
there is more than a little truth to the quip. One of Marx's earliest texts

[1] Tawney, *Religion and the Rise of Capitalism*, 36.

is a notebook in which he translated and annotated most of *De Anima*.[2] Had his political commitments and activities not rendered him ineligible for an academic post in any German university,[3] Marx planned to write a book on Aristotle.[4] And there has been a long line of commentators who have followed Ernst Bloch in reading Marx as the inheritor of a tradition of "left-wing Aristotelianism."[5] Hence, it is reasonable to think that Marx would have found in the *Inferno*'s articulation of what is wrong with the world a preestablished harmony with his own way of thinking about what is wrong with capitalism.

My argument, however, is very nearly the reverse of this. Marx adapted the *Inferno* to his own purposes, which were deeply at odds with at least several crucial elements of the moral economy of early socialism.[6] Most prominently, Marx thought the moralism of moral economy to be completely out of place in the confrontation with the capitalist mode of production. The fundamental continuity between Dante's moral ontology and socialist moral economy consisted in the attribution of responsibility for the wrongs of the world to the choices of individuals. The damned souls of Dante's poem have made their own Hell, in which they are trapped for eternity. No one is responsible for their sins but themselves. Thus their damnation is perfect and natural justice, and there is no evil in this wide world that is not attributable to one such damned soul

[2] *MEGA*, IV.1:155–82.

[3] Marx's close ties to Bruno Bauer (later severed), at precisely the time when Bauer's academic career self-destructed over his intransigent and very public atheism, eliminated whatever prospects the younger man may have had (Sperber, *Karl Marx*, 71–76).

[4] In this planned book, Marx "would refute Trendelenburg's currently influential interpretation and redeployment of Aristotle. Trendelenburg, he [Marx] writes, is 'merely formal,' whereas Aristotle is truly 'dialectical'" (Depew, "Aristotle's *De Anima* and Marx's *Theory of Man*," 137; see also McLellan, *Karl Marx: His Life and Thought*, 39).

[5] Bloch, *The Principle of Hope*. This scholarship has tended to be focused on four broad thematic comparisons: on ethics (e.g., Gilbert, "Historical Theory and the Structure of Moral Argument in Marx"; Miller, "Aristotle and Marx: The Unity of Two Opposites"; Miller, "Marx and Aristotle: A Kind of Consequentialism"); on social ontology (e.g., de Ste. Croix, *The Class Struggle in the Ancient Greek World*; Meikle, *Essentialism in the Thought of Karl Marx*; Pike, *From Aristotle to Marx: Aristotelianism in Marxist Social Ontology*; Springborg, "Politics, Primordialism, and Orientalism: Marx, Aristotle, and the Myth of the Gemeinschaft"); on the ideal political arrangement (e.g., Booth, *Households: On the Moral Architecture of the Economy*; Katz, "The Socialist Polis: Antiquity and Socialism in Marx's Thought"; Leopold, *The Young Karl Marx*, 237–41; Schwartz, "Distinction between Public and Private Life: Marx on the Zoon Politikon"); and on philosophy of science (e.g., again, Meikle, *Essentialism in the Thought of Karl Marx*; Wilson, *Marx's Critical/Dialectical Procedure*, chap. 5).

[6] The notion of the moral economy was popularized by Thompson, "The Moral Economy of the English Crowd in the Eighteenth Century." The phrase, however, goes back at least to the 1820s in Britain.

or another. The sum of evils is equal to the sum of evil deeds, performed by responsible souls. Despite all of the distance separating them from Dante, many early socialists retained the Christian notion that "disorder in society" is nothing other than "moral evil," caused by "our passions and our ignorance."[7] We are all free to educate ourselves about the workings of society and the demands of justice and thereby to eliminate the ills befalling us. Even those, like Robert Owen, who proclaimed the formation of character by circumstances, and inveighed against the doctrine of individual responsibility, thought that ignorance alone stood between the current state of social bedlam and a new moral world in which we will be able to freely form the circumstances that will form the character of the next generation.[8]

To Marx, this moralizing and individualizing tendency in socialism simply transferred to the secular world the modes of thought developed by Christian theology, applying "humanized" Christian moral categories to the social world. From as early as 1843, Marx was critical of this sort of secularization. He claimed that "this state and this society produce religion, which is an *inverted consciousness of the world*, because they are an *inverted world*."[9] In other words, it is because the social world takes a certain form that a certain form of religion arises within it; hence, the secularization of religion in the form of a humanistic morality is bound to replicate the mystification that the humanist decries in religion. If "religion is the general theory of this world, its encyclopaedic compendium, its logic in popular form, . . . [and] its moral sanction," then the secularization of that religion in the form of a humanistic morality will be the same.[10] Far from having a critical purchase on the world as it exists, this morality will merely supplement it.

If Dante's poetic tour of Hell has a special resonance with the socialists' moral criticism of the modern world, this is because Dante was, in Engels's words, both "the last poet of the Middle Ages and the first poet of modern times." His moral ontology is not merely a relic of the Aristotelian Middle Ages, but a harbinger of the new world of capital. As Marx says in *Capital* itself, "Christianity, with its religious cult of man in the abstract" is the faith most appropriate to "a society of commodity producers."[11] Dante's moral categories are the original and highest poetic expression of a religion born of exchange relations, of which the morality of the early socialists is merely a rough knock-off. Marx wants

---

[7] Proudhon, *What Is Property?*, 191, 186.
[8] Claeys, *Citizens and Saints*, 115–19.
[9] *Early Writings*, 244; *MEGA*, I.2:170; italics in original.
[10] *Early Writings*, 244; *MEGA*, I.2:170.
[11] *Capital*, 1:172; *MEGA*, II.6:109; *MEGA*, II.7:58.

to criticize the world that gives rise to such a religion and such a morality. In order to do so, he has to show, among other things, that the ills that religion and morality attribute to the free actions of the human soul—that is, to "the human essence" as an "abstraction inhering in each single individual"—can only properly be attributed to "the ensemble of social relations."[12] The responsibility that religion and morality hang on the individual, Marx places on the form of society as such. Marx's critical theory of modern society, therefore, must show how the dynamics of that society give rise both to the ills socialism is concerned to combat and to the illusion that those ills are the moral responsibility of individuals.

It took Marx over twenty years to follow through on these intuitions, which he first formulated in the early to mid-1840s. In the 1850s, in exile in Britain, he discovered Dante's *Divine Comedy* and hit upon the idea that his critique of bourgeois political economy had to take the form of a descent into the modern Inferno. Casting the proletariat as the pilgrim, he took upon himself the role of a Virgil, guiding the revolutionary class through the evils of the modern world in such a way as to reveal capital itself as the guilty party, the sinner trapped in a Hell of its own making, incapable of salvation. This katabasis would, simultaneously, constitute a proper culmination and criticism of socialism itself, revealing the ways in which its moralism derived from and supported the very world it sought to combat.

Marx wanted to publish a work that would be *both* a systematic treatment and a thoroughgoing critique of *both* the capitalist mode of production and the political economy that reflected and justified it. He wanted to do so, in part, because he thought that the existing socialist theory botched the job by oversimplifying and misidentifying the issues facing the workers' movement. Marx was convinced that capitalism was not a simple problem, amenable to simple solutions, and that the "solutions to the social question" circulating and competing for attention within the workers' movement—cooperative colonies, people's banks, monetary reform, nationalization of land—were so many mirages and distractions along the path to real emancipation. Marx's fourfold literary mission—depiction and critique, of practice and of theory—required a literary armature to support it. And Marx's sense of the scope and systematic nature of the problem required of him that he find a mode of presentation that would allow him to keep the various moments distinct from one another and properly interrelated. These multiple demands go some way toward explaining why Marx was so slow in writing *Capital*. They also suggest why Dante's poem, despite its moralism, would have been an attractive resource for Marx. The *Inferno* presents the reader with a

[12] *Early Writings*, 423; MEGA, IV.3:20–21.

descent through a systematically ordered underworld, in which the evils encountered early on are symptoms and presentiments of the evils encountered further along, in which description, diagnosis, and castigation go hand in hand, and in which scatological name-calling and eschatological first philosophy are necessary complements of each other.

This first chapter will move from this "would have been" to a more solid basis upon which to erect the argument of the book. It will canvass the evidence that Marx was well-acquainted with Dante's poem and that *Capital* and the *Inferno* bear enough resemblance to warrant suspicion. It will also indicate a precedent; Marx, on at least one other occasion, used a literary source as a model for one of his own works. Finally, it will turn to the context within which Marx, in 1859, first suggests a parallelism between Dante's *Inferno* and his own critique of political economy. By the time Marx wrote *Capital*, there was a significant tradition of socialists couching their criticisms of modern society in infernal terms. Most importantly, Marx's nemesis, Pierre-Joseph Proudhon, had cast the revolutionary task as one of escaping from an inverted underworld. Marx picked up on and developed this metaphor into an itinerary for his critique of political economy. In sum, this chapter builds the case that Marx had the motive, the opportunity, and the history to rewrite the *Inferno* as a descent into the modern social Hell of capital.

THE ELEMENTS OF THE CASE

The plausibility and value of reading *Capital* as a modern *Inferno* can only emerge from the reading itself. Nonetheless, some readers will want assurances up front that this is not a purely imaginative or speculative endeavor, and a scholar is honor bound to respect this reasonable demand. The following review of the documentary evidence—which establishes that Marx could have modeled *Capital* on the *Inferno*—is meant to provide such assurance.

There is a certain immediate resemblance between *Capital* and the *Inferno*: both are explicitly figured as descents into the depths, descents that reveal what is wrong with the world, and that trace that wrong back to its origin. This resemblance has suggested to others that Marx's project in *Capital* is akin to Dante's. We know that Marx was well acquainted with Dante's poem, and that he was reading it during the time when he was formulating and composing *Capital*. He cites all three parts of the *Commedia*, both in *Capital* and in other works contemporaneous with its composition. From the testimony of those close to him, and from his own hand, we know that Dante was among his favorite poets during this time, his exile in London. We know that, at least in part through the study of

Dante, he taught himself Italian. And we know that the conceit of treating the critical presentation of economics as a tour of Hell was one that Marx had encountered in Proudhon. There is also some evidence that Marx was willing and able to compose works in homage to literary exemplars: *The Eighteenth Brumaire of Louis Bonaparte* plays on the plot of Shakespeare's *Hamlet*. Taken together, this circumstantial evidence is strong, but not dispositive. Reading *Capital* with the *Inferno* in mind, however, proves extremely fruitful, as I hope the remainder of this book demonstrates.

Clues and Opportunities

I am not the first to have noticed similarities between Marx's *Capital* and Dante's *Inferno*. David McNally has recently written about the transition between parts two and three of *Capital*, where Marx leaves the sphere of exchange to enter "the hidden abode of production, on the threshold of which one reads, 'No admittance except on business.'"[13] McNally sees in this an allusion to the entrance of Dante and Virgil into Hell. "Marx intends us to understand that in leaving the apparently heavenly sphere of exchange . . . we are descending into a hell, and that therein resides the fundamental truth of capitalism. As with Dante, so for Marx the voyage through the sufferings of hell is essential if we are to acquire genuine knowledge of our world."[14] Before McNally, S. S. Prawer called special attention to the influence Dante exerted on Marx, especially in *Capital*.[15] What has struck these readers is the general trajectory of *Capital*, from the surface down to the depths, and the sense, again general, that the agonies Marx highlights are hellish. As we will see, both of these features are quite common in the socialist literature of the nineteenth century.[16]

What has gone unremarked is that the parallels between the two works are both more mundane and more far-reaching. Yes, they both begin on the surface, and descend beneath this surface. But they also do so in

---

[13]*Capital*, 1:279–80; *MEGA*, II.6:191; *MEGA*, II.7:143.

[14]*Monsters of the Market*, 134.

[15]*Karl Marx and World Literature*, 419–21.

[16]The theologian Arend Thomas van Leeuwen, in his unfortunately obscure Gifford Lectures, has also noticed Marx's citations of Dante, and has seen in them a précis of the trajectory of Marx's entire critique of political economy (*Critique of Earth*, chap. 8). However, van Leeuwen thinks of this trajectory in grand terms, both world-historical and biographical. "Just as Dante's journey through hell and purgatory leads to Paradise, so Marx's critical journey goes steadily forward," van Leeuwen writes, "through the spirit-realm of civil society as far as the portals of reality, the new world in which man will really be man again" (ibid., 223). There is much to be gleaned from van Leeuwen's reading, but it is the opposite of contextually situated (for an appreciation, see Boer, *Criticism of Earth*, 3n4).

thirty-three chapters, and in four major steps. When Marx went over *Capital* for the French edition—the first and last "thorough re-working" of the text that he was able to undertake[17]—he made the subsections of two chapters—four and twenty-four—into freestanding chapters, increasing thereby the number of chapters from twenty-five to thirty-three.[18] He left no indication of why he felt this change was called for. Perhaps it is coincidence, but Dante's *Commedia* is composed of three canticles of thirty-three cantos, plus a prefatory canto to make a round hundred.[19]

This curiosity would be nothing more than that, but both the *Inferno* and *Capital* can also be divided internally into four structuring sections. Dante's Hell has four major parts, arranged as a series of descending circular levels. "Upper Hell," outside the gates of Dis, is where the sins of incontinence (lust, gluttony, avarice and prodigality, sloth, envy, wrath, and pride) are punished. Dis, the walled city within Hell, holds the violent. Within and below Dis is Malebolge, where the manifold species of fraud are punished in ten concentric trenches. Finally, the central pit, Cocytus, contains those who have committed treachery, with Lucifer—the original sinner—plugging the hole at the bottom of everything.

Now, consider *Capital*. Although it has eight parts, these are not of equal import. Part one, the first three chapters, considers the capitalist mode of production from the perspective of the market. Part two, the following three chapters, is transitional, motivating a change of vantage point from the market to the site of production, the workshops and factories. Hence, these chapters form a natural unit with part three, "The Production of Absolute Surplus-Value," which comprises Marx's consideration of capitalist exploitation as the forced extraction of surplus labor. Parts four, five, six, and seven belong together, and mark another shift in standpoint; Marx is here concerned with what he calls the real subsumption of the labor process, whereby capital reconfigures how people labor—through cooperation and industrialization—and appropriates that productivity to itself in the form of accumulation. The final part, on

---

[17]Marx, *Capital*, 1:95; *MEGA*, II.6:700. It was the first because, as Marx tells us in the afterword to the second German edition, "there was no time for" fully reworking that edition, since he "was informed only in the autumn of 1871, when in the midst of other urgent work, that the book was sold out and the printing of the second edition was to begin in January 1872" (*Capital*, 1:95; *MEGA*, II.6:701). It was the last because, as Engels tells us, "Marx was not destined to get [the third German edition] ready for the press himself," dying eight months prior to its printing (Engels's "Preface to the Third Edition," in Marx, *Capital*, 1:106; *MEGA*, II.8:57).

[18]I will return to the special significance of the French edition; for some influential considerations of its status, see Anderson, "The 'Unknown' Marx's *Capital*, Volume I: The French Edition of 1872–75, 100 Years Later."

[19]For the significance of this scheme in Dante, see Freccero, *Dante: The Poetics of Conversion*, chap. 17.

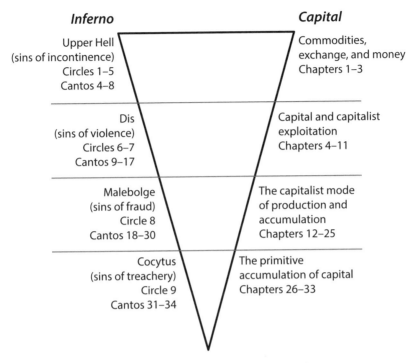

Figure 1. The structural parallels of the *Inferno* and *Capital*.

the "primitive accumulation" of capital, stands apart and plays a special role, indicating as it does the origin and tendency of capitalism in the expropriation of peasants and colonized peoples.[20] The parallel structures of the two works can be schematized as shown in figure 1.

Hence, if one goes looking for similarities between Dante's work and Marx's, one can find them. Moreover, Marx certainly had the wherewithal to put them there to be found. Wilhelm Liebknecht was, by his own account, "from the summer of 1850 until the beginning of the year 1862 . . . almost daily and for years nearly all day in the house of Marx."[21] He testifies that Dante was among the authors Marx "read almost daily," and that the elder man had the habit of declaiming aloud from *The Divine Comedy*, from which he had apparently memorized

---

[20] Identifying these four primary parts of Marx's work, and thereby cutting *Capital* at its joints, is of fundamental import. As we will see, this is what reveals the real argumentative structure of *Capital* and allows us to identify the primary opponents and interlocutors at each step of that argument.

[21] *Karl Marx: Biographical Memoirs*, 6.

"long passages."[22] There is also independent confirmation of Marx's affection for Dante: in an undated "confession," written in Marx's hand and found in his daughter Jenny's album, the Florentine heads a list of favorite poets, a list that also includes Aeschylus, Shakespeare, and Goethe.[23]

Unlike Aeschylus, Shakespeare, and Goethe, however, Dante seems to have been a relatively late discovery for Marx, coinciding basically with his term of political exile in London. Citations from Dante crop up suddenly in his writings from the 1850s and continue, off and on, throughout the rest of his life. The first published citation is in his column for the *New York Daily Tribune*, April 4, 1853, and highlights precisely the experience of living in exile.[24] Thereafter, Marx seems to have turned to the poet periodically. There is a cluster of citations in 1859 and 1860—in the *New York Daily Tribune*, the *Contribution to the Critique of Political Economy*, and, especially, *Herr Vogt*—and another cluster in the first volume of *Capital*.[25] It has been claimed that Marx taught himself Italian by reading Dante and Machiavelli.[26] According to Liebknecht, the phrase from *Purgatorio* concluding the preface to *Capital*—"*Segui il tuo corso e lascia dir le genti*"—was, throughout this time, an oft-repeated dictum of Marx's.[27] In short, Marx loved Dante, and knew the *Divine Comedy*—perhaps especially the *Inferno*—very well. He would certainly have been capable of drawing on that work for inspiration in the composition of his own.

Precedent

Besides being capable, Marx was on another important occasion willing to construct one of his own works around a borrowed literary motif. In his *Eighteenth Brumaire of Louis Bonaparte*, Marx was concerned to

[22] Ibid., 77, 130–31.

[23] Another version of the confession, from the spring of 1865, does not include Dante; *MECW*, 42:569, 672n620.

[24] *MECW*, 11:539.

[25] For commentary, see Prawer, *Karl Marx and World Literature*, 239–40, 261–64, 268, 301, 338–39, and 419–21.

[26] Ibid., 384. However, Marx did not restrict himself to the Italian original. There is a page of excerpts from Karl Lüdwig Kannegiesser's German translation, *Die göttliche Komödie dem Dante Alighieri*, in one of Marx's notebooks from 1859 or 1860 (IISG, B 93, S. 19). These excerpts, all from the *Inferno*, form the basis of the citations in *Herr Vogt*, and presumably Marx went to the German edition in order to avoid having to translate the Italian himself, since the audience for his polemics could not be expected to understand citations in the original language. Engels, by contrast with Marx, read Dante in Italian very early in life. In the course of defending his anonymous "Letters from Wuppertal" in 1839, he corrected an Italian quotation from the *Inferno* used by a critic (*MECW*, 2:29). Like Marx, he taught himself Italian by reading "with a dictionary, the most difficult classical author[s]" he could find: "Dante, Petrarch, and Ariosto," *MECW*, 47:48. The same method was used in the Marx household to teach Jenny and Laura, and, presumably, Eleanor as well (*MECW*, 41:571).

[27] *Karl Marx: Biographical Memoirs*, 83.

dissect the collapse of the 1848 revolution in France into the dictatorship of Louis Bonaparte and the Second Empire. In the course of this
dissection, Marx confronts the fact that the apparent beneficiaries of the
collapse—Bonaparte and his clique—were, by all accounts, far too in-
competent to have brought about this result by any design or stratagem.
As Marx writes:

> The Constitution, the National Assembly, the dynastic parties, the blue and
> the red republicans, the heroes of Africa, the thunder from the platform, the
> sheet lightning from the daily press, all the other publications, the political
> names and intellectual reputations, the civil law and the penal code, *liberté,
> egalité, fraternité* and the second Sunday in May—all have vanished like a
> series of optical illusions before the spell of a man whom even his enemies
> do not claim to be a magician. . . . It remains to be explained how a nation
> of thirty-six millions could be taken by surprise by three swindlers and
> delivered without resistance into captivity.[28]

The beneficiaries are not responsible for the outcome. And so Marx sets
for himself the task of explaining by what agency and by what actions
the revolution came to naught. Throughout his text, Marx figures this
task as one of revealing the parties responsible for the death of the revolution. And throughout, he models this revelation on Hamlet's revelation
of his father's murderer in *The Mouse-trap*, the play within a play in
Shakespeare's tragedy.[29] A brief retelling of Marx's tale should suffice to
establish the basic contours of the modeling.[30]

The theatrical metaphors of the *Eighteenth Brumaire* are obvious from
the opening lines, in which "the great events and characters of world history" are said to repeat themselves, "the first time as tragedy, the second as
farce."[31] The actions of 1848–51 are said repeatedly to occur on stage.[32]
Marx refers to the parliamentary roles of the Legitimist and Orleanist
parties as "*Haupt- und Staatsaktionen*," a form of popular traveling the-
ater in which the high dramas of Elizabethan and German playwrights

---

[28] *Political Writings*, 2:151–52; *MEGA*, I.11:102–3.

[29] As Prawer has rightly noted, Marx believed "that imaginative literature and other
kinds of writing are not wholly distinct and discrete, . . . that all the ways in which men
express themselves, all the institutions they call into being, all the social relations they form,
are intimately related, and that their study should form an integral whole" (*Karl Marx and
World Literature*, 421–22). Whether or not Marx was right to believe this, the fact that he
did believe it supplies a prima facie reason for approaching his own texts as if this belief
were true.

[30] I have previously discussed Marx's use of *Hamlet* in the *Eighteenth Brumaire* ("Marx
Contra the Democrats: The Force of the *Eighteenth Brumaire*").

[31] *Political Writings*, 2:146; *MEGA*, I.11:96.

[32] *Political Writings*, 2:153, 154, 161, 171, 174, 184, 194, 217, 221; *MEGA*, I.11:103,
104, 112, 119, 123, 131, 139, 160, 163.

were debased into melodramas accompanied by improvised buffoonery.[33] He also tells us that the leaders of the proletarian party were absent from the "public stage," and that the proletariat was in "the *background* of the revolutionary stage" throughout the period he is analyzing.[34]

This absence is crucial because it is the proletariat that had given the Revolution of 1848 its particular cast. The proclamation in February 1848 that the new French Republic was a "social republic" indicated "the general content of the modern revolution," a content that would reappear in a "positive form" in the Paris Commune of 1871.[35] But on June 21, 1848, the National Assembly shuttered the national workshops that had embodied Louis Blanc's "right to work." There followed four days of street battles between 50,000 armed and barricaded Parisian workers and up to 125,000 French troops and mobile guardsmen. Thousands were killed, maimed, or exiled to Algeria.[36] This was, to Marx, the moment at which the social republic, the proletarian revolution, died.

Nonetheless, death was not the end of the revolution. As he tells his readers at the beginning of the concluding section VII, "In the June days of 1848" the social republic "was drowned in the blood of the Paris proletariat, but it haunted the succeeding acts of the drama like a ghost."[37] A bit further on, he tells us which ghost he has in mind:

> "But the revolution is thorough [*gründlich*]. It is still on its journey through purgatory. It goes about its business methodically. By 2 December 1851, it had completed only one half its preparatory work; it is now completing the other half. First of all it perfected the parliamentary power, in order to be able to overthrow it. Now, having attained this, it is perfecting the *executive power*, reducing it to its purest expression, isolating it, and pitting itself against it as the sole object of attack, in order to concentrate all its forces of destruction against it. And when it has completed this, the second half of its preliminary work, Europe will leap from its seat and exultantly exclaim: "Well undermined, old mole! [*Brav gewühlt, alter Mahlwurf!*]"[38]

As everyone notes, the final exclamation is a citation of Hamlet's line, "Well said, old mole!" (I.v.162). It comes early in Shakespeare's play, just after the ghost of the king has enlisted his son to avenge his murder. After

---

[33] *Political Writings*, 2:174; *MEGA*, I.11:122; Williams, "Haupt- und Staatsaktion."

[34] *Political Writings*, 2:154; *MEGA*, I.11:104.

[35] *Political Writings*, 2:153; *MEGA*, I11:103; *Civil War in France, Political Writings*, 3:209.

[36] For a historical recounting of the June Days, see Harsin, *Barricades: The War of the Streets in Revolutionary Paris, 1830–1848*, chap. 15; and Rudé, *The Crowd in History: A Study of Popular Disturbances in France and England, 1730–1848*, chap. 11.

[37] *Political Writings*, 2:234; *MEGA*, I.11:174.

[38] *Political Writings*, 2:236–37; *MEGA*, I.11:176.

speaking with the ghost, Prince Hamlet attempts to confer with Horatio and Marcellus to obtain their silence regarding the ghost's appearance and Hamlet's interaction with it. But every time Hamlet proposes an oath of silence, the ghost pipes up from beneath the stage—Hamlet calls attention to its presence in the cellarage—impatiently commanding the trio to swear. Hamlet tries to get away from the ghost, since the impatience of its demand is continually disrupting his proceedings with Marcellus and Horatio, but the ghost is always there, under them wherever they stand. Eventually, Hamlet cries out: "Well said old mole! Canst work i' the earth so fast? A worthy pioneer!"

While commentators get pleasantly waylaid by the parallel genealogies within the two texts—a dead uncle and his eponymous nephew; a dead father and his eponymous son—or by the echo of Hegel—who characterized the work of *Geist* using the same reference—it seems that the political meaning of Marx's invocation is relatively straightforward.[39] The revolution is dead. Marx, casting himself in the Hamlet role, is the son of the dead revolution come to reveal the parties guilty of its murder and to pledge vengeance. The prime culprits belong to the bourgeois "party of order," who have replaced *fraternité* with fratricide. But the bourgeoisie has also been enabled by the petit bourgeois democrats, the workers' old coalition partners, organized under the banner of the *Montagne*.[40] Marx uses his work to call out "the bourgeois and the *épicier*" for their perfidious mouthing of republican ideals and their shameful capitulation before Bonaparte.[41] And he closes with a threat, predicting that "when the emperor's mantle finally falls on the shoulders of Louis Bonaparte, the bronze statue of Napoleon will come crashing down from the top of the Vendôme Column."[42] Just as Hamlet directed *The Mouse-trap* to "catch the conscience of a king" (II.ii.580), so Marx published *The Eighteenth Brumaire* to publicly indict and condemn the French bourgeoisie and petite bourgeoisie. He borrowed Shakespeare's plot because it served ably to condense and direct his own literary and political endeavors.

---

[39] Commentary on this passage was pioneered by Stallybrass, "Well Grubbed, Old Mole." Noteworthy additions have been made by de Grazia, "Teleology, Delay, and the 'Old Mole'"; and Harries, *Scare Quotes from Shakespeare*. Derrida, surprisingly, passes over it in silence (*Specters of Marx*). Harries has the fullest and most helpful discussion of Marx's sources and of the appropriate translation of *gewült* (*Scare Quotes from Shakespeare*, 79–89). I have followed him in rendering it as "undermined."

[40] *Political Writings*, 2:176–84; *MEGA*, I.11:124–31.

[41] *Political Writings*, 2:235; *MEGA*, I.11:177.

[42] *Political Writings*, 2:249; *MEGA*, I.11:189. In fact, it would be nearly twenty years before the Communards toppled the column, and photographs of that event would be used by the Third Republic to identify Communards for execution, imprisonment, and exile.

Hence, it seems not unreasonable to suppose that Marx might similarly have borrowed the plot of Dante's *Inferno* in order to supply himself with an order for his exposition in *Capital*. Moreover, this borrowing would have suited Marx's political aims and temperament. It would have underlined his desire to rework socialism's relationship to political economy. It would have well-captured his ambivalent admiration of that bourgeois science. It would have appealed to his perverse desire to encourage his opponents' worst thoughts about him. And it would have supplied an appropriately complex skeleton on which to hang his ambition to get to the bottom of what is wrong with capitalism. To these substantive points we must now turn.

THE SOCIAL HELL

Marx is often represented as having "created," in G.D.H. Cole's words, "that distinctively German Socialism which was soon to assume an ideological dominance over most of the continent, driving the older forms of Socialism before it as chaff before the wind."[43] One of the themes of this book, by way of contrast, is that many of the elements of Marx's work were commonplaces in the socialist and communist discourses of the mid-nineteenth century, and they retained their status as commonplaces long after Marx. Most of the phrases, tropes, and bits of technical vocabulary we have come to associate with Marx actually originated elsewhere and circulated very widely within the publications and speeches of socialists, mutualists, cooperativists, and communists. They were not in themselves the badges of a distinctive, or distinctively German, socialism, and they could not drive away the elements of the older socialisms because they were as integral to those older patterns of thinking as they were to Marx's.

This is in no way meant to imply that Marx was simply derivative of his discursive context, the amanuensis of Monsieur Nineteenth Century Socialism. Rather, Marx's specificity and originality can emerge, if at all, only on the condition that we understand what he has done with these commonplaces, how they have come to be related to one another in his works, and how this set of internal relationships gives a distinctive cast to his work. In his superb study of Greek myths of the underworld journey, Radcliffe Edmonds emphasizes "the ways in which different authors make use of myth, the way they manipulate a common set of traditional elements in various ways to achieve different ends."[44] If we follow

---

[43] Cole, *A History of Socialist Thought*, 1:222.
[44] Edmonds, *Myths of the Underworld Journey*, 4.

Edmonds in defining myth as "an agonistic form of cultural discourse, a traditional language for the communication of ideas from the author to his audience, in which competing versions vie for authority,"[45] then we can say that this book aims to articulate Marx's *Capital* against the background of the socialist myths redeployed and complicated by that text.[46] Marx's contribution to socialism can only be appreciated by following the traditional elements of socialist discourse as they enter into and are reordered by Marx's work. And this reordering can only be rendered visible as a contest with other socialists, a contest over the proper ordering of and relations among the traditional elements.

It is not by accident that I introduce this consideration of Marx's appropriation of a common set of socialist tropes by way of scholarship on Greek myths of the underworld, for a crucial case in point is Marx's appropriation of the socialist comparison of the modern social world to Hell. This trope has a long and colorful history in socialist literature, both before and after Marx. It seems to have emerged out of the idiosyncratic imagination of Charles Fourier; it found sustenance in the workers' writings of the July monarchy in France; and it was reworked significantly by Pierre-Joseph Proudhon, before Marx gave it another twist. It continued to be a staple of French socialist writing into the twentieth century. Despite its apparent heavy-handedness, it was a flexible myth, suggesting different lessons in different contexts and uses. The history I tell will be limited, picking out only a few of what I take to be the most significant instances.

Origins in Fourier and Fourierism

As with so many elements of the discourse around "the social question," the notion that modernity amounts to "a social Hell" seems to begin its public life in the works of Charles Fourier. In his *Théorie des quatre mouvements* (1808), Fourier had compared the terrors of "the first creation"—tigers, bedbugs, gout, and so on—to "a foretaste of hell."[47] With the publication of his *Traité de l'association domestique-agricole* in 1822, however, he introduced into French literature the metaphor of *l'enfer social*, a trope that would reappear in dozens of permutations over the next thirty years of Fourierist evangelism. The social Hell was

[45] Ibid., 5.

[46] I do not mean "myth" to carry any pejorative force. Myths are the stories we tell ourselves and one another to help make shorthand sense of the world. They are not true in the way that science is, but that is neither here nor there. They are action-guiding and meaning-giving, and their truth or falsity is an ethical and political question, not merely an epistemological one.

[47] Fourier, *The Theory of the Four Movements*, 45–46.

polyvalent. It named the misery of the multitude of the poor.[48] It named the "labyrinth of passions" in which we are trapped by commerce.[49] It named the barbarity of civilization under "the laws of *philosophes* and conquerors."[50] Of all these senses, that of the misery of the poor and wretched was the most appropriated, even as this shaded into a moralizing catalog of the sins that kept the multitude imprisoned in its terrors.[51]

In 1843, Victor Considérant, the dean of Fourierism in France, published, in his *Démocratie Pacifique*, a *Manifeste de la Démocratie au XIXe siècle*.[52] A plea for France to step back from the brink of social war and to organize economic production and distribution by the institution of Fourier's *phalanges*, the *Manifeste* is also a fierce denunciation of the "new feudalism" brought about by the anarchy of laissez-faire competition. This denunciation culminates in §XI, "The social Hell. Absolute necessity of a solution." Here, Considérant compares the miseries of "our regime of free competition" or "our industrial regime" to "the cruelest conceptions of the myths of antiquity."[53] The suffering of the poor masses in the midst of commercial society is compared to the torment of Tantalus. The wage laborers, driven every day to work by the recurrent threat of poverty, share the fate of Sisyphus. The wealth the workers continuously create just as continuously flows out of their hands and into the purses of the wealthy, just as the water carried by the Danaïdes flowed out of the cracked tub as quickly as they could pour it in. Drawing his lesson, Considérant writes:

> Our industrial regime, founded on competition without guarantees and without organization, is it not thus a social Hell, a vast realization of all of the torments and all of the tortures of the ancient Taenarus. There is a difference, though: the victims of Taenarus were guilty, and in the mythological hell there were judges.[54]

[48] *Traité de L'association domestique-agricole ou Attraction Industrielle*, 485.

[49] *Cités Ouvrières: Extrait de La Phalange*, 64.

[50] *Pièges et Charlatanisme des Deux Sectes Saint-Simon et Owen*, 45.

[51] Thus, in what must be one of the earliest appearances of the phrase in English, the editor of a compilation of character studies by various French authors takes the reader on the introduction on a tour of "the Parisian social hell," teeming with young girls headed to work in the workrooms, shops, attics, and cellars of the city. As the editor informs us, "Many of them become prostitutes, and are degraded to a circle of our social hell, into which we will not follow them" (Anonymous, *Pictures of the French: A Series of Literary and Graphic Delineations of French Character*, x).

[52] The *Manifeste* was republished as a pamphlet, *Principe du socialism*, in 1847, on the eve of revolution, and commentators have underlined the numerous rhetorical and tropic similarities between it and Marx and Engels's *Manifesto*.

[53] *Principes du socialisme: Manifeste de La Démocratie au XIXe siècle*, 15–16.

[54] Ibid., 16. Frédéric Bastiat, the prize fighter of nineteenth-century French liberalism, saw fit to truncate this passage, leaving off everything after "the victims" (*Harmonies*

Since he had begun the *Manifeste* in a Saint-Simonian vein, contrasting the ancient economy of slavery—"the exploitation of man by man in its most complete form"—with the modern "democratic spirit,"[55] this revelation that the modern economy embodies the worst tortures that the ancients could imagine is supposed to throw into question the reality of historical progress to date. In light of the Saint-Simonian and Fourierist attempts to marshal Christian ethics and spirituality in support of a new social order, it is not surprising that Considérant makes no mention of any Christian hellscape.[56] Hell is, for him, a place in the pagan imaginary, Taenarus, the descending path walked by Heracles. We have not avoided this survival from barbarous antiquity, and so we can only abolish it.[57]

Development by Proudhon

Three years after Considérant's *Manifeste*, Proudhon published his *Système des contradictions économiques, ou La philosophie de la misère*. This was supposed to be the positive system to follow on the scathing critique in *Qu'est-ce que la propriété?*, which had brought Proudhon great notoriety. Since, in his earlier work, Proudhon had sharply differentiated himself from both the hierarchical organizers of labor (the Saint-Simonians, the Fourierists, Louis Blanc) and those who called for a community of property (Étienne Cabet and the Icarians, Wilhelm Weitling),[58] it did seem incumbent upon him to provide some distinctive alternative to the system of private property. In this regard, the *Système* was quite a disappointment. Instead of being prescriptive, it was a long analysis of the interrelated aspects of the modern social system,[59] which aimed to highlight the destructiveness of each aspect and the potential for saving the whole by properly ordering them vis-à-vis one another.

Économiques, 45n1). By this ingenious method, he sought either to convict Considérant of "misanthropy," presumably for comparing the poor to those suffering for their sins, or else to suggest that the only difference between the Hell of antiquity and the modern social Hell was that the latter lacked victims (ibid., 45).

[55] *Principes du socialisme: Manifeste de La Démocratie au XIXe siècle*, 1–2.

[56] For citations and discussion of Fourierism's close links with social Catholicism, see Pilbeam, *French Socialists before Marx*, 44–46.

[57] For further uses of the trope of the social Hell, see Jacques Rancière's exploration of the writings of Saint-Simonian workers in the run-up to 1848, in *The Nights of Labor*, chap. 1.

[58] The organization of labor and the community of goods are at times lumped together by Proudhon, as in his attacks on the advocates of "association" (*General Idea*, 75–99; *OC*, 2:155–76).

[59] These moments are, in Proudhon's order: (1) the division of labor; (2) machinery; (3) competition; (4) monopoly; (5) police, or taxation; (6) the balance of trade; (7) credit; (8) property; (9) community; and (10) population.

There are in Proudhon's writings of the 1840s numerous invocations of the promise of an economic science that would reveal the tendency toward order in human society and catalyze the development of that order.[60] In *Qu'est-ce que la propriété?* he summed up this prospective development by coining a phrase that would have a long life as another socialist myth: "the sovereignty of the will gives way to the sovereignty of reason and ends up being replaced by a scientific socialism."[61] Proudhon's notion of this incipient social science was heavily indebted to Charles Fourier's conception of the "series,"[62] the sum of an ordered succession of elements.[63] The underlying idea is that the successive "stages" or "periods" (*époques*) of history exhibit, in turn, successive principles, and that only at the end of the series will these opposed principles come into a harmonious interrelation. As Proudhon put it, "while in nature the synthesis of contraries is contemporaneous with their opposition, in society the antithetic elements seem to be produced at long intervals, and to be resolved only after long and tumultuous agitation."[64]

Because science is supposed to grasp the series, it must proceed through the elements of the series in turn, showing how any partial summation of the series, including any element on its own, is self-contradictory and inadequate from the point of view of justice. Hence, science, in Proudhon's sense, must proceed methodically, following a determinate path, and may be said to pass from appearances—the partial aspects of the world presented by each *époque*—to the reality of the whole series. As Proudhon put it, "to explain the system of the world, . . . one must leave the circle of appearances."[65] This was the task Proudhon tried to accomplish in his *Système*.

---

[60] For examples, see *What Is Property?*, 17–20, 208–11; OC, 4:136–41, 338–42; *System*, 1:44, 55, 388–97; OC, 1:66, 75, 337–44; OC, 5:80–100, 405–51.

[61] *What Is Property?*, 208–9; OC, 4:339.

[62] Coincidentally, there were two Fouriers obsessed with series: Charles and the mathematician Joseph. Victor Hugo, in *Les Misèrables*, wrote that "There was a celebrated Fourier at the Academy of Science, whom posterity has forgotten; and in some garret an obscure Fourier, whom the future will recall" (I.III.1). This prediction has turned out to be very nearly the opposite of the truth, as the Fourier series is integral to mathematics while the other series, and the other Fourier, if not forgotten, certainly have no import in the social sciences.

[63] Hoffman, *Revolutionary Justice*, 106–9; Crowder, *Classical Anarchism*, 112.

[64] *System*, 1:129–30; OC, 1:135; compare *What Is Property?*, 19; OC, 4:19.

[65] *What Is Property?*, 18; OC, 4:138. Proudhon's self-conception as a scientist has not aged well. Even scholars very friendly to Proudhon claim, e.g., that Proudhon's "'synthesis' is quite artificial, claiming that it integrates without really doing so" (Hoffman, *Revolutionary Justice*, 109). Indeed, Proudhon himself may have been dissatisfied with this pretense, for he largely dropped his claims to science after the disappointing reception of *De la creation de l'ordre* and *Système des contradictions* (Crowder, *Classical Anarchism*, 112).

In the course of his exposition of this social science, Proudhon has recourse, like Considérant before him, to the image of Hell. Discussing the consequences of Louis Blanc's proposed right to work at a guaranteed wage, Proudhon writes:

> Certainly I do not care to deny that labor and wages can and should be guaranteed; I even entertain the hope that the time [*époque*] of such guarantee is not far off: but I submit that a guarantee of wages is impossible without the exact knowledge of value, and that this value can be discovered only by competition, not at all by communistic institutions or by a decree of the people. For in this there is something more powerful than the will of the legislator and of the citizens: that is, the absolute impossibility that man should do his duty after being discharged of all responsibility to himself: but, responsibility to oneself, in the matter of labor, necessarily implies competition with others. Ordain that from January 1, 1847 labor and wages are guaranteed to all: immediately an immense relaxation will succeed the fiery tension of industry; real value will fall rapidly below nominal value; metallic money, despite its effigy and stamp, will experience the fate of the *assignats*; the merchant will demand more and deliver less; and we will find ourselves in a still lower circle in the hell of misery of which competition is only the third turn.[66]

The lower circle of Hell to which Proudhon refers is monopoly, the fourth *époque* in his own *Système*. Here we have a striking conjunction of liberal and socialist myths. Proudhon endorses the necessity of free competition in the labor market and acknowledges that this competition is one aspect of the social Hell condemned by Considérant. He thereby casts his scientific journey from appearances to reality as a descent into this Hell, an exploration of its internal arrangement and structural necessity.

As in Considérant's text, Hell is a social reality surrounding us. However, far from being the rhetorical culmination of Proudhon's indictment, this is merely one of his many asides. Indeed, he begins his consideration of the fifth *époque*—"the police, or taxation"—by turning the trope on its head. He imagines the progress of humanity as the journey of a traveler marching up a "zigzag" path from the valley to the mountaintop. Despite its confidence, "the social genius," upon reaching "the perspective of monopoly," "casts backward a melancholy glance, and, in deep reflection, says to itself: 'Monopoly has stripped everything from the poor hireling: bread, clothing, home, education, liberty, and security. I will lay a tax upon the monopolist; at this price I will preserve him his

---

There was, however, no point at which Proudhon either gave up his notion of historical development or his valorization of science as the outcome of that historical development.

[66] *System*, 1:226–27; OC, 1:212–13.

privilege.'"[67] Far from descending through a Hell of misery, the reader is here told that we are following the social genius on its ever-ascending path, the course of which progressively corrects past errors. Proudhon betrays his affinities with the liberal thinkers of spontaneous order, intimating "that out of the common efforts of mankind, out of the struggles and collaborations among men, largely without design, intent, or self-consciousness, come the institutions, beliefs, and all that goes to make up civilization."[68] The liberal myth of providence trumps the socialist myth of Hell on earth.

However, Proudhon has not abandoned the trope of the social Hell. He ends his discussion of free trade with a passage equal in its vehemence to anything in *Qu'est-ce que la propriété?*, calling free trade

> the centralization over the whole face of the earth of this regime of spoliation and misery, . . . property in its might and in its glory. And it is in order to bring to its consummation this system that so many millions of workers are starved, so many innocent creatures turned back from the breast into oblivion, so many girls and women prostituted, so many souls sold, so many characters wasted! If only economists knew a way out of this labyrinth, an end to this torture! But no: *always! never!* like the clock of the damned this is the refrain of the economic Apocalypse. Oh! if the damned could burn hell![69]

These words cast the economists as the mouthpieces of Hell, declaring the eternity of the torments undergone by the suffering masses. They revert to the earlier metaphor, casting the journey through the *époques* as the nightmarish path through the infernal labyrinth. They suggest that, far from being a holdover from antiquity, the social Hell is a historical necessity and a trial we must undergo in order to arrive at "the exact knowledge of value" that will set us free. Finally, unlike Considérant's pagan underworld, Proudhon's Hell is obviously a Christian one. The descending circles suggest Dante's *Inferno*, while the labyrinthine structure recalls both Dante and Fourier.[70]

Five years later, imprisoned for his criticisms of Louis Bonaparte, Proudhon again turned his pen to elaborating the socialist myth, this time with considerable inventiveness and precision. "Humanity," he proposed in his *Idée générale de la révolution au XIXᵉ siècle,*

---

[67] *System,* 1:319; OC, 1:274.

[68] Noland, "History and Humanity: The Proudhonian Vision," 69–70.

[69] OC, 2:67–68.

[70] Proudhon was certainly familiar with Dante's *Divine Comedy,* referring to it in passing in several of his works. Sent a short monograph on the poem by his friend Bergmann, however, he replied (August 24, 1863), modestly, "Pour moi, je t'avoue mon ignorance; je n'avais jamais su ce que c'était que ce Dante, avec sa trilogie divine" (*Correspondance de P.-J. Proudhon,* 1875, 13:136).

in the theologico-political sphere, wherein it has been agitated these six thousand years, is like a society which, instead of being placed on the outside of a solid star, is shut up inside a hollow sphere, lighted from the interior and warmed, like the subterranean world of Virgil, by an immobile sun in the zenith common to the lands curving around it.[71]

Imagining this world, and the course of history in it, Proudhon claims that "the progress of civilization . . . would bring vast movements to these infernal regions," movements that would reveal the true scope and nature of this upside-down world, and simultaneously install in the minds of the inhabitants the conviction that "the earth is too cramped for the humanity that works it [*l'exploite*]."

> Then these men, who had at first taken their orb to be infinite, and had sung its praises, and who had nonetheless been imprisoned like a nest of beetles in a clod of earth, begin to blaspheme God and nature. . . . Menacing heaven with eye and fist, they begin audaciously to drill into the ground, so well that one day, the drill encountering only the void, they conclude that to the concave surface of this sphere corresponds a convex surface, an exterior world, which they set out to visit.[72]

This situation is, Proudhon says, a representation not of our physical existence but of our mental one, of the history of "our political and religious views." The ideas of "God and Prince, the Church and the State," have dominated and defined the sphere of our thinking. We have now exhausted our explorations of these ideas, outgrown them. "We must burst this casing if we want to arrive at a more exact notion of things and leave this hell, where the reason of man, cretinized, will end up being extinguished."[73]

Luckily for us, Proudhon thinks we have already, with "the drill of philosophy," begun to break out of "the embryonic shell" these ideas have provided for our thought. Completing this task—which is simultaneously one of society turning "from within to without," of "invert[ing]" every social relation—is the calling of the revolution. For carrying out this mission, Proudhon suggests turning to "the economists," for "they are miners by trade."[74] What is it about philosophy and economics that will help us to escape from the prison of the old ideas? Very simply, they both teach, according to Proudhon, that all authority is illegitimate. They teach "the laws of nature and of society."[75]

This may seem a puzzling lesson for Proudhon to draw, given his passionate denunciations of the economists in both *Qu'est-ce que la*

[71] *General Idea*, 289; OC, 2:340.
[72] *General Idea*, 289–90; Proudhon, OC, 2:340–41.
[73] *General Idea*, 290–91; OC, 2:341–42.
[74] *General Idea*, 291, 297; OC, 2:342, 347.
[75] *General Idea*, 292–94; OC, 2:342–45.

propriété? and the *Système*. There is certainly a knot to untie here (and I will make a suggestion about how to do this below). But what matters for present purposes is only that, in the *Idée générale*, Proudhon develops the myth of the social Hell into a comprehensive representation of both human history and the revolutionary project, one, moreover, that seems to integrate his earlier invocations of the myth with the Fourierist images. As in Considérant, the social Hell is a remnant of the past, a condition of humanity's immaturity, the limits of which we have now, finally, encountered. As in Proudhon's earlier text, only science, an excavation below the apparent surface, can show us the way out of this Hell. Finally, and also repeating a feature of the *Système*, only our very imprisonment beneath the earth could have developed our capacities to the point where we would require and seek liberation into a life above the earth. The journey through the underworld is part—if a contrapuntal part—of the providential march of human progress.

MARX'S *KATABASIS*

These developments of socialist infernalism were not unknown to Marx. He seems to have had a copy of the second edition of Considérant's *Manifeste* in his personal library, and there are marginal notations on the pages containing the discussion of the social Hell.[76] He wrote *The Poverty of Philosophy* as a response to Proudhon's *Système*, and he studied that work intensively. He read Proudhon's *Idée générale* as soon as he could get his hands on it, at the end of July or beginning of August 1851. He summarized it for Engels in a letter, then sent the book to his friend for his thoughts. Engels wrote up a lengthy critical assessment later in the year, which he sent to Marx. Marx planned to publish a long review of Proudhon's book in Joseph Weydemeyer's *Die Revolution*, but the journal went bankrupt before he could realize this intention. As I will now argue, Marx's familiarity with this trope was not barren. He himself deployed it in a novel and interesting way.

The 1859 Preface

Thirteen years after Proudhon's much-anticipated *Système*, an obscure little book was published by Franz Duncker in Berlin. Titled *Zur Kritik der politicshen Ökonomie* (*Contribution to the Critique of Political Economy*), it was written by a German exile from the revolutions of 1848

---

[76] *MEGA*, IV.32:199–200; §XI, "The social Hell," is on pp. 15–17 of the edition possessed by Marx, and page 15 and page 17 in Marx's copy contain marginalia.

who had largely disappeared from the German radical scene after 1852. Karl Marx had been making a meager living in London as a newspaper correspondent for the *New York Tribune*, the *Neue Oder-Zeitung* in Breslau, and the *Zuid Afrikaan*, a Dutch-language paper in South Africa. While this journalism was, considered in sum, the majority of what Marx would publish in his entire life, it was not addressed primarily to a working-class or socialist audience, and it was not, perforce, very heavy on either political agitation or theoretical elaboration.[77] And, as Marx said in a contemporaneous letter to Joseph Weydemeyer, he had "given up associations [and] withdrawn completely into [his] study."[78]

Marx intended this new book to return him to the partisan fray. To Weydemeyer, Marx put his aims this way:

> In these two chapters the Proudhonist socialism now fashionable in France . . . is demolished to its very foundations. Communism must above all rid itself of this "false brother." . . . I hope to win a scientific victory for our party. But the latter must itself now show whether its numbers are great enough to buy enough copies to banish the publisher's "moral scruples." The continuation of the venture depends on the sale of the first installments.[79]

The numbers of Marx's party were quite small, as it turned out. The further installments were never published, and, eight years on, when Marx published volume one of *Capital*, he had to apologize for "the long pause" between *Zur Kritik* and its "continuation," and to begin again from the beginning, recapitulating "the substance of that earlier work" at the start of the new one.[80]

Despite its having fallen apparently stillborn from the press, *Zur Kritik* was destined to deliver to later generations one of the iconic statements of Marx's project. His preface—it has come to be so detached from the work it prefaces that it is generally referred to simply as "the 1859 Preface"—comprises what Marx calls a "sketch of the course of [his] studies," an intellectual autobiography that traces his path from editor of the *Rheinische Zeitung* to surveyor of bourgeois political economy. While engaged in journalism, Marx claims, he had run up against "so-called

---

[77] Sperber, *Karl Marx*, 294–96. Marx's journalism during this period is summarized by Sperber (ibid., 302–25). The political and theoretical development of Marx's thought in and through his journalism is ably treated by the recent work of Anderson, *Marx at the Margins*.

[78] Marx to Weydemeyer, February 1, 1859; *MECW*, 40:376. The background of this withdrawal from political activity is detailed by Hunt, *The Political Ideas of Marx and Engels*, vol. 1, and Lattek, *Revolutionary Refugees*.

[79] Marx to Weydemeyer, February 1, 1859; *MECW*, 40:377–78.

[80] *Capital*, 1:89; *MEGA*, II.5:11; *MEGA*, II.7:11.

material interests" involuntarily, and, he claims further, much to his embarrassment. He resisted the first pushes of those around him toward French socialism and communism out of a principled unwillingness to embrace anything that had not first been carefully and critically studied. Only after his economic research in Paris did he come to see that "the anatomy of bourgeois society is to be sought in political economy." He reached the "general result," which "served as a guiding thread for [his] studies," in Brussels in 1845.[81] At the end of the preface, Marx casts the just completed "sketch" of his history as an apologia. It "should merely demonstrate that [his] views, however one may judge them, and however little they agree with the interested prejudices of the ruling classes, are the result of conscientious and lengthy research."[82] In sharp contrast with Marx's private communication of his hopes to Weydemeyer, the published preface portrays Marx as a scholar and conjures away any image of him as a political partisan. This gives the whole preface, as Terrell Carver notes, "a curiously de-politicized form."[83]

However, the preface ends with a veiled invocation of Proudhon, and an idiosyncratic return to the traditional motif of Hell. The final sentence, directly following Marx's apologia, incorporates a quotation from the *Inferno*: "But at the entrance to science, as at the entrance to Hell, this demand must be registered: 'Here you must abandon every suspicion; here must all your cowardice die.'"[84]

What stands out immediately is that Marx's Hell is not the social world, but the science of that world—not capitalism, but political economy. This migration, as we have seen, was previously suggested by

[81] *MECW*, 29:261–65; *MEGA*, II.2:99–103. This general result is the oft-cited passage: "In the social production of their lives men enter into relations of production that are determinate, necessary, and independent of their will, and which correspond to a determinate stage of development of their material productive forces. The totality of these relations of production forms the economic structure of society, the real basis from which rises a legal and political superstructure, and to which correspond determinate forms of social consciousness" (*MECW*, 29:263; *MEGA*, II.2:100). About this passage, Terrell Carver rightly claims that while it "can be read as the doctrinal foundation of Marxism, a science of law-like tendencies in economic and political life . . . The same propositions can also be examined as 'empirical' propositions in social science, or as attempts at such. . . . Both readings are at the heart of the academic enterprise that Marxology has become, and both have generated intensely interesting intellectual debate. Neither puts Marx into perspective as a political theorist" (introduction to Marx, *Later Political Writings*, xv).

[82] *MECW*, 29:265; *MEGA*, II.2:102–3.

[83] Introduction to Marx, *Later Political Writings*, xiv. This depoliticized form may itself have been political stratagem. As Arthur Prinz has argued, Marx was (rightfully) very concerned about Prussian censorship, and crafted the preface, and *Zur Kritik* as a whole, so as to minimize the risk of the book being seized by authorities ("Background and Ulterior Motive of Marx's 'Preface' of 1859").

[84] *MECW*, 29:265; *MEGA*, II.2:103.

Proudhon's *Système*. In that work, however, science was primarily the road through and out of Hell, not the Hell itself. Proudhon's science was supposed to lead the reader through the labyrinth of history and, unlike the pseudoscience of the economists, eventually to lead the reader out of that labyrinth again, into the new world of mutual association. Marx's science, however, is likened to Hell itself.

At other points in the course of his *Capital* project, Marx is perfectly willing to use the traditional motif in a straightforward way. Writing about the manufacture of phosphorus matches, he claims that "Dante would have found the worst horrors of his Inferno surpassed in this industry."[85] Discussing factory work, he quotes one of Engels's invocations of the motif: "The wearisome routine of endless drudgery, in which the same mechanical process is ever repeated, is like the torture of Sisyphus; the burden of toil, like the rock, is ever falling back on the worn-out drudge."[86] On the basis of texts like these, Prawer has claimed that "what Marx found most important of all in his reading of Dante was that the *Inferno* could provide points of comparison with which to characterize, standards against which to measure, the hell on earth which, he thought, the Victorians had created for the urban and rural poor."[87] This judgment certainly captures a good deal about how Marx integrates the socialist myth of the modern industrial Hell with the trappings of his own classical education. Nonetheless, it fails to encompass the novel use to which that myth is put at the end of the preface to *Zur Kritik*.

Marx's invocations of the social Hell myth register at two levels. On the first, direct level, Marx is repeating a traditional element of socialist discourse, a trope that one might find in any number of social reformers and revolutionaries, according to which the social conditions fostered by modern industry and commerce are the materialization in this life of

---

[85] *Capital*, 1:356; MEGA, II.6:252; MEGA, II.7:205.

[86] *Capital*, 1:548; MEGA, II.6:410; MEGA, II.7:363; see *MECW*, 4:467n; *MEW*, 2:398n14. Engels, in turn, is quoting from J. P. Kay's work, *The Moral and Physical Condition of the Working Classes Employed in the Cotton Manufacture in Manchester* (1832). As the title indicates, Kay's tract is fundamentally concerned with the effects of the factory on the moral character of its (Irish) prisoners. This is not the only invocation of the social Hell in Engels's *Conditions*, and not the only invocation to carry moralistic connotations. Elsewhere, he reports testimony from a father who claimed "that he would rather let his daughter beg than go into a factory; that they are perfect gates of hell; that most of the prostitutes of the town had their employment in the mills to thank for their present situation" (*MECW*, 4:441; *MEW*, 2:373). See also Engels's translation of Edward Meade's poem, "The Steam King" (*MECW*, 4:475–77; *MEW*, 2:404–5). Another source, known well by both Marx and Engels, was Thomas Carlyle, who deploys infernal imagery repeatedly in his depiction of the troubles wrought by "Mammonism" (see, e.g., *Past and Present*, 2–3, 45, 64–66, 197–99). Thanks to Gregory Claeys for calling my attention to these passages.

[87] Prawer, *Karl Marx and World Literature*, 421; compare Wheen, *Karl Marx*, 70–75.

the stories told about punishment in the afterlife. If the tortures of Hell were originally a projection of the worst features of human life into a nightmare about what awaits us on the other side of death, the socialist myth of a social Hell turns this nightmare vision into a critical judgment on the worst features of human life in modernity. However, in Marx, there is also a second, indirect level, within which the Hell invoked is not the lived, material world, but what Proudhon called "the economic Apocalypse," the scientific discourse *about* that world. At this level, political economy is the Hell into which socialists and workers—Marx's presumptive readers—must descend in order to effectively and properly orient themselves in their struggles to transform the lived, material Hell.

The Confrontation with Proudhonism

Why would Marx superimpose this second register on the traditional discourse of socialism? I think he had both partisan and principled reasons for doing so. Present in Marx's mind may have been the accusations of some of the socialists and communists with whom he had clashed in the late 1840s. One of the "True Socialists" attacked on several occasions by Marx and Engels was Karl Grün, the translator of Proudhon's *Système* into German and the author of *Die soziale Bewegung in Frankreich und Belgien* (1845).[88] While Marx was publishing scathing critiques of Grün's work, and Engels was fighting Grün's influence among the German artisan groups in Paris, Grün himself penned a story for the *Kölnischen Zeitung*, "An artisan's story." In this fable, a Mephistophelean caricature of Marx, Doctor Ludwig, enchants a young artisan, Rudolph, and leads him to his doom.[89] This incident, indicative of the passions animating the sectional struggles within the small networks of communist workers and writers, certainly did not give Marx any second thoughts. On the contrary, Grün's fears were a tonic, encouraging Marx in his hopes of winning over the artisanal militants to his own conceptions of revolution.

This episode found a sort of echo a year and a half later, toward the tail end of the upheavals of 1848. Marx had based himself in Cologne,

---

[88] Of Grün, there are only a small handful of hard-to-obtain studies (Bridenthal, "Karl Grün (1817–1887): A Neglected Socialist"; Strassmaier, "Karl Grün: The Confrontation with Marx, 1844–1848"; Strassmaier, *Karl Grün und die Kommunistische Partei, 1845–1848*; Trox, *Karl Grün (1817–1887): Eine Biographie*).

[89] For an account of Grün's story, see Strassmeier, *Karl Grün und die Kommunistische Partei, 1845–1848*, 19–22. Grün was also the author of a work on Goethe, *Über Göthe vom menschlichen Standpunkte* (1846), whose *Faust* loomed so large in the imagination of the nineteenth century. Marx might have taken comfort in Flora Tristan's novel, *Méphis* (1838), in which one of the protagonists is a heroic proletarian who calls himself Méphis, short for Mephistopheles, to signal the danger he knows society sees in him.

where he came into frequent conflict with Andreas Gottschalk, the head of the *Kölner Arbeiterverein*.[90] Gottschalk represented much the same strain of German artisanal socialism as Grün. This strain, albeit in the British context, has been aptly characterized by Craig Calhoun as "reactionary radicalism." Artisanal associations and peasant communities were most likely to engage in radical political action in the early and mid-nineteenth century, Calhoun argues, because they were seeking to protect what they had, or imagined they had, in the face of forces that were fundamentally incompatible with that protection. "Handloom weavers could not be granted their continued peaceful existence without stopping the advance of technological innovation and capital accumulation. When Parisian artisans resisted the division of labor, they were attacking the Industrial Revolution itself."[91] In the context of industrial development and the spread of commercial economies, the members of the *Arbeiterverein* were intransigent, and hence rapidly radicalized. Gottschalk was uninterested in making a strategic alliance with the liberal industrialists against the Prussian government, or in any strategy at all. He wanted an immediate and spontaneous transition to communism.[92] Marx, by way of contrast, wanted a broad democratic coalition to fight for a constitution and a unified German state, the prerequisites, he thought, of capitalist development in Germany. Only in the context of developing capitalism and a liberal constitution could the workers' fight for communism make sense and headway.[93] Gottschalk's interpretation of this strategy was incredulity: "we should really have to, as you proclaim to us, Mr. Preacher, in order to escape the hell of the Middle Ages, voluntarily plunge ourselves into the purgatory of a decrepit dominion of capital, in order to go from there into the misty heavens of your 'communist confession of faith.'"[94]

---

[90] On the life of the *Arbeiterverein*, see Hans Stein's history, *Der Kölner Arbeiterverein, 1848–1849*. There is a useful biography of Gottschalk: Schmidt, *Andreas Gottschalk: Armenarzt und Pionier der Arbeiterbewegung, Jude und Protestant.*

[91] Calhoun, *Roots of Radicalism*, 115.

[92] Schmidt, *Andreas Gottschalk: Armenarzt und Pionier der Arbeiterbewegung, Jude und Protestant.* The macho tone of Gottschalk's criticisms of Marx's party can be gathered from a letter to Engels: "Gottschalk is howling strongly against the [*Neue rheinische*] *Zeitung* here [in Cologne]. He mocks . . . the recommendation of the wusses Schneider, Hagen, Kyll as 'Democratic' candidates" (Ernst Dronke to Engels, February 24, 1849; *MEGA*, III.3, 255).

[93] These episodes have been told several times, but the best telling is, without a doubt, the careful and very insightful work of Hunt, *The Political Ideas of Marx and Engels*. For contrasting interpretations, see Gilbert, *Marx's Politics*; Felix, *Marx as Politician*; Sperber, *Karl Marx*, chap. 6.

[94] Quoted in Schmidt, *Andreas Gottschalk*, 122. This characterization is not far off the mark, at least in a certain regard. There is a strong emphasis on the need for a preparatory schooling in Marx's writings from 1845–48. In *The Holy Family* he had read this preparatory schooling into the lived situation of the laboring class, claiming that "the proletariat

It is easy to imagine Marx, a decade down the line, embracing these old charges with a renewed energy. If the petit bourgeois democrats and artisanal socialists thought of Marx as a malign influence, leading the communist workers' movement astray, so much the better. Marx took a perverse pride in being hated by those for whom he had no respect, and it is entirely in keeping with his character that he would invite such adversaries to think the worst.

These partisan reasons for Marx's transformation of the socialist trope of Hell, rooted in Marx's biography, shade into more objective or principled reasons. Proudhon had, in his works of the 1840s, articulated the terms of a problem facing the socialists and communists of the era.[95] These social revolt movements were fed by the dissolution of old ways of life under the pressure of new modes of government. Economic and political liberalism were emergent powers that fostered the conditions of revolt and raised the expectations of what revolt might accomplish.[96] At the same time, liberalization came hand in hand with a discourse of political economy that enunciated a discrete set of possible aims for government and a discrete set of possible mechanisms for attaining those aims. Political economy thus proclaimed itself the science of the possible. But this science of the possible seemed to declare *impossible* the retention of the old ways of life *and* the aspirations of the radical insurgents. The traditional boundaries of guild, municipal, and royal dominion were declared inadmissible barriers to the freedom of commerce, and, in the next breath, the desires for community, harmony, and satisfaction were ruled out of court as pitiful dreams—and barriers to the freedom of commerce!

The problem, then, was how to grapple with this novel governmental discourse, this science of the new world order. Its mode of reasoning was undeniably powerful. As a science of social mechanics, it seemed

---

can and must emancipate itself. But it cannot emancipate itself without abolishing the conditions of its own life. . . . Not in vain does it go through the stern but steeling school of *labour*" (*MECW*, 4:37; *MEW*, 2:38). In the throes of the counterrevolution in November 1848, he averred that Germans "may have to go through a hard school, but it is the preparatory school for a complete revolution" (*MECW*, 8:16; *MEW*, 6:9). By 1852, Marx had adapted Gottschalk's framing to his own ends, writing in *The Eighteenth Brumaire of Louis Bonaparte* that, while the revolution certainly seems to be over, it has in fact only gone underground, where "It is still preoccupied with journeying through purgatory" (*Political Writings*, 2:236; *MEGA*, I.11:178). Note, however, that it is the social revolution in Marx's formulation, not the proletariat, that must now go through purgatory. Here, too, there is a displacement of the original trope.

[95] Unbeknownst to Proudhon, the terms of this problem had been established fifteen or twenty years earlier in Britain, in the works of popular political economy that followed on the recession of popular radicalism of the French Revolutionary era. We will turn to this scene in the next chapter.

[96] Sperber, *Rhineland Radicals*, pt. 1.

to lay bare the actual dynamics of wealth and power. The older discourses of government—*Kameralwissenschaft*, the mercantile system—
seemed corrupt and inept by comparison. As a result, one of the most
important divisions splitting the second generation of socialist and communist writers—those who began to publish after 1830 in France and
Germany and after 1820 in Britain—is the division between those who
sought some accommodation or confrontation with political economy
and those who refused outright to engage with the new science. The vast
majority of the French and German writers were in the latter camp: most
Saint-Simonians, the Fourierists, Cabet and the Icarians, Blanc, Lamen-
nais, Buchez, Pecqueur, Hess, and Weitling.[97] Many of the most influential
British writers—Gray, Bray, Thompson, Wade, Mudie—were, with Marx
and Proudhon, among those who thought that socialist and communist
militants had to, in one way or another, study and learn from political
economy. None of these thought that this process of learning from political economy entailed an uncritical acceptance of any part thereof. Rather,
it entailed a direct confrontation with political economy, an assessment
of its strengths and weaknesses, and, for some at least, an all-out effort
to defeat it. From very early on, Marx was situated at the extreme limit
of this faction. His ecological niche, as it were, was the position of insisting that the confrontation with political economy had to be taken more
seriously than anyone else was taking it. This position, especially in the
1840s, put him into the closest proximity with Proudhon, from whom he
therefore needed most of all to differentiate himself.

Marx was initially very excited by Proudhon's *Qu'est-ce que la propriété?* It was among the first socialist works he read, and from the first
he judged it to be a "sharp-witted work" demanding "long and profound
study."[98] What he found valuable in the book at the time was that, in it,

---

[97] Engels's judgment of German socialists in his commentary on Fourier (1845) was
that they possessed a "boundless ignorance of political economy and the real character
of society" (*MECW*, 4:643; *MEW*, 2:608). Similarly, he says of French socialists in "The
Progress of Social Reform on the Continent" (1843) that they display a "total ignorance of
history and political economy" (*MECW*, 3:397; *MEW*, 1:485). These judgments are neither
charitable nor, in fact, inaccurate. Regardless, they give a sense of Marx and Engels's per-
ceptions, and of how the two situated themselves vis-à-vis other socialists at the beginning
of their collaboration.

[98] "Communism and the *Augsburg Allgemeine*" (*MECW*, 1:220; *MEGA*, I.1:240). Engels was also deeply impressed, writing in *The New Moral World*, the Owenite organ, that
Qu'est-ce que la propriété? "is the most philosophical work, on the part of the Communists,
in the French language; and, if I wish to see any French book translated into the English
language, it is this. The right of private property, the consequences of this institution, competition, immorality, misery, are here developed with a power of intellect, and real scientific
research, which I never since found united in a single volume. Besides this, he gives very
important remarks on government, and having proved that every kind of government is

"Proudhon subjects the basis of national economy,[99] private property, to a critical examination, and indeed the first resolute, ruthless, and at the same time scientific examination," an examination that "revolutionizes national economy and makes possible for the first time an actual science of national economy." He goes on to claim even more, that Proudhon's "work is a scientific manifesto of the French proletariat." The very terms in which Marx praises Proudhon are an indicator of how close to Proudhon Marx was at the time. As we will see, the desire for "an actual science of national economy" is a Proudhonian desire, and one from which Marx will progressively distance himself.

Despite all of this early praise for Proudhon's first major book, however, it would be false to claim that Marx's disagreements with Proudhon date only from the publication of the *Système* in 1846, or from their awkward and prickly exchange of letters in May of the same year.[100] In fact, Marx's assessment of Proudhon had always included a critical edge, and, if Marx sharpened this edge and drove it deeper, this is not evidence of Marx changing his mind about Proudhon. The differences between the two men simply became more important, practically speaking, as time went on.[101]

From the beginning, Marx thought Proudhon carried over too much of the standpoint of political economy into his critique of property. This is already explicit in Marx's early defense of Proudhon against Left Hegelian criticism. In *The Holy Family*, Marx writes:

> As the first criticism of any science is necessarily influenced by the premises of the science it is fighting against, so Proudhon's treatise *Qu'est-ce que*

alike objectionable, no matter whether it be democracy, aristocracy, or monarchy, that all govern by force; and that, in the best of all possible cases, the force of the majority oppresses the weakness of the minority, he comes, at last, to the conclusion: '*Nous voulons l'anarchie!*' What we want is anarchy; the rule of nobody, the responsibility of every one to nobody but himself" (*MECW*, 3:399; *MEW*, 1:488).

[99] "*Nationalökonomie*" was the nearest contemporary German equivalent to "political economy," though it betrays the extent to which the older paradigm of the *Kameralwissenschaft* retained its hold in the German context. Marx would call attention to and bemoan this fact in his afterword to the second edition of *Capital* (*Capital*, 1:95; *MEGA*, II.6:701).

[100] Marx wrote to invite Proudhon to take part in a correspondence circle among German, French, and British socialists, and to warn him off of his friendship with Karl Grün, whom Marx regarded as a "charlatan" and self-aggrandizer (Marx to Proudhon, May 5, 1846; *MECW*, 38:38). Proudhon responded with a long sermon about the need to avoid "all divisiveness, all mysticism," another sermon warning Marx and his friends against "talk[ing] like exterminators," and a hearty defense of Grün (Proudhon to Marx, May 17, 1846; *Correspondance de P.-J. Proudhon*, 2:198–202). Each managed, in short, to write as if calculating to alienate the other.

[101] The underlying continuity in Marx's criticisms of Proudhon has been noted by Thomas, *Karl Marx and the Anarchists*, 192–93.

la propriété? is the criticism of political economy from the standpoint of political economy. . . . Proudhon's treatise will therefore be scientifically superseded by a criticism of political economy, including Proudhon's conception of political economy. This work became possible only owing to the work of Proudhon himself, just as Proudhon's criticism has as its premise the criticism of the mercantile system by the physiocrats, Adam Smith's criticism of the physiocrats, Ricardo's criticism of Adam Smith, and the works of Fourier and Saint-Simon.[102]

Even at this early stage, Marx argues that Proudhon is insufficiently critical of political economy.[103] Marx will continue to differentiate himself from Proudhon in this manner right up through *Capital*, arguing that Proudhon remains captive to the principles and ideals of bourgeois society.[104]

This might appear a far-fetched complaint. Proudhon is fond of writing things like: "Political economy . . . knows nothing, explains nothing, concludes nothing. . . . For twenty-five years political economy, like a heavy fog, has weighed upon France, arresting the development of the mind and repressing liberty."[105] Nonetheless, Proudhon also "criticizes other socialists for lack of attention to economic questions,"[106] and, as we have already seen, attempts to integrate liberal political economy into his own system. As he wrote in 1858,

> Justice does not create economic facts . . . it does not ignore them; it does not misrepresent them for its purposes; it does not impose on them foreign laws. It merely records their variable and antinomic nature; in this antinomy, it seizes upon a law of equilibrium.[107]

Although abstractly presented, this contains the basis of Proudhon's approach to the works of political economy. They contain partial truths that only a developed moral sense—a conception of justice—can properly integrate with one another. He is fond of censuring economists for their obtuseness, but also of condemning socialists for their failure to acknowledge economic facts. Much like many twentieth-century interventionists, Proudhon sees economics as providing data that we would be remiss to ignore, but that does not in any way dictate what sort of outcomes we should care about and try to obtain. Economics is, in this

---

[102] *MECW*, 4:31; *MEW*, 2:32.

[103] *MECW*, 3:241, 280, 317; *MEGA*, I.2:208, 245, 428.

[104] E.g., *Capital*, 1:178n2; *MEGA*, II.6:114n38; *MEGA*, II.7:64n37. Proudhon's name is omitted in the French edition.

[105] *What Is Property?*, 106; *OC*, 4:231.

[106] Hoffman, *Revolutionary Justice*, 110.

[107] Proudhon, *OC*, 3:172.

sense, much like the natural sciences for Proudhon. It delineates the mechanics of the social world, telling us nothing about what we should do, but only providing parameters for what we should expect from our actions. It "knows nothing, explains nothing, concludes nothing" because it lacks the moral content or conception of justice that alone bridges the gap between how the world works and what we should do.

For Marx, this way of thinking gives political economy too much credit, while simultaneously absolving socialists of the responsibility of grappling with and coming to understand political economy. If economics provides "value neutral" data about the world, then socialists have to respect this data, but do not have to bother themselves with figuring out how the data are produced. Just as engineers can take physics for granted, respecting its results and knowing nothing of how they are arrived at, so too with socialists and economics. Hence Marx's frequent complaints that Proudhonists, despite their veneration of science, know nothing about it. These complaints are especially pronounced just as Marx is completing the first edition of *Capital*.[108] His letters gripe about these "faithful followers of Proudhon," who are laboring under "*la misère et l'ignorance*" "in inverse proportion to their squawking about '*science sociale*.'"[109] "They prattle incessantly about science," he writes, "and know nothing."[110] This complaint carries over into the text of *Capital* itself: "Never has a school thrown around the word 'science' more than the Proudhonists, for 'where concepts fail, a timely word steps in.'"[111]

Marx's Critiques of Political Economy

Marx's conception of political economy's significance, for the capitalist world and for the socialist attempt to overthrow that world, was quite different from Proudhon's. Marx wanted to write "an exposé and, by the same token, a critique of the system" of bourgeois economy.[112] This "economy" hovers, for Marx, between the bourgeois science of political economy and the practical economy of the bourgeois world. It can do so because Marx thought that the classical political economists had "investigated the real internal framework [*Zusammenhang*] of bourgeois relations of production," and that, hence, the concepts and categories of

---

[108] This upsurge is due to Marx's activity in the IWMA, the French section of which was dominated by Proudhonists (Braunthal, *History of the International*; Puech, *Le Proudhonisme dans l'Association internationale des travailleurs*; Stekloff, *History of the First International*).

[109] Marx to Engels, June 7, 1866; *MECW*, 42:281.

[110] Marx to Ludwig Kugelmann, October 9, 1866; *MECW*, 42:326.

[111] *Capital*, 1:161n26; *MEGA*, II.6:99n24; *MEGA*, II.7:49n23.

[112] Marx to Lassalle, February 22, 1858; *MECW*, 40:270.

the former "reflect the real social relations" of the latter.[113] Any real exposé of the problems with capitalism will require grappling with political economy, because it is in the study of political economy that one discovers how and why capitalism works the way it does.

Political economy's reflection of the real relations is not unproblematic, however, for multiple reasons. First, there are the errors and confusion that one would expect to find in any developing scientific discourse, and the special sorts of errors introduced by the fact that "the Furies of private interest" are especially engaged in economic questions.[114] Second, the reflection gives to those relations it reflects the appearance of "the fixity of natural laws of social life,"[115] whereas Marx believes them to be historically specific and transitory. Third, the theoretical reflection systematically confuses certain aspects of the practical world because the real social relations themselves produce these confusions spontaneously; what Marx calls the fetish character of the commodity is a prominent example of social relations that, of their very natures, appear to be other than what they are. For this reason, Marx refers to the political economic reflection as a "religion of everyday life."[116]

The first problem calls only for a better political economy, and so necessitates no disagreement with Proudhon on matters of principle. The second problem, however, implies that the "economic facts" to which Proudhon's justice defers are not so "value neutral" as he presumes. Proudhon's position is that mutualism (his preferred term for the solution to the social question) would be a better, more just management of the same economic reality that capitalism mismanages. The economic categories—and, especially, value—name historically constant conditions of human social life, and so there is no question of overcoming them or abolishing them, any more than there is a question of abolishing the law of gravity. But for Marx the facts of political economy and the facts of physics have radically different statuses. "Natural laws," including the natural laws of social life, "cannot be abolished at all. The only thing that can change, under historically differing conditions, is the form in which those laws assert themselves."[117] But "the natural laws of capitalist production" are not like this.[118] These laws are all based in "the value-form of the product of labor," which Marx calls "the most abstract, but also the most universal form of the bourgeois mode of production," and simultaneously the

[113] *Capital*, 1:174–75n34; *MEGA*, II.6:111n32; *MEGA*, II.7:60n32.
[114] *Capital*, 1:92; *MEGA*, II.5:14; *MEGA*, II.7:14.
[115] *Capital*, 1:168; *MEGA*, II.6:106; *MEGA*, II.7:56.
[116] *Capital*, 3:969; *MEGA*, II.15:805.
[117] Marx to Ludwig Kugelmann, July 11, 1868; *MECW*, 43:68.
[118] *Capital*, 1:91; *MEGA*, II.5:12; *MEGA*, II.7:12.

concept that "stamps the bourgeois mode of production as a particular kind of social production of an historical and transitory nature." Marx is committed to the claim that the products of human labor did not have values in ancient Athens, or in Carolingian Europe, or under the Gupta dynasty. We will have to look more closely at this claim later on. What matters here is that Marx makes it, and that he thinks classical political economy, on the contrary, "make[s] the mistake of treating [value] as the eternal natural form of social production."[119] By accepting the authority of political economy within the domain of economic facts, Proudhon does the same.

Finally, and most importantly, Marx thinks that the way in which capitalist social relations are mediated by market exchanges produces a series of systematic distortions in the relations themselves, or, better, produces an imaginary series of relations that are essential to the real relations they nevertheless occlude from analysis.[120] These imaginary relations are carried over into the scientific reflections of political economy. Marx tends to call these imaginary relations "mysteries" or "secrets" [*Geheimnisse*].[121] It is unfortunate that English cannot easily convey the double sense of *Geheimnis*. It names what is hidden or secreted away and also the very hiddenness of it, the mystery attending its absence to inspection. The root, *Heim*, is equivalent to the English "home," the private sphere, which is most familiar and most removed from public scrutiny. Thus, the *Geheimnisse* of political economy do not constitute a series of mistakes, as in the first two arenas of Marx's critique, or "a form of 'false consciousness' that merely conceals the 'real conditions.'"[122] They constitute a form of common sense or practical wisdom that is essential for people living in modern society, but which gives rise to all manner of absurdities upon analysis. They are familiar thoughts that cannot be inspected without becoming something confusing. But political economy consists, to a great extent, of the analysis of this modern common sense.[123]

---

[119] *Capital*, 1:174n34; *MEGA*, II.6:111n32; *MEGA*, II.7:60n31.

[120] For the conception of ideology as the representation of imaginary relations to the world, see Althusser, *Lenin and Philosophy, and Other Essays*, 162–65.

[121] These include: the mystery of the value-form, the mystery of commodities, the mystery of surplus value, the mystery of wages, and the mystery of primitive accumulation. I will return to the first two in the next chapter, and the third, fourth, and fifth in chapters 4, 5, and 6, respectively.

[122] Heinrich, *Introduction to the Three Volumes of Karl Marx's* Capital, 71.

[123] Thus, Marx claims that "the absurdity" of the practical attitude of buyers and sellers "is self-evident" when it is made explicit, but that the implicit absurdity is nonetheless the basis of commodity-producers' relations with one another, and that "the categories of bourgeois economics consists precisely of forms of this [i.e., absurd] kind" (*Capital*, 1:169; *MEGA*, II.6:106; *MEGA*, II.7:57; see the discussions in Wolff, "How to Read *Das Kapital*," 49; Heinrich, *Introduction to the Three Volumes of Karl Marx's* Capital, 71–79).

And so does most socialism, Proudhonism included. This situation calls for something far more radical than either a properly corrected or properly limited political economy.

We could sum up Marx's critique of political economy under three headings, then. First, and least controversially, it is a critique of particular political economists in the name of an ideal political economy, a self-critique and self-correction of political economy. Second, it is a critique of political economy as a whole, however rectified, in the name of properly historical knowledge. At this level, Marx's critique tries to locate capitalism as one mode of production among others, with its local laws and locally effective mechanisms. This is often taken to be the sum of Marx's criticism. At a third level, though, Marx's critique of political economy is the critique of the forms of thought proper to capitalism, and to the capitalism that gives rise to them, in the name of liberation. It is not just that the categories of political economy are valid only within a circumscribed historical setting; they are also the concepts proper to a system of domination, a system in which "the most complete subjugation of individuality under social conditions assuming the form of objective powers" nonetheless appears as a system of "individual freedom."[124]

In short, the third level of Marx's critique of political economy is the most properly political aspect of that critique. But this political critique demands, Marx thinks, both the most thoroughgoing engagement with political economy and the most extensive transformation of socialist thought. The "middle class prophets" "laud to the heavens [*Verhimmlung*]" the modern system of free competition. In response, the "socialists" "damn it to hell [*Verteufeln*]." Neither have actually "developed" an answer to the question of "what free competition is."[125] Marx would take his socialist readers into the Hell they have only condemned. He would show them what that Hell really is, in part to show them how their moralism and their schemes for reform are as implicated in the concepts proper to that Hell as are the apologetics of the liberals. When they demand a fair day's wages for a fair day's work, call for the exchange of equivalents, try to pin the misery of the worker on acts of force or fraud committed by the proprietors, imagine that socialism stands opposed to "the selfish man, the thief, the murder, the traitor to society,"[126] or otherwise reduce the rule of capital to acts of injustice, socialists entrap themselves, Marx thinks, in the very social system they want to escape. Marx's goal, then, is to expose political economy to his socialist readers in order to expose

[124] *Grundrisse*, 652; *MEGA*, II.1.2:537. Compare this threefold conception of critique to Douglas Kellner's sixfold understanding in "Marxism, Morality, and Ideology," 96.

[125] *Grundrisse*, 652; *MEGA*, II.1.2:537.

[126] Proudhon, *What Is Property?*, 174; OC, 4:302.

the limits of political economy and the "secret" of socialism's conceptual complicity with political economy, the way in which its tendency toward moralized criticisms of capitalism, like political economy itself, produces a religion of everyday life, an idealization of the world that supplements it and inures us to it.

Marx's citation of Dante's poem establishes this collaborative fiction according to which Marx is a Virgil-like guide for his socialist readers, introducing them into "the secret things" of political economy (l.3.21), revealing the ugly underbelly of modern capitalism and the hidden mechanisms that produce and reproduce it. Like Dante's Virgil, Marx tells his charges to disregard the social Hell's command—"Abandon every hope, you who enter"—ordering them instead to "abandon every suspicion (1.3:9–14)."[127] And, like the pilgrim in Dante's poem, the socialists who accept Marx's guidance are supposed to be so transformed by their journey that they will be able to withstand the purgatory through which the revolution was currently (and recurrently) traveling,[128] and to enter "into the misty heavens of [the] 'communist confession of faith,'" much as Gottschalk had accused. And, since Dante's pilgrim is also the poet himself, who is telling us the story of his own becoming, perhaps one or more of these remade socialists will become "the new Dante" Engels hoped for, the creator "who will mark the hour of birth of this new, proletarian era."[129]

Conclusion

This book approaches *Capital* by comparing its structure to that of Dante's *Inferno* and relating its central arguments to the contending schools of socialist theory. Marx was, in *Capital*, writing a political document, meant to be read, above all, by other socialists and activists within the workers' movement. This audience, and Marx's conception of it, are thus of decisive importance for understanding why Marx makes the arguments he does, in the way he does. To put it baldly, Marx is not trying to convince some ideal-typical bourgeois economist to come over to the side of socialism. Rather, he is trying to convince his fellow socialists to cast aside their reliance upon ideas and arguments derived from or typified by Proudhon, Considérant, Bronterre O'Brien, and other has-been and would-be leaders and theorists of the movement against capitalism.

---

[127] *MECW*, 29:265; *MEGA*, II.2:103.
[128] *Eighteenth Brumaire, Political Writings*, 2:236; *MEGA*, 1.11:178.
[129] *MECW*, 27:366; *MEGA*, I.32:208.

Marx's relationship to other socialists has certainly been the object of important studies. There are two important strands of scholarship. One treats Marx as either developing or simply borrowing the economic theories of earlier socialist writers. The other, more robust, strand examines Marx's criticisms of the political tactics of rival socialist schools.[130] In their coexistence, these strands reinforce each other and produce the apparent but erroneous conclusion that Marx largely inherited an economic theory from his predecessors even as he introduced into socialism a novel political strategy. I will argue, instead, that Marx's divergence from other socialists is greater than has been appreciated, and that this divergence cuts across the domains of theory and political practice. If *Capital* is "an impressive . . . reformulation and rationalization of a large body of earlier Socialist economic theory,"[131] this should not be understood in the sense Cole does, as implying that, for example, Marx's theory of value was merely "a refinement on the earlier theories of Thomas Hodgskin, John Francis Bray, and a number of other 'Ricardian' Socialists."[132]

Marx was radically and savagely critical of the naïveté and inadequacy of earlier socialist economic and political theory. His fundamental criticism was that other socialists had terrifically oversimplified the operations and the harms of modern capitalism by individualizing and moralizing both. As a consequence, they had also massively oversimplified the task facing the workers' movement, reducing it now to a problem of moral or scientific education, now to one of will power. As this chapter has already shown, this assessment of the challenges facing the workers' movement and of the shortcomings of the available socialist theory lies behind Marx's adoption, in 1859, of the descent into Hell as a metaphor for his task in his critique of political economy. What lies ahead of us, then, is to follow Marx on his *katabasis*, and to mark out, at each juncture, the transformation he is hoping to work on his socialist audience.

---

[130]There is much excellent and well-informed work in this second vein, e.g., Draper, *Karl Marx's Theory of Revolution*; Gilbert, *Marx's Politics*; Hunt, *The Political Ideas of Marx and Engels*; Löwy, *The Theory of Revolution in the Young Marx*.

[131]Cole, *History of Socialist Thought*, 2:300.

[132]Ibid., 2:289; this was also the claim of Menger, *The Right to the Whole Produce of Labour*. It is worth noting that both Cole and Menger were non- or anti-Marxist socialists, and that their literary efforts to collapse Marx back into his predecessors were a means by which those very trends within socialism that he tried to displace had their revenge upon Marx. Marx's name came to be the veritable name of socialism in the twentieth century, but this was a hollow victory in many respects, since many of the tendencies Marx combated came to be enshrined as part and parcel of Marxism itself.

CHAPTER 3

Styx: The Anarchy of the Market

Men were then forced to labor, because they were slaves to others; men
are now forced to labor because they are slaves to their own wants.
—James Steuart, *An Inquiry into the Principles of Political Economy* (1770)

It is our system of exchange which forms the hiding place of that giant
of mischief which bestrides the civilized world, rewarding industry
with starvation, exertion with disappointment, and the best efforts of
our rulers to do good, with perplexity, dismay, and failure . . .
—John Gray, *The Social System* (1831)

Until the human mind shall have been disabused of this insane money-
mystery, it is impossible that men can think or act like rational beings;
or that the world can be otherwise than a great lunatic asylum.
—Robert Owen, *The Revolution in the Mind and Practice*
of the Human Race (1849)

Akrasia—incontinence, weakness, lack of self-mastery or self-control—is
today a philosophical puzzle and a marketing opportunity. For Dante,
imbricated in the manifold legacies of classical political thought, it was
a moral and political problem of a high order. Getting carried away—by
lust, by anger or envy, by desire for wealth—was how the good-hearted,
who love real goods, come nonetheless to be enemies of the good and of
their fellows. Much the same could be said about the moral and political significance of *akrasia* for the early socialists, although they did not
use quite the language Dante used. Much of what disturbed them about
the newly commercial society in which they lived was caught up in the
way this society seemed out of control. The anarchy of competition be-
deviled society. Worse, perhaps, it seemed to wreck all novel efforts at
self-control, individual or collective. The well-intentioned and committed
might come together in an earnest desire to cooperate in the production
of wealth, and in the brotherly and sisterly sharing of that wealth. Nonetheless, the same "perplexity, dismay, and failure" that afflicted the larger
society also invaded the smaller.

Much as he took up and transformed the trope of "the social Hell,"
Marx inherited and reworked this socialist discourse on the *akrasia* of

commercial society. In part one of *Capital*, he integrates the two. Just as the first circles of Dante's Hell are the circles of incontinence, where those who lack self-control are tortured by their runaway desires, Marx's sphere of circulation, the market, is where producers are tormented by the movement of their products, which they cannot control. Furthering a line of thinking begun by the Owenite socialists in Britain, Marx teased apart the experience of commercial society as anarchic or *akratic* and the explanation for this experience, the impersonal domination that causes people in a commercial or market-based society to behave in an *akratic* manner. Because they are dependent for their lives upon the market, as slaves are dependent upon their masters, producers of wares for sale must keep a "weather eye" out for changing market conditions,[1] which are, at bottom, nothing but the caprices of their customers and competitors. Marx's recognition and analysis of this condition of "objective dependence" ought to be appreciated,[2] for it is the crucial argument by which he differentiates his critical *katabasis* from the moralizing criticisms of his rivals. It animates the most difficult part of Marx's book. It undergirds his discussion of the fetish character of commodities. It motivates his methodological claim to treat individuals only as the bearers or personifications of economic categories. It grounds his antipathy to all variants of labor money and mutual credit as solutions to the social question. In short, attention to the background discourse about commercial *akrasia*, and to Marx's diagnosis of this as a symptom of impersonal domination, makes sense of what Marx is trying to do in part one, and in *Capital* as a whole.

In order to substantiate this argument, I will examine the moral discourse Marx inherited from multiple sources, according to which the market is a sphere of *akrasia* and anarchy. I focus especially on two sets of intellectual influences. First, there is the moral criticism of the incontinence and slavishness of those who frequent the market. Marx knew this moral discourse from many sources: classical authors, Dante, and various Tory and republican writers. Second, there are the early socialist writers who rallied around the figure of Robert Owen, and whose writings formed the background of the British labor movement in which Marx found himself inserted by his immigration to London. These writers echoed many of the aristocratic and moralizing worries about the "social and moral problems of discipline and control" that attended the new commercial, urban, and industrial economy.[3] However, they also shared a radical republican urge to identify some sort of tyranny at work

---

[1] I here appropriate Philip Pettit's term for the insecurity and watchfulness that attends the status of a dominated agent.

[2] Marx says of modern society that it involves "personal independence founded on objective dependence" (*Grundrisse*, 158; *MEGA*, II.1.1:91).

[3] Garnett, *Co-Operation and the Owenite Socialist Communities in Britain, 1825–45*, 3.

behind the moral corruption, some arbitrary power that would explain the evident absence of virtue. Many of them laid the blame at the feet of the opaque workings of the monetary economy, which, to the republican mind, hid "the empire of force and fraud" that made staggering wealth for some and crushing poverty for many others. Hence, they proposed schemes of monetary reform, designed to make exchange transparent and free, and thereby incapable of cloaking the abuse of power.

Examining this background makes it possible to see how Marx, in part one of *Capital*, takes over the problem of commercial domination from the Owenites and transforms it by arguing that the evils they try to pin on money are actually the necessary outcome of the fair exchange of equivalent values. Commerce does not *hide* the exercise of arbitrary power,[4] it is itself the exercise of an arbitrary power, "an alien social power" produced by the individuals in the market but "standing above them."[5] Moreover, Marx's conception of impersonal market domination undergirds his concept of fetishism and his claim that people are, in capitalism, only the bearers of economic relations. Two of the most important strands of Marxist theory—the critical theory that began with Lukács and developed under the Frankfurt School, and the Marxist "structuralism" developed by and around Althusser—despite their pointed antagonism, converge in their conviction that Marx, in part one of *Capital*, has identified a form of social power hitherto unrecognized. On the one hand, *social domination*, and on the other, *structural causality*, have been identified as Marx's signal contribution, and have been derived, respectively, from his account of fetishism and from his treatment of individuals as bearers of economic relations. I hope to show, by contextualizing Marx's account, that its republican background grounds the claim that modernity is marked by a new form of social domination and makes more compelling the argument that a sort of structural causality is at work in capitalist society.

REPUBLICAN SOCIALISM AND THE MONEY MYSTERY

Marx's exiles from Germany—in France, Belgium, and, finally, Britain[6]—immersed him in a socialist movement that had emerged indecisively

---

[4] Or, rather, not only; commerce certainly hides and launders all sorts of abuse and tyranny, but that does not get to the heart of the problem, according to Marx.

[5] Marx, *Grundrisse*, 196; *MEGA*, II.1.1:155.

[6] British socialism will be at the fore in this chapter because, as far as Marx was concerned, the Owenites had accomplished more than any other socialists in the domain of analyzing the mechanisms and dynamics of the market. Nonetheless, a very similar account could be drawn out of Proudhon's work, and I will try to indicate points of convergence between Proudhon and Owenism wherever relevant.

from radical republicanism, and which was interlarded with civic republican and Christian moralism.[7] This hodgepodge of discursive influences
expressed itself, among other ways, in a tension between moralistic condemnation and naturalistic explanation running through early socialism.
The anarchy of the market was, like the *akratic* merchants and artisans
of antiquity, subject to two contrary but intertwined political judgments.
On the one hand, this anarchy was indicative of slavishness and corruption and could be rectified only by a strong and rational will, issuing in
a new self-mastery. On the other hand, commercial anarchy embodied
and promulgated a condition of lawlessness and domination, which individuals could not be expected to resist, and which therefore had to be
regulated by a new set of institutions, inaugurating a new freedom. The
former judgment expressed the continued salience of moral perfectionism; the latter the vitality of a republican problematic that was in principle, if not in practice, independent of moral judgments.[8] In premodern
political thought, markets had figured more prominently as a symptom
of servile vice than as a threat to freedom. Hence, we must first examine
the moralizing discourse to which socialism was heir.

Incontinence and the Need to Be Ruled

From Plato's *Republic* onward, *akrasia*—the lack of *enkrateia*, self-
mastery—has been a problem for political theory, and thinking about
akrasia has always been keyed to the market as a place teeming with men
without masters.[9] For most classical political thinkers, the market was

[7]The republican background of socialism is controversial in the British context, though
it is implicit, to some extent, in the story told by Thompson's *Making of the English Working Class*. Even there, the emphasis on republicanism is purchased by the sidelining of
Owen. The best studies of Owenism are those of Gregory Claeys (*Machinery, Money, and
the Millennium*; *Citizens and Saints*), which trace the manifold ways in which the republican tradition informed Owen's politics (and antipolitics), as well as the cooperative and
communitarian movements that formed around him. My own account of Owenism in this
chapter owes an immense debt to Claeys's research and arguments. In the French context,
by contrast, the influence of republicanism is acknowledged by many of the major studies,
even if the content of that republicanism remains vague (e.g., Vincent, *Proudhon and the
Rise of French Republican Socialism*; Pilbeam, *French Socialists before Marx*). This is in
part due to the fact that the French socialist parties have always traced their lineage back
to 1789; Jean Jaurès, influential leader of the first unified socialist party there, claimed—
echoing Tocqueville—that "the French Revolution contains the whole of socialism" (quoted
by Pilbeam, *French Socialists before Marx*, 26).

[8]On the tension within early socialism between antipolitical perfectionism and political
republicanism, see Claeys, *Citizens and Saints*, 7.

[9]Hannah Arendt noted the importance of Plato's "maxim that only a man who could
both command and obey himself should have the right to command others, but be under no
obligation to obey the behests of other men. This self-control or alternatively, the conviction

where the vulgar, who lacked the self-mastery and virtue to live honorably, made a living by bowing and scraping for their customers, making and selling things to please others without any independent thought about what is actually worthwhile. That artisans and merchants, not to mention wage laborers, depended upon the desires of others to such a degree was proof of their slavishness, and of the wisdom of excluding them from the body politic. Conceived this way, the problem of what to do with the *akratic* was centrally important for the history of political thought. How ought we to keep the vulgar subordinate and at arm's length from political power, with minimum bother and without compromising the humanity and virtue of those capable of self-mastery? Within this line of thought, the phenomenon of *akrasia* finds its place in a conceptual polarity of slavishness and self-mastery. The *akratic* is seen as lacking the moral and/or physical strength to take what he needs, to assert himself in war and politics, and to be responsible for himself.[10] This problematic of *akrasia* is moralistic and, in the terms of contemporary political theory, strongly perfectionist. It focuses its scrutiny on the condition of the individual soul and expects no changes in politics except those that spring from the power of the soul's decision to rightly order itself and, subsequently, the world around it.[11]

In Dante, this problematic of *akrasia* appears as the sins of incontinence. Situated beyond Limbo, where the virtuous who do not know God "live in desire" but "without hope" (4.42),[12] the four circles of upper Hell punish the sins of "incontinence" (11.82): lust (circle II); gluttony (circle III); greed and prodigality (circle IV); pride, envy, wrath, and sloth (circle V).[13] Since this is where the greedy and the spendthrift are punished, and these are essentially sins of the marketplace, this part of the

---

that self-control alone justifies the exercise of authority, has remained the hallmark of the aristocratic outlook to this day" ("Freedom and Politics," 202). Obviously, *akrasia* has been the topic of an immense amount of philosophical writing in the past fifty years, ever since R. M. Hare revived interest in the Socratic question of whether one can do what one really knows one ought not to do (*The Language of Morals*). Nonetheless, there has been almost no attention paid to *akrasia* as a problem for political theory. The only exception I know of is Amélie Rorty's discussion of "The Social and Political Sources of Akrasia." In a very different way, Philip Pettit's work on *akrasia* in collective agents is also relevant; see "Akrasia, Collective and Individual."

[10] I have reverted to the masculine pronouns, since, for most classical thinkers, there was no doubt but that only men could possess *enkrateia* in this way.

[11] This classical problematic did not disappear with antiquity; it finds a forceful expression, for instance, in Shakespeare's *The Tempest*, in which Caliban's lack of self-mastery is equated with suitability for enslavement (see Holbrook, *Shakespeare's Individualism*, pt. III).

[12] I have used Robert M. Durling's edition of Dante's *Inferno* throughout; citations will follow the standard practice of noting the canto and the line(s).

[13] Adopting the interpretation proposed by Russo, *Sussidi Di Esegesi Dantesca*.

Inferno seems to maintain the classical association of *akrasia* with the market. In fact, this association extends beyond greed and profligacy. Look, for instance, at Dante's description of what those who are tortured by the winds in the second circle did to condemn themselves. These are "the carnal sinners, who submit their reason to their talent [*che la ragion sommettono al talent*]" (5.38–39). For us, a talent is a natural or spontaneous propensity or ability, but for the ancients, a talent was a weight, especially of a metal used as a money of account, or the value or wealth that this weight embodied. For Dante, it was somewhere between these poles, the weight of one's inclination, and the momentum this weight had in action. Virgil's description fits not only the lustful, but all of the incontinent. And the fact that this description is in terms that are still recognizably, if obliquely, monetary, opens the way to seeing incontinence in general—and not only the special forms of incontinence punished in the fourth circle—as a phenomenon keyed to the market, to commodity exchange, to monetary wealth, and to all that these allow or encourage.[14]

Akratics act against their better judgment, seduced by a present pleasure, about which they have not made any deliberate decision. Seeing and choosing the better, the akratic does the worse anyway. Hence, Dante repeatedly describes the souls punished in these circles as having faults or diversions of vision. The lovers Paolo and Francesca gave in to their desire after their reading of the Lancelot romance "many times . . . drove [their] eyes together" (5.130–31). The eyes of Ciacco turn "oblique" (6.91). Gluttons are called "blind ones" (6.93). The greedy are "cross-eyed of mind" (7.40–41), and led an "undiscerning life" (7.53). To adapt one of Aristotle's illustrations of judgment and action, incontinents are like archers who, having picked out and aimed at the target, are distracted by something close at hand, take their eyes off the target they have chosen, and, therefore, shoot errantly. The incontinent are fatally distracted from what they know to be the good. Nonetheless, these sinners are in Hell, not in Purgatory. Their vice may be temporary,[15] but it is deadly. Their unreliability, their susceptibility to temptation, means they are bad marriage partners and bad citizens.[16] Out of crooked timber like this, nothing straight can be built.

The harshness of Dante's judgment is reinforced by another detail. In the encounter with the greedy and prodigal, Virgil digresses for a time

---

[14] As mentioned in the previous chapter, Proudhon seems to have noticed the special significance of these circles of Hell, comparing the evils of competition to those of greed and the evils of monopoly—"a still lower circle in the hell of misery"—to those of indolence (*System*, 1:227; OC, 1:213).

[15] Kent, "Transitory Vice."

[16] Note, for instance, Martinez and Durling's comment on Ciacco, whose gluttony bespeaks a "disregard of civic responsibility" (editorial notes to *Inferno*, 1:111).

on the role of Fortune in distributing the "empty goods [*ben vani*]" of the world (7.79). He is at pains to underline the inscrutability of Fortune's providential role in governing the sphere of sublunar goods (7.61–99). Both the greedy and the prodigal try to hoard up earthly goods; the greedy grasp after monetary wealth while the prodigal throw money away in an effort to assimilate as much "use value" as possible. Both are distracted from the pursuit of the good life by the passionate desire to master their own fortunes. Virgil insists, however, that Fortune's ability to take away wealth is "beyond any human wisdom's power to prevent," that "her judgment . . . is hidden," and that "Your knowledge cannot resist her" (7.81–85). Plutus, god of wealth, is "the great enemy" (6.115) because greed for "empty goods" metonymically stands in for all wrongdoing. The pursuit—whether deliberate or incontinent—of what we cannot happily and stably possess is the basic form of human folly and misery. Thus, the incontinent are of a piece with all the damned.[17]

In Dante, then, we find a Christianized version of the classical problem, for what matters is how to secure a proper ordering of the soul, and then how to secure a proper political order that reflects this order of the soul. Self-mastery is Christianized, for the achievement of continence depends upon grace; the disorder of the soul is a heritage of original sin. Only the advent of a new truth, known by faith, can dispel the darkness of the soul and set humankind on the righteous path. Despite the historical distance separating them, and as we will see in some detail below, there are echoes of this theme reverberating still in the "new view of society" outlined by a writer who thought that Dante's religion had otherwise "made the earth a Pandemonium."[18] Indeed, Pilbeam's claim about "nearly all" French socialists can be broadened even further; early socialists "were moralists first and based their critique of their favorite enemy, *concurrence*, capitalist competition, on moral grounds."[19]

Republicanism's Problem

Alongside this moralism, however, early socialism also inherited a tradition of republican political thought that contained the germ of something very different: an analysis that preempts moralism by insisting that slavishness is a consequence of domination, rather than its cause and

[17]Indeed, the pilgrim's entire passage through Hell can be said to be for the sake of achieving continence, the subordination of his desire to reason. Purgatory, then, is where his desire is made righteous, or where he becomes temperate. Paradise, finally, rectifies his reason, or makes him blessed. Again, incontinence, or the rebellion of desire against reason, is the figure of all Hell (Freccero, "Dante's Pilgrim in a Gyre," 180).

[18]Owen, *A New View of Society and Other Writings*, 311.

[19]*French Socialists before Marx*, 9.

justification.[20] Republican thought is politically concerned more with re-moving certain barriers to virtue—those barriers constituted by arbitrary power—than with promoting it positively.[21] As Eric MacGilvray has put it, "republican thought centers around the problem of securing the prac-tice of virtue through the control of arbitrary power."[22] Traditionally, of course, this problem did not contain anything like a categorical judg-ment that arbitrary power was the only threat to the practice of virtue. On the contrary, the republican concern to secure some people's freedom and capacity for virtue always went hand in hand with the conviction that many other people are incapable of freedom, and ought rightfully to remain in subjection. That is, as Alex Gourevitch argues, "Historically and conceptually 'enslavement and subjection are the great evils' not be-cause the free citizen hates slavery but because he thinks that he does not deserve the servitude that others *rightfully deserve*."[23] But while this is certainly true historically, some strands within the workers' movements of the nineteenth century challenged the conceptual linkage between one person's virtue-enabling freedom and another person's justified servitude. They tried to universalize the claim on freedom, and, in so doing, they ran up against the hypothetical inversion of the aristocratic conviction that slavery and servitude are explained by the slavishness and servility of the underclass. The republican problematic was radicalized as the conviction emerged that, in fact, servitude explains servility.

As republicans have long noted, being at the mercy of an arbitrary power has a tendency to corrupt the character of the subjected, to make them "increasingly unable and even unwilling to resist" that power.[24] This is so because the practice of virtue entails a more-or-less predictable alignment between "being good and doing good," between the actions that will perfect one as a person and those that will successfully achieve one's ends.[25] This alignment is disrupted if the achievement of one's ends is dependent upon the caprice of someone with the power to interfere in one's life at will. Achieving one's ends, in such a context of domination, requires staying on the sweet side of the powerful, and there is no reason to think that this sweet side will coincide, in any nonaccidental way, with one's own flourishing as a person. If one is concerned to promote virtue, and one recognizes that virtue is threatened in this way by the presence

---

[20]Skinner, *Liberty before Liberalism*, 93; van Gelderen and Skinner, *Republicanism: A Shared European Heritage*, 1:2.

[21]At least, not as an end in itself; see Skinner, "The Idea of Negative Liberty."

[22]*The Invention of Market Freedom*, 22.

[23]Gourevitch, *From Slavery to the Cooperative Commonwealth*, 14; Gourevitch is quot-ing Pettit, *Republicanism*, 132.

[24]MacGilvray, *The Invention of Market Freedom*, 35.

[25]Garver, *Confronting Aristotle's Ethics: Ancient and Modern Morality*, 2–3.

of arbitrary power, then eliminating arbitrary power is a prerequisite to human flourishing, and trying to achieve this task for the sake of that end means tackling the problem of republicanism.[26]

However, even if one grants that early socialists inherited these notions from the tradition of republican thought, they did so in a radically changed and rapidly changing world. The attempt to radicalize republican thought and universalize republican freedom emerged from but also stumbled over "the difficulties involved in pursuing republican ends in a world that is largely governed by and through markets."[27] Indeed, since most early socialists were relatively unconcerned with the purely political, institutional arrangements traditionally advocated by republicans, some have claimed that this disavowal of a "merely political standpoint" constitutes a disavowal of republicanism as such.[28] The socialists with whom I am concerned certainly saw republican government as only a partial and preliminary requirement for human emancipation. This only indicates, however, that the scope of domination in modern commercial society seemed to them so enhanced that to confront it with political freedom alone was tantamount to restraining an elephant with sewing thread.

There is nothing surprising in the fact that the amplification of commercial society in the eighteenth century should evoke from critics moralizing denunciations of the sins encompassed by Dante's circles of incontinence.[29] Money could be made from and spent in the service of lust and gluttony. Monetized wealth could be accumulated without apparent limit and frittered away with impressive alacrity. It could purchase indolence as easily as its lack could fuel envy and rage. But these complaints did not remain the province of priests and parsons. They were amplified and put on a new footing with the emergence of a new genre of tracts, populist and working-class treatments of political economy, what Noel Thompson has called "the people's science."[30] Classical political economists had, in the words of one writer, "bewildered themselves and the world in endeavoring to prove that hireling labor at the lowest possible rate, is the

[26] I am following MacGilvray here, *The Invention of Market Freedom*, chap. 1, but also extending his argument. The specific nature of the threat posed to virtue by arbitrary power is not spelled out by MacGilvray, and I hope my effort here might supplement his. I think my account is also harmonious with Pettit's discussion of freedom as fitness to be held responsible, since the presence of arbitrary power distorts decision making in precisely the sort of way that renders one *unfit* to be held responsible (*A Theory of Freedom*).

[27] MacGilvray, *The Invention of Market Freedom*, 21.

[28] Isaac, "The Lion's Skin of Politics: Marx on Republicanism," 476.

[29] Pocock, *The Machiavellian Moment*, chaps. 13–14; MacGilvray, *The Invention of Market Freedom*, chap. 3.

[30] Thompson, *The People's Science*.

proper condition of the vast and overwhelming portion of our race, from whom proceed all the wealth and strength of our communities."[31] What was needed was a working-class counterweight to this political economy of the capitalists and landlords, a political economy from below.[32] Using a phrase that was just as commonly found in the mouths of the priests and parsons, William Thompson claimed that:

> The ultimate object [of production] is not accumulation, is not capital, but enjoyment immediate or future. Herein differ the mere political and the moral economist. The accumulation of wealth or capital, and particularly in large masses, is the sole object of the mere political economist: happiness, health, particularly of the productive many, are with him secondary.[33]

Basing themselves in the conviction that labor is the source of all the wealth and strength of a community, these popular moral economists set out to defend the laborers against the depredations of the wealthy and powerful, who enjoyed the greater part of that wealth and strength.[34] Gone was the faith of the older republicans that the social fabric was basically intact, and that the expulsion of a few usurpers or a reform of the government would bring things back into shape. A penny paper quoted by the Tory *Quarterly Review* measures the depth of the dissatisfaction and the scope of the remedies entertained:

> Supposing, now, the whole body of the people were to rise in like manner—all the laboring classes against their masters—into what a terrible state of misery would the country be plunged, aristocrats and all! would it not be universal ruin? Could the aristocrats culture the earth for themselves, or provide themselves with clothing, if the laboring classes refused any longer to sacrifice themselves for the exclusive advantage of their masters? what could be done?—but if the present outrages are continued, and become general—if the people not only refuse to produce further, but destroy what is already produced—what *then* will be done? Will not the aristocrats find

[31] "Senex" (probably J. E. "Shepherd" Smith and James Morrison), "Letters on Associated Labour," *Pioneer* 28 (1834): 244; cited by Thompson (*The People's Science*, 23). Thanks go to Gregory Claeys for the identities of the authors of these letters.

[32] This being the title of Rob Knowles's study of the somewhat later Proudhonian and post-Proudhonian mutualist tradition (Knowles, *Political Economy from Below*). Marx viewed the British popular political economists as the original (and best) expositors of many of the positions he associated with Proudhon (see, e.g., *Grundrisse*, 135–36; *MEGA*, II.1.1:71–72; and *The Poverty of Philosophy*, *MECW*, 6:138).

[33] Thompson, *Inquiry*, 299.

[34] Anton Menger later saw in these defenses what he thought to be the core doctrine of socialism, the right of the producer to the whole produce of labor. Menger, *The Right to the Whole Produce of Labour*. As I will argue below, Menger's reading distorts the positions taken by, at least, the Owenites among this group of writers.

out then, when it is too late, that they are not better than the mass of their fellow-creatures; but that, on the contrary, they are dependent on them for everything they enjoy or require! What would avail the government's standing army, if they could no longer supply it with food and clothing? would it not be the first to turn upon them?—and this must happen, unless society is so altered, that machinery shall no longer be used as the means of amassing great wealth for individuals, instead of relieving the people at large;—and this can only be effectually done by universal equality. It is, indeed, time to listen to the voice of the people, and that voice is, in a very great degree, directed and instructed by Robert Owen and his disciples, who have taught them to know their own rights.[35]

This invocation of Owen is both instructive and surprising. It instructs us that, if the earliest British socialists of the 1820s and '30s were "Ricardian" in their conviction that the present social order entailed a discord of class interests,[36] they were Owenite in their conviction that "to gather the delicious food for ourselves will be far more desirable and advantageous, and by so doing we shall enjoy the fruits of our labor in the winter of age, instead of the grudging and scanty pittance of a parish workhouse. We shall then be surrounded with every necessary comfort, encircled *with friends in equality*, and our children amply provided for; all this shall we effect by our united efforts in the cause of co-operation."[37] It ought to surprise us, though, with its free intermingling of the older republican themes—the arrogance and corruption of the upper classes, the need for a rebalancing of society, the tribune of the people—with the new socialist language of the Owenites.[38] Since socialism is widely regarded as one of the modern political ideologies that emerged after the demise of—or even helped to displace—the older republican tradition, the conjunction of the two languages in one statement is noteworthy. It is hardly an aberration.

---

[35] Quoted in a long review of the *Doctrine de Saint Simon: Exposition*, the fourth article in the *Quarterly Review* 45, no. 90 (1831): 436.

[36] I will consider the question of Ricardo's influence on socialism in chapter 5.

[37] The words of an address published by the Committee of the British Association for Promoting Co-Operative Knowledge, quoted in the *Quarterly Review* 45, no. 90 (1831): 437.

[38] Throughout what follows, my characterization of Owenism will focus almost exclusively on Owen, William Thompson, John Francis Bray, and John Gray. The literary output of Owenism was massive; journals, penny-papers, and pamphlets promoted and debated cooperative production, moral economy, education and marriage reform, and many other topics of concern. Besides the works of Claeys and Thompson, J.F.C. Harrison, Edward Royle, and Barbara Taylor have produced significant studies of the movement. However, despite Engels's early acquaintance with such figures as John Watts, only the works of Owen, Thompson, Bray, and Gray were studied by Marx (Claeys, *Machinery, Money, and the Millennium*, chap. 7). These were the arguments with which he was most familiar.

The usual story of Owen's popular reception is one of generational transition. As E. P. Thompson has documented, Owen's panacea was received by many of the British radicals of the older generation like cheap patent medicine—with incredulity, scorn, and not a little anger. But it was enthusiastically received and promulgated by a new type of radical: optimistic, millenarian, and rationalistic. This picture of generational transition reveals much about the relationship between the Owenites and the older species of radial republicanism. However, it also obscures the extent of the continuity between the two traditions, and makes it hard to see how they managed to appeal to the same constituency of working people, or how someone like William Thompson could so easily go from being under Godwin's tutelage to being the chief theorist of Owenite cooperation. Rather than stressing only the generational shift, it is important to underline the conceptual and tropological continuity between old republicanism and the new moral world of Owenism.[39]

For present purposes, the most important continuity between republicanism and Owenism is contained in their analysis of the ills of commercial society, according to which the pursuit of gain gives rise to force and fraud, and to the vices bred by both luxury and poverty. On republican grounds, this calls for some explanation. If the world has become, thanks to commerce, "a great lunatic asylum,"[40] then this does not, for the Owenites, justify, as it did for the aristocratically inclined, the subjection of the working class whose character has been so corrupted. On the contrary, the Owenites, universalizing the thought of their republican forebears, believed that "a servile character need not be the result of any personal failing," for it may instead "follow from the fact that one is not able to display one's true character as long as one is in the presence and under the thumb of an arbitrary power."[41] The arbitrary power that explains the "ignorance, poverty, corruption, and wretchedness" of the present system,[42] the "constant source of caprice" that has turned "the mass of mankind into ignorant contented drudges,"[43] must be sought out. The Owenites—and in this they were followed by Proudhon and by a hundred other socialists—thought they had found this arbitrary power and source of caprice in "the money-mystery,"[44] the "occult operations"

[39] Claeys sees some cases where Owen moves "closer to the language of radicalism," but reads these as tactical shifts on Owen's part (*Machinery, Money, and the Millennium*, 43). I think these continuities are both native to Owenism and more basic.

[40] Owen, *The Revolution in the Mind*, 35.

[41] MacGilvray, *The Invention of Market Freedom*, 34. MacGilvray is describing the way of thinking that gives rise to the republican tradition, not Owenism.

[42] Owen, *The Revolution in the Mind*, 143.

[43] Thompson, *Inquiry*, 155, 133.

[44] Owen, *The Revolution in the Mind*, 35.

of which exposed the producer "to the mercy of uncontrolled and uncontrollable circumstances."[45] This mystery is what Marx seeks to explicate by his account of the fetish character of commodities, which, inserted into this republican lineage, becomes a theory of the impersonal domination of all those who must depend upon the market.

The Owenites generally argued that if market transactions were actually free and voluntary exchanges between equals, then there would be no problem. They presumed that such free and voluntary exchanges would proceed from "the necessity of sharing with others, of mutual aid, or mutual insurance."[46] They presumed, further, that such exchanges would be governed by "the only equitable principle," "to exchange the supposed prime cost of, or value of labor in, one article, against the prime cost of, or amount of labor contained in any other article."[47] However, they also argued that such "free, voluntary exchanges, founded on equal knowledge of the parties, . . . no where prevail."[48] On the contrary, the present commercial system is an "empire of force and fraud,"[49] "one vast Babel of interests, in which true charity, and morality, and brotherly love, have no existence,"[50] "a covered civil warfare."[51]

There is here a significant continuity between the Owenites and the old advocates of "civic or Machiavellian moralism," like William Godwin, who wags his finger at the commercial producer for studying "the passions of his customers, not to correct but to pamper them."[52] Thus, William Thompson wrote that, "consequent on the over-anxious pursuit of wealth, are the servility and corruption to which excessive wealth gives rise throughout the community in which it exists."[53] Similar sentiments could be found in all of Owen's premier followers.[54] Hence, John

[45] Bray, *Labour's Wrongs and Labour's Remedy*, 139, 142, 183.

[46] Thompson, *Labour Rewarded*, 13.

[47] Owen, *A New View of Society and Other Writings*, 268. "Like the commercial ideologists, many critics evinced an underlying belief in the salutary psychic effects of both exchange and property and their critique of capitalism often rested upon the argument that the psychic, moral, and social benefits of property and equal exchanges had been both denied and deferred" (Jaffe, "Commerce, Character, and Civil Society," 260).

[48] Thompson, *Labour Rewarded*, 11.

[49] Thompson, *Inquiry*, 255.

[50] Bray, *Labour's Wrongs and Labour's Remedy*, 28.

[51] Owen, *A New View of Society and Other Writings*, 358.

[52] Claeys, "The Concept of 'Political Justice' in Godwin's Political Justice: A Reconsideration," 566; Godwin, *Enquiry concerning Political Justice and Its Influence on Morals and Happiness: In Two Volumes*, 766.

[53] Thompson, *Inquiry*, 148.

[54] This is a challenge to Jaffe's view that it is a special property of Hodgskin's "unique brand of radicalism" that it was so "stamped by eighteenth-century debates on virtue, vice and luxury" ("Commerce, Character, and Civil Society," 257). It also suggests that the "transition from republican radicalism to socialism," which Bevir locates only in the

Gray has this to say on the subject of "Shopkeepers and Tradesmen retailing goods":

> Certain it is, that these men are not unproductive, for never, upon the face of the earth, was there any thing half so productive of deception and falsehood, folly and extravagance, slavery of the corporeal, and prostitution of the intellectual faculties of man, as the present system of retail trade. In these particulars certainly, tradesmen are productive enough.[55]

Nor was Owen averse to using a similar rhetoric of civic moralism. The same man who never tired of proclaiming his necessitarian doctrine that "the character of man is formed for him, and not by him," could also characterize his detractors thus:

> Vociferators for freedom while subjected to the lowest mental slavery—chained to the earth by the most violent and injurious passions—bound hand and foot by the worst habits and most degrading ignorance—and existing amidst intellectual and physical wretchedness, cry out to their deliverers not to touch their bonds, and beseech them to leave them in possession of all the liberty they enjoy! Mistaken hapless beings! They must not, they shall not, be left thus! Their deliverance is near at hand, and they shall enjoy true liberty, both of body and mind.[56]

It would not be hard to read into these condemnations of servility, prostitution, and mental slavery an aristocratic contempt for the *akrasia* of the modern denizens of the market. Indeed, one could read the Owenite movement's many failures to establish working cooperative communities and labor exchanges as the tale of an akratic at odds with itself. Owen would be the higher self of the movement, possessed of a rational grasp of the good, but incapable of controlling the movement's lower self, the thousands who signed on to move to New Harmony or Orbiston, or who set up shop in a labor bazaar. These members, each actuated by his or her own desires, pushed the movement this way and that and frustrated everyone's stated desire to establish a new moral world. All that was lacking, as Gray said, was "the will of the people."[57]

Nonetheless, this aristocratic reading would have to set aside a crucial element of the Owenite analysis.[58] For, as Gray also says, "as society is now constituted, man is trained to be anything but a rational creature," for, "as

---

Democratic Federation in the 1880s ("Republicanism, Socialism, and Democracy in Britain," 354), was actually an ongoing and multiply instantiated movement, a path that existed and could be followed.

[55] Gray, *The Social System*, 26–27.

[56] Owen, *A New View of Society and Other Writings*, 207.

[57] *Lecture on Human Happiness*, 19.

[58] Claeys, *Citizens and Saints*, chap. 2.

all exist in bondage, each in his brother sees a fellow slave, and cries, alas! 'it is the lot of man.'"[59] The difficulty is that the members of commercial society cannot *see* what is being done to them. We are not slavish by nature but have been rendered so by our position in society, whereby we are subject to powers we cannot check or oversee. The "occupations" of everyone dependent upon the market "are perfect slavery," for "their minds are in a state of continual anxiety"; they are so "tortured by fears" of losing to their competitors or their debtors that "every effort of body and mind must be exclusively devoted to the laudable, admirable, and glorious pursuit of *getting money.*"[60] There is something compulsory about the monetary system, according to the Owenites, and this compulsion explains the corruption and servility we find all around us. It is this system, and its operations, that came to occupy more and more of the Owenites' attention, for they sought to explain how the opaque and mysterious workings of the monetary system could subjugate the multitude, and how this subjugation could explain the mass slavishness of modern society.

The Money Mystery

Scholars of Marx often presume that his frequent recourse to the language of "mysteries" and "secrets" is a stylistic peculiarity, however significant.[61] Whatever this language may reveal about Marx, however, it is far from unprecedented. Precisely in the arena in which Marx most famously tried to lay bare the mysteries of the social world—the arena of exchange and money—many had come before, seeking to do the same. For instance, in 1818, William Cobbett had inveighed in his *Political Register* against the Bank of England as the "great tool of tyrants" and "a sort of partner with them in cruelty and plunder." He continued:

> This thing was . . . a *mystery* as complete and almost as sacred, as any other of those mysteries, by the means of which artful and impudent knaves have contrived to rob the laboring part of mankind. This paper-money mystery is now laid as bare as were the miracles of the monks, when . . . their pegs, wires and wheels were exposed at Charing Cross.[62]

Cobbett thought of the bank and its paper money in much the way that Patrick Henry had thought of the "intricate and complicated nature" of the American Constitution, as a thicket in which it was nearly impossible to determine what was really going on. As a potential or actual

---

[59] *Lecture on Human Happiness*, 9, 57.
[60] Ibid., 36.
[61] See, for instance, Sperber, *Karl Marx*, 404–8.
[62] William Cobbett, *Cobbett's Political Register* 34 (November 28, 1818), 285.

hiding place for conspiracy, the bank ran counter to the republican concern "that citizens be able to determine where the responsibility for a bad outcome actually lies."[63]

Worries about currency manipulation and financial conspiracy were probably as prevalent among Owenites and other early socialists as they had been among older radicals. Thompson, for example, seems to be channeling Cobbett when he argues that, "there is not one of the old expedients of force and fraud practiced on the Industrious Classes, not even the iniquities of human wholesale butchery under the name of wars, that has produced, and is at every moment liable to produce, more extensive misery to those classes, than arbitrary alterations in the currency by the portion of the Idle who form the governing classes."[64] But there is also a shift underway, for the mystery of money is no longer sought only, or even primarily, in central bank machinations, but in the "occult operations" of money itself, as it circulates in society.[65] Gray reports that when he arrived as a young man in bustling, commercial London, the city presented itself to him as "a puzzle"; although "some enormous error" seemed to pervade "this moving mass of flesh and blood," Gray admits that he was "unable to penetrate the unfathomable mystery with which everything seemed to be invested."[66] The puzzle is well articulated by Thompson's disciple William Pare, who asks, in 1850, "How comes it that the fruits of labor of the industrious, after years of incessant and successful exertion, are mysteriously—and without imputation of fault to them, without any convulsion of nature—swept away?"[67] This is the "strange anomaly of human affairs" that exercises not only the Owenites but also Proudhon and many other early socialists.

The facts that seemed, to the Owenites, to reveal the inner workings of this strange anomaly were two: there is a class of people who, by their know-how and hard work, make all of the good things enjoyed as wealth, and there is also a class of people who, by their possession of the medium of exchange, are empowered to buy up and enjoy the vast majority of those good things. It is the misfortune of the former class that they do not possess the medium of exchange, and cannot buy what they need directly with their own products. They are therefore dependent upon selling their products to the money owners. The money owners, for their

---

[63] MacGilvray, *The Invention of Market Freedom*, 41–42. I am, once again, extending MacGilvray's discussion, which concerns only the republican demand for transparency in political government.

[64] Thompson, *Labour Rewarded*, 62.

[65] Bray, *Labour's Wrongs and Labour's Remedy*, 139.

[66] Gray, *The Social System*, 339.

[67] Preface to Thompson, *Inquiry*, xxviii.

part, make nothing, but still possess the means of obtaining whatever they want. How do they come to possess these means? Let Bray explain:

> The present circulating medium, . . . as the economists confess, is made by a class of capitalists called bankers—some of them acting independently, and others in connection with the established government—and for this medium of exchange, or money, it is acknowledged that the bankers receive commodities of certain parties. These *second* parties, in turn, exchange the money for other commodities from some *third* party; and upon the same principle, of giving value for value, the exchange goes on among all succeeding parties. Thus *real value* is rendered in exchange for real value in every case except the *first transaction*—that between the banker and the person who receives his medium—and in this first negotiation, according to the showing even of the economists, there is a vile and cunning robbery committed upon the productive classes; . . . Thus the productive classes give to the banking and trading capitalists their labor—their very sweat and blood—and the latter give to them in exchange—what? They give them a shadow—a rag—a "bank-note!"[68]

This is what Bray means when he says that money is "the secret of the almost omnipotent might of the capitalist."[69] Despite his much more subtle grasp of many subjects, it is also what Thompson means when he calls commercial society an "empire of force and fraud." The near monopoly of the wealthy over the means of exchange is a self-perpetuating engine of unequal exchanges. The bargaining power it gives to the wealthy ensures that the poor producers are never able to exact a fair price for their products, leaving them in the same penury and need of purchasers as before.

The remedies entertained by the Owenites and like-minded socialists— easy fiat money, free credit, labor exchanges, combinations, cooperative communities—were all aimed at allowing the workers to get out from under this need for money, either temporarily or permanently. Except for the first, they were intended to empower the industrious classes to produce their own means of exchanging their commodities among themselves. What was imperative was to withdraw "the tacit and voluntary consent" that has made gold and silver and their paper representatives, "which may be hoarded up without injury to any one," into the wealth itself.[70] Because the money mystery rests on the consent of the producers, what Owen says of religion he could just as easily have said of money; "when [it] is stripped of the mysteries with which the priests of all times and countries have invested it, and when such is explained in terms

---

[68] *Labour's Wrongs and Labour's Remedy*, 147–48.
[69] Ibid., 136.
[70] This characterization of money comes from Locke's *Second Treatise*, chap. 5, sec. 50.

sufficiently simple that the common mind can fully comprehend it, without fear or alarm from the misguided imagination, all its divinity vanishes; its errors become palpable; and it stands before the astonished world in all its naked deformity of vice, hypocrisy, and imbecility."[71] The slavishness of the people is explained by their ignorance of the secret of the money mystery. Once this mystery is revealed, however, both their subjugation and their slavishness will vanish like a bad dream. Only a false consciousness of their situation keeps "the laboring classes" from "refus[ing] any longer to sacrifice themselves for the exclusive advantage of their masters."

This conception of the problem facing working people received a renowned and very public enunciation on the last day of July 1848. Rising to address the Constituent National Assembly in Paris, in lonely support of his own motion to establish a free credit bank financed by a one-third tax on rents and interest,[72] Proudhon argued that the only way to guarantee the right to work—enshrined in the Constitution, Articles 2, 7, and 132—was to guarantee the demand for work's products. This demand was *virtually* present, Proudhon asserted; "the power to consume, in society and in the individual alike, is infinite." What prevents us from actuating our "love of comfort and effective enjoyment," and thereby guaranteeing to the producers of the means of that comfort and enjoyment a rich reward for their efforts, is the fact that goods can only be circulated between producers and consumers by the intercession of "gold and silver as instruments of exchange." This has the effect of creating a bottleneck in the circulation of goods. The monopoly power of the holders of gold and silver allows them to charge interest and to buy up large holdings of capital and land, for which they can charge rent. The poor producers, meanwhile, are stranded on the shores of their own products, which they can neither enjoy directly nor exchange directly for what they need. Free credit would deliver them from their enforced hermitage, and allow them to bring home the good things that others have created. By this means, "consumption will be relieved of all burdens, as will the faculty of enjoyment," and the labors of all will be guaranteed to be fruitful. All that is needed, Proudhon proclaimed, between bouts of *"laughter and sundry exclamations"* from the Assembly, was to allow "the fetishism of gold [*le fétichisme de l'or*]" to give way to "the realism of existence."[73]

[71] Owen, *A New View of Society and Other Writings*, 310.

[72] Half of the revenue raised by the tax would be transferred directly to the payers of rent and interest. The remaining half would, besides paying for the free credit bank, partially replace other taxes. Proudhon's bill, together with Adolphe Theirs's negative report for the Finance Committee, and Proudhon's floor speech can be found in OC, 10:343–406.

[73] *Property Is Theft!*, 347–48; OC, 10:366. Marx published an unsigned report on "Proudhon's speech against Thiers" for the *Neue Rheinische Zeitung*, number 66, on

MARX'S INNOVATIONS

Against this background of popular concern about the mystery of money and the fetishism of gold, I think it is possible to make out more clearly Marx's real contributions to the socialist discourse about the market. These contributions are concentrated in the notoriously difficult first chapters of *Capital*. Much of what Marx seeks to accomplish therein—and this is where much of the difficulty lies—is to demonstrate that commodities are already money in "germ,"[74] and that, therefore, generalized exchange of commodities is impossible without a general equivalent or a money commodity, which can, of course, be hoarded up, lent out, and so forth. Marx needed to make this argument because the Owenites, Proudhonists, and many others denied the necessity of these connections.[75] Underlying the whole discourse on the money mystery and the fetishism of gold was the conviction that money was an alien presence in the economy, obscuring both the good and the bad reality thereof. Money was supposed to obscure the real labor of the workers, which created all of the wealth being exchanged, and to create a "hiding place" for force and fraud.

Marx agrees, in a sense, that force and fraud lurk "behind" the apparently free and fair exchanges in the marketplace,[76] but he denies (1) that this obscurity of the market is a feature of money, and that markets can be rid of money. He also denies (2) that the "good" reality supposedly obscured by money—the reality of labor creating all wealth—is actually there to be found. Labor does not create all wealth, and the labor that "forms" the value of wares on the market is not the hard labor and skillful craftsmanship of the individual workers, so obvious to every socialist. Instead, the labor that forms value can only ever appear as the prices of wares on the market. Let us look at each of these denials in turn.

The Secret of the Money Mystery

According to the Owenites and Proudhon, a money-driven divergence between price and value makes it impossible for producers to know that their efforts will be rewarded, and all too possible for money owners to

---

August 5, 1848 (*MECW*, 7:321–24); in German translation, Proudhon decries "*der Fetischismus des Geldes*" (*MEW*, 5:306).

[74] Marx, *Capital*, 1:163; *MEGA*, II.6:102; *MEGA*, II.7:52.

[75] Marx was most concerned about the form these denials took among the followers of Proudhon and Bronterre O'Brien. Taken together, these two groups formed a significant bloc within the IWMA. Marx lumped together the writings of "Bray, Gray, Bronterre O'Brien, etc., in England and of Proudhon in France" as purveyors of "money nonsense" (Marx to Friedrich Adolph Sorge, September 1, 1870; *MECW*, 44:57–58).

[76] The force obscured by capitalist exchange will be the focus of chapter 4, the fraud of chapter 5.

pay too little for goods. Because monetary prices do not accurately reflect labor values, no one can deliberate well about how hard they ought to work or whether the objects of their desires are worth the trouble of obtaining them. The data are skewed, and so the rational calculations of producers are likewise. As Proudhon puts it:

> It results from the relation of useful value to exchangeable value that if, by accident or from malice, exchange should be forbidden to a single producer, or if the utility of his product should suddenly cease, though his storehouses were full, he would possess nothing. The more sacrifices he had made and the more courage he had displayed in producing, the greater would be his misery.[77]

Marx agrees that deliberation is systematically distorted by commercial society, and that the market is a sphere of anarchy. He also agrees that the market gives rise to something like an irrational compulsion to pursue ever more monetary wealth, a "lust for gold" that replaces the "lusts of the flesh."[78] But he does not attribute these phenomena to any price/value divergence, or to the intercession of money in what would otherwise be transparent exchanges of labor time. Every evil that his predecessors pin on money is, according to Marx, a feature of generalized exchange as such, of which money is a necessary and automatic concomitant. Rather than being imposed from above by bankers, "money necessarily crystallizes out of the process of exchange," and so commercial society "sweats money from every pore."[79] The source of the problem lies in the fact that producers are related to one another by exchange itself. It is, therefore, the purpose of sections three and four of chapter one of *Capital* to reduce "the enigma of money" to the "enigmatic character of the product of labor, as soon as it takes the form of a commodity."[80]

Marx's argument in these sections has given rise to an "immense literature," but this "has produced disappointing results."[81] The sections are often read in isolation, from the rest of *Capital* and from any direct interlocutors. Interpretations float in a vacuum, so grappling among them only produces more and more eccentric trajectories and increasing confusion.[82] The context I have traced above provides a fixed background, against

---

[77]Proudhon, *System*, 1:76; *OC*, 1:93.

[78]*Capital*, 1:229, 231; *MEGA*, II.6:153, 155; *MEGA*, II.7:104, 106.

[79]*Capital*, 1:181, 208; *MEGA*, II.6:116, 137; *MEGA*, II.7:66, 88.

[80]*Capital*, 1:139, 164; *MEGA*, II.6:81, 103; *MEGA*, II.7:31, 53. I am following the French translation, which uniformly renders the German *Rätsel* as *énigme* (*MEGA*, II.7:31, 53); the English translation uses *mystery* and *enigma* indifferently, but I would prefer to reserve *mystery* for *Geheimnis*.

[81]Bidet, *Exploring Marx's Capital*, 231.

[82]That is not to say there are not excellent works of scholarship, however. I have learned an immense amount, especially, from Suzanne De Brunhoff's *Marx on Money*.

which most of Marx's claims in these sections gain a cogency and determinacy that they might otherwise appear to lack. Marx's point of departure is his claim that the value of a commodity does not inhere in the commodity itself. A useful object in isolation has no value.[83] If one wishes to understand value, one must instead look at how the value of a commodity is "expressed" in something else, that for which it is or could be exchanged.

This—the expression of the value of x in y—is Marx's entire object in section three.[84] In a series of steps, he tries to show that, whether the value of x is expressed (A) in y alone, or (B) in each member of the series of a, b, c, and so on, or (C) in the same z that also expresses the values of a, b, c, and so on, it all comes out the same.[85] Whichever commodity expresses the value of the first—Marx calls it *the equivalent form*—takes on, by that very fact, a peculiar appearance. Because value is expressed in it, it seems to be valuable in itself. If twenty yards of linen are exchanged for one coat (Marx's illustration), then the coat seems to have what the linen obviously lacks, value inherent in its own being. Since value, as all the socialists agree, represents labor, the labor that makes coats here becomes the measure of the labor that creates linen, the form of labor that weaving emulates and is equated with in exchange. The weaver proves that he, too, labors, that his labor counts as labor, when his product, the linen, is exchanged for the coat. It is always the *other* commodity, and the labor embodied in it, that assume in exchange the character of being valuable, something the original commodity proves only by being exchanged for its equivalent, in which its value is expressed.

Marx's analysis of the equivalent form is meant by him to prove that the commodity in the equivalent form always functions as a protomoney.[86] Only the equivalent instantiates socially average abstract labor, the determinant of value. It is only by being actually exchanged for the equivalent that the first commodity proves to be of value. Hence, the labor embodied in the original commodity only counts as value-forming labor once it has been equated with—by being exchanged with—the labor embodied in the equivalent.

[83] In an idiom more familiar to contemporary ears, valuation requires choice.

[84] A fact that Bidet has stressed, even if his reading also spins in the vacuum to quite an extent (*Exploring Marx's* Capital, chap. 9).

[85] This is not all he tries to show. He also claims that the latter form—that of the general equivalent—is a more adequate expression of value than the prior forms. This has led commentators to argue about whether this sequence of ever-more-adequate forms is supposed to be a logical progression, dialectical or not, or whether Marx is tracing the historical development of exchange. This question is largely irrelevant to Marx's *Auseinandersetzung* with the other socialists, however, and can be left aside.

[86] As he put it elsewhere, "all commodities are perishable money" (*Grundrisse*, 149; *MEGA*, II.1.1:155).

Hence—and this is, I think, the point of the argument—the Owenites and Proudhon are mistaken in thinking that the uncertainties and calamities of commercial exchange can be avoided by getting rid of the means of circulation, money, or by declaring all commodities directly exchangeable with one another. As soon as one commodity is equated with another in exchange (even if only prospectively), the peculiar forms of relativity and equivalence come into play, and with them the uncertainty of each producer as to what expression the value of their commodity will find. The producer always needs what the other has, and what the other has always appears, therefore, as the medium through which exchange becomes possible. A system of exchange without money, if it were possible, would present all of the same difficulties as a system of monetary exchange.

And vice versa: money does not escape its origin in the commodity. The difficulty of counting on a "double coincidence of wants" is supposed to make monetary or commercial exchange rationally preferable to direct barter.[87] But, as Marx points out, following the socialists this time, commercial exchange certainly does not guarantee that one will find a buyer for one's product or a seller willing to take one's cash. Money does not cease to be a commodity by being the money commodity, and "like every other commodity, cannot express the magnitude of its value except relatively in other commodities."[88] A commercial economy is a liquid economy, but one that always harbors the danger of freezing up, of commercial or monetary crises.[89]

The dream of perfect liquidity unites "the modern bagmen of free trade,"[90] the Owenites, and Proudhon. As Marx points out in the *Grundrisse*, the "time-chit men" believe labor money to be "the ultimate product of the 'series,' which, even if it corresponds to the 'pure' concept of money, appears last in reality."[91] That is, labor money is supposed to realize what cash has only promised, to turn every commodity into money, to "republicanize specie" in Proudhon's phrase.[92] Every product of labor is to be, as such, as liquid as currency. The double coincidence of wants is supposed to be a matter of course, and so no coincidence any longer, but an iron necessity. The perfect liquidity that is imagined to already exist

---

[87] Jevons, *Money and the Mechanism of Exchange*; Menger, "On the Origins of Money."

[88] *Capital*, 1:186; *MEGA*, II.6:120; *MEGA*, II.7:70.

[89] See Marx's discussions in *Capital*, 1:208–9, 235–37; *MEGA*, II.6:137–38, 158–60; *MEGA*, II.7:88–89, 109–11.

[90] As Marx refers to Bastiat (*Capital*, 1:153; *MEGA*, II.6:92; *MEGA*, II.7:43), in whom one might see a premonition of the marginal revolution of Jevons and Menger.

[91] *Grundrisse*, 153; *MEGA*, II.1.1:86.

[92] Hence, Proudhon's claim that "A value really [constituted]—like money, first-class business paper, government annuities, shares in a well-established enterprise—can neither be increased without reason nor lost in exchange" (*System*, 1:105; *OC*, 1:116).

by Jevons and Menger is, by Gray, Bray, and Proudhon, projected into the future of mutual credit and the chamber of commerce.

Marx denies the very possibility of a perfectly liquid market.[93] The *inability* to buy and the inability to sell are necessary concomitants of the ability to buy and the ability to sell. The dream that a social nexus constructed behind our backs might become so perfect as to never bind us or press us into the dirt is just that, a dream. There is no way to reform commercial society so as to eliminate the uncertainty and frustration that bedevil the producer. And so Marx thinks that freedom can only come with the elimination of the producers' dependency upon the market as such.[94]

A Value Theory of Labor, Not a Labor Theory of Value

Marx is just as critical of the role played by the labor theory of value in Owenism and Proudhon.[95] His criticism on this point has not been appreciated because Marx has generally been read as a proponent of this same theory.[96] I cannot hope to dislodge this widely held opinion here, although I think it is highly misleading.[97] However, I do want to show that

[93] "The difficulties inherent in barter can be overcome [*aufheben*] by money only insofar as it generalizes these difficulties, makes them universal" (*Grundrisse*, 149–50; *MEGA*, II.1.1:83).

[94] But what is supposed to stand in the market's place? How is the social division of labor to be established and regulated if not through market forces? Everyone knows the answer: central planning. In fact, Marx dismissed the notion of a central planning body—deduced by him as the logical outcome of Bray and Gray's labor money schemes—as "a despotic ruler of production and trustee of distribution" (*Grundrisse*, 155–56; *MEGA*, II.1.1:89). I will return to this question in chapter 7, where I will outline Marx's preferred alternative.

[95] I borrow the chiasmus in the section heading from Diane Elson, "The Value Theory of Labour."

[96] G. A. Cohen's formulation of the labor theory of value can be taken as definitive: "the exchange-value of a commodity varies directly and uniformly with the quantity of labor time required to produce it under standard conditions of productivity, and inversely and uniformly with the quantity of labor time standardly required to produce other commodities, and with no further circumstance" ("The Labor Theory of Value and the Concept of Exploitation," 339).

[97] I will say that almost all criticisms of Marx on this front presuppose that Marx advances a labor theory of value as an economist, and, since "the central problem of economic inquiry" is "the explanation of the formation of price" (Roll, *A History of Economic Thought*, 373), the criticisms assume that Marx intends to explain the formation of price by appeal to the labor time necessary for the items bearing prices. It will be easy enough to see from my argument in the main text that I do not think Marx is at all interested in explaining price formation, and that, therefore, the vast majority of criticisms simply miss the target. In this conviction I follow the lines of what is generally called value-form theory. An influential early partisan of the position is Elson, who writes: "It is not [for Marx] a matter of seeking an explanation of why prices are what they are and finding it in labour. But rather of seeking an understanding of why labour takes the forms it does, and what the

what Marx does with the labor theory of value renders it inadmissible as a normative principle to which society might or might not measure up. But this is precisely what the Owenites and Proudhon need the labor theory of value to be. They need labor to be the normative truth of value, the truth obscured and falsified by the mysterious formation of monetary prices in exchange. Marx argues, as we have seen, that the mystery attends any and all generalized exchange relations, even if those were direct barters or were mediated by labor certificates. But he also argues that the labor that the Owenites and Proudhon want to find *behind* the mystery is, in fact, the mystery itself; value just is the form taken by social labor in capitalism. The labor theory of value does not support the claim that the laborers are getting bilked, or getting anything less than their due.[98]

There are two steps to Marx's argument here. First, he denies that a divergence between price and value hides any systematic shifting of value away from the rewards of labor and toward money owners. Rather, this divergence is the mechanism by which price comes to reflect value dynamically and on average.[99] In a competitive commercial economy, overpriced goods lose market share until they are no longer overpriced.

---

political consequences are" ("The Value Theory of Labour," 123). Marx bases himself in a social ontology of cooperation, according to which he can say, for instance, that "social" "denotes the co-operation of several individuals" (*MECW*, 5:43; *MEGA*, I.5:19). Different forms of society, including the global bourgeois society constituted by market interactions, are different forms of cooperation. It is this notion of society as shared labor, that grounds Marx's conviction that the value of commodities, which mediates their circulation in commercial society, must be the form labor takes in that society.

[98] This is the same conclusion that Cohen arrived at, though he thought he was disagreeing with Marx. Cohen, however, wanted to hang on to the notion that the workers are getting bilked, and so he advanced what he called "the plain argument" for the workers' exploitation ("The Labor Theory of Value and the Concept of Exploitation," 356), which is nothing other than the right to the whole produce of labor, which even the Owenites were sophisticated enough to avoid! In general, my reading of chapter 1 diverges from Cohen's in two regards. First, Cohen thinks Marx is an economist trying to explain the formation of average prices, whereas I think he is a social theorist trying to explain the form that social cooperation takes in capitalism. Second, Cohen thinks that Marx's socially necessary labor time—the determinant of value—can be fully specified technically, by an empirical survey of the prevailing production technology and the consequent average productivity of different forms of labor. I disagree: socially necessary labor time is keyed to satisfying social needs, which are only manifested in effective demand in the market. Hence, socially necessary labor time can only manifest itself in prices themselves. In short, Cohen, like most commentators, does not take seriously enough Marx's claim that exchange value is the necessary form of appearance of value.

[99] "The relationship between demand and supply thus explains on the one hand simply the divergence of market price from market value, while on the other hand it explains the tendency for these divergences to be removed, i.e., for the effect of the demand and the supply relationship to be cancelled" (*Capital,* 3:292; *MEGA*, II.15:190; see also *Grundrisse*, 137; *MEGA*, II.1.1:72–73).

Second, Marx denies that the value of commodities is determined by the labor actually spent on them; it is rather the labor necessary to produce them in a socially average way that determines their value. Moreover, "if a thing is useless, so is the labor contained in it; the labor does not count as labor, and therefore creates no value."[100] Socially necessary labor must fulfill a social need, not just a technical requirement. But, if I am producing for exchange, I cannot know beforehand whether or not my labor will be useful to others, or whether my product will fulfill someone's need. As Marx puts it, "only the act of exchange can prove whether that labor is useful to others, and its product consequently capable of satisfying the needs of others."[101] Therefore, there can be no way of observing and measuring the labor time exhibited by the value of a commodity. It is impossible to know what place one's labor has in the social division of labor, and how it compares to the labors of others, until one enters the market and sells—or fails to sell—one's produce.[102] In Marx's terms, one's own labor is private labor, but value is determined by social labor. It does no good to assume a priori that one's private labor is immediately identical with social labor. That someone worked really hard for twenty hours to produce a commodity is irrelevant for the determination of its value, especially if most producers can make an equivalent commodity in half the time, or if no one wants that commodity in the first place.[103]

But this is fatal for the Owenite and Proudhonian dream of reforming commerce. The socialists are mistaken in thinking that the value of commodities can be ascertained directly by a measurement of the time spent in their production, or, indeed, by any sort of empirical observation. "In effect, the very idea of the time-chits supposes that the labor-time

[100] *Capital*, 1:131; *MEGA*, II.6:74; *MEGA*, II.7:24.

[101] *Capital*, 1:180; *MEGA*, II.6:115; *MEGA*, II.7:65. From this one can see how mistaken is the notion that Marx fatally ignores utility in his discussion of value (e.g., Elster, *Making Sense of Marx*, 139–40).

[102] "Every hour of labor measured by a clock is an hour of a particular concrete labor. . . . Abstract labor, on the other hand, cannot be 'expended' at all. Abstract labor is a *relation of social validation*." Hence, only in the moment of exchange "does the individual producer find out to what extent his individually expended labor time corresponds to the socially necessary labor-time" (Heinrich, *Introduction to the Three Volumes of Karl Marx's* Capital, 50–51). We will return to this theme in the next section.

[103] The same goes for Marx's example of the capitalist possessed of "the fantasy of using golden spindles instead of steel ones" (*Capital*, 1:295; *MEGA*, II.6:202; *MEGA*, II.7:155). Proudhon actually appreciates this, up to a point. According to him, competition is necessary to drive down production costs to the point at which they are identical with what he calls the "constituted value" of the commodity. Once value has gone through this process of constitution, however, he thinks it can be fixed by law or convention: "Commerce, free and competitive, is but a long operation of redress, whose object is to define more and more clearly the proportionality of values, until the civil law shall recognize it as a guide in matters concerning the condition of persons" (*System*, 1:122; *OC*, 1:129).

provided by the worker can be compared with the time embodied in the commodities withdrawn. The question of comparing individual labor with social labor, however, can only be resolved by the transformation of one into the other, by socialization."[104] The value of a commodity can only be expressed in the terms of another commodity, which serves as its equivalent.[105] This equivalent is the "mirror" in which the first commodity appears as a thing having value.[106] As Bidet has put it, "Value is not 'measured,' but *established* in the confrontation of the market."[107] It is this "peculiar social character of the labor that produces" commodities— the fact that it is indirectly social, or socialized only in exchange—that gives rise to "the fetishism of the world of commodities."[108] Hence, this fetishism, and the attendant opacity and uncertainty of the social production process, would be features of a world of labor exchanges and mutual credit, no less than of the commercial society those schemes seek to displace. So long as we labor to produce goods for exchange on the market, our labor will prove itself to be social labor only after the fact, and only in terms of the other goods that its products can be exchanged for.[109]

---

[104] Bidet, *Exploring Marx's* Capital, 65; compare Marx, *Grundrisse*, 168; *MEGA*, II.1.1:99–100.

[105] Marx's way of putting this is to say that value "can only appear in the social relation between commodity and commodity" (*Capital*, 1:139; *MEGA*, II.6:80; *MEGA*, II.7:30–31). Alternately, he claims that exchange value—the proportion in which one sort of commodity exchanges for another (*Capital*, 1:126; *MEGA*, II.6:70; *MEGA*, II.7:20-1)—is "the necessary mode of expression, or form of appearance, of value" (*Capital*, 1:128; *MEGA*, II.6:72; *MEGA*, II.7:22).

[106] *Capital*, 1:144; *MEGA*, II.6:85; *MEGA*, II.7:35.

[107] Bidet, *Exploring Marx's* Capital, 64. To put this in a very different way, we could say that there is no such thing as a single commodity. If there is one commodity, there must be many commodities. And the values of these commodities can only appear in the relation between them, in the form of *x* commodity *A* = *y* commodity *B*. This equation, or point of equivalence between two different sorts of things, is the norm of all market exchanges. When people exchange things in the market—when I buy a soda at the *dépanneur*, giving $1.50 in exchange for the soda—no one is supposed to leave feeling like they owe something to the other, or deserve something more from the other. Market exchange is not gift giving, or charity, or theft. The immanent norm of the practice—giving as good as you get—is obfuscated by the marginal utility analysis that insists that, since each prefers the other's goods to their own, each party to an exchange gets better than they give. This confuses the subjective motivations of the parties with the principle that regulates those motivations such that the outcome is an exchange rather than a battle to the death.

[108] *Capital*, 1:165; *MEGA*, II.6:103. This phrase is omitted from the French edition (*MEGA*, II.7:54).

[109] Paul Thomas recognizes at least the basic contours of this analysis as an argument against Proudhon. "The consumer and producer," Thomas writes, "cannot in fact be what Proudhon would like to make of them, that is free agents able to make up their own minds about the prices of what they produce and what they consume, and to act freely upon their decisions, for the good and simple reason that their respective positions are in large part

FETISHISM AND DOMINATION

Marx's understanding of the dynamics of competitive exchange destroys the basis of the Owenite and Proudhonian plans for getting producers out from under the thumb of the market. However, this does not mean that Marx breaks with the underlying republican diagnosis of market anarchy as a manifestation of mass domination. On the contrary, Marx grounds this diagnosis. If "the exchange of commodities implies no other relations of dependence than those which result from its own nature," this presupposes that understanding these new relations of dependence, proper to commercial society, requires understanding the nature of exchange.[110] Exchange has given birth to new powers, which are no longer "based on personal relations of domination and servitude," but are, rather, "impersonal."[111] These powers, of money and of commodities, despite their impersonality, are still "exercise[d] over" people whenever they enter the market.[112] Just as the Owenites intuited, the subjection of producers to these impersonal powers gives rise to the characteristic *akrasia* of market society.

The impersonality of this modern form of domination manifests itself in what Marx called the fetish character of commodities, the way in which they function as the conduits of social power and of the information necessary for practical deliberation. Because of this fetishism, and the domination it reflects, market actors are not fit to be held responsible, but are, according to Marx, merely the bearers of economic relations, the playthings of alien forces. It is because members of commercial society are subject to impersonal domination that they are precluded from pursuing the sort of human self-development, or virtue, that can only be the fruit of freedom. Impersonal market domination is, thus, the key to Marx's concept of fetishism and to his so-called structuralism or economic determinism.

Marx's concept of fetishism has been developed by German critical theory into a suggestive account of *social domination*, "the domination of people by abstract social structures that people themselves constitute."[113]

---

determined by the existence of a market economy. . . . [P]roducer and consumer, far from inhabiting separate islands within which their separate decisions hold sway, are in fact linked or joined together by their mutual involvement in the process of exchange, which, again, operates as an exchange mechanism independent of the will of either" (*Karl Marx and the Anarchists*, 223).

[110] *Capital*, 1:270–71; *MEGA*, II.6:183; *MEGA*, II.7:135–36.

[111] *Capital*, 1:247n1; *MEGA*, II.6:165n1; *MEGA*, II.7:117n1.

[112] *Capital*, 1:262; *MEGA*, II.6:177; *MEGA*, II.7:129.

[113] Postone, *Time, Labor, and Social Domination*, 30. This strand of critical theory has been reconstructed in a doctoral thesis by Chris O'Kane, to which I am indebted, "Fetishism

His structuralism was taken up by Louis Althusser as an indicator of Marx's theoretical antihumanism, and of his separation of science from all ideology. In both of these developments, Marx's criticism of other socialists is correctly seen to imply the emphasis Marx placed on reaching a correct understanding of the dynamics of capitalist society, and of the political economy that expressed these dynamics theoretically. In both cases, however, the erasure of the republican problematic undergirding Marx's theory has had distorting effects. The critical theory of social domination has never clarified how abstractions can dominate people, or why we should care about an abstract domination. Althusser's reconstruction of Marx, because it proceeds on the assumption that Marx's theory of the capitalist mode of production is, as such, nonideological, severs the link between social structure and domination that motivates Marx's project. In both cases, therefore, Marx's political theory is occluded by theory at an irreducible distance from politics. An important consequence of this chapter's analysis of part one of *Capital* is that it makes possible a recovery of the political theory that is the obscure origin of "Western Marxism."

The Microfoundations of Social Domination

The socialist criticism of the market boils down to the claim that, using Dante's phrase, commerce submits reason to talent. To be more precise, commercial society renders the deliberate choice of an agent—socialists were most concerned with the choices of direct producers—ineffective in the domains covered by the market.[114] Deliberate choices are ineffective because the market compels agents to fall in line with the social division of labor, which is not and cannot be an outcome of deliberate choice. The better judgments of individual agents as regards earthly goods are subjected not to Fortune, but to the forces of the market, the aggregated preferences—passions—of the owners of money and the producers of commodities, which "evaluations, though constant and public, [are] too irrationally performed to be seen as acts of political decision or virtue."[115]

---

and Social Domination in Marx, Lukács, Adorno, and Lefebvre."

[114] This includes the deliberate decisions of corporate agents, at least up to a certain threshold. I will return to this point in my discussion of cooperative production in chapter 7.

[115] Pocock, *The Machiavellian Moment*, 464. Because of their approximation to one another, it is worth underlining the crucial differences between the limits set on deliberate action by Fortune and those set by the market. Both Fortune and the market can be said to confound human beings, in the sense of frustrating their desires and ruining their plans. And both are amenable to providential readings, in which the pain and frustration they deal out is, in the long run, for the best. However, Fortune, whether it is Aristotle's unintelligible chance or Dante's disguised providence, is supposed to make us, its victims, better off only

Hence, the discipline imposed on desire by the market is a recognizable descendant of the classical problem of *akrasia*. Hayek, the premier defender of the market, provides us with a useful illustration:

> Assume that somewhere in the world a new opportunity for the use of some raw material, say, tin, has arisen, or that one of the sources of supply of tin has been eliminated. It does not matter for our purpose—and it is very significant that it does not matter—which of these two causes has made tin more scarce. All that the users of tin need to know is that some of the tin they used to consume is now more profitably employed elsewhere and that, in consequence, they must economize tin. There is no need for the great majority of them even to know where the more urgent need has arisen, or in favor of what other needs they ought to husband the supply.[116]

The users of tin know only that the price of tin has risen. They do not know, on the other hand, whether the short supply and consequent high price of tin is due to a use of which they would approve, or for which there are good reasons. Neither do they know whether, if all users of tin got together and discussed things, they would be able to agree as to the merits of the various uses to which tin is being put.

Because they are ignorant of these matters, the users of tin are in a position analogous to the akratic.[117] Giving them the benefit of the doubt, they have individually come to deliberate judgments about the place of tin in their lives, and the role it is to play in their pursuit of the good life. However, due to the rise in price, they all act, and are economically compelled to act, contrary to those deliberate judgments. They must either forsake other deliberately chosen goods in order to retain their commitment to the use of tin, or they must forsake this for the sake of the others. But all of the other material goods and services that figure in their plans are equally susceptible to market pressures. Taken together, these pressures are so many uncontrollable factors as to make deliberate judgments

---

in a transformative sense, only, that is, insofar as it demonstrates to us that possession of the goods ruled by Fortune is not worth taking seriously, or ought to be subordinated to the pursuit of other sorts of goods. In the Boethian formulation underlying Dante, Fortune is composed of "a series of challenges to faith and philosophy, which the individual overcomes and integrates in the pattern of his redeemed life as a citizen of the heavenly city. All fortune is good fortune only in the sense that every circumstance can be so used" (Pocock, *The Machiavellian Moment*, 42). The forces of the market, on the other hand, are supposed to make us better off in the aggregate by *satisfying* rather than by working any transformation on our desires for the goods distributed by the market. The person impoverished by Fortune is supposed to learn that happiness lies not in whatever money can buy. The person impoverished by an inability to compete in the market is supposed to learn to produce goods more pleasing to consumers, and at a price lower than other producers.

[116] "The Use of Knowledge in Society," 526.

[117] To be clear, I am not attributing this reading of the situation to Hayek, for whom *akrasia* cannot exist in the market.

about the place of commodities in a decent life extremely fragile, and to render the subjects of these deliberate judgments—be they individuals or polities—incontinent.[118]

Marx sees in this exposure of decisions to market forces—the price sensitivity of buyers and sellers—an encroachment upon the sphere of deliberate action. He thinks that the compelling reasons for action provided by the prices of things are more like the compulsions of ir-rational or corrupted desires—"general venality, corruption . . . general prostitution"[119]—than they are like the good reasons offered in delibera-tion. And, like the Owenites before him, he thinks this generalized *akra-sia* and corruption bespeaks a generalized form of domination, novel to modernity. In *Capital*, Marx calls the market-goer's decisive sensitivity to price signals the fetish character of commodities. It is built into exchange on any large scale and becomes "visible and dazzling to our eyes" in the form of the universal desire for money.[120] Hence, I am arguing that fetish-ism ought to be understood as a form of domination, rather than a form of false consciousness. Fetishism is, on my reading of Marx, a political problem first and foremost, and an epistemic problem only derivatively. Fetishism, in short, is the impersonal domination suffered by members of commercial society, the domination that explains how *akrasia* becomes generalized in such a society.

---

[118] It seems that many people have intuitions that line up with this concern. When your favorite independent bookstore closes down in the face of competition from discount and Internet booksellers, you might moan about how good it was for your town to have such a place, and how unfortunate it is that the shop was not a profitable venture anymore. And yet you might also have done much of your own book buying on the Internet. In a similar vein, a family member recently posted the following rant on Facebook: "You know how the Ben Davis label used to say 'union made, plenty tough'? Then it said 'USA made, plenty tough.' Looking at my jacket, I realized now it just said 'Plenty tough' and was made in China! I am pissed off now." There is no reason to think that the owners of Ben Davis are not also upset that they can no longer stand by their old commitments. On a larger scale, there has been some reporting to the effect that certain oil company executives think hydraulic fracturing is a dangerous and unsustainable practice, but that it must be pursued regardless because it is the only economically viable avenue for exploiting the remaining petroleum reserves. In each of these cases, something (buying books from the local bookstore, having a unionized and local workforce, refraining from fracking) is not done, not because the agents involved don't think it is worth doing, but because they feel compelled to bow to economic impera-tives. We can set aside the question of whether or not these particular judgments about what is worth doing are correct. The bare-bones structure of the intuition is only that there may be some divergence between what is worth doing and what is economically advantageous, and that, when the two come into conflict, people might feel both compelled to follow the economic incentives, and regret at forsaking their previous judgment about what is worth-while. Thanks to Arash Abizadeh for helping me to clarify this point.

[119] Marx, *Grundrisse*, 163; *MEGA*, II.1.1:95.

[120] *Capital*, 1:187; *MEGA*, II.6:121. This sentence is omitted from the French edition. *MEGA*, II.7:71.

To some extent, it is easy to show that Marx thought of fetishism as a sort of domination. He claims, for instance, that, in fetishism, the producers are under the "control" of the "movement of things," instead of controlling this movement.[121] But the most commonly encountered discussions of fetishism treat it not as a form of domination but as a form of illusion or false consciousness. According to this reading of Marx, "The fetishism of commodities is . . . the [false] belief that commodities *have* value in the same sense as they *have* weight or color."[122] On this reading, as Arthur Ripstein has said, fetishism is "an epistemic problem—the mistaking of appearance for reality."[123] Some such assimilation of fetishism to illusion is incredibly widespread, even if the character of the illusion varies with commentators.[124]

This illusion interpretation assimilates Marx's use of fetishism to Proudhon's use—remember that Proudhon counterposed the fetishism of gold precisely to the realism of existence—and this ought prima facie to raise suspicions about the illusion interpretation's correctness. More importantly, however, it trips over Marx's explicit claim that, in fetishism, "the social relations between [the producers'] private labors appear *as what they are*."[125] Where social relations are mediated by commodities,

---

[121] *Capital*, 1:167–68; *MEGA*, II.6:105; *MEGA*, II.7:56.

[122] Elster, *Making Sense of Marx*, 96; compare Cohen, *Karl Marx's Theory of History*, 116–17; Carver, "Marx's Commodity Fetishism," 53. Elster both attributes this notion of fetishism to Marx and attributes to him the error of thinking that the value of commodities is contained in them by virtue of the labor expended upon them. Apparently, Marx was so inattentive to his own writing that he managed to criticize fetishism and fall prey to it on the same page.

[123] "Commodity Fetishism," 736.

[124] "The interpretation of fetishism as 'false consciousness' has a long history and can be seen as far back as Karl Kautsky's highly influential *The Economic Doctrines of Karl Marx*." It is also the dominant interpretation in the analytical Marxist tradition (O'Kane, "Fetishism and Social Domination in Marx, Lukács, Adorno, and Lefebvre," 16). For Gould, fetishism is the "false appearance" that "causal agency" inheres in objective conditions rather than in labor alone (*Marx's Social Ontology*, 95). According to others, Marx's account of fetishism "ascribes to commodities . . . the automatic tendency to successfully obscure the real relations between people simply by the act of exchange itself" (Wayne, "Fetishism and Ideology," 198; compare Mohun, "Ideology, Markets and Money"; Tanner, "Marx's Theory of Commodity Fetishism as the Unstated Premise of What Is to Be Done?"). De Angelis asks, rhetorically, "Does the social character of the private producers' labour originate in exchange?" No, "it only *appears* in exchange. It is in fact an obvious thing that the labour of the 'private producers' is also a moment of 'social labour'" ("Social Relations, Commodity-Fetishism and Marx's Critique of Political Economy," 19). For De Angelis, apparently, the social character of labor is a self-evident truth, and so fetishism is not only an illusion but an exceedingly poor one.

[125] *Capital*, 1:166; *MEGA*, II.6:104; *MEGA*, II.7:54; emphasis added. The warrant for the illusion reading comes from the last two pages of the section on fetishism, culminating in Marx's jests about Samuel Bailey and the other Dogberrys of political economy,

exchanges *are* the real relations between the producers of commodities.[126] And, where exchanges are the real relations between producers, the only way to have any knowledge of the social division of labor is by means of the information contained in the exchanges of commodities. There is a social division of labor, but it is not subject to direct intervention, deliberation, collective decision, or control. It plays out behind the backs of the producers, as Marx says repeatedly. The manifold intricacies of this social division of labor "do not appear as direct social relations between persons in their work, but rather as thingly relations between persons and social relations between things."[127] But why should anyone care that the social relations amongst persons are mediated by things?

I think this significance lies in a remark made by Lukács. For Lukács, fetishism is "the essence of the commodity-structure," and, as such, represents "the central, structural problem of capitalist society in all its aspects."[128] He describes this commodity structure as "the abstract, quantitative mode of calculability,"[129] and claims that "the essence of rational calculation is based entirely upon the recognition and the inclusion in one's calculations of the inevitable chain of cause and effect in certain events."[130] What Lukács indicates, ever so barely, is that "the mysterious character of the commodity-form" is also the basis of all rational calculation in a commercial society.[131] In short, the fetishism of the commodity is the capacity of the commodity, via its price, to convey information to participants in commercial society. This information is, as Hayek and the other Austrian neo-Smithians emphasized, the raw material of a form of "rational" planning, carried out in a decentralized way by the participants in the market. The reality of "thingly" relations among people finds its significance in the fact that, in a commercial society, in order for

---

the economists who say that value is a property of things (*Capital*, 1:176–77; *MEGA*, II.6:112–13; *MEGA*, II.7:63). Marx refers to illusions and mistakes in the fetishism section *only* in pointing out the ways in which economists are "deluded" (*täuschen*) by the fetishism of commodities (*Capital*, 1:176; *MEGA*, II.6:112; *MEGA*, II.7:62). I think this is significant. Fetishism is not itself an illusion, but it may give rise to illusions among those who seek to give an account of the economic order.

[126] Geras, "Essence and Appearance: Aspects of Fetishism in Marx's 'Capital,'" 75–76.

[127] Marx, *Capital*, 1:166; *MEGA*, II.6:104; *MEGA*, II.7:54. On the basis of these texts alone, we can conclude that Ripstein is closer to Marx than are Elster and Cohen, since he argues that "the problem is not that social relations between people *seem to be* relations between things, but that in an important sense they *are* relations between things." "Commodity Fetishism," 739.

[128] Lukács, *History and Class Consciousness*, 83.

[129] Ibid., 93.

[130] Ibid., 98.

[131] *Capital*, 1:164; *MEGA*, II.6:102; *MEGA*, II.7:53.

individual agents to weigh different courses of action they must base their calculations on the prices of commodities.

Commodity fetishism, then, is essentially a matter of practical reason, not a theoretical error.[132] Indeed, Marx's text emphasizes again and again the ways in which the practice of exchange runs ahead of any theory of exchange.[133] From the practical standpoint of the members of commercial society, the phenomenon of prices is both the central concern and the most mysterious aspect of exchange. "What practically interests the exchangers of products in the first place is the question: how much alien product do they get for their own product, and thus in what proportions do products exchange? . . . These change constantly, independently of the will, foreknowledge, and actions of the exchangers."[134] What Ripstein says about the seller of labor power could be said about any seller:

> Each individual faces the labor market in just the way an individual faces the weather. The market sets parameters within which one must operate. And the only way to turn these parameters to one's advantage is . . . by exploiting their very inexorability. The individual can only attain his or her ends by ensuring that his or her labor power is marketable, by making herself or himself available and useful.[135]

However, as MacGilvray rightly points out, "markets do not in fact make it possible for individuals to foresee the consequences of their economic choices—of training for a certain line of work, taking or refusing a certain job, making certain investment decisions, and so on."[136] Therefore, there is no way to *ensure* that one's labor power, or one's commodity in general, is marketable. That is precisely the problem. There is no way of knowing whether one's wares will be "available and useful" to buyers until after the fact.

---

[132] If fetishism finds primary expression in a practical attitude of the representatives of commodities, it is this practical truth of fetishism that gives rise to the theoretical illusions that are the focus of the standard interpretations of fetishism. If, as Ripstein puts it, "The best way to succeed in capitalist society is to think of economic interactions as interactions between individual agents and natural forces" ("Commodity Fetishism," 748), then we ought not be surprised when economists like Bailey claim that value is "a property of things" (*Capital*, 1:177; *MEGA*, II.6:112–13; *MEGA*, II.7:63).

[133] E.g., *Capital*, 1:166–67, 180; *MEGA*, II.6:104–5; *MEGA*, II.7:54–56. Money, for example, as a universal equivalent, is not and could not have been the product of deliberate action, individual or collective. Practice precedes theory, in the sense that the practice of exchange gives rise to a more-or-less justified conviction that all goods can be exchanged for one good in particular, the money commodity. This conviction was not true before the social practice of exchange made it true, and it remains true because we continue to act as if it were true.

[134] Marx, *Capital*, 1:167; *MEGA*, II.6:105; *MEGA*, II.7:55.

[135] Ripstein, "Commodity Fetishism," 746.

[136] *The Invention of Market Freedom*, 171.

It is this uncertainty of market interactions that so bothered early socialists, and that Marx underlines when he discusses commerce. He writes, for instance, that, "The division of labor converts the product of labor into a commodity, and thereby makes necessary its conversion into money. At the same time, it makes it a matter of chance whether this transubstantiation succeeds or not."[137] That the prices of things provide agents in commercial society with the only bearings they can come by does not mean that these bearings are certain to any very great degree. Marx goes to great lengths to make this point in chapter three of *Capital*. He calls the sale of the commodity "the commodity's *salto mortale*," but is quick to point out that, "If the leap falls short, it is not the commodity which takes a hit [*ist geprellt*] but rather its owner."[138] What follows is Marx's partial elaboration of the factors that can explain the hit taken by a commodity owner who fails to sell her product:

> The social division of labor makes the nature of [the commodity owner's] labor as one-sided as his needs are many-sided. . . . But [his product] cannot acquire universal social validity as an equivalent-form except by being converted into money. That money, however, is in someone else's pocket. To allow it to be drawn out, the commodity . . . must above all be a use-value for the owner of the money. The labor expended on it must therefore be of a socially useful kind . . . But the division of labor is an organization of production which has grown up naturally, a web which has been, and continues to be, woven behind the backs of the producers of commodities. . . . Today the product satisfies a social need. Tomorrow it may perhaps be expelled partly or completely from its place. . . . Moreover, although our weaver's labor may be a patented branch of the social division of labor, yet that fact is by no means sufficient to guarantee the use-value of his 20 yards of linen. . . . One does not look a gift horse in the mouth, but our friend does not frequent the market to give gifts.[139]

These are just some of the ways in which circulation can go wrong. They are necessary concomitants to the social division of labor being mediated by commodity exchange. Assuming that none of them prevent the sale from taking place, nonetheless the sale price realized will also reflect the same factors.[140] Marx sums up his whole discussion of this uncertainty by

---

[137] *Capital*, 1:203; *MEGA*, II.6:133; *MEGA*, II.7:84.

[138] *Capital*, 1:200–201; *MEGA*, II.6:131; *MEGA*, II.7:82. The Fowkes translation has "is defrauded" for "*ist geprellt*," but this is incorrect; *prellen* is much vaguer in its connotations. Obviously, the commodity owner is not defrauded by being unable to sell her wares, and Marx does not think otherwise.

[139] *Capital*, 1:201; *MEGA*, II.6:131; *MEGA*, II.7:82.

[140] "What was yesterday undoubtedly labour-time socially necessary to the production of a yard of linen ceases to be so today, a fact which the owner of the money is only too eager to prove from the prices quoted by our friend's competitors. . . . If the market cannot

returning to the theme of commodities' appetitive nature: "We see then that commodities are in love with money, but that 'the course of true love never did run smooth.'"[141]

I can sum up the preceding by concluding that, for Marx, commerce has two distinct but interrelated effects upon deliberation. First, it quantifies deliberation by imposing the price form on it; one has to think not only of the particular characteristics of the goods with which one is concerned, but of the quantitative relations of equivalence in which they stand vis-à-vis all other goods. Second, it compels deliberation to take account of a new sort of uncertainty, the uncertainty of the movements of these relations of equivalence.

The quantification of deliberation is the abstract rationality that concerned Lukács. For Lukács, what matters is that "the 'coordination of action . . . is imposed from outside by the autonomous movement of things on the market (*cash nexus*).' This leads 'actors' to 'adopt the objectifying attitude of instrumental-strategic action towards themselves and others' and for 'thingness' to become the determining modality of thought."[142] The emphasis here is on the objects exchanged, and on the quantitative relations of equivalence among them. In Adorno's later works, much more explicitly than in Lukács, one can find a theory of fetishism as social domination, keyed to exchange as a practice.[143] As in Lukács, however, this

---

stomach the whole quantity at the normal price . . . this proves that too great a portion of the total social labour-time has been expended in the form of weaving. . . . As they say: caught together, hung together" (*Capital*, 1:202; *MEGA*, II.6:132; *MEGA*, II.7:83). Marx introduces further considerations in volume three (the manuscript of which, to remind the reader, Marx wrote *before* drafting volume one). Considering demand, Marx writes: "It appears . . . that there is a certain quantitatively defined social need on the demand side, which requires for its fulfilment a definite quantity of an article on the market. In fact, however, the quantitative determination of this need is completely elastic and fluctuating. Its fixed character is mere illusion. If means of subsistence were cheaper or money wages higher, the workers would buy more of them, and a greater 'social need' for these kinds of commodity would appear, not to mention those paupers, etc., whose 'demand' is still below the narrowest limits of their physical need" (*Capital,* 3:289–90; *MEGA*, II.15:188–89). In a commercial society, there is no way to feel the existence of a social fact like *social need* except through the mediations by which it appears as effective market demand.

[141] *Capital*, 1:202; *MEGA*, II.6:133; *MEGA*, II.7:83–84. Marx's citation is from Shakespeare, *A Midsummer Night's Dream*, Act 1, scene 1, line 134.

[142] O'Kane, "Fetishism and Social Domination in Marx, Lukács, Adorno, and Lefebvre," 28; quoting Vandenberghe, *A Philosophical History of German Sociology*, 148. This concern fed into the Frankfurt School's Weber- and Nietzsche-inspired obsession with bureaucracy and "one dimensional" rationality, and with "the quantitative, rationalized and rationalizing character of modern institutions" (Postone, "Lukács and the Dialectical Critique of Capitalism," 6).

[143] This may indicate the influence of Alfred Sohn-Rethel's work, *Intellectual and Manual Labour*, which argued that the practice of commodity exchange was the womb of all

domination is fundamentally conceived as a process of subject formation, whereby individuals become integrated into capitalist society by internalizing, or, better, by *becoming* ideology.[144] This process is understood, moreover, as the creation and maintenance of a certain relationship between people and things. This understanding of social domination generates real confusion, both theoretically and regarding Marx's argument.

The theoretical confusion is apparent in two of the most sophisticated followers of Lukács and Adorno: Moishe Postone and Michael Heinrich. Both insist that capitalism must be grasped as "a system of abstract, impersonal domination,"[145] or of "impersonal, objective domination."[146] But both are quite vague about where this domination comes from and why it counts as domination. Heinrich says, in the same breath, that modern domination takes the form of "an overwhelming social interaction that cannot be controlled by individuals," *and* that "people (all of them!) are under the control of things." Moreover, he traces this objective domination back to the fact that, in modern society, "people relate to things in a particular way—as commodities."[147] But why do people relate to things as commodities, and how does this constitute such a problematic situation that it merits the name of domination? Because he understands objective domination as a relationship between people and things, he does not make clear that the things in question only mediate relations with other people, and that it is the relationship to other people, the dependency upon their arbitrary and incontestable actions and desires, that makes this into an instance of domination.

Postone runs into a similar problem. His argument, that "social domination in capitalism does not, on its most fundamental level, consist in domination of people by other people, but in the domination of people by abstract social structures that people themselves constitute,"[148] might have led to a real breakthrough if he had realized that domination, in

---

abstract thought. Adorno championed Sohn-Rethel for a time, but was unable to overcome Horkheimer's objections to including him in the Institute for Social Research.

[144] O'Kane, "Fetishism and Social Domination in Marx, Lukács, Adorno, and Lefebvre," chap. 4. Despite Althusser's antipathy to the humanist, Hegelian tradition out of which the Frankfurt School arose, there is a similar impulse in his work, and that of his students, to see in fetishism the rudiments of a theory of ideological subjection as subjectification (Althusser and Balibar, *Reading* Capital; Balibar, *The Philosophy of Marx*). Rather than finding in Marx's discussions of objective dependence and the domination of exchange relations an elucidation of the mechanics of modern, generalized servitude, both schools find an intimation of a social ontology in which social macrostructure is replicated via individual microstructure.

[145] Postone, *Time, Labor, and Social Domination*, 125.

[146] Heinrich, *Introduction to the Three Volumes of Karl Marx's Capital*, 75.

[147] Ibid.

[148] *Time, Labor, and Social Domination: A Reinterpretation of Marx's Critical Theory*, 30.

order to be something we care about, must be domination by other people, and that, therefore, the constitution of a social structure by people must be understood as a mediated relationship among people.[149] Domination mediated in this way is indirect or impersonal, but it is still the domination of people by people. Instead, however, Postone goes in the opposite direction, claiming that capitalist domination "subjects people to impersonal, increasingly rationalized structural imperatives and constraints. It is the domination of people by time."[150] Domination here loses all reference to an arbitrary, incontestable will, and becomes nothing more than a metaphor.[151]

Marx, despite his proclivity for arresting turns of phrase, was much more precise and careful than Lukács and his followers. Although Marx does refer to "objective" or "external" dependency or domination,[152] he also clarifies that objective domination is not domination *by objects*, but domination by "social production," or by the "social relation of individuals to one another."[153] The key texts from *Capital*, in this regard, are tolerably straightforward. Of the members of commercial society Marx says that "their own social movement has for them the form of a movement of things, and instead of controlling it, they are under its control."[154] That

---

[149] As Marx put it in his Paris notebooks, "If the product of labor does not belong to the laborer, if it is over against him as an alien power, then this is only possible because it belongs to a man other than the laborer. If his activity is a torment to him, to another it must give satisfaction and the joy of life. Not the gods, not nature, but only man himself can be this alien power over man" (*Early Writings*, 330–31; *MEGA*, I.2:371).

[150] "Lukács and the Dialectical Critique of Capitalism," 18. This is surely due to the fact that Postone's reading of Marx is determined by his opposition to what he thinks of as traditional Marxism, which he understands to have conflated the impersonal, abstract domination of capitalism with class domination veiled by market interactions. Thus, he writes at one point: "Abstract domination . . . cannot simply be equated with the workings of the market; it does not refer simply to the market-mediated way in which class domination is effected in capitalism" (*Time, Labor, and Social Domination*, 126). While I wholeheartedly agree that, for Marx, modern, impersonal domination is not itself a form of class domination (even though it makes possible a new form of class domination), Postone makes a major error in treating the market as if its relevance were exhausted by the question of whether it transmits class domination.

[151] "In Postone's account . . . it is unclear how abstract labour and capital are constituted in their historical specificity and how this pervasive process, and its dynamic structures, compels and dominates society" (O'Kane, "Fetishism and Social Domination in Marx, Lukács, Adorno, and Lefebvre," 12n5).

[152] E.g., *Grundrisse*, 158; *MEGA*, II.1.1:91.

[153] *Grundrisse*, 158, 197; *MEGA*, II.1.1:91, 146. Postone lays heavy emphasis on these texts, but he denies, without any evidence or argument, that the dominating social relationships can be understood as market relationships (*Time, Labor, and Social Domination*, 125–26).

[154] *Capital*, 1:167–68; *MEGA*, II.6:105; *MEGA*, II.7:56. Fowkes, like Moore and Aveling before him, mistranslates this passage, turning it into an affirmation of Lukács's position,

is, individuals fall under the control of the social movement, the changing relations of interdependency, of people. Thus, "there develops a whole circle of social-natural interrelations, uncontrollable by the people involved. The weaver can only sell his linen because the farmer has already sold his wheat, the hothead can only sell his Bible because the weaver has already sold his linen, the distiller can only sell his firewater because the other has already sold the water of everlasting life, and so forth."[155] These interrelations are social because they are among people; they are natural because, as he put it in the *Grundrisse*, "as much as the individual moments of this movement [of circulation] arise from the conscious wills and particular purposes of individuals, so much does the totality of the process appear as an objective interrelation, which arises spontaneously from nature."[156]

Because the domination of market society is impersonal, the specific individuals on whom one is dependent are of no import; what remains the same, no matter who one's customers and competitors are, is the relationship of all-around dependence on one another's production and consumption. Thus, Marx calls this modern social domination, this "objective dependence," the "domination of relationships." Because "relationships can naturally be expressed only in ideas," Marx thought it unsurprising that "philosophers have seen the peculiarity of modern times in the individuals' being dominated by ideas," or "abstractions."[157] While it would be tendentious to claim that Lukács and those who follow him have fallen back into this "German ideology," it would be both fair and productive to say that, in the absence of an analysis of the market as a system for aggregating *arbitria*, the diagnosis of social domination is little more than a vague and unpersuasive complaint, cut off from any articulable interest or political constituency.

---

that "things, far from being under [the exchangers'] control, in fact control them." The German is ambiguous: "*Ihre eigne gesellschaftliche Bewegung besitzt für sie die Form einer Bewegung von Sachen, unter deren Kontrolle sie stehen, statt sie zu kontrollieren.*" Does *deren* refer to *Form* or *Bewegung* or *Sachen*? The French, however, clears up this grammatical ambiguity: "*leur propre mouvement social prend ainsi la forme d'un mouvement des choses, mouvement qui les mène, bien loin qu'ils puissant le diriger.*"

[155] *Capital*, 1:207–8; MEGA, II.6:136–37; MEGA, II.7:88.

[156] *Grundrisse*, 196; MEGA, II.1.1:126. In Marx's earliest articulations of the intuitions that would eventually become the account of impersonal domination, he does claim that, via the alienation of labor, "the labourer becomes a slave to his object." However, even in 1844, he concludes, as noted above, that "if the product of labour . . . confronts him as an alien power, this is possible only because this product belongs to a man other than the labourer. . . . Not gods, not nature, but only man himself can be the alien power over man" (*Early Writings*, 325, 330–31; MEGA, I.2:365, 371).

[157] *Grundrisse*, 164; MEGA, II.1.1:96.

The Sense of Structuralism

According to Marx, commercial exchange becomes the social nexus just to the extent that producers come to "exist for one another merely as representatives . . . of commodities." As representatives of their commodities, they are "characters who appear on the economic stage," "merely personifications of economic relations," or "bearers of these economic relations."[158] As characters on stage, the lines they speak do not show their minds, but the minds of the commodities they represent. When a seller prices his or her commodities, for example, Marx says the seller "must stick his tongue in their heads."[159] And commodities are utterly without judgment, "ready to exchange not only soul, but body, with each and every other commodity."[160] By being a representative of his commodities, therefore, a member of commercial society is hamstrung in his judgment, and becomes, "socially," the "creature" of economic relations, "however much he may subjectively raise himself above them."[161]

There is a familiar line of early modern thinking that saw in the spread of commerce the prospect of restraining the vices of the powerful. Montesquieu summed up this hope in his prognosis that princes would be "cured of Machiavellianism," that "great acts of authority" were, thanks to "the avarice of princes," no longer so common or so likely.[162] In Aristotelian terms, this amounts to the hope that, due to commerce, the passion for gain would undermine the vicious judgments of the wicked. This hope is, therefore, the obverse of Marx's worry about commerce. Montesquieu, though he never put it in these terms, hoped that princes would be compelled to act against their worse judgment, and that incontinence would moderate vice. Marx sees the knife cutting both ways. The commodity is "a born leveler and cynic."[163] By becoming the representatives of commodities, we compromise our freedom to be virtuous *or* vicious.[164]

---

[158] *Capital*, 1:178–79; *MEGA*, II.6:113–14; *MEGA*, II.7:64.

[159] *Capital*, 1:189; *MEGA*, II.6:122; *MEGA*, II.7:73. This is Marx's grotesque way of saying that, "the value judgments—the prices—with which we are confronted in a commercial society are not made in most cases by identifiable people but rather by the market itself, that is, by a decentralized and largely anonymous mechanism for aggregating information about the economic decisions of an indefinite number of people" (MacGilvray, *The Invention of Market Freedom*, 102).

[160] *Capital*, 1:179; *MEGA*, II.6:114; *MEGA*, II.7:64.

[161] *Capital*, 1:92; *MEGA*, 1983, II.5:14; *MEGA*, II.7:14.

[162] *The Spirit of the Laws*, sec. XXI.20; see Hirschman, *The Passions and the Interests*.

[163] *Capital*, 1:179; *MEGA*, II.6:114; *MEGA*, II.7:64.

[164] I will return to this question in chapter 6, for it is centrally important for Marx's account of primitive accumulation.

This aspect of Marx's argument in *Capital* has given rise to immense controversy and misunderstanding. This is "Marx at his most austerely structural," as Alex Callinicos put it, "rigorously abstracting from individual's perspectives and purposes."[165] These passages are the touchstones of Althusser's argument that,

> The structure of the relations of production determines the *places* and *functions* occupied and assumed by the agents of production, who are never anything more than the occupants of these places, insofar as they are the "supports" (*Träger*) of these functions. The true "subjects" (in the sense of the constitutive subjects of the process) are therefore not . . . "concrete individuals," "real men"—but . . . *the relations of production* (and political and ideological social relations).[166]

This argument, in turn, has been subjected to the most strident and vituperative criticisms, from Marxists and non-Marxists alike. The debate over Althusser's structural Marxism—insofar as there has been anything except a litany of accusations and attacks—has centered on the question of where agency lies. If individual human beings, and no other beings, are admitted as agents, then structural Marxism falls apart, since it attributes agency to social structures, or to relations of production. On the other side, to emphasize structures and structural causality is to underline the limits of human agency, the ways in which individuals suffer their situation in society.

For Marx, this debate, oriented by the "polarity between structure and agency,"[167] would have been utterly beside the point. The significance of his comments about individuals in modern commercial society being bearers of economic relations is not that these individuals suffer an impairment of their *agency*, but that they suffer an impairment of their *freedom*. Commodity producers in a commercial society are *dominated* agents, not nonagents. Only after the forgetting of the republican conception of freedom could freedom come to be so conflated with the mere capacity to act that any qualification of the claim that human beings are free to make their own history might be taken to run afoul of the axiom that "those subject to the power of dominant groups themselves are knowledgeable agents, who resist, blunt, or actively alter the conditions of life that others seek to thrust upon them."[168] If domination leaves freedom intact, then there is no such thing as domination.

---

[165] *Making History: Agency, Structure, and Change in Social Theory*, ix.
[166] Althusser and Balibar, *Reading* Capital, 180; Althusser et al., *Lire* "Le Capital," 393.
[167] Callinicos, *Making History*, 2.
[168] Giddens, *A Contemporary Critique of Historical Materialism*, 172.

Marx does not argue that economic relations manipulate individuals like puppets,[169] but that economic relations dominate their decision making. Commodity producers in a commercial society face competitive pressures from other producers. These competitive pressures predictably incentivize certain courses of actions. Moreover, competition replaces producers who are insufficiently susceptible to those incentives with producers more susceptible to them. Under these conditions, producers—regardless of their personal idiosyncrasies or perfect-world preferences—will tend to act on market incentives, and to be price sensitive in their decision making. Their agency remains intact. They continue to make decisions based on their beliefs and desires, and to have all the characteristics attributed to persons by the standard accounts of agency. But they are not, for all that, fit to be held responsible for their actions in view of the market. They are not *forced* to act as they do,[170] but they are subject to a kind of hazard that rules out discursive deliberation except within arbitrarily narrow parameters. If not making or selling x, in y manner, means risking one's livelihood, then there is not much room for wondering whether making or selling x, in y manner, is worth doing. Nor is there much reason for anyone else to believe one's claim that it *is* worth doing; no one trusts a salesperson.

The problem is not that individuals cannot do exactly what they each want to do, but that they cannot get together and talk about what sorts of things that should and should not be done, and what sorts of reasons should and should not count as good reasons. Having to take the beliefs and desires of others into account is, in itself, no threat to one's freedom; the question is whether one can challenge those beliefs and desires before having to take them into account. (I will discuss this further below.) Hence, although people continue to make decisions based on their beliefs and desires, these beliefs and desires are not especially salient as explanatory factors, because the macroregularities of market societies—all of the tendencies or laws of economic development—will hold regardless of

[169] Neither does Althusser, in fact. The usual criticisms of Althusser assume that when he denies that individuals are the subjects of the economic process he is denying individual agency and attributing agency instead to structural regularities (e.g., Pettit, *The Common Mind*, 132). A careful reading of Althusser's text, however, will show that he is only denying that individuals have *control* over the economic roles available to them. When he claims that the relations of production are the "subject" of the economic process—he always keeps the word in scare quotes—he means that the relations of production have a formal coherence that unifies a mode of production. It is the functional coherence of society, the way a social formation is reproduced, and the obstacles to this reproduction, that interest Althusser. Denying human agency is neither here nor there for this project.

[170] One might say that individuals are forced to be market agents *in general*, but not forced to make *any particular* market decisions. They are, as it were, forced to be free.

which individuals play which parts.[171] The great irony of modern market societies is that they give rise to the cult of the individual at the same time that, through their institutional order, they render the specificity of any individual irrelevant to social scientific explanation. What matters for the predictable dynamics of the modern economy is that there are individuals. *Who* those individuals are does not matter at all.

Liberal defenders of freedom tend to respond by assimilating submission to the market to submission to natural forces, and opposing it to submission to the arbitrary will of another person. This is certainly where Hayek goes, following Spencer and Mises, as when he argues that, except in the case of a monopoly over "an indispensable supply," the "power of withholding a benefit" cannot by itself be coercive, for,

> Though the alternatives before me may be distressingly few and uncertain, and my new plans of a makeshift character, yet it is not some other will that guides my action. . . . So long as the act that has placed me in my predicament is not aimed at making me do or not do specific things, so long as the intent of the act that harms me is not to make me serve another person's ends, its effect on my freedom is not different from that of any natural calamity—a fire or a flood that destroys my house or an accident that harms my health.[172]

This conclusion is reached not only by libertarian liberals. Philip Pettit has also defended the notion that market offers are noncoercive, and that, for this reason, the discipline of the invisible hand is not a form of domination, and hence not a form of domination with which republicans ought to be concerned. The core of Pettit's argument is the claim that,

> Making a market offer is different in a normatively significant way from making a threat. If we embrace the ideal of republican freedom, arguing for the value of protection against the control of others, then we will naturally adopt a very different view of offers and threats. The influence I have on you when I make a market offer need be no more inimical to your status as an undominated agent than the influence I have on you in revealing a mistake in your deliberative assumptions or transitions. The influence I have on you when I make a threat, however, is the influence of an alien, dominating source of control.[173]

---

[171] Contra Geras, *Marx and Human Nature.*

[172] Hayek, *The Constitution of Liberty*, 136–37. Compare also Hayek's admonition: "Unless this complex society is to be destroyed, the only alternative to submission to the impersonal and seemingly irrational forces of the market is submission to the equally uncontrollable and therefore arbitrary power of other men" (*The Road to Serfdom*, 224).

[173] Pettit, "Freedom in the Market," 144. See also Pettit's *Republicanism*, where he restricts dominating power to the power possessed by an agent who is able to intentionally

Despite their many differences on the question of state regulation and the possibilities of freedom outside the market, Pettit and Hayek agree that market forces do not impinge upon our freedom because they are not like the freedom-robbing imposition of an alien will.[174]

Although he expresses himself much less clearly, Proudhon seems to agree with Hayek and Pettit. He calls legal limits on production "a violation of liberty: for, in depriving me of the power of choice, you condemn me to pay the highest price."[175] He complains about the French tobacco monopoly, equating "the very fact that the [tobacco] administration's worker has no competitors and is interested neither in profit nor loss" with "the fact that he is not free."[176] Furthermore, he looked upon contracts as the purest expression of mutual liberty and argued that it is only in a social order built entirely out of contracts "that I may remain free; that I may not have to submit to any law but my own, and that I may govern myself."[177]

Marx disagrees. In doing so, he casts a sideways glance, as it were, at the interaction that fixates the attention of mutualists, libertarians, and liberal republicans alike. It is striking that both Hayek's and Pettit's claims about the freedom-preserving character of market interactions treat them as one-on-one interactions between buyers and sellers. The question, for them, is whether some identifiable person, either in making me an offer or in considering my offer, is a threat to my freedom. The "central theme" of Marx's criticism of fetishism, on the other hand, "is that dependence is no less dependence for the absence of an identifiable individual to be depended on."[178] This dependence is a threat to freedom because, no matter

---

influence what another does by means of imposing costs on them (52–53, 79). Since market forces are neither possessed by individual or corporate agents (except in the case of monopoly power), nor intentionally wielded against anyone in particular, domination by market forces is impossible on Pettit's reconstruction of republicanism.

[174] In Pettit's terms, the market, "like the fertility of the land, the hospitality of the weather, the cleanliness of the water," conditions but does not compromise freedom ("Discourse Theory and Republican Freedom," 74, 77). For a much fuller discussion of Pettit's integration of the market within his republicanism, see Gourevitch, "Labor Republicanism and the Transformation of Work." Although he—or the American labor republicanism upon which he draws—does not identify the market itself as a form of domination, Gourevitch is, to my knowledge, the only person to argue explicitly that we do not need to identify a specific individual upon whom an individual is personally dependent in order to diagnose a case of domination.

[175] *System*, 1:81; OC, 1:97.

[176] *System*, 229; OC, 1:215.

[177] *Property Is Theft!*, 579; OC, 2:267.

[178] Ripstein, "Commodity Fetishism," 747. In discussions of the confrontation between republicanism and commercial society, it is an article of almost universal affirmation that Rousseau represents the ne plus ultra of republican antipathy to commerce, and so it especially gratifying to see Ripstein point out that Rousseau's *Emile* contains a spirited defense

how impossible it is to attribute responsibility for price levels to any identifiable set of human beings, price levels nonetheless mediate the desires
and preferences of multitudes, and those multitudes, being anonymous
and dispersed, cannot be challenged to defend their desires and preferences, no matter how much these might spell the ruin of a whole class of
people.[179] This is the significance of Marx's oft-repeated indication of the
social processes going on behind the backs of the producers. What goes
on behind your back cannot be contested.

Hence, Marx's attention is not on the identifiable person with whom
I am transacting business, but on all of the unknown buyers and sellers
whose choices have established the parameters of this transaction. By
focusing narrowly on the personal interaction, the defenders of the market have missed the drama of the situation entirely. The defenders worry
only about the possibility that a *monopolist* might threaten the freedom
of market agents; hence, the freedom of the market is only threatened by
a force alien to—and, supposedly, ameliorated by—market competition.
Marx's worry is about the threat to freedom posed by a market agent's
competitors and customers, and hence about a threat to freedom proper
to the market as such, and which would be more of a threat the more
perfect the market became.

Buyers and sellers on the market are not asked to justify their preferences for money or goods. I think it is safe to say that we would all find
it very strange if the cashier at a store asked us to supply reasons for our
purchases: "Why do you want that? Do you really think it is the best
thing for you?" If anything, we expect our counterparts in exchange to
justify our desire for us, to give us a litany of reasons for wanting what
they have to offer. To a large extent, we offer money and commodities in
exchange precisely as an alternative to offering reasons for wanting what
we want.[180] This is something Smith saw quite clearly, even if he put it in

---

of the proposition underlying the Smithean and neo-Smithean defense of the market, that
impersonal dependence "does no injury to liberty and begets no vices" (Rousseau, *Emile*,
58; Ripstein, "Commodity Fetishism," 747).

[179]Pettit (like most liberals) assimilates economic processes to the social situation, and
sees no difference, from the standpoint of freedom, between the social situation and the
physical situation ("Discourse Theory and Republican Freedom," 73–77). Threats to freedom arise, on the other hand, from interpersonal relationships. Many Marxists have gone
to the opposite extreme, seeing threats to freedom arising from both the physical and the
social situation, as well as from interpersonal relationships. Marx, for his part, puts the
social situation together with interpersonal relationships (even if he does not assimilate it
to the latter), but he does *not* see in the physical situation a source of threats to freedom. I
will argue for this last claim, which is controversial, in chapter 7.

[180]Proudhon embraces this aspect of the market, declaring that, "I, as a free purchaser,
am judge of my own wants, judge of the fitness of the object, judge of the price I wish to
pay" (*System*, 1:82; OC, 1:97).

very different terms. In the famous line near the beginning of *The Wealth of Nations*, he claims, regarding our fellows in commercial society, that "We address ourselves, not to their humanity but to their self-love, and never talk to them of our own necessities but of their advantages."[181] Smith portrays the appeal to humanity as a servile appeal to the benevolence of one with power, but to talk of our necessities is also to articulate reasons for them, or to justify them, and perhaps in terms with which the other can equally identify. Smith and the other eighteenth-century advocates of commercial society saw freedom in the market's erosion of personal dependence and of the consequent need to justify oneself, which had for them the air of slavish pleading. With the nineteenth-century socialists, Marx saw the reverse of the medal, the equally slavish pandering to the desires of the money owners, and the correlative muting of the discursive mediation of social life.[182] Thus he claims that, in commercial society, "the individual carries his social power, as well as his connection with society, in his pocket."[183]

MacGilvray has aptly christened the difference between the pro-market conception of freedom and the political conception of freedom I find in Marx as the difference between a freedom modeled on irresponsibility and a freedom modeled on responsibility.[184] I think Marx's concern about

[181] *The Wealth of Nations*, bk. 1.I.ii. Much commentary on this passage focuses on the way in which the market offer is a sort of reason-giving. What is occluded here is the difference between offering you an *incentive* to do what I want (market offers) and offering you *grounds* for doing what I want (offering reasons). Thanks to Jacob Levy for pressing me on this point.

[182] There is in Marx's 1844 excerpt notebooks on James Mill's *Elements of Political Economy* a very striking premonition of this insight, and perhaps the clearest indication of the role of fetishism in Marx's thought: "The only intelligible language we speak to one another is that of our objects in their reference to one another. A human language we do not understand, and it remains without effect. On one side, it would be understood, felt as a plea, as begging, and as *humiliation* and hence uttered with shame and a feeling of supplication; on the other side, it would be heard and rejected as *shamelessness* and *madness*. We are so far mutually alienated from human nature [*Wesen*] that the immediate language of this nature seems to us an *injury to human dignity*, while the alienated language of material values seems to be the righteously justified, self-confident, and self-recognized human dignity" (*Early Writings*, 276–77; *MEGA*, IV.2:464). (Thanks go to Alex Gourevitch for recalling this passage to me and noting its importance as an early attempt by Marx to articulate the argument I find in part one of *Capital*.) Despite his appreciation of the market, Pettit's understanding of freedom as discursive control, as spelled out in *A Theory of Freedom*, resonates with the concerns about the market I am here outlining (*A Theory of Freedom*, chap. 4).

[183] *Grundrisse*, 157; *MEGA*, II.1.1:90. One might say that the democratization of distinction that went along with the rise of commercial society—calling all men and women "Sir" and "Ma'am," for example—carried with it the habit of not expecting or asking Lords and Ladies to give any reasons.

[184] *The Invention of Market Freedom*, 190–98.

the anarchy and incontinence of the market can be summed up neatly by saying that commercial society leaves us unfree because it renders us systematically irresponsible for our economic life. It is this systematic irresponsibility that Marx pinpoints when he treats individuals as the personifications of economic relations. Of course, as Marx says, "a single individual can, by chance, cope [*fertig werden*] with" these "thingly relations of dependence"; however, "the mass of those dominated by them cannot, since their very existence expresses the subordination, and the necessary subordination, of the individual to them."[185] The freedom of the market is the domination of the mass of producers. This is the political theoretical core of Marx's structuralism.

CONCLUSION

Marx finds two wrongs inherent in capitalism considered as a commercial society. First, because value is determined by abstract, socially necessary labor time, no producer can know until after the fact whether or not their labor was productive at the socially necessary level. This exposes every producer's judgment to a form of uncertainty and compulsion that makes him or her act incontinently. Second, this exposure to the market renders each producer a slave to the decisions of others, made without any consultation or debate. The preferences of others impose themselves on each producer without any need to justify themselves, and without any possibility of being contested. There is no way to ask whether the activities that set the terms of sale are themselves worthwhile. Thus, Marx's understanding of commodity fetishism, on the reading I have proposed, retools the republican criticism of domination for the modern situation of expanding markets.

Moishe Postone has argued that, "Analyzing the structures of abstract domination as the ultimate grounds of unfreedom in capitalism, and re-determining the Marxian categories as critical categories that grasp these structures, would be first steps in re-establishing the relationship between socialism and freedom, a relationship that has become problematic in traditional Marxism."[186] While I disagree with how Postone has carried out this analysis, and think he has misidentified both the origin of "abstract domination" and its consequences for class-based politics, it is hard to disagree with the claim that the relationship between socialism and freedom has become problematic. By identifying the republican roots of Marx's criticisms of the market, I hope to have located the point of

---

[185] *Grundrisse*, 164; *MEGA*, II.1.1:96.
[186] Postone, *Time, Labor, and Social Domination*, 127.

connection, and to have made possible a radical reconsideration of socialism as an attempt to escape domination.

This reading transforms the opening chapters of *Capital*. Instead of containing only highly abstract (and perhaps wrongheaded) economics, or neo-Hegelian conceptual mastication, these chapters compose the beginnings of a critical political theory of capitalism. They contain, not a theory of price, but an account of the structure of human relations in commercial society. The concept of value they elaborate is, first and foremost, a tool for understanding the dominating form that these relations take. Marx identifies the mechanisms by which a competitive market affects the decision making of everyone who enters into it to sell their products. He takes seriously such a producer's experience of being dominated by the unchallengeable choices of anonymous others. And he argues convincingly that the proposals put forward by socialists to alleviate this domination by abolishing the privileges of money would in fact do nothing to address the problem. The problem is rooted in the fact that the social nexus is constituted by relations of exchange. To the extent that our contributions to society are mediated by exchange, we will find ourselves trapped in a giant collective-action-problem-generating machine, a machine that we have inadvertently created and from which it will be extremely difficult to extricate ourselves. We all suffer for the sin of a social form, for which no particular set of agents can be held responsible.

Thus, the impersonal domination embodied in the market is not a form of class domination. Instead, the dominant class in modernity, the class of capitalists, is as subject to this impersonal domination as are the laboring classes. This has major, and largely unrecognized, consequences for Marx's argument in the rest of *Capital*. First, it motivates Marx to reconceptualize the socialist concept of exploitation. The specifically capitalist form of exploitation grows up on the basis of commodity exchange and extends the exchange nexus to encompass society as a whole. Capitalist exploitation cannot, therefore, be understood as the exercise of a personal or collective power of extortion. The capitalist, dominated by market imperatives, is compelled thereby to exploit labor, and to do so within the confines of competitive market transactions that secure for the laborer the fair value of his or her special commodity, labor power. The transformation this works on the concept of exploitation will be the topic of the next chapter. But the impersonal domination of the market, felt by capitalists and laborers alike, does not abolish class domination. Just as it encompasses and mediates a novel form of exploitation, the modern "domination of relationships" is also "transformed into certain personal relationships of dependence" within the workplace.[187] The direct

---

[187] *Grundrisse*, 164; *MEGA*, II.1.1:96–97.

"despotism" of the capitalist at the site of work makes the laborer into a slave of a slave, beholden to the market-driven desires of the boss. This new form of class-bound, personal domination will be the topic of chapter 5. We have barely entered the modern social Hell, barely scratched the surface of capital's sins.

CHAPTER 4

Dis: Capitalist Exploitation as Force Contrary to Nature

"Exploitation" is a word which we cannot translate, it literally means the working of mines, land, etc.; but metaphorically applied, it means the working the value out of a man for your own ends, "making a chop" of him, or "bleeding him," as the vulgar say. . . . We think the word would be adopted by the English if it were not harsh in sound.
—*London Phalanx*, vol. 1 (May 1, 1841)

Ideas are made definite by their contraries.
—Proudhon, *General Idea of the Revolution in the Nineteenth Century* (1851)

In *Capital*, as in the *Inferno*, the realm of anarchic desire proves difficult to leave. For Dante and Virgil, the difficulty lay in their attempt to enter the gates to the city of Dis, which contains the lower reaches of Hell. Devils bar the gates and call upon the Furies to keep the pilgrim from going any further. Only the intercession of an angel makes it possible for the journey to continue.[1] This is the point where Dante's *katabasis* diverges from, and surpasses, that of Aeneus, his model. Aeneus turned aside here "where the path splits itself in two." He followed the "road to Elysium, that runs beneath the walls of mighty Dis," rather than taking the one that "works punishment on the wicked, and sends them on to godless Tartarus."[2] Dante, however, has to take the path his predecessor did not, descending into the circles of malice, where the sins of force and fraud (*forza e frode*) are punished.[3]

Marx must also transgress a boundary at the end of part one and take his readers where, he claims, previous authors have not. The marketplace

[1] This is a much discussed crux of the poem. For commentary, see Freccero, *Dante: The Poetics of Conversion*, chap. 7.

[2] *Aeneid*, VI.540–44.

[3] According to Dante's Augustinianism, the ancient world did not have to confront the evil of the will, the perversions of theoretical and practical rationality that signify the denial of the revealed God and mark the boundaries of the circles of *forza* (see Freccero, "Dante's Pilgrim in a Gyre").

manifests but also obscures the existence of capital and capitalists. Capitalists are, according to most socialists of the mid-nineteenth century, "persons living by the interest of money";[4] or "profitmongers" and "lazy, worthless, swindling villains";[5] or those who, by power of their ownership of the means of production, "exacted . . . under the name of rent or profits, . . . taxes on industry," abstractions from the laborers' product.[6] These depictions fit naturally with the picture of commerce painted by early socialists. If commercial exchanges take place at prices that regularly diverge from labor values, monopolies in land and machinery fundamentally distort market interactions, and force and fraud are communicated in the prices of things, then it is easy to believe that extortion and chicanery explain most or all stories of economic success. But Marx, by taking seriously the ideal of the market—values are exchanged for equivalent values, disruptions correct themselves—has made these depictions hard to believe. Part one of *Capital* has painted socialism into a corner. If the market really is a place where free and fair exchanges rule the day, and where competition disciplines sellers who mark wares up in an unwarranted manner, then the usurer, the profit monger, and the taxer of industry seem out of place, marginal figures at best. How can Marx write a critique of capital if there is no room in his account of the market for the classic character of the capitalist villain?

Marx plays up this tension, highlighting it. He spends all of chapter five running his reader up against the same roadblock from many different avenues. If equivalents are exchanged in the market, "it is plain that no one abstracts more value from circulation than he throws into it."[7] But, supposing the exchange of nonequivalents, still there will be "no change in the sum of social values."[8] The money owner of part one can become a capitalist only if he buys and sells commodities "at their value, and yet at the end of the process withdraw[s] more value from circulation than he threw into it at the beginning."[9]

Marx then claims to surmount this roadblock in chapter six, with his observation that "our money-owner must be so lucky as to find within the sphere of circulation, on the market, a commodity whose use-value possesses the peculiar quality of being a source of value, whose actual use, therefore, would itself be an objectification of labor, hence a creation of value." The only commodity that fits the bill is labor power, "the epitome

[4] Gray, *Lecture on Human Happiness*, 21.

[5] O'Brien, *Human Slavery*, 102, 144.

[6] Thompson, *Inquiry*, 125.

[7] *Capital*, 1:262; *MEGA*, II.6:176; *MEGA*, II.7:129.

[8] *Capital*, 1:266n18; *MEGA*, II.6:180n31; *MEGA*, II.7:132n31, quoting Say.

[9] *Capital*, 1:269; *MEGA*, II.6:182; *MEGA*, II.7:134.

of those mental and physical abilities existing in the corporeality, the living personality, of a human being, and which he sets in motion whenever he produces a use-value of any kind."[10] But, as he notes, "the consumption of labor-power, like the consumption of any other commodity, takes place outside the market or the sphere of circulation."[11]

> Let us therefore, in the company of the owner of money and the owner of labor-power, leave this noisy sphere, residing on the surface and accessible to the eyes of all, and follow them into the hidden site of production, on whose threshold one reads, "No admittance except on business." . . . He who was formerly the money-owner now strides out in front as the capitalist; the owner of labor-power . . . is timid and unenthusiastic, like someone who carried his own hide to market and now has nothing to expect but the—tannery.[12]

Beyond the market, Marx must lead us into the realm of capitalist production, depicted here as a place where the workers' very flesh will be stripped from them in order to become a saleable ware.[13] The money owner will become a capitalist, and money will acquire "the occult quality of generating value because it is a value,"[14] but only on the condition

---

[10]*Capital*, 1:270; *MEGA*, II.6:183; *MEGA*, II.7:135. Marx's claim that labor power is the only commodity that is "a source not only of value, but of more value than it itself has" (*Capital*, 1:301; *MEGA*, II.6:206; *MEGA*, II.7:159), has been criticized on the basis of the claim that, in a growing economy, any basic commodity adds more to production than is required to reproduce that commodity (e.g., Roemer, *A General Theory of Exploitation and Class*, chap. 6, appendix). Marx's specification of labor power has been defended, however (Schweikart, "On the Exploitation of Cotton, Corn, and Labor"). Given a definite level of production technology, the quantity of any nonlabor input will determine the quantities of all other nonlabor inputs. The quantity of labor power purchased, however—e.g., one day's labor—determines nothing, both because the goods necessary to reproduce that labor power contain a social or historical element ("habits and expectations"; *Capital*, 1:275; *MEGA*, II.6:187; *MEGA*, II.7:139), and because, as we will see, the length and intensity of the working day is indeterminate.

[11]Richard Biernacki convincingly argues that Marx's identification of the purchase and use of *Arbeitskraft* as the source of capital's profits had numerous precedents in the German workers' press around the time of the 1848 revolutions (*The Fabrication of Labor*, 411–12). Biernacki does not claim that Marx knew of these early articulations of what would become the Marxist theory of exploitation, but that the conception of wage labor as the sale of the capacity to work for a given time was natural to the German context in which pay scales for weaving were according to the number of shuttle passes made by the weaver (as opposed, for example, to Britain, where pay scales were according to the length and density of the produced cloth; ibid., chap. 2).

[12]*Capital*, 1:279–80; *MEGA*, II.6:191; *MEGA*, II.7:143–44.

[13]This was telegraphed in chapter 1, where value was referred to repeatedly as a gelatin (*Gallerte*) of human labor (e.g., *Capital*, 1:128; *MEGA*, II.6:72). If you know how gelatin is made, the factory-as-slaughterhouse analogy should already be in your mind by the time you get to chapter 6.

[14]*Capital*, 1:255; *MEGA*, II.6:172; *MEGA*, II.7:124.

that the laborers are subjected to torture and slaughter within the production process. From the realm of incontinent desire, we must descend into the realm of force or violence, made possible by the sale of labor power.

In Dante, the *forza* punished within the walls of Dis is depicted as the denial or perversion of the divine order of generation. Heretics pervert the mind with doctrines denying the soul, the principle of the body; murderers and tyrants pervert the human community; suicides and wastrels deny their own lives and livelihoods; blasphemers and sodomites deny or rebel against God and nature. The final perpetrators of this violence against natural generation are the usurers, who made money grow unnaturally and are now reduced to the status of strange grazing animals oppressed by a rain of fire (l.17.34–75).

It is this old issue of usury that confronts Marx as the problem of capital; in the modern world, money has somehow become productive, wealth that grows of its own accord.[15] If the pushing and pulling of the avaricious and the prodigal neatly illustrates the *akrasia* of exchange, it is inadequate as a representation of usury. Within exchange, one holds, another tosses, but this is only a back-and-forth movement, not growth. It is only after Dante and Virgil have passed into Dis that they begin to encounter transformations and monstrosities. Likewise, in *Capital*, there is movement in the market, but no growth. One can take from another, but no wealth is created thereby. But Marx upends the traditional problem regarding the growth of money, for he regards usury as "derivative" of "the modern primary form of capital."[16] Marx inscribes usury within capitalist production, thereby reconfiguring the terms by which its violence against the natural order is understood and criticized. No longer is usury an inexplicable or even unholy breeding of money; instead, self-augmenting wealth is dependent upon "making a chop" of or "bleeding" the workers, "as the vulgar say."

But if Marx reveals, in part three, that *force* is "the secret of profit-making,"[17] this revelation is the inverse of the Owenite contention that money conceals the empire of force and fraud, or the Proudhonian attacks on "capitalistic feudalism." Socialists before Marx had explained the abstraction of the laborers' product, and the perpetuation of their poverty, by appealing to a series of preeconomic facts: the feudal conquest of the land and the extortion this allowed the landed to exact from the poor producer. Hence, it is what has happened *before* the laborer and capitalist enter into exchange that explains the laborer's vulnerability to

---

[15] Marx cites Aristotle's paradigmatic criticisms of money making, commerce, and usury (*Capital*, 1:253n6, 267; *MEGA*, II.6:170n6; *MEGA*, II.7:122n6).

[16] *Capital*, 1:267; *MEGA*, II.6:181; *MEGA*, II.7:133.

[17] *Capital*, 1:280; *MEGA*, II.6:191; *MEGA*, II.7:143.

exploitation, and exploitation happens when this vulnerability is taken advantage of, such that the laborer gets less out of the exchange than he or she ought. Force precedes and distorts exchange, which ought to be—but is not, yet—an exchange of equivalents.

For Marx, on the other hand, force comes into the picture *after* the laborer and capitalist negotiate their exchange. Exchange precedes and licenses the force relevant for capitalist exploitation. The workplace relation between capitalist and wage laborer is one of force because it is one in which the boss directly controls and uses the worker's labor power—that is, the worker's body—for the end of making a profit. Just as, and just because, Marx's critique of market domination takes aim at competitive and fair markets, so his critique of capitalist exploitation takes aim at "cleanly generated" capitalism. It is what capital *does* with and to labor power, rather than any distributional causes or effects, that constitutes exploitation. Capital bends labor power to an alien and unnatural end, using it to generate a surplus excessive of the aims and needs of the laborers. The monstrous productivity of capital—in particular, the overwork it enforces—is inherent in this mode of exploitation. Hence, Marx condemns capitalist exploitation in very old-fashioned terms—it is an unnatural use of labor power—even as he tries to take seriously the novelty of the capitalist epoch, and its irreducibility to previous modes of injury, extortion, and plunder.

EXPLOITATION BEFORE *CAPITAL*

Marx did not coin the phrase, "the exploitation of labor,"[18] but he may be significantly responsible for its entry into English. As late as 1865, he called attention to its foreignness, telling his audience—the General Council of the IWMA, hardly neophytes of the socialist movement and its terminology—"you must allow me this French word."[19] Sixteen years later, John Rae, a journalist who regularly wrote on socialism for the liberal *Contemporary Review*, could treat as a matter needing no explanation that "Marx and his disciples" systematically formulate "their theories of the exploitation of labor by capital."[20]

[18]It appeared, for instance in Jules Lechevalier's October 3, 1849, report on France for George Holyoake's *The Reasoner* ("What Can the Pope Do?" 218). Lechevalier was a former Saint-Simonian and Fourierist who had collaborated with Proudhon in setting up his "Banque du Peuple."

[19]*Value, Price, and Profit*, MECW, 20:136.

[20]Rae, "Ferdinand Lassalle and German Socialism," 921. There is a convergent development in the history of Marx's texts. If you examine an early text in which he is beginning to formulate his criticism of capitalism, *Wage Labour and Capital* (1847), you find that

Prior to the 1870s, then, *exploitation* was a word obviously marked by its French origins. In particular, it carried a Saint-Simonian association. It brought to mind the assertion that, in the words of *The Doctrine of Saint-Simon*, "The empire of physical force and the exploitation of man by man are two contemporaneous, mutually corresponding facts. The latter is the consequence of the former."[21] According to the leading Saint-Simonians, the exploitation of the worker by the capitalist is the vestigial consequence of the conquest of the land by the warrior lords preliminary to the establishment of the ancien régime. Between 1865 and 1875, Marx tried to wrest the word away from these origins and to give it an entirely new sense within his own critical theory of capitalism.

He was motivated, not by a concern with the Saint-Simonians per se, but by his ongoing effort to displace Proudhon. Proudhon had taken over the Saint-Simonian historical schema wholesale, and with it the conviction that the exploitation of labor was rooted in the premodern conquest of the land. Marx thought this way of thinking misdirected the working class in its struggle for self-emancipation by figuring capitalist exploitation as just another form of rent seeking. Rather than an index of the persistence of the precapitalist world, Marx argued, the exploitation of labor takes a special form in modernity.[22] Before we can explore Marx's effort

---

Marx generally referred to exploitation using the word *Ausbeutung*, the standard German equivalent of the French word. In 1850, Charles Dana, soon to be Marx's editor at the *New York Tribune*, wrote a defense of Proudhon's "People's Bank" proposal in which he claimed that "the Germans are better off than we [English-speakers], the flexibility of their language allowing them to express new ideas by new combination, which are still purely German. For *exploitation* they say *Ausbeutung*" ("The Bank of the People," 342n). By the time Marx wrote *Capital*, however, his writing had absorbed the French loan-word to the exclusion of the "purely German" expression. *Ausbeutung* does not disappear entirely, but *Exploitation* has displaced it in five out of every seven cases, and entirely in chapter and section headings.

It is also worth noting that *Exploitation* appears only once—as "the exploitation of women and children" (in the preface; *Capital*, 1:91; *MEGA*, II.5:13)—prior to part three, and that the four appearances of *Ausbeutung* prior to part three refer to the exploitation of diamond mines (130; *MEGA* 1987, II.6:74), of theoretical difficulties (146n21; *MEGA*, II.6:87n20), of monetary crises (237n52; *MEGA*, II.6:256n101), and of the writings of the Physiocrats (266n18; *MEGA*, II.6:180n31). That is, none of the appearances of either word have a specific theoretical sense.

[21] Bazard, Enfantin, and Barrault, *Doctrine of St-Simon*, 63; *Doctrine de Saint-Simon*, 151.

[22] It is in his writings about the French Revolution of 1848—in the *Neue Rheinische Zeitung* (1848–49) and the *Neue Rheinische Zeitung-Revue* (1850)—that Marx began to foreground class exploitation and class domination as conjoint factors in the analysis of the modern world. Nonetheless, no specialized use of the term develops. Both *ausbeuten* and *exploitieren* are used very broadly to refer to any sort of plunder or theft (*Political Writings*, 2:38, 49, 110; *MEGA*, 1.10:121, 129, 181) as well as to the more neutral using or taking advantage of something or someone (*Political Writings*, 2:70, 102, 105; *MEGA* 1.10:147, 174, 176–77). The exceptional case is Marx's discussion of the French peasantry in *The Class Struggle in France*. There he claims that the exploitation of the peasant "differs from

to develop a concept of capitalist exploitation, then, we must examine the meaning of exploitation prior to *Capital*, in the Saint-Simonians and in Proudhon.[23]

The Doctrine of Saint-Simon Regarding the Exploitation of Man

The first public appearance of the famous phrase, "the exploitation of man by man," was in a public lecture on December 17, 1828, the first of seventeen lectures in which Amand Bazard presented a systematic expo-sition of the doctrine he and several close associates attributed to Henri de Rouvroy, Comte de Saint-Simon.[24] Bazard and company, in the course of their account of the history of art and culture from Greek antiquity through the French Revolution, claim that the decline of the ancien ré-gime saw "the laymen," armed with the weapons of science and wealth, overthrow "the ungodly coalition," the clergy and the nobility, "which had trusted in the eternity of the exploitation of man by man."[25] This first occurrence, although it barely hints at the Saint-Simonian theory of exploitation, contains a couple of important clues.[26]

First of all, the exploitation of human beings is associated with the fail-ure of the strong to protect the weak, and with a consequent rule of force. Both clergy and nobility had made themselves the instruments of imperial or political powers, "the successors of Caesar," rather than defending the

---

the exploitation of the industrial proletariat only in form." He continues: "The exploiter is the same: capital. The individual capitalists exploit the individual peasants through mort-gages and usurious interst; the class of capitalists exploits the class of peasants through state taxes" (*Political Writings*, 2:117; *MEGA*, I.10:187). Exploitation does not have a special meaning here, but Marx does indicate that capital exploits the smallholding peasantry in a different way than it does wage laborers. This very basic indication of different *forms* of exploitation is the seed of something that will grow in Marx's research leading into *Capital*.

[23] The Owenites, without using the word *exploitation*, also insisted on the abstraction of the produce of labor from the laborer. Their theory of how this happened is fragmentary and implicit, but so far as it can be made explicit, it generally coincides with Proudhon's theory (McNally, *Against the Market*). Hence, I will indicate what I take to be the crucial points of comparison along the way, but will not devote space to a full reconstruction.

[24] The first course of lectures (1828–29) was followed by a second, leading up to the es-tablishment of the Saint-Simonian church in December 1829, with Bazard and Barthélemy Prosper Enfantin as "Pères suprêmes."

[25] *Doctrine of St-Simon*, 18; *Doctrine de Saint-Simon*, 96–97.

[26] There has not been much scholarship on the Saint-Simonian theory of exploitation, but the essay by Cunliffe and Reeve is generally accurate. As they correctly note, while the word is new to the *Doctrine*, this is merely the renaming of an older "analysis focused on the unjust monopoly over the means of production which enabled a minority of unproduc-tive but wealthy parasites to live from the labour of the productive but impoverished major-ity" ("Exploitation: The Original Saint-Simonian Account," 62).

weak against these powers.[27] They did so, the lecture suggests, because they thought submission to physical force was inescapable, and exploitation is nothing but "the consequence" of "the empire of physical force."[28] Second, the presumption of eternity enjoyed by this hierarchy of force and exploitation was shattered by the growth of new powers, the powers of knowledge and wealth. Hence, there is here an opposition between brute powers, the powers of making war and compelling obedience, and the civilized or peaceful powers of science and commerce, together with a progressive conviction that these civilized powers have won the decisive contest and will continue to displace force in human affairs: "Antagonism, by preparing the way for a larger association and hastening the day of universal association, devours itself bit by bit and tends definitively to disappear."[29]

However, this disappearance is for the future, for the third "organic state" in the "series of civilization," in which common thought and collective action will again become the rule.[30] In the present, in the wake of the French Revolution, surrounded by "the debris of the middle ages, living debris, which still expresses some regret" about its fallen state,[31] the Saint-Simonians detected an antipathy to "anything that seems destined to re-establish order and unity," a desire for "permanent anarchy" and "universal slackening of social ties."[32] These signs mark the present as a critical epoch in which collective action is at first destructive of the previous order and then impossible, in which egoistic mutual antagonism reigns.[33] The old relations of force persist in "forms of government, in

[27] *Doctrine of St-Simon*, 18; *Doctrine de Saint-Simon*, 96.

[28] *Doctrine of St-Simon*, 63; *Doctrine de Saint-Simon*, 151.

[29] *Doctrine of St-Simon*, 62; *Doctrine de Saint-Simon*, 150. This conviction takes the form, in the *Doctrine*, of a secular theodicy. The "bonds" that held together the feudal world were indeed "healthy" for it, but the victory of the laymen shows that those bonds "had become obstacles to [mankind's] development" (*Doctrine of St-Simon*, 51; *Doctrine de Saint-Simon*, 136). This development is in the direction of "a vast association of workers constantly perfecting its means of action on the globe, and thus tightening the social bond for the sake of the best combination of efforts" (Enfantin, "Considérations II," 243). Hence, periods of crisis and dissolution are only the growing pains of this development of association.

[30] On the *series*, see chapter 1. See, also, Henri de Saint-Simon, *Mémoires sur la science de l'homme* (*Oeuvres choisies* II, 52).

[31] *Doctrine of St-Simon*, 18; *Doctrine de Saint-Simon*, 97. The Saint-Simonians may have shared much with de Maistre, but they certainly did not share the reactionary's desire to transmute the losses of the old higher orders into a claim of authority for precisely those losers. This is another point on which they remained very close to their master, for whom functionality was the only claim to authority (Hart, "Saint-Simon and the Role of the Elite").

[32] *Doctrine of St-Simon*, 2–3; *Doctrine de Saint-Simon*, 77.

[33] For example, in science and industry, each individual seeks to monopolize discoveries by shrouding them in "mystery," one of many present "obstacles" to industrial and scientific progress (*Doctrine of St-Simon*, 12; *Doctrine de Saint-Simon*, 88–9).

legislation, and above all in the established relations between the sexes."[34] Finally, and most importantly for our purposes,[35] "antagonism, the empire of physical force, and man's exploitation by man" continue into the present to "manifest themselves," howsoever "tempered and transformed," in the "relations between proprietors and laborers, masters and wage earners."[36]

What about these relations was exploitative?

> The worker is not like the slave, the direct property of his master. His condition, always temporary, is fixed by a transaction concluded between them. But is this transaction free on the part of the worker? It is not, since he is obliged to accept it under pain of death, reduced as he is to only expecting his food each day from his labor of yesterday.[37]

Workers are exploited because, and just so far as, they are compelled, "under pain of death," to accept an offer of employment from some master. They are so compelled because they own nothing but themselves and their wage,[38] and having no recourse to any other source of subsistence. Thus, the root of exploitation, in the present as in the past, is force or compulsion.[39] The empire of physical force has been "considerably" and "successively weakened," but it has also taken on new forms, and "in these forms," "its intensity is still very strong."[40] The proprietor no longer has the right to directly compel the laborer to support his or her idleness, either through forced labor or through the compulsory taking of some portion of the product. Nonetheless, the proprietor can rely upon the law—"a delegation of force"[41]—to compel the propertyless to keep their hands off his or her property, and, because of this, the propertyless

[34] *Doctrine of St-Simon*, 81; *Doctrine de Saint-Simon*, 174.

[35] And, also, for the purposes of many rank-and-file Saint-Simonians, the artisans and wage-laborers who attended the meetings, formed the associations, wrote for the journals, and imbibed the hope of the coming of *la Mère* (see Faure and Rancière, *La Parole Ouvrière, 1830–1851*). However, as Pilbeam has stressed, the Saint-Simonian movement under Enfantin was devoted almost equally to "the joint objectives of the liberation of women and workers" (*French Socialists before Marx*, 78; see also Cunliffe and Reeve, "Exploitation: The Original Saint-Simonian Account," 66–67).

[36] *Doctrine of St-Simon*, 81–82; *Doctrine de Saint-Simon*, 173–74.

[37] *Doctrine of St-Simon*, 82; *Doctrine de Saint-Simon*, 175.

[38] *Salaire* had a broad meaning in the early nineteenth century, covering almost any wage or fee (*Dictionnaire de l'Académie française*, 6th ed. [1835]). For the Saint-Simonians, and for Proudhon, the primary referent seems to be the daily wage of the journeyman artisan, who owned his tools but not his materials, and had to work for a *maître*, being forbidden by guild rules from selling his own product.

[39] Saint-Simonian gestures at a theory of exploitation, thus, figured "exploitation-as-extortion" (Godels, "Marx, Engels, and the Idea of Exploitation, 511).

[40] *Doctrine of St-Simon*, 81, 86; *Doctrine de Saint-Simon*, 173–74, 179.

[41] *Doctrine of St-Simon*, 92; *Doctrine de Saint-Simon*, 187.

are compelled by need to come looking for work and to accept the terms offered.[42] Under those terms, the proprietor retains "the privilege of living without doing anything, that is to say, of living at the expense of others."[43]

Werner Stark has emphasized that "a correct philological understanding of Saint-Simon is an indispensable condition of a correct interpretation of his ideas," since, "in his writings many words have a meaning essentially different from the one predominant today."[44] Despite the numerous and important differences between the doctrines actually propounded by Saint-Simon and those attributed to his name by Bazard, Enfantin, and company,[45] this hermeneutical principle is equally crucial for an understanding of the Saint-Simonians. An object lesson in the application of this principle is the Saint-Simonians' apposition, in this context, of "the proprietor, the capitalist."[46] The proprietor remains for the Saint-Simonians, as for their namesake, the *landed* proprietor, especially the one whose title to the land is inherited, who is born with the privilege of idleness. For the Saint-Simonians, therefore, *capitalist* is little or nothing more than another word for *landlord*. Insofar as the exploitation of man by man persists in a new form in postrevolutionary France, it reduces to this: the landlords, by their inherited titles to property, enforced by the state, compel the workers to sustain them in their idleness.

This interpretation is verified by Enfantin's studies of classical political economy in *Le Producteur*. For example, in his first article, "On the progressive decline of rent of movable and immovable property," he had concluded, from his reading of Say and Ricardo, that "the proprietors who farm out their land, by means of rent, levy a portion of the products of the work of industrious men; such is indeed the result of the rental of capital, and this means that workers pay some people to sit, and for this [payment of rent] they [the owners] leave at their [the producers'] disposal the materials of production."[47] It is also attested by the *Doctrine* itself, which asks, "by virtue of what authority does the present proprietor enjoy his wealth and transfer it to his successors?"

> By virtue of legislation, the principle of which goes back to conquest, and which, however distant it may be from its source, still manifests the exploitation of man by man, of the poor by the rich, of the industrious producer

---

[42] This is also the model one finds, piecemeal, in William Thompson, writing in England just a few years earlier. This is revealed by his insistence that any abstraction of the product from the laborer reduces the incentive to labor (*Inquiry*, 46–54).

[43] *Doctrine of St-Simon*, 86; *Doctrine de Saint-Simon*, 179–80.

[44] "Saint-Simon as a Realist," 49n23.

[45] Iggers, *The Cult of Authority*, 7; Proudhon, *General Idea*, 123; OC, 2:197.

[46] *Doctrine of St-Simon*, 86; *Doctrine de Saint-Simon*, 180.

[47] "Considérations II," 243.

by the idle consumer: the advantages which property confers, whether it comes from inheritance or is acquired through labor, are thus only the delegations of the right of the stronger, transmitted by the accident of birth, or ceded to the laborer under certain conditions.[48]

The "living debris" of medieval society, mentioned above, is here revealed to be the class of landlords, the last beneficiaries of the ancient conquests, who, farming out their capital, live at the expense of the industrious, exploiting both "the entire mass of laborers" and "the leaders of industry."[49]

Hence, when the Saint-Simonians called for the end to the exploitation of man by man, they intended by this slogan to indicate the eradication of the last vestiges of conquest. Where the right of inheritance is eliminated, and where all land is managed by a central bank, which would delegate its use to those most capable of improving it, there would be no exploitation of man by man, since no one would live at the expense of another.[50] Indeed, the Saint-Simonians foresaw even the end of the exploitation of the earth itself:

> In the industrial society, thus conceived, one will see everywhere a leader, everywhere inferiors, patrons and clients, masters and apprentices; everywhere *legitimate* authority, because the leader is more capable; everywhere *free* obedience, because the leader is loved; order everywhere. No worker is without guidance and support in this vast workshop. All have instruments they know how to use, labor they love to do. All labor, no longer to exploit men, no longer even to exploit the globe, but to embellish the globe by their efforts, and to embellish themselves with all the riches the globe gives them.[51]

In this vision of a world without exploitation we should see, first and foremost, a hope for a world without violence, a world that has left all forceful extraction of benefits behind. Industry will beautify the world and benefit each and every without harming any. The negative will have negated itself completely. Creation will proceed, as if ex nihilo, without any destruction.

Proudhon and Capitalistic Feudalism

The Saint-Simonian eschatology would be little more than a curiosity of history were it not the original and most explicit formulation of an account of exploitation that would be reiterated by many socialists

[48] *Doctrine of St-Simon*, 92–93; *Doctrine de Saint-Simon*, 187–88.
[49] *Doctrine of St-Simon*, 83; *Doctrine de Saint-Simon*, 176.
[50] *Doctrine of St-Simon*, 92–112; *Doctrine de Saint-Simon*, 187–213.
[51] *Doctrine of St-Simon*, 106n; *Doctrine de Saint-Simon*, 205n.

up to the present day.[52] Most crucially, it was reproduced in all its essentials by Proudhon, who, despite his derisive criticisms of the Saint-Simonians on many points, followed them closely in their project of replacing the military or feudal organization of society with the peaceful and industrial organization thereof.[53] This continuity between the Saint-Simonians and Proudhon is indicated already by *Qu'est-ce que la propriété?*,[54] but comes to the fore in *Idée générale de la revolution au XIXe siècle*, which Proudhon wrote while imprisoned after the Revolution of 1848.[55] Marx and Engels studied this book immediately upon its publication in 1851. Marx intended at the time "to publish 2–3 sheets about the book,"[56] or even to serialize his criticisms in Joseph Weydemeyer's *Die Revolution*,[57] an intention he never fulfilled. Proudhon claims in *Idée générale* that the "regime of exploitation" is "synonymous" with the "feudal regime, governmental regime, [or] military regime," and that, "whatever phraseology is used," "doing away with farm-rent and lending at interest" would eliminate "the last vestiges of the ancient slavery," and, with them, "the sword of the executioner, the hand of justice, the club of the policeman, [and] the gauge of the customs officer."[58] Marx disagrees vehemently. In order to see why, we must first review Proudhon's argument.

In the work that brought him his initial fame, Proudhon generally, and in keeping with common French practice at the time, uses *exploiter* and derivative words simply to refer to the cultivation of a field, operation

---

[52]This influence has been stressed by Bernstein, but in a very different sense ("Saint Simon's Philosophy of History"). Where he finds the forces of class and economics at the bottom of the Saint-Simonian theory of history, I see almost nothing about classes in the Marxian sense, and even less about economics.

[53]The relationship between Proudhon and Saint-Simonianism has not received much scholarly attention. The major exception is *Les fondateurs français de la sociologie contemporaine: Saint-Simon et P. J. Proudhon*, a work by Georges Gurvitch, "the dean of French Proudhon scholars" (Bowen, "Review: L'Actualite de Proudhon; Colloque Des 24 et 25 Novembre 1965," 630). Gurvitch does not even mention exploitation, however.

[54]See, especially, the final chapter.

[55]The new prominence of Saint-Simonian themes in *Idée générale* is probably due to the intervention of Pierre Leroux, who dedicated a series of articles on Saint-Simon and the history of French socialism to Proudhon, beginning in the December 30, 1849, issue of *la République*. These articles, especially the article of February 10, 1850, called Proudhon's attention to the proximity between his thought and that of Saint-Simon. See Aimé Berthod's note in Proudhon, *OC*, 2:399–400.

[56]Marx to Engels, August 14, 1851; *MECW*, 38:423–24.

[57]Marx went so far as to write to Weydemeyer that, "you can announce a serialised work of mine, to appear article by article, namely, *Neuste Offenbarungen des Sozialismus, oder 'Idée générale de la Révolution au XIXe siécle' par J.P. Proudhon.—Kritik von K.M.*"; Marx to Weydemeyer, December 19, 1851 (*MECW*, 38:519). *Die Revolution* was canceled, however, and nothing came of Marx's proposal.

[58]*General Idea*, 287; Proudhon, *OC*, 2:337.

of a factory, or utilization of a material.[59] However, he also deploys the Saint-Simonian phrase, "the exploitation of man by man." In one case, he takes it to be a synonym for "slavery, usury, or the tribute levied upon the conquered by the conqueror."[60] In another, it is interchangeable with "oppression" and "slavery."[61] In a third, he is discussing the difference between the wages of the agricultural laborer, which provide only for "immediate subsistence," and the "preparation of the land and manufacture of implements of production," which provide the landowner with "a promise of independence and security for the future." The owner's "fraudulent denial" of this same promise to the laborer is "above all" what is meant by "the exploitation of man by man."[62] These replicate the Saint-Simonians' use of the phrase. Exploitation of the laborer is figured in terms of a monopoly power derived from conquest. Exploitation is a remnant of feudalism. It is present in the entitled security of the landlord and the enforced precariousness of the farm laborer.

Providing labor with the guarantee it lacks would eliminate, on this line of thinking, the exploitation of man by man. Precariousness makes the laborer vulnerable, and this vulnerability allows the possessors of secure property, through loans and leases of what the laborer lacks, to perpetuate the laborer's precariousness. Proudhon saw very well that it was expensive to be poor. He hoped, by reducing this expense, to get the poor out from under the thumb of the wealthy. The program of cheap credit—Proudhon wanted his People's Bank to lend at 0.25 percent to 0.5 percent—and land reform—he proposed a Land Bank and a mandate that rent paid would always establish a lien upon the property—follows from this intuitive starting point.

These are also recognizably republican responses to a recognizably republican problem. The poor, lacking property—"a promise of independence and security for the future"—are dependent upon the wealthy proprietors. Proudhon's program aims to secure the independence of every family.[63] Hence, near the end of his life, he describes his ideal of mutuality in this way:

[59] *What Is Property?*, 90, 91, 96, 99, 113, 214n; OC, 4:214, 215, 221, 224, 238, 345n. The English translations of Proudhon do not treat *exploiter* with any care; there is no general correspondence between Proudhon's use of the word and appearances of English cognates in the translations.

[60] *What Is Property?*, 202; OC, 4:333.

[61] *What Is Property?*, 213n; OC, 4:344n.

[62] *What Is Property?*, 91–92; OC, 4:216.

[63] These independent families would be frankly and thoroughly patriarchal. Proudhon's misogyny and antifeminism are notorious. During his time as a radical editor he would attack prominent Saint-Simonian women on the theory that women should be either secluded in the privacy of the home as daughters and wives, or, if they made themselves known in public, declared "public women" that is, prostitutes; Pilbeam, *French Socialists before Marx*, 98.

For there to be perfect mutuality, it is necessary that each producer, in taking on a commitment with respect to others, who on their side are committed in the same manner with respect to him, retains his complete and total independence of action, all his freedom of movement, his whole personality: mutuality, according to its etymology, consist rather in the exchange of good offices and products than in the grouping of forces and the community of labor.[64]

This ideal of independent producers exchanging fairly with one another is, as we have seen, widespread among the socialists of the nineteenth century.[65] In Proudhon, however, this ideal is wed to the Saint-Simonian picture of history as the progressive replacement of force by labor.[66]

Imprisoned for sedition by Louis-Napoléon's government, Proudhon wrote *Idée générale de la revolution aux XIXe siècle* in 1851 in order retrospectively to justify the Revolution of 1848 as the latest attempt to continue the work of the Revolution of 1789, and to plead that this work be finally completed. The events of 1789 had abolished "the feudal regime," and had "proclaimed the principles of liberty and civil equality," for it had decreed that "birth no longer counted." Following the Saint-Simonians, Proudhon understands the feudal regime to have been "entirely military," a society organized "for politics and war."[67] Hence, the abolition of this order in 1789 should have led to a new social order dedicated to "labor" and to "perpetual peace."[68] However, "the revolutionaries failed in their own mission," hobbled as they were by "the absence of economic notions." They knew how to destroy, but not how to

---

[64] *OC*, 3:141–42.

[65] Contra Schapiro ("Pierre Joseph Proudhon, Harbinger of Fascism," 723), who, with many others, conceives nineteenth-century socialism via a backward projection of twentieth-century Leninism; compare Vincent, *Pierre-Joseph Proudhon and the Rise of French Republican Socialism*, 11–12.

[66] Proudhon's conceptions of history and of war have been examined in great detail by Noland ("History and Humanity: The Proudhonian Vision"; "Proudhon's Sociology of War"), who is one of the most trustworthy Proudhon scholars to have written in English. A more recent appreciation is found in Prichard, *Justice, Order, and Anarchy*.

[67] Marx and Engels noticed this Saint-Simonian theme in their correspondence over Proudhon's new work: "I am half way through the Proudhon and heartily endorse your view. His appeal to the bourgeoisie, his reversion to Saint-Simon and a hundred and one other matters in the critical section alone, provide confirmation that he regards the industrial class, the bourgeoisie and the proletariat as virtually identical and as having been brought into opposition only by the fact that the revolution was never completed" (Engels to Marx, August 21, 1851; *MECW*, 38:434).

[68] *General Idea*, 43; *OC*, 2:125–25. Proudhon's debt to Adam Smith, one of his "real masters" (Proudhon to J. A. Langlois, 1848; cited in *What Is Property?*, 1970, xxxiii), is evident in his notion that "the separation of industrial functions" conduces to peace (*General Idea*, 48; *OC*, 2:130). The division of labor produces partial persons, dependent upon exchanges with one another, and hence peaceful. The complete human beings lauded by the ancients are not prone to exchange, and make war instead.

build. Therefore, "the society which the Revolution in '89 should have created, does not exist; it is yet to be made."[69]

Hence, the France of 1850 is "a still feudal society."[70] Contemporary feudalism has two linchpins. First, there is the state and its government, with its taxes, police, customs duties, and institutional corruption. But "government . . . is the mirror of society."[71] If government is still feudal, this is because society is still feudal. And, indeed, in society itself, "the ancient hierarchy of classes has been replaced by an ignoble feudalism, based on mercantile and industrial speculation [*l'agiotage mercantile et industriel*]."[72] And, like all feudalism, this contemporary feudalism is rooted in the land:

> It is through the land that the exploitation of man began, and it is in the land that it has laid its solid foundations. The land is still the fortress of the modern capitalist, as it was the citadel of feudalism and of the ancient patriciate. It is the land, finally, that gives authority, the governmental principle, an ever renewed force whenever the popular Hercules has overthrown the giant.[73]

It is the destruction of this last fortress of exploitation—it will fall like the walls of Jericho before Joshua's trumpets[74]—that Proudhon prophesies in his recommendation of Land Banks and rent equity.

Proudhon is never explicit about the mechanisms by which landed property subtends all exploitation, but he doubtless had a more complicated understanding of the problem than the Saint-Simonians. Of course, he agrees with them that the landed proprietor directly exploits others via rent, and via any capital investments paid for by rents. But Proudhon also suggests that, as these rents circulate through society, they allow others—those from whom the proprietors have purchased goods—to, in

---

[69] *General Idea*, 44–45; OC, 2:127.

[70] *General Idea*, 58; OC, 2:140.

[71] *General Idea*, 60; OC, 2:142.

[72] *General Idea*, 73; OC, 2:153. *Agiotage* is generally translated as *usury*, but this is misleading; it is, in particular, the practice of speculating by hoarding, especially currency. During the period of the hyperinflation of *assignats*, in 1791–92, Parisians of means would stock up quantities of candles, cloth, and the like, in order to resell them within a couple days against the ever-falling *assignats* (Rambaud, *Histoire de La Civilization Contemporaine en France*, 311). Henri de Saint-Simon nearly lost his head to the Terror for larger scale *agiotage* in the Church lands that underwrote the *assignats*.

[73] *General Idea*, 195; OC, 2:258.

[74] The comparison is Proudhon's (*General Idea*, 195; OC, 2:258). Perhaps this passage was in Marx's mind when, in his *Eighteenth Brumaire*, he accused the petty bourgeois democrats of "endeavor[ing] to repeat that miracle" of the trumpets (*Political Writings*, 2:178; *MEGA*, I.11:126). Remember that Marx's critical dissection of Louis Bonaparte's rise to power was published in the same year and in the same short-lived journal, *Die Revolution*, in which he hoped to publish his critical commentary on Proudhon's *Idée générale*.

turn, accumulate a fund for the exploitation of others. Moreover, rents also provide a motive for exploitation, since a farmer leasing land will be pressured into exploiting farmhands in order to make the payment of rent worthwhile. Wherever any accumulation gives one member of society an advantage over a fellow, Proudhon senses the possibility, at least, of exploitation.[75] This is why exploitation is so intimately associated by him with *agiotage*, speculation, which Proudhon calls "commercial arbitrariness."[76] Everyone has a motive to buy cheap and sell dear, to mark their goods up, to accumulate a hoard. Everyone is constantly trying to exploit others, or, via "*l'agio, le vol*," to accrue the means of exploiting others.[77] While Proudhon certainly recognizes many instances of *agiotage* and even exploitation that do not involve property in land, he thinks of the monopoly power attending land ownership as both the purest exemplar and the causal first principle of exploitation. All other cases of exploitation are recognized as such by an analogy or likeness to this first principle.[78]

Capitalist Exploitation in *Capital*

Against this background, we can appreciate the novelty of what Marx does with *exploitation* in *Capital*. *Exploitation* crops up in *Capital* for the first time in the first section of chapter nine, "The Rate of Surplus-Value."[79]

[75] Hence, for example, the passage in his *Système* that Iain McKay takes as evidence that "like Marx, but well before him," Proudhon had explained exploitation by reference to "the hierarchical relationship of the capitalist workplace" (*Property Is Theft!*, 8–9): "I have shown the contractor [*entrepreneur*], at the birth of industry, negotiating on equal terms with his comrades, who have since become his workmen. It is plain, in fact, that this original equality was bound to disappear through the advantageous position of the master and the dependence of the wage earners [*salariés*]" (*System*, 1:201; *OC*, 1:193). It is a difficulty for McKay's reading of this passage that Proudhon takes himself to be explaining, not the rise of the capitalist workplace, but the fact "that the guilds and masterships were established in the Middle Ages" (*System*, 1:202; *OC*, 1:193).

[76] *General Idea*, 228; *OC*, 2:286.

[77] Proudhon was far from alone in seeing all accumulation as problematic. Auguste Blanqui argued that everyone is under a moral duty to consume all that they produce, since all saving up potentially creates an opportunity to exploit others. This is of a piece with the moralism of French republican socialism; see Vincent, *Pierre-Joseph Proudhon and the Rise of French Republican Socialism*, 41–47, 121–23.

[78] For a sophisticated neo-Proudhonian account of exploitation as "making money out of being a nuisance to others," see Van Donselaar, *The Right to Exploit*.

[79] The chapter numeration differs across the various editions of *Capital*. I will refer to chapter numbers according to the French and English editions. Thus, for example, "The Modern Theory of Colonization" is chapter thirty-three, not chapter twenty-five, as in the German editions. Comparisons among the various editions can be made on the basis of *MEGA*, II.5–II.10.

"The rate of surplus value is," Marx tells us, "an exact expression for the degree of exploitation of labor-power by capital, or of the worker by the capitalist."[80] The exploitation of the worker by the capitalist—of concern to all French socialists—is here equated by Marx with the exploitation of labor power by capital, the exact expression for which is the rate of surplus value, which was, in the 1860s and '70s, a matter of concern to no one other than Marx. By equating the two, Marx is attempting to make a substitution, to appropriate a common trope of socialist literature and, by definitional fiat, to make that trope interchangeable with an abstruse element of his critique of political economy.[81]

In particular, he is playing for the ear of those tutored in theory by the French socialists and their epigones.[82] It is Proudhon's recitation of the Saint-Simonian theory of exploitation that Marx is seeking to displace. From the founding of the IWMA on, Marx was confronted anew with Proudhon's influence within the French and Belgian workers' movement, and with the resonances between Proudhonism and British popular radicalism (especially as found among the followers of Bronterre O'Brien and his National Reform League). Marx's intervention in part three of *Capital*, like many of his theoretical interventions, attempts to seize the means of theoretical production, to transform how socialists talked and

---

[80] *Capital*, 1:326; *MEGA*, II.6:226–27; *MEGA*, II.7:179.

[81] This is suggested by the way Marx uses *exploitation* throughout part three of *Capital*. The word crops up in clusters, enlivening the most technical passages of the whole. Hence, it appears nine times in section one of chapter nine, where it motivates Marx's presentation of his "method for calculating the rate of surplus-value" (*Capital*, 1:327; *MEGA*, II.6:227; *MEGA*, II.7:179). There is a smattering of instances (eight) in the much longer and historically detailed chapter ten, and then fourteen uses in the short and technical chapter eleven, on "The Rate and Mass of Surplus-Value." In the latter, the word is clustered around Marx's explication of the three laws by which the rate and mass of surplus value are related to one another.

[82] Although the word was French, the theory of exploitation propounded by the Saint-Simonians and by Proudhon had a recognizable parallel and precursor, as I have mentioned, in the Owenite literature. The Owenite theories of exploitation have been capably treated by several writers, however, and so I will pass over them here. On the school as a whole, see N. Thompson, *The People's Science*, chaps. 4–6; and *The Market and Its Critics*, chap. 3; Biernacki, *The Fabrication of Labor*, 394–410; McNally, *Against the Market*, chap. 4; and King, "Utopian or Scientific?" On William Thompson and John Gray, see Claeys, *Machinery, Money, and the Millennium*, chaps. 4–5. On John Francis Bray, see Reeve "Thomas Hodgskin and John Bray: Free Exchange and Equal Exchange." The epitome of the Owenite theory of exploitation is contained in Bray's claim that "all the wrongs and the woes which man has ever committed or endured, may be traced to the assumption of a right in the soil, by certain individuals and classes," since, "wherever one man possesses land, and another has none, the latter must always be the slave of the former" (*Labour's Wrongs and Labour's Remedy*, 34; compare Thompson, *Inquiry*, 68–110).

thought about exploitation by associating the term with a new conceptual apparatus.

As I hope to show, this appropriation and transformation had a series of theoretical effects. First, and in accordance with his understanding of the market as a sphere of impersonal domination, and with his attempt to displace the popular moral economy of censure away from individuals and onto capital as a form of society, Marx de-personalizes exploitation, making it a relationship that obtains between classes, rather than between individuals. Second, he directs attention to the novel and revolutionary effects of capitalist exploitation, to the ways in which capitalism harnesses the powers of the human body to transform what and how it produces. Third, he establishes an explanation for the "boundless thirst for surplus labor" that attends this new mode of exploitation and that underlies many of the abuses suffered by workers in the capitalist workplace.[83] Finally, he does all of these things while tying the concept of exploitation into an Aristotelian moral language that links force to the violation of nature, and that therefore condemns capitalist exploitation as an unnatural seizure and use of the laboring body.

De-personalizing Exploitation

In the immediate context in which he introduces *exploitation*, the first section of chapter nine, Marx is seeking "to exercise the reader in the application of [a] novel principle."[84] This novel principle is that the rate of surplus value differs from and underlies the rate of profit. The rate of profit is the rate of return on the total capital advanced, and was and is familiar to anyone concerned with political economy or business. The rate of surplus value, however, was Marx's own coinage. Because Marx believes that the constant capital advanced—the value of the means and materials of production—is transferred to the product without any augmentation, he argues that it must be ignored for the purposes of calculating the return that matters, the return on capital advanced as wages for the purchase of labor power.

What is distinctive about the capitalist mode of production is that it operates on the principle, articulated by Montesquieu, "that everything can be done by freemen, however arduous the work that society requires."[85] Or, as Marx puts it, "as a producer of alien industriousness, as a surplus-labor-pump and an exploiter of labor-power, [capital] surpasses—in its energy, measurelessness, and effectiveness—all earlier

[83] *Capital*, 1:345; *MEGA*, II.6:242; *MEGA*, II.7:194.
[84] *Capital*, 1:326; *MEGA*, II.6:227; *MEGA*, II.7:180.
[85] *The Spirit of the Laws*, 252 (III.15.8).

systems of production based on direct forced labor."[86] It is this phenomenon that Marx wants to get at, the fact that moderns freely do what ancient peoples had to enslave others to get done. In the French edition, he calls it "the great secret of modern society."[87] But this great secret is kept secret by looking at the whole mass of capital advanced rather than just at the capital advanced in the form of wages. If one attributes capital's productivity to its marshaling of human labor, then it makes sense to look at the ratio between the return on capital and the capital advanced on wages. This is Marx's rate of surplus value.

When Marx says that this rate of surplus value is "the exact expression" for the degree of exploitation, he means that it is the scientific expression of the efficiency with which hired labor is put to work producing the basis of profits. However, despite his examples of the method of calculating it, Marx is committed to denying that the rate of surplus value can be measured.[88] This is because the rate of surplus value requires as its basis, of course, a measure of value. The measure of value, according to Marx, is the labor time socially necessary to produce the valuable commodities given the current means of production.[89] But, as I argued in the previous chapter, it is a basic element of Marx's theory of value that value, while it is determined by labor time, only ever appears as exchange value, as "the social relation between commodity and commodity."[90] There is no direct, empirical measure of labor time, since there is no way to know whether any given instance of labor actually performed—and hence empirically measurable—counts as an equivalent amount of socially necessary labor. Moreover, the fact that commodities sell on the market does not guarantee that they sell at their values. Hence, neither the prices of commodities (including the wages of labor), nor the empirically measurable hours of labor performed give us access to the value of things. Abstract labor and the value it determines are invisible gods, essences that must take on phenomenal forms, but that never appear as such. Therefore, the exact expression of the degree of exploitation is, by virtue of its exactness, never present in such a way that it can be measured. It is conceptually rigorous, not empirically precise.[91]

---

[86] *Capital*, 1:425; *MEGA*, II.6:309; *MEGA*, II.7:263.

[87] *MEGA*, II.7:143.

[88] Harvey, *A Companion to Marx's Capital*, 132.

[89] *Capital*, 1:129; *MEGA*, II.6:73; *MEGA*, II.7:22–23.

[90] *Capital*, 1:139; *MEGA*, II.6:80; *MEGA*, II.7:31.

[91] Thus the caveats in Marx's footnote: "The calculations given in the text are intended merely as illustrations," *Capital*, 1:329n9; *MEGA*, II.6:229n13; *MEGA*, II.7:181n36. This same issue arises in Marx's presentation of the laws pertaining to the rate and mass of surplus value. Indeed, Marx says of the third law that it "obviously contradicts all experience grounded in what appears to the eye" (*Capital*, 1:421; *MEGA*, II.6:306; *MEGA*, II.7:261).

What is at stake, then, in Marx's effort to exercise the readers of his book in the application of his novel principle? If socialists and reformers are concerned about "the exploitation of man by man," or with "the exploitation of women and children,"[92] why ought they to practice calculating a counterfactual rate of surplus value? After all, Marx himself, in chapter ten, compiles a mass of compelling testimony to the empirically verifiable and very concrete ways in which laborers are taken advantage of by their bosses. He reports the depositions made by children employed in the potteries of Staffordshire.[93] He directs us to the story of "Mary Anne Walkley, 20 years old," who was worked to death "by a lady with the pleasant name of Elise."[94] Regarding the laborers "who throng around us more urgently that did the souls of the slain around Odysseus," he claims that we can "see at first glance" how overworked they are, "without referring to the Blue Books under their arms," much less to the rate and mass of surplus value, the exact expressions of their exploitation.[95] If the suffering and overwork of the wage laborer are apparent to the investigator of concrete facts, what is gained by chaining exploitation to the theoretical apparatus of the rate of surplus value?[96]

One part of the answer lies in the account of exchange Marx developed in part one. The impersonal domination undergone by producers in the market renders them irresponsible for their actions. But if capital only begins to function as such in production for the market, then capital's relationship to labor is mediated by those same impersonal forces of all-around dependence and irresponsibility. The concrete facts of overwork and abuse, however powerful they may be as testimony, direct us to the relations between *this* boss and *these* workers, in *this* place and time. But the theory of commodity fetishism as impersonal domination tells us that these particularities are consequential, not causal to the basic dynamics of the situation, and that any boss similarly placed would likely relate to any workers in a similar manner, not because all bosses share a special psychology, but because the forces of the market *dominate* producers in certain ways.[97] Indeed, the fact that value

---

[92] *Capital*, 1:91; *MEGA*, 1983, II.5:13; *MEGA*, II.7:13.

[93] *Capital*, 1:354; *MEGA*, II.6:249–50; *MEGA*, II.7:202–3.

[94] *Capital*, 1:364; *MEGA*, II.6:253; *MEGA*, II.7:211.

[95] *Capital*, 1:364; *MEGA*, II.6:253; *MEGA*, II.7:211.

[96] The ill-repute of the labor theory of surplus value is obvious in the frequency with which one encounters arguments that the Marxist theory of exploitation is independent of Marx's value theory (Carver, "Marx's Political Theory of Exploitation," 74–75; Cohen, "The Labor Theory of Value and the Concept of Exploitation"; Roemer, *A General Theory of Exploitation and Class*; Wood, *Karl Marx*, 240).

[97] This social domination can end up selecting for a special psychology, by predictably rewarding that psychology and starving its competitors, but then again the psychology is the effect of the social domination, not its cause.

is invisible in production, and only realizes itself through market exchanges, is crucial for understanding *why* bosses are inclined to overwork their laborers.[98] Therefore, the concrete facts are misdirecting us, making it out as if capitalist exploitation were just a series of instances of individual capitalists taking advantage of individual wage laborers, using their accumulated wealth to hold sway over those who need to work in order to live.[99] Marx, by inserting exploitation into his surplus-value theory, de-personalizes exploitation and thereby argues against the tendency to moralize over it.[100]

In particular, he does so by passing over from empirically identified and morally blameworthy cases of the exploitation of laboring individuals to the exploitation of the laborer as a representative of the class of laborers. These are not identical. Mary Anne Walkley was exploited in the everyday sense that she was taken advantage of. Her youth, gendered socialization, and poverty made it such that she was willing to work in conditions that were detrimental to her health and to which she succumbed. Her employer took advantage of her vulnerability in the hope of making a pretty penny off the pretty things she and her fellow milliners produced, and the employer can be the object of censure for doing so. But Mary Anne Walkley did not suffer *capitalist* exploitation in her own individuality, but only qua laborer. Her particular labors counted as productive labor from the standpoint of capital only insofar as they formed an aliquot part of the total labor of society, or of the laboring class. Mary Anne Walkley suffered and died from the particular circumstances that attended her particular labors, but she suffered *capitalist* exploitation, if at all, only insofar as she was a member of a class of laborers, producing all manner of things in all manner of circumstances, many of which are not nearly as injurious as those in which she worked. Recognizing the concrete form of her exploitation does not require any special theoretical apparatus, but only the acknowledgment that her employer took

---

[98] A point to which I will return below.

[99] Here is where Marx's account diverges decisively from the account of wage slavery that Alex Gourevitch finds in the labor republicanism of the United States. Despite Gourevitch's terminology ("structural domination," for example), the labor republican account pinpoints only the personal domination experienced by the worker on the job and the class domination whereby the legal and political preconditions of that personal domination are secured ("Labor Republicanism and the Transformation of Work"; *From Slavery to the Cooperative Commonwealth*, chap. 4).

[100] Thus, my argument differs from that offered by Alan Ryan, for whom it is Marx's explanatory holism that is reflected in his "impatience with moralizing" ("Justice, Exploitation, and the End of Morality," 126–27). Marx does not have a generalized sociological holism according to which the social system "dictates to . . . individuals what aspirations and beliefs to adopt"; he has an account of the market as a motivating and selecting machine, a form of impersonal domination.

advantage of Ms. Walkley.[101] Recognizing that it is an instance of capitalist exploitation requires, however, that one recognize her membership in
a class of exploited laborers and recognize further that it does not matter
what or in what manner the members of that class produce. This recognition requires a leap, an abstraction.

This de-personalizing abstraction runs counter to the model of exploitation articulated by earlier socialism. On that model, modern exploitation may be less personal than in feudal or slaveholding societies, since
the application of force is now delegated to the state, which merely enforces property titles, leaving poor individuals to draw their own conclusions about how their lack of property compels them to accept the terms
of employment offered. Nonetheless, the monopoly power enjoyed by the
proprietors allows them to exploit the poor producer without compelling
them to. They may not know better than to do as they do, but they could
act otherwise. And so Proudhon thinks that mutual consent would be
sufficient to establish a just price regime.[102] Even the Owenite doctrine
of the blamelessness of individuals does not prevent Bray from calling
the capitalist "grasping."[103] Capitalists have the power to exploit, and so
they exploit. Anyone with the power to exploit will do so. It is the circumstance of having the power that creates the character of the exploiter.
But exploiting is something done by individuals with that power. That is
why the reform of society must ensure that no one is able to accrue that
power. For Marx, on the contrary, it is capital that exploits labor, not the
individual capitalists, for whom the drive toward increasing exploitation
is "an external coercive law."[104] It is not the *power* to exploit that matters
to Marx, but the *imperative* to exploit.

The Revolutionary Capacity of Capitalist Exploitation

In addition to being essentially the exploitation of a laboring class, capitalist exploitation is essentially the exploitation of "human labor in the

---

[101] As G. A. Cohen has forcefully argued; see "The Labor Theory of Value and the Concept of Exploitation."

[102] *General Idea*, 230–33; OC, 2:288–91.

[103] *Labour's Wrongs and Labour's Remedy*, 114.

[104] *Capital*, 1:381; MEGA, II.6:273; MEGA, II.7:226. Marx had long insisted upon the
new predominance of economic power over political power. See, for instance, his polemi-
cal back and forth in 1847 with Karl Heinzen, who "argued that Marx and Engels did not
recognize that the rule of force dominates capitalistic property relations, which caused them
to focus too intently on the bourgeois accumulation of capital while ignoring those who
truly hold power, the aristocracy" (Bessner and Stauch, "Karl Heinzen and the Intellectual
Origins of Modern Terror," 151). Heinzen, unlike Proudhon, applied this judgment also to
the condition of women. For Heinzen, "war and violence have been the essential reasons
why women have been and remained deprived of their rights" (Bessner, "Zarte Hände" 68).

abstract,"[105] and, in the final analysis, the exploitation of the basic capacity for labor, labor power, however that capacity might express itself. Marx begins part three with a well-known discussion of the labor process. What he underlines there is the specific intentionality that defines any human labor process as such.

> At the end of every labor process, a result emerges that was already in the imagination of the laborer at the beginning, thus was already present ideally. Not only does he effect [bewirkt] a change in the form of natural things, he simultaneously actualizes [verwirklicht] in the natural things his purpose, of which he is aware, which determines the type and manner of his activity as a law, and to which he must subordinate his will.[106]

Every human labor process proceeds under the guidance of an end in view, a particular object or result that fulfills a particular need. As Marx put it in the manuscript version of part three, "Every actual labor is a *particular* labor."[107] However, within the capitalist production process, this particularity of every actual labor is subordinated to the aim of capital, self-valorization, and submerged in the virtual reality of the abstract labor that forms value.

Not all members of the laboring class perform the same sort of labor. If they did, there could be no exchange of their products against one another, and hence no realization of value, much less surplus value, and hence no capital. If the members of the laboring class perform different types of labor, and their products exchange against one another, then, as Marx says, there must be something in virtue of which they exchange, some common denominator. This is value. But if value is the *name* of the common denominator, the *substance* of this name is the fact that all the various labors that went into all the products being exchanged are, despite their variety, identically modes of labor as such. The labors of one can aid or replace the labors of another. The exchange of commodities is, at base, "nothing else but the exchange of labor for labor," as Benjamin Franklin put it.[108]

As we have seen in chapter 2, this is the intuitive basis of Marx's much maligned labor theory of value. In this context, it entails that the capitalist exploitation of the laboring class is the exploitation of labor in general, or of abstract labor. In other word, it means that the aim of capital—the realization of surplus value—is indifferent to the particular aim of the labor on which it depends. The capitalist exploitation of labor requires

---

[105] *Capital*, 1:128; *MEGA*, II.6:72; *MEGA*, II.7:22.
[106] *Capital*, 1:284; *MEGA*, II.6:193; *MEGA*, II.7:146.
[107] *MECW*, 30:55; *MEGA*, II.3.1:48.
[108] Cited by Marx, *Capital*, 1:142n18; *MEGA*, II.6:83n17a; *MEGA*, II.7:60n31.

that what labor produces does not really matter, "that all commodities, when taken in certain proportions, must be equal in value."[109] The capitalist exploitation of labor transmutes this indifference to the product into an indifference to the production. Capital is mobile and flexible, capable of exploiting any branch of labor that promises a return. It "can come into relation with every *specific* labor; it confronts the *totality* of all labors *dunamei*, and the particular one it confronts at a given time is an accidental matter."[110] Indeed, labor is productive, in capitalism, just to the extent that it creates capital, just to the extent that capital can exploit it to create and recreate itself.[111] The concrete product is "irrelevant";[112] what matters is the susceptibility to production by wage labor for profitable sale.

Capital's indifference to the concrete form and end of labor implies, for Marx, that capitalist exploitation can only be understood by retreating from labor's performance back to the potentiality for that performance. In *Capital*, the most important formula for capitalist exploitation is "the exploitation of labor-power." Unlike "the exploitation of the laborer" and "the exploitation of labor," Marx never uses this formula to refer to precapitalist systems of production and exploitation. The exploitation of labor power is the peculiar mode of capitalist exploitation. That is why the rate of surplus value can be the exact expression for it; there is no rate of surplus value in any mode of production other than the capitalist one. Only capital exploits labor power, because only capital rests on the commodification of "human labor-power without consideration of the form of its expenditure":[113] its sale, purchase, and use as a means of valorization.

The genesis and exploitation of labor power signifies, for Marx, the genesis and exploitation of human capacities as forces of nature, or as "the material of nature transposed into a human organism."[114] Labor power is nothing other than the "bodily organism" of a human being, his or her "brains, muscles, nerves, hands, etc."[115] This bodily organism may be turned to this or that end. For this reason, Marx also refers to the exploitation of labor power as the exploitation of "human material," which he claims is "capital's most proper field of exploitation."[116] No previous

[109] *Capital*, 1:136; *MEGA*, II.6:79; *MEGA*, II.7:28.

[110] *Grundrisse*, 296–97; *MEGA*, II.1.1:217.

[111] *Capital*, 1:644; *MEGA*, II.6:479–80; *MEGA*, II.7:440–41; see also *Grundrisse*, 308–9; *MEGA*, II.1.1:227–28.

[112] *Capital*, 1:297; *MEGA*, II.6:203; *MEGA*, II.7:156.

[113] *Capital*, 1:128; *MEGA*, II.6:72; *MEGA*, II.7:22.

[114] *Capital*, 1:323n2; *MEGA*, II.6:224n27; *MEGA*, II.7:177n30.

[115] *Capital*, 1:134–35; *MEGA*, II.6:77; *MEGA*, II.7:27.

[116] *Capital*, 1:518; *MEGA*, II.6:385; *MEGA*, II.7:338. In Paolo Virno's formulation, labor power "effectively designates the ensemble of generically human psycho-physical

mode of production has exploited—or taken advantage of—what the human body can do, as such. This open-ended exploitation of the human body and its powers is contained, in germ, in the existence of the labor market. The more extensive this market, the broader the field of corporeal powers open to profitable employment by capital.[117] With his formula, "the exploitation of labor-power," Marx indicates, in short, the specificity of capitalist production.[118]

Because of the specific way in which capital takes advantage of the human body and its capacities, the capitalist mode of production is inherently revolutionary. This was one of the first things that Marx noticed about the rise of the bourgeoisie, that this new ruling class "cannot exist without constantly revolutionizing the instruments of production, and thereby the relations of production, and with them the whole relations of society."[119] This will become especially important in the following chapter, where we will have to consider what Marx calls the production of relative surplus value, the transformation of the production process in order to make it better suit the requirements of capital.

For the moment, it is enough to underline the discontinuity between Marx's emphasis upon the exploitation of labor power and the older socialist tendency to divide society into the productive and the unproductive, the useful and the useless. Previous accounts of the exploitation of the workers, or of the abstraction of their product, presupposed a demarcation of the working class in terms of what it produced, and how its product satisfied the real needs of humankind. Thus, for example, Gray argued that makers of "useful wearing apparel" are exploited, but that makers of lace dresses are not, since lace dresses fulfill no real need and

---

faculties, which are precisely considered as mere *dynameis* that have yet to be applied" ("Natural-Historical Diagrams," 143).

[117] The post-workerist or autonomist lineage in Italian Marxism and feminism has been most attentive to this basic dynamic. The concepts of "affective labor," "intellectual labor," "social labor," and "immaterial labor," whatever their shortcomings, indicate, to this line of thinking, the ongoing extension of capitalist exploitation into powers of the bodily organism that had previously operated under the guidance of tradition and custom.

[118] John Roemer thinks that Marx generalized from exploitation in feudalism and slavery in order to arrive at a theory of exploitation that held even in capitalism, that is, "even when one relaxed the institutional specification of an economy concerning the coerciveness of its institution of labor exchange" (*A General Theory of Exploitation and Class*, 7). I think this gets Marx's procedure exactly backward. Instead of beginning with a historically specific, institutionally thick concept of (feudal) exploitation, which he generalized and thinned out until it could describe capitalist conditions as well, Marx started with an apparently generic conception of exploitation and then worked toward a historically specific, institutionally thick concept of capitalist exploitation.

[119] Marx, *Political Writings*, 1:70; *MEW*, 4:465.

thus command no just recompense.[120] For Marx, however, this whole problem of dividing real from spurious labor, real from spurious needs, is beside the point.[121] It is the usefulness of a branch of labor for capital that is alone relevant to the question of whether workers in that branch suffer capitalist exploitation. Whether their products satisfy needs arising "from the stomach, or from the imagination, makes no difference."[122]

The Boundless Need for Surplus Labor

Despite the fact that he de-personalizes capitalist exploitation by emphasizing its difference from any observable abuse that might be addressed by moral censure, and despite his appreciation of the revolution it works on the labor process, Marx has neither a normatively neutral account of capitalist exploitation nor a laissez-faire attitude toward it. He thinks that the capitalist exploitation of labor power is a wrong that has horrendous consequences for the laborers.

The primary consequence is overwork. Because capital's concern is valorization, rather than the production of use values, and because the surplus realized by the capitalist takes the form of money, of which there is no measure, capitalist production gives rise to a "boundless need for surplus labor."[123] This is why Marx's treatment of the working day follows immediately on the heels of his introduction of the exploitation of labor power. Having purchased labor power on the market and for a fixed period, the capitalist wants to "extract the maximum possible advantage" from this purchase while he or she can dispose of it.[124] Having sold for a time the use of his or her body, the wage laborer is interested to ensure that today's labor will not make tomorrow's impossible, that, in other words, his or her labor power is not so depleted by its use today that it cannot be set in motion again every day for the foreseeable future.

---

[120] Gray, *Lecture on Human Happiness*, 25. This is hardly an isolated instance. Similar attempts to isolate real, exploitable labor from unproductive or useless activity—which is therefore not really labor—can be found throughout, especially, the British literature (e.g., Gray, *The Social System*, 50–51; O'Brien, *Human Slavery*, 135; Thompson, *Inquiry*, 149–57, 240–41, 388; *Labour Rewarded*, 24). For the common British reliance upon Colquhoun's taxonomy of productive and unproductive classes, see Claeys, *Machinery, Money, and the Millennium*. The French had no such social statistics to draw upon, but Proudhon, like the Saint-Simonians, made similar demarcations.

[121] Of course Marx did have opinions about the real needs of humankind, and these opinions are a part of his political anthropology worthy of study (see Leopold, *The Young Karl Marx*, 223–34; Heller, *The Theory of Need in Marx*). These opinions do not play into his account of capitalist exploitation, however.

[122] *Capital*, 1:125; *MEGA*, II.6:69; *MEGA*, II.7:19–20.

[123] *Capital*, 1:345; *MEGA*, II.6:242; *MEGA*, II.7:194.

[124] *Capital*, 1:342; *MEGA*, II.6:240; *MEGA*, II.7:192.

The struggle to define a normal working day—both its length and its intensity—is built into the sale and purchase of labor power.[125]

In what may be yet another *détournement* of Proudhon, Marx characterizes capital as "dead labor, which, vampire-like, lives only by sucking up living labor, and lives the more, the more of this it sucks up."[126] In his *Système*, Proudhon had said of the master in the guild system that he, "like the fabled vampire, exploit[ed] the degraded *salarié*," just as "the idle devour[ed] the substance of the laborer."[127] Marx takes the metaphor out of the feudal setting in which Proudhon had placed it and relocates it squarely in the capitalist world, the only place where he thinks it is generally appropriate.[128] While there were certainly many cases of "frightful" overwork in the premodern world, these were, Marx claims, "exceptions." Wherever "the use-value rather than the exchange-value

[125] Roemer has argued against making "the struggle between worker and boss on the factory floor over the extraction of labor from labor power" the central point of the theory of exploitation, since this is a mere "dispute over the terms of the labor contract," and Marx assumed "frictionless markets with costlessly enforced contracts" ("Exploitation, Class, and Property Relations," 198). This is of a piece with Roemer's assumption that labor inputs can be technically specified (see note 10, above). While I agree that Marx assumes competitive markets, I think one of Marx's central points in part three is that labor inputs can be neither technically nor contractually specified. The wage labor contract is essentially underspecified because capital "needs the *agency* of labour" (Arthur, *The New Dialectic and Marx's Capital*, 52). This is not a matter of enforcing a fully determinate contract; it is a matter of determining what must be indeterminate in advance, how much labor one can get out of labor power in a set time.

[126] *Capital*, 1:342; *MEGA*, II.6:239; *MEGA*, II.7:192. Marx's use of the vampire metaphor has, of course, drawn plenty of attention (e.g., Panichas, "Vampires, Werewolves, and Economic Exploitation"; Carver, *Postmodern Marx*, chap. 1; Neocleous, "The Political Economy of the Dead"; McNally, *Monsters of the Market*, chap. 2). Nonetheless, I know of no one who has drawn attention to the Proudhonian precedent for the metaphor. It has other precedents, as well, some of which are cataloged by Neocleous, "The Political Economy of the Dead," 672–77. Blanqui, in a text from 1869–70, but unpublished until 1885, equates the profits of capital with usury and calls both "*le vampirisme*" (*Maintenant, Il Faut des Armes*, 194). Bray, thirty years earlier, claimed that the modern form of tyranny, the inequality of rights, "enables one or two classes of the community to suck into their own substance, unobserved, unceasingly, and unmercifully, the wealth which has been created by the toils and privations of the working class" (*Labour's Wrongs and Labour's Remedy*, 20).

[127] *System*, 1:414–15; *OC*, 1:357. As Julius Sensat has noted, the vampire is a particularly apt incarnation of the exploiter ("Exploitation," 29). Exploitation is a type of social relationship or interaction, not merely a matter of the distribution of benefits among otherwise unrelated parties or coalitions, à la Roemer (*A General Theory of Exploitation and Class*).

[128] As Neocleous notes, all three of Marx's explicit uses of the vampire metaphor appear in chapter ten ("The Political Economy of the Dead," 681). Neocleous also reveals one esoteric use in the chapter: the Wallachian boyar who, "drunk with victory," declares that "the twelve *corvée* days of the *Réglement organique* amount to 365 days in the year," turns out to have been none other than Vlad Dracula (ibid., 673; *Capital*, 1:348; *MEGA*, II.6:245; *MEGA*, II.7:196).

of the product predominates, surplus labor will be restricted by a more or less confined set of needs." It is only where exchange value becomes the aim of production—either in the mining of silver and gold, or where older modes of production "are drawn into a world market"—that overwork, the depletion of the life of the laborer for the sake of the wealth of the boss, becomes the rule.[129] Overwork is a phenomenon proper and essential to the capitalist world.[130]

Indeed, while he entertains the possibility that "the interest of capital itself points in the direction of a normal working day"—it would seem that quickly burning through labor powers would raise the costs of reproduction—Marx argues that, aside from "significant gaps in certain epochs of feverish expansion," "what experience generally shows to the capitalist is a constant excess of population."[131] He cites E. G. Wakefield to the effect that the overworked "die off with strange rapidity; but the places of those who perish are instantly filled, and a frequent change of persons makes no alteration of the scene."[132] Even if it were better, in the long run, for capitalists to agree to limit the working day, the collective action problem endemic to production for the competitive market makes it impossible for capitalists, individually or severally, to voluntarily enact those limits. The same is true for workers, who, if they want to work at all, must do so on the terms dictated by the labor market. Only "a law of the state, an overpowering social deterrent," can establish a limit to labor time under capitalism.[133]

This was not true under any previous social system, Marx thought. The intentionality of actual or concrete labor is concerned with the satisfaction of particular needs, and labor is, therefore, according to its own nature, episodic and for the sake of enjoyment, even when it is enforced by lord or master. The capitalist production process, on the other hand, is, according to its nature, continuous and for the sake of accumulation. Capitalist production is, therefore, a gigantic make-work project, for it needs above all to produce labor itself. Because it is abstract labor that forms value, the surplus labor performed by the laboring class "is not directly visible."[134] It cannot be observed and measured at the point of

---

[129] *Capital*, 1:345; *MEGA*, II.6:242; *MEGA*, II.7:194–95.

[130] There has been, recently, a renewed attention to the phenomenon of overwork as a problem for political theory; see, especially, Weeks, *The Problem with Work: Feminism, Marxism, Antiwork Politics, and Postwork Imaginaries*.

[131] *Capital*, 1:377–80; *MEGA*, II.6:270–72; *MEGA*, II.7:223–26.

[132] Quoted by Marx, *Capital*, 1:380n79; *MEGA*, II.6:272n111; *MEGA*, II.7:225n118. Marx does not make this clear, but Wakefield is describing the situation of children employed in the factories of northern England (*England and America*, 1:54–55).

[133] *Capital*, 1:415–16; *MEGA*, II.6:302; *MEGA*, II.7:256.

[134] *Capital*, 1:346; *MEGA*, II.6:243; *MEGA*, II.7:195.

production, but only realizes itself, if at all, in the profitable sale of the products. Because of this uncertainty, from the standpoint of the capitalist, more labor is always better.[135] Every extra moment of labor is treated like the straight gate through which the messiah—that is, the profits—may come. "Moments are the elements of profits," in the words of one factory owner.[136] This is what the law must now address.

But things are more complicated than setting a beginning and ending hour for the day. The expenditure of labor power can be sped up and intensified, such that what used to be two hours' labor is now done in one. Moreover, the labor process itself can be transformed by dividing and mechanizing the labor. This decomposition of labor in its traditional forms demolishes entirely the temporality of the project, the cyclical time of labor, determined by performing tasks at the right time,[137] and in the right way.[138] One of the greatest perversities of the capitalist mode of production, according to Marx, is that the capitalist use of machinery, instead of reducing labor time, "sweeps away all customary and natural limits to the length of the working day."[139] The struggle to limit work does not end, therefore, with the passage of eight- or ten-hours regulations, but is an endemic feature of capitalism. This dynamic is, according to Marx, specific to the capitalist mode of exploiting labor power, and arises under no other form of exploitation.[140]

Contrary to what earlier socialists thought, then, the exploitation of the laborer by the capitalist is neither an echo nor a renaissance of feudalism. Capitalist exploitation is a novelty. It is based in the impersonal domination of the market, not the personal domination of the local monopolist.[141] It is open-ended and flexible, indifferent to the particularity

---

[135] The fact that "people do not calculate surplus value accounts" is, thus, *pace* Roemer, a reason for capitalist exploitation to give rise to class struggle ("Should Marxists Be Interested in Exploitation?," 279n34). If exploitation were unequal exchange, then Roemer would be right to say that fetishism would render this inequality invisible, and hence make it impossible that exploitation could underpin or explain class struggle.

[136] Quoted by Marx, *Capital*, 1:352; *MEGA*, II.6:248; *MEGA*, II.7:201.

[137] The "critical moments" so important for both Plato and Marx (*Capital*, 1:445; *MEGA*, II.6:325; *MEGA*, II.7:280–81).

[138] Booth, "Economies of Time: On the Idea of Time in Marx's Political Economy"; Postone, *Time, Labor, and Social Domination*, chap. 5; Sohn-Rethel, *Intellectual and Manual Labour: A Critique of Epistemology*, pt. III.

[139] *Capital*, 1:532; *MEGA*, II.6:396; *MEGA*, II.7:349.

[140] For a recent study vindicating the continued relevance of Marx's framework, see Philip, "Marxism, Neoclassical Economics and the Length of the Working Day."

[141] Marx does not deny that the Saint-Simonian concern about accumulated economic power is valid. He denies only that it captures the capitalist exploitation of labor power in its specificity. What Marx says about the labor process in its simple and abstract elements—that it does not reveal the social relations under which it took place—can also be said about the abstract account of exploitation as use of economic power to extract surplus product.

of what is produced or how it is produced, rather than conservative and tradition bound. It contains an immanent drive toward overwork that is alien to other forms of exploitation. Doing away with this exploitation cannot be a matter of providing cheap credit and cheap land, for it is neither interest nor rent that establishes the relationship of wage laborer to capitalist. At the bottom of the pre-Marxian account of exploitation are the convictions (a) that individual persons exploit individual persons; (b) that they ought not to do so; and (c) that exploitation can be rooted out only by limiting each individual's power to exploit others.[142] Marx's account of impersonal market domination rules out this individualized and moralized understanding of capitalist exploitation. Which is not to say that Marx does not sound like a moralist when he discusses capitalist exploitation. "Indeed, it is hard not to feel that the passion with which he describes and denounces the appalling suffering experienced by workers in Victorian England is a moral one."[143] The question remains, then, what sort of moralist does Marx sound like?

The class power of the capitalist is different in an important way from that of the Athenian *kalos k'agathos* or Wallachian boyar. The individuals of the latter classes are able to exploit individually only because their membership in a class of masters (Vrousalis, "Exploitation, Vulnerability, and Social Domination," 143–44; a point made by Plato in book VIII of his Republic). The capitalist, however, is as dominated as the wage-laborer; modernity is not a world without domination, but, as Deleuze and Guattari say somewhere, it is a world without masters.

[142] Many have also attributed these convictions to Marx and to Marxists (e.g., Arneson, "What's Wrong with Exploitation?"; Geras, "Bringing Marx to Justice"; Logar, "Exploitation as Wrongful Use: Beyond Taking Advantage of Vulnerabilities"). Even Nicholas Vrousalis, in his recent article on exploitation—which is in many respects congenial to my reconstruction of Marx's argument—attributes to Marxists the belief that capitalists exploit workers when capitalists exercise their economic power to appropriate the fruits of workers' labor ("Exploitation, Vulnerability, and Social Domination," 135–36). This formulation retains the notions that, in capitalism, individuals exploit laborers by taking their products, and that this is enabled by an economic power exploiters possess. I think it also implies, though Vrousalis does not say this, that individuals are culpable for using their power in this way. Certainly these three claims can be attributed to many Marxists, for the socialist account of exploitation against which Marx intervened was certainly not done away with by his intervention, and continued to exist alongside and even in precedence over Marx's own account from *Capital*, even amongst Marxists. Engels, who did much more to popularize Marxism than did Marx himself, was much more sympathetic to Saint-Simoniansim than was Marx, and, on many points, replicated Proudhon's view that "a society of independent, proprietor farmers and craftsmen could form the basis of a commodity-producing society and that capitalism distorted commodity production" (Weeks, *Capital and Exploitation*, 46; see also 50–62). The resurgence of socialism in Britain in the last decades of the 1800s also largely reproduced the political economy of the Owenites. Even the avowedly Marxist Social Democrat Federation, under the leadership of Hyndman, propagated the notion that profits arose in capitalism because "the capitalist was able to buy labor power . . . 'on the cheap,' due to the competition among workers for subsistence" (Biernacki, *The Fabrication of Labor*, 409).

[143] Callinicos, "Marxism and Contemporary Political Thought," 274.

Exploitation as *Forza contra Natura*

It has long been a sticking point for those discussing Marx's theory of exploitation that he claims explicitly that the capitalist exploitation of labor power is "by no means an injustice towards the seller" of labor power, the laborer.[144] One standard way of dealing with this claim has been to say that Marx had a "technical" or "descriptive" concept of exploitation, which differed from the normal, morally loaded sense of the term.[145] Another has been to say that he thought moral norms such as justice to be ideological, and relative to the mode of production, and hence means to say that capitalist exploitation is not an injustice from within the bourgeois conception of justice that prevails in capitalist society.[146] Both of these approaches have been roundly criticized by Norman Geras, who adduces the dizzying array of texts from *Capital* itself where Marx characterizes capitalist exploitation as "unpaid labor" or labor "appropriated without equivalent."[147] These, he says, show without a doubt "that, irrespectively of whether or not Marx characterized the relation of exploitation as an unjust one, he did certainly treat it as being a relation of unequal exchange," or of "robbery."[148] "Was Marx confused? How could he think . . . that the capitalist robs the worker but treats the worker justly?"[149]

On the basis of the arguments above, I think this debate has largely missed the point. When he denies that capitalist exploitation is an injustice toward the seller of labor power, Marx's target is Proudhon, not Rawls.[150] That is, he has in view not a theory of justice as the first virtue of the basic structure of society, but a transactional conception of justice according to which justice is embodied in reciprocal exchanges of goods and services at or near the cost of production. His point in chapters six and seven is to show that capital's exploitation of labor power satisfies Proudhon's criterion of justice.[151]

Nonetheless, if Marx succeeds in this local and internecine attack on the utility for socialist theory of Proudhonian justice, then his theory

---

[144] *Capital*, 1:301; *MEGA*, II.6:207; *MEGA*, II.7:159.

[145] For example, Cohen, *Karl Marx's Theory of History*, 182–203; Reiff, *Exploitation and Economic Justice in the Liberal Capitalist State*, 29.

[146] For example, Brenkert, *Marx's Ethics of Freedom*, chap. 5; Wood, *Karl Marx*, chaps. 9–10.

[147] "Bringing Marx to Justice," 50–51.

[148] Ibid., 48.

[149] Young, "Doing Marx Justice," 251.

[150] A fact appreciated, or at least brought forward for consideration, by Callinicos, "Marxism and Contemporary Political Thought," 274.

[151] This was not a new concern for Marx, going back as it does to *The Poverty of Philosophy*; see Thomas, *Karl Marx and the Anarchists*, 228–29.

of capitalist exploitation also ought to challenge those, like Geras, who want to construe exploitation as "an uncompensated taking of what belongs, by right, to someone else."[152] Or, indeed, those, like Wood, who want to construe it as a "shameful" or "degrading" taking advantage of another's vulnerability.[153] For, these conceptions, whatever their merits, figure exploitation as something one person does to another person, and for which the exploiter is responsible. This is may be generally appropriate for noneconomic exploitation and for noncapitalist economic exploitation. As I have argued, however, both the agent and the victim of *capitalist* exploitation are impersonal. The individual wage laborer has no right to what he or she produces,[154] and so the "someone else" in Geras's definition can only be the class of wage laborers as a whole.[155] Likewise, the one doing the "taking" is the capitalist class as a whole, since there is no way of determining with certainty, at the level of each firm, how much surplus value has been produced.[156] Similar difficulties attend the de-personalization of Wood's definition.[157] Fundamentally, both of these definitions, like Proudhon's, seek to pin the responsibility for capitalist exploitation on some set of individuals who are empowered to exploit or not, as they choose. This presumption of individual responsibility is one of "the ideals of bourgeois society" that Marx castigated Proudhon for

---

[152] "Bringing Marx to Justice," 53.

[153] *Karl Marx*, 257–63.

[154] Indeed, Marx claims that "equal exploitation of labour-power is the first human right of capital"; *Capital*, 1:405; *MEGA*, II.6:294; *MEGA*, II.7:247. Aside from his mocking mentions of "the pompous catalogue of 'inalienable human rights,'" Marx's only references to human rights in the whole of *Capital* are his claims that capital declares its own human right to equal conditions of exploitation (*Capital*, 1:416; see also 280, 520, 903; *MEGA*, II.6:416, 191, 386–87, 665–66; *MEGA*, II.7:257, 143–44, 340, 658–59). Even if Marx did not deny—as he did—that labor entails a right to possess the full product, this right could not be individualized, for the individual's product is unidentifiable. Even Hodgskin recognized that "there is no principle or rule . . . for dividing the produce of joint labour . . . but the judgment of the individuals themselves" (*Labour Defended*, 24; cited by Thompson, *Labour Rewarded*, 5). That is one reason Hodgskin preferred individual, petty production.

[155] A greedy farmer, as Marx says, robs the soil of its fertility (*Capital*, 1:376; *MEGA*, II.6:269; *MEGA*, II.7:222). This does not mean that the soil has a property right in its fertility. If the farmer engages here in a wrongful taking, the wrongfulness does not consist in the violation of someone's rights. The fact that Marx claims that capital robs the soil in the same sentence in which he says it robs the laborer ought to have given Geras more pause (*Capital*, 1:638; *MEGA*, II.6:477; *MEGA*, II.7:438–39).

[156] As Marx says, in a different context, "'capitalist' appropriation and 'personal' appropriation, whether of science or of material wealth, are completely different things" (*Capital*, 1:508–9n23; *MEGA*, II.6:377n108; *MEGA*, II.7:331n114).

[157] Wood appreciates the difficulties posed by Marx's de-personalization of exploitation when he is criticizing the notion that exploitation must involve coercion (*Karl Marx*, 252–53).

wishing to transmute into the principles of socialism.[158] It is incompatible with Marx's account of the competitive market as a sphere of impersonal domination. This is one of the crucial lessons of his recapitulation of Dante's *Inferno*. Capital, the ensemble of modern social relations, is the sinner. No individual or set of individuals is responsible for capital's exploitation of labor power. Hence, whatever is wrong with capitalist exploitation—whatever makes Marx think "that it is hateful and ought to be abolished"[159]—is embodied in its systematic features.

The hatefulness of capitalist exploitation, I argue, is that it is contranatural or monstrous. Pay heed to the language Marx uses. Capital is "an animated monster."[160] It is "vampire-like."[161] It is "werewolf-like," and guilty of "monstrous outrages."[162] It quotes Shylock's arguments for a cutting of flesh.[163] It is bloodthirsty and cannibalistic. This language is new to part three.

By contrast, the labor process is consistently portrayed by Marx as both natural and full of life. In the labor process, a human being—"a natural object, a thing, if also a living, self-conscious thing"[164]—"confronts the stuff of nature as a force of nature," "works on external nature" and "simultaneously changes his own nature."[165] Labor is "an appropriation of what exists in nature for human needs," "the metabolism between human being and nature," "an eternal natural condition of human life."[166] It is the "living agent of fermentation," which is incorporated into the "dead objectivity" of the factors of production.[167] Indeed, the natural labor process is so full of life that "it raises the means of production from the dead merely by entering into contact with them, ensouling them."[168] Even the instruments of this process have a "life" and a "death"; their "vitality [*Lebenskraft*]" continuing so long as they are able to serve in the labor process.[169]

---

[158] *Grundrisse*, 248; *MEGA*, II.1.1:171.

[159] Wood, *Karl Marx*, 245.

[160] *Capital*, 1:302; *MEGA*, II.6:208; *MEGA*, II.7:160.

[161] *Capital*, 1:342, also 367, 416; *MEGA*, II.6:239, 261, 302; *MEGA*, II.7:192, 214, 256.

[162] *Capital*, 1:353; *MEGA*, II.6:249; *MEGA*, II.7:201.

[163] *Capital*, 1:399–400; *MEGA*, II.6:289; *MEGA*, II.7:242–43.

[164] *Capital*, 1:310; *MEGA*, II.6:214; *MEGA*, II.7:166.

[165] *Capital*, 1:283; *MEGA*, II.6:192; *MEGA*, II.7:145.

[166] *Capital*, 1:290; *MEGA*, II.6:198; *MEGA*, II.7:151.

[167] *Capital*, 1:292, 302; *MEGA*, II.6:199, 208; *MEGA*, II.7:152, 160.

[168] *Capital*, 1:308; *MEGA*, II.6:212; *MEGA*, II.7:164.

[169] *Capital*, 1:311–12; *MEGA*, II.6:214–15; *MEGA*, II.7:167–68. "Instead of dignifying the human being and setting him or her at the apex of the universe, instead of spiritualizing nature via a human force different in kind, labor [for Marx] situates the human in continuity with nature and natural force" (Wendling, *Karl Marx on Technology and Alienation*, 84; see also Rabinbach, *The Human Motor*, chap. 3).

When capital employs labor, rather than this natural life overflowing and enlivening the dead factors of production, the dead seizes hold of the living, reanimating itself to the detriment of the source of its animation. This is why Marx sees capital as a vampire.[170] It is the "inversion, indeed derangement" of the natural relationship between "dead and living labor," by which "the mere transformation of money into objective factor of the production process" transforms these objective factors into "a rightful claim and a compulsory claim on alien labor and surplus-labor."[171] Motivated by some of these textual considerations, Chris Arthur has identified capitalist exploitation with "the subjection of workers to alien purposes."[172] In a closely related manner, Julius Sensat has argued that "workers are exploited in capitalism because they are used as means of expanding value, and this use is contrary to their nature."[173] I think this line of argument is insightful and wish to extend and clarify it.

There is, of course, an ancient tradition of condemning capital precisely in terms of use contrary to nature. In Aristotle, one finds the claim that both usury and commerce—Marx's "antediluvian forms" of capital[174]—are contrary to nature. Commerce, Aristotle claims, "is justly blamed since it is not according to nature" (*Pol.*, 1258b1–2). Usury, likewise, "is most reasonably hated because one's possessions derive from money itself and not from that for which it was supplied. For it came into being for the sake of exchange, but interest actually makes more of it" (*Pol.*, 1258b2–6).[175] Commerce—buying cheap and selling dear—is wrong because it violates the nature of exchange, which is to be a giving and getting of equivalents. Usury violates the nature of money, which

---

[170]Contrary to the argument of Wendling (among others), Marx's use of the vampire metaphor does not contain "a subtle anti-Semitism" (*Marx on Technology and Alienation*, 152). I am happy to grant that the metaphor has anti-Semitic roots; even if this is not true, it is certainly true of the Shylock comparison, which Marx also deploys. However, the force of Marx's use of these tropes goes directly contrary to the actually existing anti-Semitism of the workers' movement (Proudhon was notoriously anti-Semitic, as were many of the radicals around Bronterre O'Brien). In his criticism of Bruno Bauer's anti-Semitic modernism, Marx had adopted what Leopold calls a strategy of linguistic extension (*The Young Karl Marx*, 165–7); he extended the contemporary associations of *Jude, jüdisch*, etc., to include the Christian population of Germany, thereby tarring the Christian population with the brush Bauer wished to reserve for the Jews. He is doing something similar in *Capital*, making capital—an impersonal economic force—the object for prejudicial images that others would reserve for Jewish persons. Even Shylock gets rehabilitated by Marx: where he speaks for the capitalist exploiter in chapter ten, in chapter fifteen he speaks for the exploited worker (*Capital*, 1:618n30; *MEGA*, II.6:466n307; *MEGA*, II.7:423n320).

[171]*Capital*, 1:425; *MEGA*, II.6:309–10; *MEGA*, II.7:264.

[172]*The New Dialectic and Marx's* Capital, 56.

[173]"Exploitation," 36.

[174]*Capital*, 1:266; *MEGA*, II.6:180; *MEGA*, II.7:132.

[175]Marx quotes Aristotle's claims; *Capital*, 1:267; *MEGA*, II.6:188; *MEGA*, II.7:133.

is supposed to be a mere means by which to facilitate the reciprocity of exchange, not an end. Here, the notion of being contrary to nature means misusing something, failing to see or respect that to which it is, in and as itself, directed. It is this sense of *nature* and its violation that Sensat locates at the core of the notion of exploitation. And violating something's nature means, as Arthur says, subjecting it to an alien purpose. Hence, there is no anachronism in saying that commerce and usury are, for Aristotle, forms of exploitation.[176]

Of course, Aristotle did not call the misuse of things *exploitation*. Rather, Aristotle called the disruption of the natural constitution or action of things *bia*, force or violence.[177] In his *Physics*, *bia* is defined as a motion proceeding from an external source. It is opposed to natural motion, which proceeds from an internal source, the nature of the thing moved. Hence, "what is by force (*biai*) and what is contrary to nature are the same."[178] This principle—the opposition of force and nature—is also centrally important in the thinking of subsequent Aristotelians, including in Dante's demarcation of the lower reaches of Hell as proper to the sins of *forza*, as opposed to the sins of *incontenenza*, defined as the immoderate pursuits of natural desires (11.70–90).

Thus, my claim that the capitalist exploitation of labor power is best understood as the use of labor contrary to its nature[179] is bolstered by the fact that Marx locates violent force, not *prior to* the selling of labor-power, but *after*, within the capitalist's control of production itself. Together with the contraposition of natural, living labor to monstrous, dead capital, part three is marked by an upsurge in Marx's emphasis upon coercion, compulsion, force, and struggle. As a crude index, consider the rate at which the most common German words for these concepts appear in parts one and two combined (122 pages in the *MEGA* edition) in comparison to part three (118 pages). *Zwang* appears six times in parts one and two, but twenty-seven times in part three. *Kampf* shows a similar increase in frequency, from three appearances to thirteen. *Gewalt*, which shows up

---

[176]Note that commerce is the exploitation of exchange, and usury is the exploitation of money. For Aristotle, exploitation does not have to exploit *people* in order to be blameworthy or hateful. This will be important further on.

[177]I am indebted to Francis Wade's instructive article on the history and meanings of *violence*, "On Violence."

[178]*De Caelo*, 300a23; see also *Phys.* I215a1-3 and 230a29–30; *Gen. An.*, 788b27. "To force something means to make a thing move against its own 'natural internal tendency'"; Walter, "Power and Violence," 354.

[179]The transition from "the end of the power to *x*" to "the end of *x*-ing" is unproblematic. The power or capacity to make a chair, for instance, has no other end than the end of making a chair. The activity and the power to undertake the activity are oriented toward the same end.

five times in the first two parts, is used eighteen times in part three.[180] The production of surplus value is a violent and conflictual process.

The length of the working day is the crucial point of contestation. Surplus value arises out of surplus labor, labor that continues beyond the point at which it has reproduced its wage. This quantitative extension of the production process is the quantitative extension of "the process of consuming labor-power."[181] But due to "the special nature" of the commodity labor power, due, that is, to the fact that it is only available in the living body of the laborers themselves, this extension can only come about by somehow getting the laborers to work longer than they would if they were under their own direction.[182] Getting the laborers to work *more* is the concern of capitalist superintendence and oversight.[183] This superintendence takes the length and rhythm of the working day out from under the aegis of the individual workers.[184] While the "general nature of labor is not evidently changed" thereby,[185] the chapter on the working day reveals that this general nature is certainly disrupted in an important sense.[186] Because the aim of capital is the accumulation of surplus value, the capitalist is compelled to view all of the laborer's available time as "by nature and by right labor-time."[187]

[180] These counts include derivative words.

[181] *Capital*, 1:302; *MEGA*, II.6:207; *MEGA*, II.7:160.

[182] This might be thought to be a counterfactual of ambiguous epistemic status. However, the point is a purely pragmatic one for any capitalist employer. The point of workplace discipline is always to extract more and better work from workers than if they were left to their own devices. The specificity of capitalist discipline is that there is no limit to the demand for *more*. That is, the forcing of labor in capitalism is exploitative in the specific sense that it is oriented toward accumulation, toward a purpose that could not possibly spring from human deliberation among the workers themselves. As Marx noted in 1844, alienated labor, because it belongs to and is directed by another, "is thus not voluntary, but compelled, *forced labour [Zwangsarbeit]*" (*Early Writings*, 326; *MEGA*, I.2:367). As Jacques Bidet puts it, "the compulsion to produce is established to the extent that the abstract purpose [value] is asserted" (*Exploring Marx's Capital*, 62). Thanks to Alex Gourevitch for pushing me on this point.

[183] As Marx wrote in response to Adolf Wagner's misreading of *Capital*, "The capitalist . . . not only 'deducts' or 'robs' but enforces the production of surplus value, thus first helping to create what is to be deducted" (*MECW*, 24:535; *MEW*, 19:359).

[184] "The problem for capital is that it needs the *agency* of labor. It is not really a matter of reducing the worker to the status of a mere instrument of production, like a machine, or like an animal whose will has to be *broken*. It is a matter of the *bending* of the will to an alien purpose. . . . The former 'subjects' of production are treated as manipulable objects; but it is still a question of manipulating their activity, not of depriving them of all subjectivity" (Arthur, *The New Dialectic and Marx's Capital*, 52).

[185] *Capital*, 1:290; *MEGA*, II.6:198; *MEGA*, II.7:151.

[186] In part four, the nature of labor will be shown to undergo profound modifications, which will be treated in the next chapter.

[187] *Capital*, 1:375; *MEGA*, II.6:268; *MEGA*, II.7:221.

Instead of the normal maintenance of labor-power determining the limits of the working-day, the greatest possible daily expenditure of labor-power, howsoever sick, violent, and painful, determines the limits of the resting-time of the laborers. Capital asks not after the life-span of labor-power. What interests it is simply and only the maximum labor-power that can be made liquid in a working-day. It achieves this aim by shortening the duration of labor-power, as a greedy farmer achieves a higher yield by robbing the soil of its fertility.[188]

The aim of capital and the aim of labor are divergent. Thus, when capital takes command over labor, this divergence in aim becomes a conflict, and the victory of capital in this conflict manifests itself as the "unnatural extension of the working-day,"[189] and the precise length of this unnatural extension cannot be established by any right, but only by "force," by a continuous "struggle" between capitalist and laborer.[190] This struggle between opposed forces gives rise, in turn, to the necessity that the working class "compel a law of the state, an overpowering social deterrent by which they are deterred from selling themselves and their families, by a voluntary contract with capital, into death and slavery."[191] The violence capital does to labor under its control reverberates through social struggle until it issues in the state's enforcement of factory legislation.[192]

Concern for this violence might seem scholastic in the bad sense. Surely, the labor process has no right to its own integrity. I assume that this is why Sensat connects exploitation directly to the nature of human beings. If capital violates or disrupts *human* nature, then it is easier to see why it might be wrong. Human beings are beings who can make claims on us, and to whom it does not seem strange to attribute rights, including perhaps the right to self-realization, or the right to fulfill their natures. Labor,

---

[188] *Capital*, 1:376; *MEGA*, II.6:269; *MEGA*, II.7:222.

[189] *Capital*, 1:377; *MEGA*, II.6:269; *MEGA*, II.7:222.

[190] *Capital*, 1:344; *MEGA*, II.6:241; *MEGA*, II.7:194.

[191] *Capital*, 1:416; *MEGA*, II.6:302; *MEGA*, II.7:256.

[192] There is here another contrast with the Saint-Simonian/Proudhonian conception of exploitation. For the French socialists, the state's role was fundamentally that of enforcing property rights, and thereby compelling the propertyless to work for the proprietors. Certainly, Marx does not deny the state this role, but he tends to relegate it to an earlier point in the transition to capitalism (e.g., *Capital*, vol. 1, chap. 28; *MEGA*, vol. II.6, chap. 24.3; *MEGA*, vol. II.7, chap. 28). As capital develops, the role of the state changes; "the longer working-day which capital tried to impose on adult workers by acts of state violence from the middle of the fourteenth to the end of the seventeenth century is approximately the same length as the shorter working-day which, in the second half of the nineteenth century, the state has here and there imposed as a barrier to the transformation of the blood of children into capital" (*Capital*, 1:382; *MEGA*, II.6:274; *MEGA*, II.7:227). On the fight with the Proudhonists over the desirability of general laws, enforced by the power of the state, and on the utility of trade unions, see Marx, *Political Writings*, 3:89.

as such, seems incapable of making any such claims on us. However, as we have seen, Marx argues that capitalist exploitation of labor power has a horrific effect on the laborers, since it contains an intrinsic tendency toward overwork. One might read Marx as making a simple consequentialist argument; capitalist exploitation of labor is wrong because it has terrible consequences. According to another way of reading Marx, however, he is making a slightly different argument; the fact that the capitalist exploitation of labor has terrible consequences reveals that it is wrong, and gives us a reason to care about its wrongness, but does not get to the bottom of this wrongness. Rather than the consequences constituting the wrongness, they give rise to the suspicion that there is something wrong with the principle of action itself.[193] There must be something wrong with the capitalist production process if it predictably and consistently leads to terrible overwork, and hence to a constant struggle to limit work. This something is that it does violence to the labor process.

Indeed, it is a *strength* of Marx's account of exploitation that it is not formulated as the exploitation of human nature. This is an advantage of Marx's account because it is much easier to admit that labor has a teleological nature than to admit that humanity does. As a form of instrumental action, labor only makes sense as a means to an end outside itself, the final product, and to the enjoyment of that product. This teleology does not depend upon the intentions of the laborer, either, but is a norm to which the laborer's intention must conform in order for the action to count as labor. In other words, it is not my intention to construct a table that makes the construction of a table a teleological action, but the objective tendency of my actions to actually bring about a table that gives content and actuality to my intention. Intending a table in such a way that no table is produced is not labor but a failure to labor.

In order to make sense as labor, therefore, our laboring activity must give way to a type of enjoyment that is not itself for the sake of returning to labor. This implies a hierarchy of ends. The ends of enjoyment, of the uses of things made, are higher than the ends of labor. This hierarchy is implicit in the activity of labor itself.[194] Labor is absurd without it.

---

[193] This is similar to Kant's procedure for testing maxims of action, but without the insistence that noncontradiction be the only test.

[194] Hence the oft-quoted claim from the manuscript to volume three of *Capital*: "In fact, the realm of freedom actually begins only where labour which is determined by necessity and mundane considerations ceases; thus in the very nature of things it lies beyond the sphere of actual material production. . . . Freedom in this field can only consist in socialised man, the associated producers, rationally regulating their interchange with Nature, bringing it under their common control, instead of being ruled by it as by the blind forces of Nature; and achieving this with the least expenditure of energy and under conditions most favourable to, and worthy of, their human nature. But it nonetheless still remains a realm of

Marx's criticism of capitalist exploitation presupposes such a hierarchy of ends. Capital, by exploiting labor power for the sake of accumulation, makes labor absurd or pointless for the laborer. This conclusion can be drawn without implying any claim about the point or purpose of human existence as such. To be sure, Marx is committed to the claim that the purpose of human existence is not labor, but labor itself tells us that. Beyond this negative claim Marx is not committed by his criticism of capitalist exploitation to any teleological doctrine of human nature.[195]

CONCLUSION

Overwork and meaningless work are the rule and tendency of capitalist production, according to Marx, because the end for which capital exploits labor power is the augmentation of surplus value, something of which there is never enough. This criticism of capitalist exploitation does not commit Marx to a teleological account of human nature, but only to the claim that, in fact, human beings do engage in labor, and that, in fact, capitalism rests upon turning our capacity for labor into a resource for the endless accumulation of wealth. Neither is it based in a claim that laborers possess a right to their full product, but only on the claim that there is a fundamental conflict between the commitment of the laborers to pursue the means of enjoyment and the commitment of the capitalists to pursue the endless accumulation of wealth.[196]

This indicates that Marx was quite an odd socialist. In the face of the predominant socialist demand that the laborer receives the full product of his or her labor, Marx insists that, both as useful things and as values, the products of labor cannot be traced to any discrete set of individuals. In the face of the socialist complaint that capitalism is, like feudalism

---

necessity. Beyond it begins that development of human energy which is an end in itself, the true realm of freedom, which, however, can blossom forth only with this realm of necessity as its basis. The shortening of the working-day is its basic prerequisite." *Capital*, 3:958–59; *MEGA*, II.15:794–95.

[195]This is not to say that Marx never said anything that might commit him to such a doctrine, but that such a doctrine is not necessary for Marx's theory of capitalist exploitation to make sense.

[196]Postone has rightly claimed that "Marx's analysis of production in capitalism is not based upon a labor theory of wealth." But because he assumes that any theory of economic exploitation will share the Saint-Simonian assumptions, he adds to this that Marx's "critique should not be understood as one of exploitation alone. . . . Capitalist production, according to Marx is characterized not only by class exploitation but also by a peculiar dynamic, rooted in the constant expansion of value" (*Time, Labor, and Social Domination*, 282). On the basis of my argument in this chapter, one can say that capitalist exploitation is characterized not only by class exploitation!

before it, based on the exploitation of man by man, Marx emphasizes the specificity of capitalist exploitation, the way in which it is an unprecedented marshaling of labor power as a natural resource. In the face of the socialist project of eliminating exploitation, Marx sets the more modest goal of eliminating the exploitation of labor power for the production of surplus value.[197]

The uneasy fit between Marx's concept of exploitation and the standard socialist picture drives home Terrell Carver's point that "Marx's theory of exploitation is political" insofar as it "may function within a political struggle which might not have been perceived as such . . . until the theory had, as Marx said, seized the masses and become a material force."[198] Marx was hardly the first person to talk about exploitation in capitalism. He was active in a political movement within which the existence and evil of capitalist exploitation were articles of faith. Marx's intervention was not to name a previously unknown evil, but to take this circulating and recognized evil and to insert it into a framework of new concepts. This insertion changed the significance of the evil by giving to exploitation a new center of gravity. No longer is "the exploitation of man by man" first and foremost a violation of the rights of persons. Instead, the exploitation of persons takes the form it does because of the misuse of labor power within capitalist production. In part, Marx's political aim must have been to use the existing terminology to carry his own critical theory into the workers' socialist movement. This would reflect a concern that the everyday speech of those in the movement—the language of its demands, promises, and proclamations—articulate and imply a true or scientific understanding of the present order. Such a concern is evident throughout Marx's writings. This indicates that, for Marx, the language of politics was itself a political matter.

This does not mean that Marx was trying to impose a new way of talking on the socialist movement. He did not even try to impose such

---

[197]Indeed, given the Aristotelian lineage of Marx's concept of exploitation, it would make no sense to attempt to eliminate every form of exploitation. A world without force and exploitation would be a world in which we did not eat or engage in any labor whatsoever. You think the nature of those plants and animals is not frustrated by you eating them? You think the tree is meant to become a table? For the most part, the plants and nonhuman animals of the world cannot rebel against our exploitation of them, and are therefore dependent upon our own prudence to ensure that the consequences of that exploitation is not catastrophic. On Marx's analysis, however, capital, being subject to the impersonal domination of the market, is incapable of prudence, and laborers are very capable of rebelling. The wake of such a rebellion—a postcapitalist world—would not be free of exploitation, but only free of the sort of exploitation of labor power that frustrates its immanent drive to supply the means of enjoyment (compare Vrousalis, "Exploitation, Vulnerability, and Social Domination," 135).

[198]"Marx's Political Theory of Exploitation," 77.

a way of talking on himself; he continued to use *exploitation* in ways that suggest nothing other than using one's power to take advantage of another's vulnerability. Instead, it means that, on Marx's understanding of the capitalist mode of production, what the socialist movement as a whole is concerned about under the name of *exploitation* is best treated as a consequence of the subordination of the labor process under capital. The rational kernel of the concern with the exploitation of man by man is a concern with the exploitation of labor power for the production of surplus value.

This de-personalized reconstruction of capitalist exploitation is a crucial moment in Marx's larger project in *Capital*. His understanding of impersonal domination by the market begins to push strongly against the moralized accounts of exploitation predominant among socialists. Rather than being restricted to the level of economic theory, it is becoming clear that the conflict between Marx's critical theory of capital and the existing socialist discourses ranges across the practical and normative registers as well. Here, too, Marx can lay claim to having carried out the materialist critique he had always called for. He has shown how the moralizing discourse about exploitation presupposes and supplements the very world that gives rise to it as a reflex. The socialist who reduces exploitation to—and decries it as—"the right of the strongest,"[199] inadvertently, but unavoidably, sanctifies *capitalist exploitation*, which, proceeding on the basis of the exchange of equivalents, escapes the censure directed at it. By condemning *individuals* for the sins of capital, these moralists unwittingly trap socialism within the Hell that capital has made.

However, this is not the whole story. For it is not as if *personal* and *political* domination and abuse have disappeared under the reign of capital. Capitalism means more, to Marx, than the impersonal domination of the market and the de-personalized exploitation of labor. The reign of capital also empowers and impels capitalists to exercise a sort of personal dominion over the workplace, and over the labor process that occurs there. It gives rise to a labor market that is stratified by gender, age, race, and nationality, and to an immense population dependent upon wages for survival. It usurps the political power of the state, which comes to be dependent upon capital accumulation for its operations, and, therefore, deploys force of arms to establish the conditions of that accumulation. Capital's social Hell is labyrinthine, and its recesses hold many monsters.

Part of Marx's challenge in *Capital* is to integrate the horrors still to come within the framework established by the first three parts. Part and parcel of reworking Dante's *katabasis* is the notion that the various levels

---

[199]Proudhon, *What Is Property?*, 202; OC, 4:333.

of Hell do not merely rest on top of one another like an inverted wedding cake. The descent into the realm of violence does not leave incontinence behind, for the circles of the incontinent also contain the circles of the violent. And we have seen that the impersonal domination of the market continues to mediate the violence of capitalist exploitation; the market contains the site of production, even though the site of production necessarily introduces new complication. The same pattern will emerge again in the following chapters. The new personal and political relations established on the basis of the market and of the sale of labor power, whatever new vistas they may open up, never remove us from these realms.

CHAPTER 5

Malebolge: The Capitalist Mode
of Production as Fraud

At length, casting away his guise of terror, this much cursed power revealed itself in its true form and looks to men. What graciousness was in its aspect, what benevolence, what music flowed from its lips: science was heard and the savage hearts of men were melted; . . . and as science spoke, the multitude knelt in love and obedience.
  —Douglas Jerrold, "The Factory Child" (1840)

Machines promised us an increase in wealth; they kept their word, but gave us at the same time an increase of poverty. They promised us liberty; I will prove that they have brought us slavery.
  —Proudhon, *Système des Contradictions Économiques*, I.IV.ii (1846)

One must say that because man is a social animal, by nature each man owes to the other that without which human society cannot be preserved. For men cannot associate with each other unless they believe they are telling each other the truth.
  —Thomas Aquinas, *Summa Theologica*, 2a 2ae, q. 109, a. 3

As we have seen, Marx turned the socialist diagnosis of "the empire of force and fraud" on its head. Because he took commerce to realize the exchange of equivalent values, he could not, as his precursors had, understand capitalists' massive accumulations of wealth to be explained by past acts of conquest, acts that gave capitalists an unfair bargaining power by which they could continually get the better of their poor fellows in exchange (thereby preserving and augmenting their advantage, ad infinitum).[1] Instead, Marx locates the rule of force within capitalist production itself, *after* exchange. Having purchased at a fair price the workers' only salable commodity, their labor power, the capitalists set them to work in the production of new commodities. Because the aim of capital is the realization of surplus value, this production process forces

[1] Capitalists may seek (and find) rents, but this is not what makes them capitalists.

labor power to be active beyond the point at which it has produced the means of its own reproduction. That is, capital bends labor power to an alien goal and forces it to produce more than it otherwise would. This is the specifically capitalist form of exploitation, and it constitutes a forceful seizure of labor power, a use of labor contrary to its nature.

What, then, of *fraud*, the twin of force in Thompson's slogan? The premise that labor power is purchased at its value might seem to rule fraud simply inadmissible in Marx's critical theory. It befits Proudhon to claim that "from the right of cunning arose the profits of industry, commerce, and banking; of mercantile frauds and pretenses which are honored with the beautiful names of 'talent' and 'genius,' which ought to be regarded as the highest degree of falsity and deception; and, finally, of all kinds of social inequalities."[2] Marx's argument, very much to the contrary, is that even "the valorization of the merchant's capital is not to be explained by mere frauds."[3] However, the question of fraud is not so easily dismissed. Given that Marx has transformed the moral categories of incontinence and force into de-personalized critical concepts, applicable to capital as an ensemble of social relations, why cannot something similar be done with fraud? That personal acts of fraud have no explanatory value for Marx does not entail that a de-personalized concept of fraud has no place in his account of capital.[4]

Indeed, Marx's account of capital has constant recourse to the dichotomy that furnishes the basic conceptual materials of any account of fraud. The sine qua non of fraud is a certain discrepancy between *appearances* and *reality*, *seeming* and *being*. A fraud promises one thing and does another, passing off a harm as a benefit, or something paltry as something grand. Unlike force, which is naked, fraud is sophisticated, tricky. It should require no argument to convince the reader of *Capital* that the distinction—and the discrepancy—between appearance and reality is a crucial one for Marx. Basic to his whole enterprise is the

---

[2] Proudhon, *What Is Property?*, 203; *OC*, 4:333.

[3] Marx, *Capital*, 1:267; *MEGA*, II.6.181; *MEGA*, II.7:133.

[4] De-personalized fraud is not alien to everyday speech, either. The Securities and Exchange Commission can investigate hedge fund managers for "unintentional fraud," that is, for negligent misrepresentation of material facts about investments (Comstock, "Meet the First Big Exec to Pay for 'Unintentionally Defrauding' during the Credit Crisis"). But one might also go further and say, for example, that "global finance capitalism is a fraud," not because of the criminal intentions of anyone in particular, but because the institutions and practices out of which it is constituted are based on simplified assumptions and faulty analyses, such that it cannot possibly deliver the benefits it is supposed to deliver, regardless of the intentions and good faith of the people running the institutions and engaged in the practices (Shakespeare and Russia Today, "Global Finance Capitalism Is a Fraud"). The mismatch between apparent benefits and actual (but less apparent) harms is enough to mark something as fraudulent.

conviction that things are not what they appear to be, that, for example, "the surface process of market-exchange camouflages the depth-process of exploitation."[5]

This discrepancy between appearance and reality is not, by itself, enough to hang a concept of fraud on. As I pointed out in chapter 1, Marx thinks science is necessary wherever appearances dissemble reality, but it would be bizarre to say that gravity is a fraud because the laws of motion of bodies actually depart from and contradict the rules of thumb derived from how things appear to casual experience. Besides a discrepancy between appearance and reality, fraud always has a temporal character. First there is the bait, then the switch. Things seem to be good for a while, but then turn bad. Fraud is, inherently, a process. Applications of violence or force, by contrast, while they may endure, remain self-same events from beginning to end. The forced extraction of labor is just as forced at the beginning of the workday as it is at the end, and just as much forced labor if it ends after five minutes as if it lasts twelve hours.[6] Being defrauded, however, takes time.

In his *Inferno*, Dante presents the reader with an "image of fraud" in the beast, Geryon, who transports Virgil and the pilgrim into Malebolge, the ringed field where the sins of fraud are punished:

> Its face was that of a just man, so kindly seemed its outer skin, and the rest of its torso was that of a serpent; it had two paws, hairy to the armpits; it had back and breast and both sides painted with knots and little wheels: ... so the wicked beast rested on the rim of stone that encloses the sand. In the emptiness all its tail was wriggling, twisting upward the poisoned fork that armed its tip like a scorpion's. (*Inf.* 17.10–15, 23–27)

This image well captures the process character of fraud. The victim is taken in by the initial appearance of a good, then confused by the intricacies, and caught in the grip of something unforeseen, before being impaled. The harm can be dissembled by the good because, while the two are connected, they are also at some remove from each other.

This is the key to a marked—but unremarked—shift in Marx's project between parts three and four of *Capital*. With the opening of part four, historical process enters into Marx's presentation in a new way. The production of relative surplus value—"which arises from the curtailment

[5] Maguire, *Marx's Theory of Politics*, 144.

[6] Hence Marx's delightful demolition of Nassau Senior's claim that "the whole net profit is derived from the last hour" of an eleven-and-one-half-hour working day, and that a Ten Hours' Bill would therefore put all the manufacturers of Manchester out of business (*Capital*, 1:333–38; *MEGA*, II.6:232–36; *MEGA*, II.7:184–89).

of the necessary labor-time"[7]—introduces diachronic development into Marx's account. Capital develops the productivity of labor. Capital introduces machinery into production and causes mechanization to spread and intensify. Capital progressively conquers the various fields of production. Capital accumulates and becomes more concentrated. These essentially diachronic tendencies define Marx's concerns in parts four through seven. Because the first three parts of *Capital* identified the cyclical dynamics of the market that mediate all of capital's processes, and the constant compulsion to grow that defines capital's forceful seizure of the labor process, they treated capital sub specie aeternitatis, as it were, and looked at it in forms that were "no less effectual [*wirksam, active*] in the old-fashioned bakeries than in the modern cotton factories."[8] But the whole thrust of parts four through seven is that capital operates to very different effect in old-fashioned bakeries and in modern cotton factories, that the differentiation between these—indeed, much of the difference between "old-fashioned" and "modern" as such—arises from the operations of capital, and that the diversity of capitals, of working classes, and of labor processes is essential to the capitalist mode of production. Capital is the matrix of a history, of a diachronic development, that forces the observer to grapple with the relationship between the first appearance of the capitalist mode of production, or what it seems to be at any point, and its long-term tendencies, far-flung consequences, and far-from-immediate results. This temporalization of the distinction between seeming and being makes it possible for Marx to incorporate and de-personalize the socialist accusation of fraud.

If, according to Marx, the force of capital lies within its free contractual relationship with wage labor, then its fraud hides behind its most beautiful promise, the promise to deliver prosperity and human development to the laborers. This promise was most famously articulated by Adam Smith. The division of labor occasioned by the exchange of products, and developing with every extension of the market, enables a progressive increase of national wealth, and this increase keeps up demand for labor and the wages of the laborer, while simultaneously cheapening commodities. The liberal reward of labor, going along with the increase in wealth, encourages this wealth to further increase, since a liberal reward encourages industry.[9] A concern for the least well off, even more than a concern for the inviolability of private property, has animated liberal defenses of capitalism ever since. "Optimism and conscience" complement each

---

[7] *Capital*, 1:432; *MEGA*, II.6:313–14; *MEGA*, II.7:269.
[8] *Capital*, 1:425; *MEGA*, II.6:309; *MEGA*, II.7:263.
[9] Smith, *The Wealth of Nations*, chaps. 1–3, 8; for commentary see Hont and Ignatieff, "Needs and Justice in the Wealth of Nations: An Introductory Essay."

other.[10] The claim that mobilizes this concern for the defense of modern capitalism is that only in capitalism are the incentives established whereby technological changes can be harnessed for steady improvements in the productivity of labor. Progress in technology means progress in wealth.

This promise of wealth is not crudely materialistic, either, as Marx appreciated from early on.[11] What the technological revolution in production provides is "the mightiest means of shortening labor-time."[12] Echoing Godwin's claim that "the genuine wealth of man is leisure,"[13] Marx looks to the length of the working day as the key index of wealth and well-being of the laborer. The promise of free time, and of the "integral development" thereby made possible, is the "revolutionary side" of the industrial revolution.[14] Beyond mere material prosperity, then, capital's transformation of production promises humanization.

This humanization was extoled by Marx and Engels in 1848 as the "evaporation" of "everything corporative and long-standing."[15] In their "panegyric upon bourgeois achievement,"[16] they could not resist telescoping what they took to be the tendency of the capitalist mode of production into accomplished facts: "Gender and age differences no longer have any social validity for the working class. . . . Modern industrial labor, modern subjection to capital, the same in England as in France, in America as in Germany, has stripped [the proletarian] of every national character."[17] In these passages—and in many others—Marx seems to claim that the capitalist mode of production is doing communism's work for it by creating a new sort of human being, the first class of universal persons,[18] "the

---

[10] Berg, *The Machinery Question*, 18.

[11] Heller, *The Theory of Need in Marx*, 104–5.

[12] *Capital*, 1:532; *MEGA*, II.6:396; *MEGA*, II.7:349.

[13] *The Enquirer: Reflections on Education, Manners, and Literature*, 167; cited by Claeys, *Machinery, Money, and the Millennium*, 32.

[14] Marx, *The Poverty of Philosophy*, MECW, 6:190.

[15] *Manifesto, Political Writings*, 1:70; *MEW*, 4:465. This phrase—*Alles Ständische und Stehende verdampft*—is usually translated as "All that is solid melts into air." I agree with Sperber when he argues that, within the context of Germany in 1848, Marx meant primarily that "economic power deriving from the capitalists' steam engines . . . would terminate the anachronistic society of orders" [*Stände*] (*Karl Marx*, 206–7). That Sperber thinks it means *nothing more* than this requires tearing it from the text in which it is embedded. The *Stände* are not merely a German phenomenon, and they have many analogues (whatever is *stehende*) in other social relations.

[16] Schumpeter, "'The Communist Manifesto' in Sociology and Economics," 209.

[17] *Political Writings*, 1:74, 78; *MEW*, 4:469, 473.

[18] I do not say *the first universal class*. In Marx's usage, any class whose particular interests coincided with the interests of the whole society—understood by him, generally, along the lines of political states—was, for just so long as this coincidence obtained, a universal class (Llorente, "Marx's Concept of 'Universal Class': A Rehabilitation").

contemporary, and final, realization of universality."[19] All of this is supposed to result from capitalism's revolutionizing of production.

That this is not the whole story, however—that, in fact, there is significant uncertainty about Marx's understanding of the relationship between capitalism and communism—is apparent from the fact that two diametrically opposed doctrines are attributed to him. Alongside the optimistic doctrine, according to which capitalism produces processes of automation and scientific management that render the capitalist and the market unnecessary—that is, communism grows within capitalism until it is ready to supplant its host—there is also the catastrophic or apocalyptic doctrine, according to which the steady immiseration of the proletariat, and the ever more severe crises of capitalism, will force, at some point, a complete scrapping of the capitalist system, compelling the desperate to invent a new social system to put in its place. Thus, the bourgeoisie, "incapable of assuring its slave any kind of existence within his slavery," leaves the proletariat with "nothing to lose" in the communist revolution "but their chains."[20]

This uncertainty about capitalism's contribution to the communist project, is, I think, understandable. Marx's argument in parts four through seven of *Capital*, is that the capitalist mode of production is, as far as the workers are concerned, a gigantic fraud. It develops the productive powers of labor to an extraordinary degree, but rather than lightening the burden of labor, this increase in productivity becomes a means of making labor more onerous and less rewarding. It rests on and reproduces the wage relation, which falsifies the picture by making the constant plunder of the laboring class appear as a series of voluntary exchanges. It accumulates the wealth of nations, but only by simultaneously accumulating the misery of the "relative surplus population," the reserve army of the unemployed by which both the technical transformations of the production process and the operations of the labor market are mediated. On Marx's account, the goods promised and delivered by capitalism are inseparable from the evils that follow in their train.

The essential condition of this fraud is the attractiveness of exchanges and mutually voluntary contracts as a form of social mediation. Exchange is the "sheep's clothing" that "covers up the wolf most perfectly," such that no one can charge the capitalist with "adultery, robbery, murder, sacrilege, or anything that the world or reason would censure," even

---

[19] Avineri, *The Social and Political Thought of Karl Marx*, 59.

[20] Marx, *Political Writings*, 1:79, 98; *MEW*, 4:473, 493. Claiming that these two doctrines are rendered compatible by a dialectical inversion is an admission that one has failed to understand what is at stake.

as workers slave away and the unemployed starve, rot, and languish.[21] This is why part six, on wages, is the pivot between Marx's discussion of the objective domination found inside the capitalist workplace and his analysis of the misery that accompanies capitalist accumulation in society at large.[22] It also underscores Marx's disagreement with those socialists who, like Proudhon, called for workers to associate with one another on the basis of contracts and fair exchanges, or who counseled the working class to police their own rate of reproduction for the sake of keeping the population of workers within the confines of the so-called wage fund. So long as exchange constitutes the social nexus, producers will be dominated by market forces, workers will suffer overwork and despotism in their work, and masses will be excluded from access to the means of subsistence.

This split within socialism reflects a much broader disintegration of the republican tradition of political thought out of which socialism grew. Proudhon, like many socialists and radicals in Britain, understood republican freedom to require a sort of individual independence that was not merely compatible with but also reinforced by the practices of contract and exchange.[23] In this, they reiterated the move made by the commercial republicans of the eighteenth century, and, like those predecessors, prepared the way for a conception of market freedom.[24] Marx, by contrast, represents another path, one that sees in exchange a mode of social

----

[21] These phrases come from Martin Luther's "Sermon on the Gospel of the rich man and poor Lazarus," excerpted by Marx in the notebooks from the early 1860s, which were published posthumously as *Theories of Surplus Value* (*MECW*, 32:532–33).

[22] By way of contrasting judgment, David Harvey finds part six to be "fairly obvious" and "rather pedestrian," and hence sees in it nothing but a disappointing lull before part seven, which "is, unquestionably, the culminating argument" of the book (*A Companion to Marx's Capital*, 243). In this, Harvey echoes (intentionally or not) a long line of interpreters who, discerning little in Marx's treatment of wages in *Capital*, fall back on his claim in the 1859 preface that, after treating capital, Marx will go on to survey "landed property, wage-labour; state, foreign trade, world market" (*Contribution to the Critique of Political Economy*, *MECW*, 29:261; *MEGA*, II.2:99). This six-part plan, these interpreters claim, was never realized by Marx, and volume one of *Capital* constitutes only the first part of the first book of his theory, which would have included a full treatment of wage labor; see Wilbrandt, *Karl Marx: Versuch Einer Würdigung*; Rubel, *Rubel on Karl Marx: Five Essays*; McLellan, "Introduction"; and Lebowitz, *Beyond Capital*. As I argued in the introduction, I do not take this view. Marx's account of wages, if it does not do everything some commentators would like it to do, is neither missing nor uninteresting.

[23] Of course this individual independence was really, for Proudhon, only the independence of individual patriarchal families; women's freedom was conditioned by their nature.

[24] This has led to some rather amusing results, as when Lew Rockwell Jr., one of the deans of American right-libertarian fusion, citing with approval Proudhon's dictum that liberty is the mother, not the daughter of order, calls the French socialist "an American essayist" (*The Left, the Right, and the State*, 21).

mediation that threatens the very possibility of freedom, which "can only be enjoyed in the company and through the cooperation of other people."[25] The fraud of which the capitalist mode of production is guilty is, at bottom, that of passing off a wage-contract-mediated form of mass slavery and mass precariousness as the realization of all-around social cooperation, freedom, and security.

CAPITAL WITH A HUMAN FACE

Marx arrives at his considerations of the revolution wrought by capitalism in the mode of production by considering what capital must do in order to pursue valorization once the length of the working day is established by law. If the working day cannot be extended, then the only way to increase surplus labor is by increasing the productivity of labor, such that the laborer is able to reproduce his own necessities more quickly,[26] and "this cannot be done except by an alteration in his tools or in his mode of working, or both. Hence, a revolution must be introduced in the conditions of production of his labor, i.e., in his mode of production, and thus in the labor process itself." By this route, Marx arrives at what he calls "the fundamental form of the capitalist mode of production."[27]

It would seem obvious that this fundamental form of the capitalist mode of production must be proper to capitalism, in the sense that it must be hegemonic in capitalism and only exceptionally present in other modes of production. For instance, if communism differs from capitalism, it must differ at this level: it must be defined by a *different* mode of production. After all, "the mode of production of material life conditions the general process of social, political, and intellectual life,"[28] and where all of these remain essentially the same, there could hardly have been a radical social revolution. And yet Marx calls this fundamental form of the capitalist mode of production—which conditions all of capitalism, and which must be revolutionized if there is to be a social, political, and intellectual revolution—*cooperation*.

This ought to have shocked Marx's early readers. *Cooperation* was the English equivalent of the French *association*, a term that was truly

---

[25] MacGilvray, *The Invention of Market Freedom*, 179. MacGilvray is not characterizing Marx's conception of freedom with this phrase; I am the one who thinks it appropriate for that task.

[26] I will retain the male pronoun for now. One of the issues with which Marx grapples in part four is the transformation of the gender of the laborer.

[27] *Capital*, 1:431, 454; *MEGA*, II.6:313, 332; *MEGA*, II.7:268, 287.

[28] Marx, *Contribution to the Critique of Political Economy*, *MECW*, 29:263; *MEGA*, II.2:100.

overfull of import,[29] a veritable shibboleth of the workers' movement.[30] It was already in 1827 what it would be for Lenin almost a century later, a synonym or near synonym for socialism itself.[31] In his "Inaugural Address of the International Working Men's Association," Marx had called "the co-operative factories raised by the unassisted efforts of a few bold 'hands'" a great "victory of the political economy of labor over the political economy of property."[32] A decade later, in his criticisms of the Gotha Programme, he would treat as interchangeable "communist society" and "cooperative society based on common ownership of the means of production."[33] Texts like these—and they could be multiplied—have led commentators to argue that "Marx looked upon cooperation as a new production mode superseding capitalism."[34] Certainly many members of his intended audience would have looked upon it in this way. And yet Marx claims precisely the opposite in *Capital*, that cooperation is not a new mode of production superseding capitalism, but the capitalist mode of production itself.

This underscores the difficulty the reader faces in making political theoretical sense of these crucial sections of *Capital*. This problem is more frequently noted in discussions of chapter fifteen, on "Machinery and Large-Scale Industry," where Marx seems to say "that machines are in themselves neutral" between capitalism and communism, and that "technologies and social relations are integral to one another."[35] My suggestion is that the ambiguity of these sections is a function of Marx's thesis, that the capitalist mode of production is a fraud. Fraud is especially fraud if the good and the evil are really both there. The task is to clarify the

[29] Palmer, cited by Vincent, *Proudhon and the Rise of French Republican Socialism*, 128.

[30] The word may have been coined by Robert Owen in 1817 (Vincent, *Proudhon and the Rise of French Republican Socialism*, 275n46). As detailed by Vincent, the centrality of *association* for French socialism may itself have been spurred by the propagation of Owen's ideas in France in the 1820s (even though it was already a keyword for Fourier as early as 1808). The Saint-Simonian organ, *Le Producteur*, for instance, ran two articles by Joseph Rey, in 1826 and 1828, on Owen's notions of cooperative production (ibid., 134–36).

[31] *The Co-Operative Magazine and Monthly Herald*, 2:11 (November 1827), 509n: "The chief question . . . between the modern (or Mill and Malthus) Political Economists, and the Communionists or Socialists, is, whether it is more beneficial that . . . capital should be individual or in common?" Lenin's declaration that "cooperation is socialism" comes in his 1923 text, "On Cooperation"; see Jossa, "Marx, Marxism, and the Cooperative Movement."

[32] Marx, *Political Writings*, 3:79–80.

[33] *Political Writings*, 3:345–46; *MEGA*, I.25:13.

[34] Jossa, "Marx, Marxism and the Cooperative Movement," 4.

[35] Harvey, *A Companion to Marx's Capital*, 218. Cohen attempts to dissolve the ambiguity by saying that sometimes Marx uses *mode of production* in a purely material sense, sometimes in a social sense, and sometimes in a mixed sense (*Karl Marx's Theory of History*, 79–84). This attempt seems to me to fail, in that the interpretation of individual instances is more difficult than Cohen lets on.

ambiguity inherent in this fraud—in this case, the mutual imbrication of material powers and social relations of domination—without dispelling it. In order to do this, it will help to compare Marx's discourse on cooperation and production technology to that of Proudhon, for this will help to pinpoint the specificity of Marx's approach.

Amy Wendling has claimed that "it is Proudhon who supplies the impetus for Marx's turn to the study of machines and, more broadly, to science and technology."[36] Certainly Marx's studies of machinery, technology, and large-scale production—including especially large-scale industrial agriculture—seem to coincide with his critical encounters to Proudhon's works and followers.[37] The persistence of Proudhon shows up in the fact that, aside from part one (which clearly recapitulates Marx's earlier *Zur Kritik*), no part of *Capital* has such an obvious ancestor text as does chapter fifteen, which closely tracks the section of *The Poverty of Philosophy* on "The division of labor and machinery."[38]

The mutual imbrication of Marx's study of production techniques and his argument with Proudhon is not merely critical. In *Qu'est-ce que la propriété?*, Proudhon had noted that the cooperative labor of a large workforce accomplishes what the sum of individuals would not be able to separately, and he notes that wages do not reflect this "collective force [*force collective*]," the "immense force that results from the union and

[36] *Karl Marx on Technology and Alienation*, 66.

[37] Wendling seems to locate this turn in 1846. In particular, she connects it to Marx's study of Charles Babbage's *Economy of Machinery and Manufactures* (1835), which he excerpted first in 1845 and again in 1860 (*Karl Marx on Technology and Alienation*, 182). Marx first mentions Babbage in print in *The Poverty of Philosophy*, so it is unclear whether he was prompted to read Babbage because of Proudhon, or if Proudhon simply gave him the opportunity to use what he had been reading independently. Proudhon's discussions of the division of labor and of machinery in the *Système* provided the occasion for Marx to draw on Babbage, Ure, and Lemontey for the first time. Five years later, having read Proudhon's criticisms of "the principle of association" in the *Idée générale*, Marx prompted Engels for his thoughts on the book: "your *vues* on Proudhon . . . are of particular interest to me since I am now in the throes of working out the Economy. By the way, during my recent visits to the library, which I continue to frequent, I have been delving mainly into technology, the history thereof, and agronomy, so that I can form at least some sort of an opinion of the stuff" (Marx to Engels, October 13, 1851; *MECW*, 38:475–76).

[38] *MECW*, 6:178–90. This is no doubt tied up with Marx's confrontation with Proudhonism in the IWMA during its first five years of existence. This confrontation came to a head at the Brussels Congress in 1868, where machinery, cooperation, and large-scale industry dominated the discussions, and at Basel in 1869, which rejected Proudhonist protests against the resolutions taken at Brussels. For an account of the Brussels Congress, see Braunthal, *History of the International*, 133–36. It was the Belgian César de Paepe who spearheaded the resolutions on common ownership and on cooperative production. Marx was not present. Nonetheless, de Paepe's resolutions signaled the defeat of the more orthodox Proudhonism of the French sections of the IWMA, who were opposed to any "crude communism." On the Basel Congress, see ibid., 136–41.

the harmony of the laborers, from the convergence and the simultaneity of their efforts."[39] The descendant of this claim is Marx's own argument in chapter thirteen of *Capital* that "combined labor" constitutes "the creation of a new productive power, which in and of itself must be a power of the masses [*Massenkraft*]," and which "costs capital nothing."[40] Given these connections, and in order to appreciate Marx's distinctive approach to these matters, it is first necessary to return to Proudhon's writings.

Collective Force

Proudhon was always forthright about what he took to be his own discoveries. Alongside his much more famous discovery of anarchy as the truth of government, he took special pride in being "the first to accentuate the importance" of what he termed *the union of forces*, or *collective force*.[41] He first highlighted this issue in the central section of *Qu'est-ce que la propriété?*, in which he seeks to show that labor, far from being the origin of private property, is antithetical to it. Considering the capitalist's claim to the product of labor above and beyond the amount of wages, Proudhon points out, among other things, that the capitalist "has paid nothing for that immense force that results from the union and the harmony of the laborers, from the convergence and the simultaneity of their efforts. . . . When you have paid all the individual forces, you have not paid the collective force; as a consequence, there always remains a right of collective property, which you have not acquired, and which you enjoy unjustly."[42] In 1851, he would reiterate that "A hundred

---

[39] *What Is Property?*, 93, 91; *OC*, 4:217, 215. In *The Holy Family*, Marx commended Proudhon on this point, claiming that "Proudhon was the *first* to draw attention to the fact that the sum of the wages of the individual labourers, even if each individual labour were fully paid, does not pay for the collective power [*die Kollectivkraft*], which is objectified in their product, that therefore the labourer is not paid as a *part* of the *labour-power of the community* [*der gemeinschaftlichen Arbeitskraft*]" (*MECW*, 4:52; *MEW*, 2:55).

[40] *Capital*, 1:443, 451; *MEGA*, II.6:323, 330; *MEGA*, II.7:279–80, 285. The French text certainly echoes Proudhon in its invocation of "*travail commun . . . une force nouvelle ne fonctionnant que comme force collective.*" By 1867 Marx no longer believed that Proudhon was the first to call attention to this fact; that honor now went to several other writers, including John Bellers, whose *Proposals for Raising a Colledge of Industry* (1696) was an important precursor of the cooperative movement in Britain, and was reprinted by Owen in 1818. The fact that Marx does not cite Proudhon in this context should not be taken as a slight or as a case of plagiarism, as, e.g., in McKay's introduction to Proudhon, *Property Is Theft!*, 66.

[41] *General Idea*, 81; *OC*, 2:161. Proudhon claims to have first encountered the concept of collective force in the work of Germain Garnier (*OC*, 5:300–301). Another influence may have been a Saint-Simonian text from 1840, *Premiere memoir sur la propriété*; see Noland, "History and Humanity: The Proudhonian Vision," 94n38.

[42] *What Is Property?*, 91, 93; *OC*, 4 :215, 217.

men, uniting or combining their efforts, produce, in certain cases, not a hundred times as much, but two hundred times, three hundred times, a thousand times."[43] We might call this the *narrow* meaning of collective force in Proudhon. It is presented by Proudhon as a simple application of physics to the labor process.

However, Proudhon thinks that the concept of collective force extends far beyond this narrow application, to every instance in which the social whole might be said to be greater than the sum of its parts. Far from being a matter of physics, it has a "metaphysical" side, and is, indeed, "essentially immaterial."[44] Collective force emanates from "collectivities that exist wherever and whenever a society takes form."[45] It is significant that Proudhon pairs the discovery of "the law of collective force" with Adam Smith's discovery of "the law of the division of labor."[46] Just as the labor of each individual becomes more effective when the whole task is divided among many, so the labor of the whole becomes capable of new feats just insofar as it is social.[47] As the development of the social division of labor is not a purposeful outcome of the designs of individuals, but an unintended side effect of uncoordinated individual action, so the collective force of the social body is perceived by Proudhon in all of the spontaneous orders—"political, moral, religious, intellectual"—that have "governed civilization" from its rudest beginnings.[48] We can call this the *broad* meaning of collective force.

However, we must appreciate the fact that, for Proudhon, the narrow sense of collective force is but an instance of the broad sense. That is, Proudhon sees something spiritual or metaphysical in the fact that ten people pushing together can move a massive object that no subset of them would be able to budge. Thus, he asserts that the existence of this phenomena and others like it certify "the fundamental dogma of the Christian theory, creation *de nihilo*."[49] Thus, also, he characterizes collective

---

[43] *General Idea*, 81–82; OC, 2:161.

[44] *General Idea*, 82; OC, 2:161–62.

[45] Noland, "History and Humanity: The Proudhonian Vision," 69.

[46] See the discussion in Knowles, *Political Economy from Below*, 124–28.

[47] Proudhon, *Property Is Theft!*, 744; OC, 3:185–86.

[48] Noland, "History and Humanity: The Proudhonian Vision," 69.

[49] When Engels made his critical notes on *Idée générale*, he was confounded by these passages. He wrote: "It is strange that Proudhon, p. 88, calls these relationships essentially non-material forces, and makes this non-materiality the basis for hymns to the effect, for example, that the economists by their theory of industrial forces 'have, without suspecting it, demonstrated the fundamental dogma of Christian theology, creation *de nihilo*,' (ex ??) (p. 87), and earlier [he speaks] of the 'purely moral' act of 'commerce, which is also a creation' (p. 86)" (MECW, 11:555). Marx did not respond to this point in his letters, but, in the second edition of *Capital*, he inserted a footnote in chapter nine: "What Lucretius says is self-evident: *nil posse creari de nihilo*. Out of nothing comes nothing. 'Creation of value'

force as "an impersonal act" rather than "a voluntary engagement."[50] To Proudhon, the increased power of the collective laborer is an emergent property of the gang of laborers, unanalyzable into their individual efforts, an unmistakable sign of the reality of collective beings.

Proudhon thinks that only such "essentially immaterial forces" are economically productive. Any force, "the effect of which is to multiply the power of labor far beyond what it would be, if it had been left entirely to individual liberty," is classed by Proudhon among the economic forces.[51] Thus, commercial exchange, because it is "a direct excitation of consumption," is an economic force, and the honest merchant has a just title to remuneration for his service. The same goes for competition, machinery, credit, and money.[52] Whatever pertains to relations among individuals is, in Proudhon's way of writing, immaterial. Whatever augments those relations, making the *relata* more effective, is itself a force and, by making the collectivity so-related more powerful and more real, issues in a collective force.

Association

Within this schema, Proudhon vacillates over the ontological status of association. In the *Idée générale* he calls it a dogma, "in its nature sterile, even injurious," a mode of government by which both the liberty of the individual and the power of the collectivity is curtailed.[53] In *De la capacité politique des classes ouvrières*, written fourteen years later, he claims that, "by virtue of the confidence and the security it inspires," it is an economic force.[54] Nonetheless, even at his most pessimistic, he

---

is the transposition of labour-power into labour. Labour-power is itself, above all else, the stuff of nature transposed into a human organism" (*Capital*, 1:323n2; *MEGA*, II.6:224n27; *MEGA*, II.7:177n30). It is hard not to see in this Marx's response to Proudhon.

[50] *General Idea*, 82; OC, 2:162, 161.

[51] *Property Is Theft!*, 744; OC, 3:185.

[52] Hence, also, by the converse, labor itself, which creates by "changing the form" of something, is also "immaterial" (*General Idea*, 80–81; OC, 2:160), since, it modifies the relations among individual beings—worker, tools, object—so as to increase their collective ability "to attract and be attracted, to repulse and be repulsed, to move, to act, to think, to produce, at the very least to resist, by [their] inertia, influences from the outside" (*Property Is Theft!*, 654; OC, 8:257). This metaphysics of relations bears comparison to certain Deleuze-inspired currents on the European far left, as for instance in the recent essay by the collective Tiqqun (*Introduction to Civil War*, 16–27).

[53] *General Idea*, 83; OC, 2:162.

[54] *Property Is Theft!*, 745; OC, 3:186. This vacillation is partly due to the shifting lines of polemics among the French socialists during these years. But the ambivalence with which he approached association was also due to the fact that Proudhon's thoughts on labor and cooperation are indelibly marked by his biography. A printer by trade, he thought labor necessarily implied "gravity" and "taciturnity," and that it, therefore, could not be aided

also recognized that, "in the near future," large undertakings (railroads, factories, building projects, and even theaters) would command a larger share of the working population than at present, and that these depend upon "the combined intervention of several industries, professions, different specialties; . . . a combination in which man meshes with man as wheel with wheel; the ensemble of laborers forms a machine." In these cases, association seems to Proudhon to be a matter "of necessity and of right." In this "new land" of large industry, "discovered or created, all of a sudden and out of thin air, by the social genius," workers' associations ought to be established. Proudhon even proposes the rules according to which these ought to operate,[55] rules that Marx copied out in his notes to Engels. Thus, even in the *Idée générale*, where Proudhon expresses greater skepticism about workers' associations than in any of his other texts, he still concludes that they are "indispensable."[56]

However, because *association* was a term so laden with disparate connotations, we must ask which of these connotations ruled Proudhon's mind when he alternately commended and criticized association. Here it is his distinction between natural and artificial communities that becomes crucial. Communities are natural when they proceed spontaneously from the tastes and interests of the members. This naturalness shows itself in the fact that the increased power of the collectivity redounds equally to the benefit of each member. Each member is enlarged and made more capable by his or her membership, and hence there is no need for any special, formalized power that would bind members to the group, or impose terms upon them. This is what Proudhon means by saying that "power is immanent in society." However, as this social power grows in primitive, natural societies, its immanence is not recognized; it is attributed first to

---

by "the cheerfulness of companionship." He went so far as to declare that, "labour is, with love, the most secret, the most sacred function of man; it is strengthened by solitude, it is dissolved by prostitution." Since he generally, and in accordance with his experience of it, held labour to the standard of the solitary workings of the craftsman, it is unsurprising that he saw in it "the negation of fraternity," the principle of association. Furthermore, he could lean on the demographics of France, where, he thought, of thirty-six million people, twenty-four million were employed in agriculture and six million more in craft production, and hence would have no interest in workers' associations (*General Idea*, 87–88, 97–98; OC, 2:165–66, 174–75).

[55]Proudhon, *General Idea*, 98, 219, 221–22; Proudhon, OC, 2:175, 279, 281–82; *MECW*, 38:414–15.

[56]Proudhon to Langlois, December 1851; quoted by Vincent, *Proudhon and the Rise of French Republican Socialism*, 191. Vincent is right to argue that Proudhon was an associative socialist, "contrary to the image presented in much of the secondary literature" (ibid., 127). And Marx seems to find very little in this worth criticizing. His letters to Engels do criticize Proudhon's book, but, despite taking note of everything it says about associations, no strong judgment is forthcoming on this topic.

the gods, then to the chiefs, the fathers of the various family groups. Relations can then be imposed on the unwilling. The whole community grows yet more powerful, but the growth in collective power is not distributed equally. Those with little—the poor, the exploited, the compelled—still feel the social power as their only guarantee; "it is obvious" to them that, "however intense may be the tyranny, . . . it is better for each to remain in the group than to leave it." Nonetheless, the disintegration of the collectivity begins to be a real threat. More and more coercive power seems necessary. But this "artificial constitution of power" is futile; government is, in the long run, impossible, and accomplishes nothing but "disorder."[57]

The lesson Proudhon draws from this growth and alienation of power is not that the natural community is good and the artificial bad, but that the natural community's propensity to expand must be checked by a new artificial principle, one that retains all of the benefits of the natural community of interests. This new principle is what Proudhon calls *reciprocity* or *mutuality*, and it is embodied in the contract of exchange. The natural unity of interests lives on in the family, where Proudhon sees a natural complementarity between male and female, parents and children, and "association for its own sake, as an act of devotion."[58] But this cannot possibly be extended very far without degenerating into the "superstition" that thinks of society as a large family. Instead of being presupposed, the commonality of interest must be found freely by each person in each situation.

For this free discovery of community Proudhon self-consciously appropriates the language of the social contract. The social contract is not, for him, an all-at-once agreement to form a society, much less a contract stipulating the terms under which one agrees to be governed. It is the ever-renewed formation of society out of the oft-repeated "act whereby two or several individuals agree to organize among themselves, for a definite purpose and time, that industrial power we have called exchange, and in consequence have obligated themselves to each other, and reciprocally guaranteed a certain amount of services, products, advantages, duties, etc., which they are in a position to obtain and give to each other; recognizing that they are otherwise completely independent."[59] All such contracts—acts of commutative justice, or of commerce—imply to Proudhon that all parties "abdicate all pretension to govern each other," and that "each citizen pledges to the association his love, his intelligence, his work, his services, his goods, in return for the affection, ideas, labor,

---

[57] This paragraph draws on the second instruction in Proudhon's "Little Political Catechism" (*Property Is Theft!*, 660–66; OC, 8:263–71).

[58] *General Idea*, 87; OC, 2:166.

[59] *General Idea*, 113; OC, 2:188.

products, services and goods of his fellows."[60] For this reason, Proudhon's affirmation of association is explicitly conditional: association, within mutuality.[61]

Hence, the principle according to which such associations might be formed—contracts of mutual benefit or reciprocity—is the principle by which all of society ought to be constructed. Only the family, the sphere proper to authority and religion, is excluded from the scope of mutuality. Every other interaction, whether momentary and isolated or established and ongoing, whether between two people or among ten thousand, ought to take the form of a contract of mutual benefit.[62] And, as Proudhon makes clear many times, every such contract takes place against the backdrop of competition, since you and I can only be of mutual benefit to each other if benefit is ascertainable by comparison with other offers. What matters for Proudhon is that social relations be properly mediated. The only proper mediation—the one that excludes all force, all fraud, and all authority, and therefore preserves the independence of the parties—is the contract.[63]

This result epitomizes what Marx disliked about Proudhon's approach. Surveying modern society, Proudhon sees, on the one hand, that the independent, artisanal labor he valorizes is endangered, and, on the other, that fair exchanges and free contracts seem to preserve the mutual independence of the parties. He therefore believes that independent labor and social mediation by exchange can go hand in hand, and support each other. To Marx, this amounts to making "the illusion of the honest bourgeois the ideal that he seeks to realize." The ideal of free and fair exchanges among independent producers is but "an embellished shadow" of actually existing capitalism, for which the exchange of commodities constitutes the social nexus. Seeking to establish a society on the basis of this shadow means fleshing it out with mutually supporting institutions

---

[60] *General Idea*, 112, 114; *OC*, 2:187, 188. Here one sees the affinity between the path taken by Proudhon and that taken by the inventors of market freedom, for whom consent is "something that is given day to day and moment to moment in the market" (MacGilvray, *The Invention of Market Freedom*, 147).

[61] See Part II, Chapter XIII of *De la capacité politique* (*Property Is Theft!*, 744–53; *OC*, 3:185–97).

[62] Proudhon's caution regarding associations is, at bottom, a skepticism about the general utility of the sort of long-term contracts that would, to his mind, constitute large-scale associations of workers—what we would call today worker-managed firms. Associations are just a special form of society, appropriate for certain purposes and inappropriate for others.

[63] For Proudhon, as Paul Thomas notes, "Free mutual exchange . . . would secure a balance of interests in society so long as neither state nor monopoly interfered. It has been pointed out that many passages in Proudhon's writings are hymns to contract excluding government, that 'not even Sir Henry Maine had a more lyrical conception of contract than did Proudhon'" (*Karl Marx and the Anarchists*, 191; citing Brogan, *Proudhon*, 60).

and practices, and, "in proportion as this shadow becomes substance," Marx thinks, "it is seen that this substance . . . is nothing but the body of existing society." Not to put too fine a point on it, "there is no individual exchange without the antagonism of classes," that is, without the pro-letarianization of the laborers and their subordination to the capitalist within production.[64]

Marx's criticism of Proudhon can be recast in the terms of Dante's image of Geryon. The mutualist is taken in by capital's human face, the free exchange of goods and services, which he assumes to be something apart from the beast with the poisoned tail, the despotism of the factory, wage slavery, and the misery of the masses. Proudhon, according to Marx, has failed to examine or appreciate the inner connections that make the human face the face *of* the beast. Those "inner connections" are inves-tigated by political economy,[65] by the study of which Marx believes he has armed himself to both reveal and confront capital's fraud. However, political economy is taken in by, and even complicit in, the same fraud as Proudhon. While Marx refers at several points in *Capital* to bourgeois economists being confused by or reliant upon the *Schein* on the surface of society, he usually has in mind the vulgar or apologetic economists.[66] There is only one place in the book where he indicts the classical school with contributing to the misapprehension of how capital works. In chap-ter eighteen, Marx claims that "the habit of presenting surplus-value and the value of labor-power as fractions of the total value product dissimu-lates the main matter, the exchange of variable capital for labor-power," thereby giving to the capital relation "the false appearance of a relation of association."[67] It is only by attending to capital's temporal development, tracing its convolutions through time, that the dissimulation inherent in the classical school's presentation can be revealed. Thus, as Marx will in-sist in chapter twenty-three, as soon as capital is viewed in the process of its reproduction—even if this is merely the "repetition" or "continuity" of the production process—it will become apparent why it is "systematically misleading to call the worker-capitalist transaction an 'exchange' at all."[68]

---

[64] Marx, *The Poverty of Philosophy*, MECW, 6:144. These lines are actually directed by Marx at Bray, but Marx makes clear that he is treating Bray as "the key to the past, present, and future works of M. Proudhon" (ibid., 138).

[65] Marx, *Capital*, 1:174n34; MEGA, II.6:111n32; MEGA, II.7:60n31.

[66] For example, *Capital*, 1:176, 177n38, 420, 569, 679; MEGA, II.6:112, 113n36, 306–7, 424, 501; MEGA, II.7:62, 63n35, 260, 380, 464.

[67] *Capital*, 1:670; MEGA, II.6:496; MEGA, II.7:459. The language of this passage is significantly different in the French edition, which I have followed here. The Fowkes trans-lation is extremely loose, and at equal distance from both the German and the French.

[68] *Capital*, 1:712; MEGA, II.6:523; MEGA, II.7:492; Maguire, *Marx's Theory of Poli-tics*, 145.

In order to depict the nature of capital's fraud, therefore, capital must be observed in its historical development.

THE MONSTERS OF FRAUD

Geryon, Dante's personification of fraud, appears by name in *Capital*, in a footnote to chapter twenty-four, "The Transformation of Surplus-Value into Capital." He is one of three monsters named there, alongside Cacus and Antaeus. These three are linked in myth, as well as in the text, by their deaths at the hands of Hercules in the course of his tenth and eleventh labors. Geryon was a three-headed or three-bodied giant, living on the far western island of Erytheia, where he owned a herd of cattle, which were red from the setting sun. Hercules was charged with taking these cattle as his tenth labor, and he slew Geryon in the process. Driving the cattle back to Greece, he had some of them taken from him by Cacus, a fire-breathing monster living in the hills that would eventually be the site of Rome. Cacus dragged the cattle backward into his lair, so as to make it seem that their trail led out from there, rather than in. But Hercules figured out where the cattle had gone, and, tearing off the top of the hill, killed Cacus in his home. While performing his next labor—taking the golden apples from the garden of the Hesperides, in the valley of what is now called the Draa River, in Morocco—Hercules encountered Antaeus, who wrestled and slew every traveler, and who was invincible so long as he remained in contact with his mother, the Earth (Gaia). Learning the secret of his strength, Hercules lifted Antaeus off the ground and crushed him while holding him aloft.[69]

Geryon, Cacus, and Antaeus appear in Marx's text because he quotes from Martin Luther's writings on usury, claiming that these writings capture "the desire to dominate" inherent in the "*auri sacre fames*." For Luther, these three monsters of antiquity are benchmarks for the destruction wrought by usury, which "lays waste to all," even while the usurer "would be thought pious, so that people do not see where the oxen have gone, that he drags backwards into his den."[70] And, although Luther's text brings Cacus to the fore as "the villain that is the pious usurer, and steals, robs, and eats everything," and thus as the archetype of fraud, there is an important precedent for considering these three monsters, as a trio, as *the* monsters of fraud: this is how they appear in the *Inferno*.

---

[69] Further details, including a compendium of the existing textual evidence for each of these myths, can be found on the website Theoi Greek Mythology (http://www.theoi.com/, accessed May 15, 2014).

[70] *Capital*, 1:740n22; *MEGA*, II.6:543n34; *MEGA*, II.7:514n47.

Geryon, as I have mentioned, carries Virgil and Dante from the circle of violence, where they left the usurers, into the circle of fraud. Cacus appears in canto XXV as a raging centaur/dragon hybrid, a thief meting out punishment on thieves. Antaeus, finally, lifts the pilgrim and his guide out of Malebolge in his giant hand and sets them down in Tartarus, the frozen heart of Hell. These are the only three classical monsters to appear in the Malebolge, and it is striking that Geryon and Antaeus, by carrying the heroes into and out of the circle, bookend Dante's treatment of fraud. While the fraud of Cacus is obvious in the tale told of him, this is not so with Geryon and Antaeus. Geryon's association with fraud arises only in Dante and Boccaccio (who claims he was a king of Spain who killed his guests after receiving them with the appearance of friendship). Antaeus was traditionally allegorized as a figure of lust; in order to make him out as a fraud, Dante must rely on the detail that he used a secret trick to defeat his opponents.[71]

Picking up on Luther's reiteration of these monstrous figures of fraud within his "naïve polemic" against usury,[72] Marx bends the allegory to his own ends, associating Geryon, Cacus, and Antaeus with capital as a mode of "direct and indirect domination."[73] I propose to read sections four through seven along these lines, highlighting, according to Marx's presentation, the threefold fraud inherent in the historical development of the capitalist mode of production.

In part four, Marx argues that, while capital's domination of the production process vastly increases the productive powers of labor, unleashes the "capacities of the species," and contains "the germ of the education of the future"—and thereby promises wealth, leisure, and human development—it also, by its very nature, transforms "the entire lifetime of the laborer and his family into disposable labor time," even while it turns labor into a "torture" and productivity into a "misfortune."[74] Then, in parts five and six, he details the "mystery of wages," by which it seems that the laborers get paid for what they do, and paid better the more productive

---

[71] On the allegorical tradition behind Dante's use of the Herculean monsters, see Miller, "Hercules and His Labors as Allegories of Christ and His Victory over Sin in Dante's Inferno." I have drawn on Miller's work liberally throughout this section.

[72] Marx turns to this seemingly unlikely source because "Luther's naïve polemic against interest's ingrown being in capital" is "*superior* to Proudhon" (*MECW*, 32:526, 531; compare *MECW*, 37:391).

[73] In the French edition, he even calls it a form of "*domination personelle*," claiming that, for the capitalist, "to accumulate is to conquer the world of social wealth, to extend his personal domination, to augment the number of his subjects, who are sacrificed to an insatiable ambition" (*MEGA*, II.7:514).

[74] *Capital*, 1:447, 614, 532, 548, 644; *MEGA*, II.6:326, 462–63, 396, 410, 479; *MEGA*, II.7:282, 420, 349, 363, 441.

they are.[75] The wage transaction is the very mechanism that serves capital so well in maintaining the pretense "that what he has taken from others and brought into his den, *emanates from him*, and by causing it to go *backwards* he gives it the semblance of having *come from his den*."[76]

Finally, Marx turns to the process by which the product of wage labor is reconverted into capital, such that capital accumulates. This accumulation of wealth is perhaps the most striking fact about modernity. It is what Douglass North termed the "Second Economic Revolution," the first being the rise of settled agriculture ten thousand years ago.[77] While this transformation is most often portrayed as glorious—the unequalled prosperity of the modern West, generalized luxury and leaps in life expectancy, constant innovation in both production processes and opportunities for consumption—it has also always called forth some horror from observers, and massive protest from those newly caught up in its grasp. For Marx, this tremendous accumulation of wealth draws its power from its roots in the labor market. Because of this, he argues that the accumulation of capital is inseparable from the accumulation of misery in the form of a relative surplus population, those cast out of work by the very dynamism of capital's growth, but still dependent upon wages for their subsistence.

Hence, capital embodies a threefold fraud. It promises an increase in the productivity of labor and a consequent increase in material wealth, which it delivers only via the despotism of the capitalist workshop and factory. It promises that real wages will increase in step with increases in productivity, but neglects to mention that, insofar as this is true at all, it is subordinated to increases in the rate of exploitation. Finally, it promises that generalized abundance will bring in its train generalized equality and cosmopolitan association, while it delivers an accumulation of social misery. The liberal defenders of capitalism are wrong, but so, too, are those, like Proudhon, who think socialism can salvage from the wreckage the ideals of free contracts and exchanges among independent producers.

Geryon: In the Realm of "the Factory Lycurgus"

Near the end of part three, Marx points out that "not every sum of money, or value, can be turned into capital at will." In order to make it worthwhile to exploit labor in the capitalist manner, via the extension of labor time, there must be materials and laborers enough to bear the extra labor necessary to support the capitalist. This requires stores of

---

[75] *Capital*, 1:681; *MEGA*, II.6:503; *MEGA*, II.7:466.
[76] *MECW*, 32:539; *MEGA*, II.3.4:1536.
[77] *Structure and Change in Economic History*, chaps. 12–13.

money to advance on materials and wages. "Hence," Marx concludes, "the possessor of money or commodities turns into a capitalist only where the minimum sum advanced for production greatly exceeds the known medieval maximum," since guild rules limited the number of journeymen employable by any master.[78] This quantitative prerequisite is the jumping-off point for Marx's consideration of the capitalist mode of production as such, for, as he puts it, "capitalist production first begins, in fact, . . . when each individual capital simultaneously employs a larger number of workers, when, thus, the labor-process expands its scope, and yields products on a greater quantitative scale."[79]

Marx initially presents this quantitative expansion in a positive light. The simultaneous employment of a large number of laborers makes production more regular and allows for economies of scale.[80] Most importantly, wherever "many labor according to a plan, next to and with one another," one finds "not only a heightening of the individual productive power, but the creation of a productive power which must be, in and as itself, a power of the masses."[81] Because capitalist production requires the simultaneous employment of a large number of laborers, it requires and brings about this power of the masses, the "collective power" of cooperation. Marx ends his appreciation of the combined working day with what seems to be a throwback to his early Feuerbach-inspired lyric humanism: "In working together with others, according to a plan, the laborer strips off his individual limits and develops his species-capacities [*Gattungsvermögen*]."[82] Besides sounding like his own younger self, Marx seems to be treading on Proudhon's toes. Is this not the collective force Proudhon emphasized?

Perhaps. But Marx differentiates himself from his younger self and from Proudhon by the argument that takes up the rest of part four. What seems at first to be the development of the productive powers of humanity is, in fact, the subjection of the working class to the despotic command of the capitalist, and the development thereby of the means of production into a form of objective domination. "Wage-laborers cannot cooperate without being employed simultaneously by the same capital, the same capitalist, who thus buys simultaneously their labor-powers."[83]

[78] *Capital*, 1:422–23; *MEGA*, II.6:308; *MEGA*, II.7:262.
[79] *Capital*, 1:439; *MEGA*, II.6:319; *MEGA*, II.7:276. This underscores the fact that *Capital* does not present a temporal development of capital; Marx proceeds via the excavation of material conditions for the free development of the previously considered aspect of capital.
[80] *Capital*, 1:440–43; *MEGA*, II.6:320–23; *MEGA*, II.7:276–79.
[81] *Capital*, 1:443; *MEGA*, II.6:323; *MEGA*, II.7:279.
[82] *Capital*, 1:447; *MEGA*, II.6:326; *MEGA*, II.7:282.
[83] *Capital*, 1:447; *MEGA*, II.6:326; *MEGA*, II.7:282.

Hence, it is the concentration of capital that makes the cooperation of labor possible, and it is only through this concentration of capital that cooperation develops. Proudhon had said that "collective force is an impersonal act." Marx responds that it is indeed, in modernity, an impersonal act *from the standpoint of the laborer*, since "the cooperation of wage-laborers is entirely brought about by the capital that employs them. Their unification into a collective productive body . . . lies entirely outside them, in capital, which brings them together and keeps them together."[84] The collective laborer is not a voluntary act of the individual laborers. It is an inevitable concomitant of the impersonal domination of the market, and of the exploitation of labor power this domination motivates. To the laborers, therefore, cooperation signifies "the power of an alien will, which subjects their acts to his end." It appears as the "plan" and the "authority of the capitalist," and is, therefore, "in form, purely despotic."[85]

Marx's inheritance of the Hegelian—and, prior to that, generically republican[86]—conception of "Oriental despotism," which structured his earliest writings on India,[87] shows up in *Capital* only here, as a characteristic of the capitalist's authority within the workshop.[88] Despotism is not simply another word for tyranny or dictatorship. Marx, following Hegel, considered despotism to be a specific form of tyranny in which constant flux in the person of the despot did nothing to disturb the overall structure of society, or in which "an unchanging social infrastructure [is] coupled with unceasing change in the persons and tribes who manage to ascribe to themselves the political superstructure."[89] It might seem strange, therefore, that Marx would use this term to characterize the capitalist workshop, where the infrastructure is being constantly transformed. What the characterization does, however, is call attention to the irrelevance of the person of the capitalist to the structure of power within the workshop. The boss may change; that there is a boss, and that the

---

[84] *Capital*, 1:449–50; *MEGA*, II.6:328; *MEGA*, II.7:284.

[85] *Capital*, 1:450; *MEGA*, II.6:328; *MEGA*, II.7:284.

[86] The history of the term up until the beginning of the nineteenth century is sketched by Venturi, "Oriental Despotism."

[87] Anderson, *Marx at the Margins*, chap. 1.

[88] *Capital*, 1:452; *MEGA*, II.6:330–31; *MEGA*, II.7:286. *Despotism*, in fact, is a keyword for part four; of twelve appearances in the book, half are in chapters thirteen to fifteen (*Capital*, 1:450 [x2], 477, 526, 550n9 [citing Engels], 564 [citing Ure]; *MEGA*, II.6:328, 351, 391, 412n190, 421; *MEGA*, II.7:284 306 344–45 364n198376 ["despotisme" has gone missing in the French translation of Ure]). Three more refer back to these chapters (*Capital*, 1:793, 799, 904; *MEGA*, II.6:583, 588, 667; *MEGA*, II.7:563, 568, 659). Of the remainder, two refer to a form of political government *Capital*, 1:894n33, 919; *MEGA*, II.6:659n220, 677; *MEGA*, II.7:651n38, 671). Finally, one is ironic *Capital*, 1:825; *MEGA*, II.6:611n137; *MEGA*, II.7:592n170.

[89] "Chinese Affairs," *Die Presse*, July 7, 1862; *MECW*, 19:216; *MEW*, 15:514.

boss is beholden to the pursuit of surplus value, does not. Hence, also, the personal characteristics of the capitalist are irrelevant. "The capitalist is not a capitalist because he is a leader [*Leiter*] of industry; rather, he is a commander [*Befehlshaber*] of industry because he is a capitalist."[90] Oriental despotism may always have been a republican projection—the threat of what our republic was in danger of becoming, or the mirror revealing what our monarchy already is—but Marx claims to have found this peculiar "power of Asiatic and Egyptian kings" welling up within modern society, bestowed upon anyone with the money to command labor on a large scale.[91]

This "primordial" form of bourgeois rule, "the command of capital over labor in the workplace,"[92] does not merely collectivize the labor process. It also transforms how things are made by de-composing the handicrafts into a multitude of simple operations, and replacing the agents of those simple operations with machines. Under the rule of capital, the "shuttle [has] dropped from the fingers of the weaver and [fallen] into iron fingers that ply it faster."[93]

If there is one point at which Marx has the reputation of a modernist, not merely ambivalent about capitalism's progressive bona fides, but enthusiastic about them, it is here. However, as Amy Wendling has noted,[94] this enthusiasm does not seem to be much in evidence in *Capital*. In place of the *Grundrisse*'s invocation of the "social individual," who, "as watchman and regulator" of production, appropriates "his own general productive power, his understanding of nature and his mastery over it,"[95] *Capital* claims that "machine labor exhausts the nervous system to the utmost" and "confiscates all free bodily and intellectual activity. Even the lightening of labor becomes one of the means of torture, since the machine does not free the laborer from labor, but frees the labor of content."[96] So far, in fact, from freeing the laborer from labor, the machine "turns into the most infallible means of transforming the entire

[90]*Capital*, 1:450; *MEGA*, II.6:329; *MEGA*, II.7:285.

[91]See also Marx's discussion in chapter fourteen (*Capital*, 1:477–79; *MEGA*, II.6:351–53; *MEGA*, II.7:306–8). Once again, consideration of the "despotism" within the factory leads directly into a discussion of the ancient Indian communities, the structure of which "remains untouched by the storms of the cloudy regions of politics."

[92]Hunt, *The Political Ideas of Marx and Engels*, 2:91–92.

[93]Carlyle, *Critical and Miscellaneous Essays*, 15:474.

[94]*Karl Marx on Technology and Alienation*.

[95]Marx, *Grundrisse*, 705; *MEGA*, II.1.2:580.

[96]*Capital*, 1:548; *MEGA*, II.6:410; *MEGA*, II.7:363. The contrast between the *Grundrisse* and *Capital* ought not be overplayed; there are many passages in the earlier notebooks that are as pessimistic as anything found in the published text. Nonetheless, the contrast has been of historical importance, since it was precisely in the *Grundrisse*'s "fragment on machines" that Antonio Negri and his fellows found the intimations of a theory of the

lifetime of the laborer and his family into labor-time available for the valorization of capital."[97]

Because the despotic command of the capitalist is premised on the capitalist being him- or herself under the sway of market imperatives, the subordination of the production process to the needs of capital recreates the workplace not just as a site of despotic power but as a form of objective domination.[98] In the machine, the fact that "the conditions of labor employ the laborer" acquires "a technical reality you can grasp with your hand."[99] It is the machine that directs production, that paces the work, that imposes mind-numbing tasks on the laborer, that denudes labor of all intellectual content, and that confronts it with an apparatus embodying intellectual powers unfathomable to its operator. Workers' control of the factory alone would not be sufficient to make any of these aspects of the machine go away.[100]

While Marx implies time and again that communist society will preserve—and even expand—the large-scale, scientifically and technically advanced industry developed by capital,[101] he does not provide any clear guidance on the question of what this preservation and expansion might look like. His argument tends in another direction entirely. What interests Marx is the extent to which the capitalist development of machinery motivates, and even compels, the laborers to embrace Marx's own vision of political organization by precluding a return to independent artisanal production. It is not the positive development of the productive powers of labor that undergirds Marx's argument in part four, but the erosion of the productive powers of individuals. To put it bluntly, the Marx of *Capital* is less interested in the novel productive capacity of technically advanced cooperation than in the novel incapacity of individuals and small groups to produce anything independently.

Such an interpretation seems to fly in the face of one of the central tenets of historical materialism: that only the development of the productive powers of labor will make anything like a liberating communism possible, and that only capital's rule develops these productive powers to

---

social factory, in which labor time had ceased to play the role of measure of value, and in which social and "immaterial" labor had displaced manual labor.

[97] *Capital*, 1:532; *MEGA*, II.6:396; *MEGA*, II.7:349.

[98] In the sense that, "as objects," the forces and means of production "are independent of the labourers whom they *dominate*" (*Capital*, 1:1054; "Results"; *MEGA*, II.4.1:121–22).

[99] *Capital*, 1:548; *MEGA*, II.6:410; *MEGA*, II.7:363.

[100] It is one of the many virtues of Harry Braverman's work to have made this argument with great clarity and force; see *Labor and Monopoly Capital: The Degradation of Work in the Twentieth Century*.

[101] For examples, see *Capital*, 1:515n33, 616–18, 621, 635n46; *MEGA*, II.6:382n166a, 464–66, 468–69, 475n322; *MEGA*, II.7:335, 422–24, 426, 437n334.

the extent necessary.[102] This version of historical materialism rests, however, on a narrow and reified notion of what the material conditions of communism might be. There are three chief instances where Marx seems to make this claim about the preconditions of communism in *Capital*.[103] Each must be carefully examined.

> With the material conditions, and the social combination of the production processes, [factory legislation] ripens the contradictions and antagonisms of their capitalist form, thereby simultaneously ripening the rudiments of the formation of a new society and the impulses to overturn the old.[104]

> The capitalist mode of production completes the breaking up of the original family bond between agriculture and manufacture, which embraced the childish, undeveloped shape of both. But at the same time it creates the material presuppositions for a new, higher synthesis, for the union of agriculture and industry on the basis of the shapes worked out by their opposition.[105]

> As a fanatic for the valorization of value, [the capitalist] ruthlessly compels humanity to production for the sake of production, thus to a development of the productive forces and to a creation of the material conditions of production which alone can form the real basis of a higher form of society, the fundamental principle of which is the full and free development of each individual.[106]

In each of these cases, Marx does *not* seem to mean by the material conditions or presuppositions of the new society the technological apparatus of production as such, nor even the forces of production more broadly, which would include the abilities and knowledges embodied in the collective working body. Notice in the third passage, for instance, how Marx sets the material conditions of production next to the productive forces as the two things developed by capitalist production. Notice, also, the context of the first two passages. In the first, while Marx claims that factory legislation gives a "monstrous spur to technique," this is not introduced by Marx as an independent consideration but is tied immediately to the consequent magnification of "the anarchy and catastrophes of capitalist production, the intensity of labor, and the competition of machinery with

---

[102]The most careful and sophisticated defender of the claim that capitalism's mission is to produce the technological presuppositions of socialism is, of course, G. A. Cohen, *Karl Marx's Theory of History*; see especially 193–207.

[103]There is also a fourth, critically important instance (*Capital*, 1:927–30; *MEGA*, II.6:681–83; *MEGA*, II.7:677–79). I will discuss it in the next chapter.

[104]*Capital*, 1:635; *MEGA*, II.6:475; *MEGA*, II.7:437.

[105]*Capital*, 1:637; *MEGA*, II.6:476; *MEGA*, II.7:438.

[106]*Capital*, 1:739; *MEGA*, II.6:543; *MEGA*, II.7:514.

the laborer."[107] In the second, the only material condition of a new synthesis of agriculture and industry indicated by Marx is the urbanization of the population, which both concentrates "the historical motive power of society" and "kills the metabolism between humans and the earth."[108]

In none of these places does Marx point to the power humanity has acquired through capitalism in a positive manner. Nowhere in *Capital* does he argue or imply that capitalism has developed human productive powers to the point where we can meet everyone's needs, or that such a development would constitute a threshold before which the attainment of communism would be impossible. Instead, the power developed by capitalism is the power to destroy workers' lives, to expose large swaths of humanity to immiseration and sudden desolation, and to undermine the earth's capacity to sustain us all. The development of this power of destruction is, nonetheless, the development of the material conditions of communism, for the simple reason that capitalism gives to the laboring class a powerful motive to cooperate in the construction of a new society. It does so, on the one hand, by destroying the laborers' capacity for going it alone, and, on the other, by creating disasters so immense in scale that only massive collective efforts could possibly address them.[109]

While the current confrontation with anthropogenic climate change makes the latter sort of motive most salient to the twenty-first-century reader, it is the first sort of motive that would have had the greater punch in the context of Marx's day. Both worker separatism and the yeoman republican ideal of independent peasants and artisans were powerful ideological currents within the workers' movement, and Proudhon represented these elements powerfully. The insufficiency of this ideal of independence, according to Marx, is shown by its failure to appreciate capital's power to bring workers into cooperation where workers would themselves have no independent motive to cooperate. Journeymen, owning their own tools, and used to working in a master's shop with one or two of their fellows, have no interest on earth in cooperation. Proudhon appreciates this. But capital overcomes this lack of motive and produces

---

[107] *Capital*, 1:635; *MEGA*, II.6:475; *MEGA*, II.7:436–37.

[108] *Capital*, 1:637; *MEGA*, II.6:476; *MEGA*, II.7:438.

[109] This underscores the importance of reading *Capital* as Marx's public declaration of his views. We know from his earlier, unpublished texts—especially the "German Ideology" manuscripts and the *Grundrisse*—that Marx had, at times, a proclivity for certain techno-utopian lines of thought, which would see in the industrial capacity for producing absolute abundance the precondition of escaping capitalism. And yet Marx does not make anything like those arguments in *Capital*. The discipline imposed by writing for public consumption, and for the sake of influencing the workers' movement, compelled him to make deliberate choices about what to include and what to exclude. Those choices are instructive regarding both his considered views and his sense of the discourse into which he was intervening.

cooperation anyway. One can't build up cooperative labor piece by piece, adding skilled artisans one at a time. It is capital that strips off the limits of the laborer's individuality, making a mass worker out of an artisan, against the artisan's expectations or designs.

The result—"the command of capital over labor"—is something Proudhon hated as much as Marx did. But Proudhon did not, in Marx's opinion, grapple with the fact that, through the development of cooperation, "the command of capital develops into a requirement for carrying on the labor process itself, into an actual condition of production."[110] The larger scale at which production is carried out has revealed a new, collective power. Artisans and peasants, owning their own tools and materials, are barred from access to this power, but they have to confront in the market the products of this collective power. They have to compete with this power. Proudhon's principles seem to require him to accept the outcome of this competition.

Marx thinks the outcome of this competition is the capture of an ever greater share of production by the despotic command economies of capitalist firms. The independent producer loses out to the power of the masses. Moreover, this seems to be a one-way road: the development and growth of cooperation, via the division of labor within the workshop and the mechanization of production, render the individual ever less capable of regaining the independence lost. If the only two possibilities for the mediation of association are competitive exchange on the market and the authority of the capitalist, it seems that most people will end up foot soldiers in one industrial army or another, appendages of the workshop and the machine. This outcome of the development of large industry makes direct, cooperative association attractive in a way it never could be to peasants and skilled artisans. Thus, while Marx thinks that the capitalist mode of production—the form that cooperation, the division of labor, and machinery take under the command of capital—is a thoroughgoing fraud, which will never deliver on the promise of less and more attractive labor, he also thinks that the tortures inflicted by that mode of production upon the laboring class has made some form of large-scale, cooperative, and mechanically transformed labor inescapable. Ironically, the cooperation imposed despotically by capital compels laborers to search for a new form of cooperation.

Cacus: The Wage Fraud

In stark contrast to the extensive and intensive scope of part four, parts five and six are quite brief, and seem, at first glance, to add little to what has come before. Part five underscores what Marx takes to be the three

---

[110] *Capital*, 1:448; *MEGA*, II.6:327; *MEGA*, II.7:283.

political lessons of parts three and four. First, the development of the capitalist mode of production—cooperative, large scale, mechanized—does not do away with, but rather magnifies the capitalist's need and power to extend the working day, imposing overwork on the laborers. That is, capitalist domination in the workplace intensifies capitalist exploitation. Second, the shortening of the working day is not generally detrimental to the capitalist class, even if it is always a gain for the workers, while a prolongation of the working day (or its intensification) is almost always bad for the workers. Therefore, Marx's argument implies that the workers' movement ought to focus its agitation on this question of the length of the working day. The struggle to work less will spur capitalist development and win free time for the workers.[111] Third, a proper conceptualization of capitalist exploitation is critical for revealing the domination inherent in the relationship between labor and capital. While it is natural enough to see capital and labor (and land) sharing in the total product according to some proportion more or less properly arrived at, Marx is insistent that labor has no share in the product, as usually understood, that the exchange of wages for labor power entails this exclusion of the worker from the product, and that the appearance that there is some "relationship of association" between the capitalist and the laborers is only a "*falsche Shein*."[112]

Part six, picking up at this last point, examines the mechanism by which the surplus labor of the proletariat disappears into the perception that, in a market society, everyone's reward is commensurate with their contribution, that the wages of labor are the market equivalent of the service performed, or, in the language of the day, that wages express the value of labor. This perception was crucial to the liberal defense of capitalism, since that defense rested upon the conviction that gains in the productivity of labor would bring with them increases in real wages.[113]

---

[111]That these first two lessons seem to push in opposite directions reveals something of Marx's political strategy. If the development of large industry increases the power of the capitalist to impose overwork, then directing working-class struggle toward the aim of reducing working time might seem to undercut itself. Capital, faced with the necessity of a shorter working day, will redouble efforts to improve productivity, which will, as those gains in productivity are generalized, give new impulse to the attempt to lengthen the working day, taking the struggle back to square one. But Marx seems to think this fight does not go around in a circle so much as it ratchets up the pressure on capital. If, at each round of the fight, workers will be fighting for a shorter working day, which Marx thinks will speed the concentration of capital, then the fight will, by this logic, become sharper, with more and more workers fighting fewer and fewer capitalists.

[112]Marx, *Capital*, 1:670; *MEGA*, II.6:496; *MEGA*, II.7:459.

[113]In chapter twenty-two, Marx singles of Henry Charles Carey as the mouthpiece of this doctrine that "wages everywhere rise and fall in proportion to the productivity of labour" (*Capital*, 1:705; *MEGA*, II.6:520; *MEGA*, II.7:486).

The bargain offered the worker by political economy was: make yourself useful and you, too, will find your reward.

A congruent if apparently very different argument found voice within the IWMA, and more broadly in the workers' movement, in the form of skepticism about the utility of workers uniting to try to raise their wages.[114] In the midst of composing *Capital*, Marx undertook to debate John Weston, a carpenter and member of the General Council, on the question of what ought to be the IWMA's attitude toward workers' strikes for higher wages. Weston argued that such strikes were pointless, since any rise in wages would induce the capitalists to raise also the prices of their wares, so that the increase of wages would dissipate itself in the increased prices workers encountered when they went shopping. Otherwise, any local rise in wages would be offset by wage cuts imposed on other sections of the working class. Ferdinand Lassalle preached a similar notion to German workers in the guise of "the iron law of wages." Although Proudhon did not oppose combinations and strikes on this basis, such arguments also offered a "practical" buttress to Proudhonist "moral" arguments against strike activity. Marx was motivated to attack these doctrines, both for the sake of cementing an alliance with the British trade unionists in the IWMA, and because he believed that proletarian self-emancipation depended upon and grew out of local struggles to reform and ameliorate workers' conditions.[115]

Marx is concerned in part six to deny what he takes to be the presupposition of the liberal consolation that wages will follow productivity and the socialist serenity prayer that there is no point in fighting for higher wages, that only a complete transformation of the system will be any change at all. That wages will rise with productivity, thinks Marx, amounts to the claim that "the price of labor" is "regulated . . . by the quantity and supposed value of the work," while fatalism about wage struggles rests on the claim that the price of labor is, instead, regulated by "the price of the necessaries and conveniences of life" that wages must purchase.[116] Both of these claims presuppose that wages are the value of labor, and that this value is regulated by either the value of labor's product

---

[114]This is the pessimistic flip side of the liberal providentialism above. It was expressed also by political economists in the form of the doctrine of the "wage fund," or "labor fund," which will be Marx's target in part seven.

[115]A summation of the history behind Marx's debate with Weston, and the fate of Marx's essay, can be found in Lapides, *Marx's Wage Theory in Historical Perspective*, 168–73.

[116]Both of these claims about regulation come, of course, from chapter VIII of Smith, *The Wealth of Nations* (83, 95). Proudhon had endorsed the former (normatively), claiming that "labour is said to have value not as a commodity itself, but in view of the values which it is supposed potentially to contain" (*System*, 1:101; *OC*, 1:113).

or the value of labor's requirements.[117] That is, the value of labor is regulated by another value, "'value is determined by value,' and this tautology means that, in fact, we know nothing at all about value."[118] As he tells his audience in the IWMA, "All of you feel sure that what they daily sell is their Labor; that, therefore, Labor has a Price, and that . . . there must certainly exist such a thing as the Value of Labor. However, there exists no such thing as the Value of Labor."[119]

What the worker sells is not his or her labor, but him- or her*self*. The capitalist uses the worker for a time, and then pays his or her wages. The wages seem to be payment for what the worker has done, for the time and effort he or she has given over to the capitalist, or for the service performed. In fact, argues Marx, wages are merely what is required to bring the worker back to square one, ready and able to sell him- or herself again. They make recompense for what the worker has lost in being worked; they do not in any way represent the value of what the capitalist has gained from the working. Hence, the form of the contract for exchange spontaneously and very effectively hides the capitalist exploitation of labor power, or the fact that the worker does not stop working when he or she has produced the equivalent of his or her wages, but keeps on working, to the exclusive benefit of the capitalist. Thus, for Marx, the form of the wage contract is, as Richard Hunt has noted, the "disguise" worn by the slavery of the laborers in capitalism.[120] The forceful extraction of surplus labor is hidden by the wage, and this passing off of force as freedom is the essence of fraud.[121]

---

[117] Weston had explicitly affirmed the notion that wages regulate the prices of necessaries, and that, hence, a rise in wages will raise the cost of necessaries, canceling out the wage increase. Marx responded: "First he told us that wages regulate the price of commodities and that consequently when wages rise prices must rise. Then he turned round to show us that a rise of wages will be no good because the prices of commodities had risen, and because wages were indeed measured by the prices of the commodities upon which they are spent. Thus we begin by saying that the value of labour determines the value of commodities, and we wind up by saying that the value of commodities determines the value of labour" (*Value, Price, and Profit, MECW*, 20:119–20).

[118] Ibid., 20:120.

[119] Ibid., 20:127–28.

[120] Hunt, *The Political Ideas of Marx and Engels*, 2:94.

[121] This structural fraud is independent of—even as it encourages—the individual frauds committed by individual capitalists on particular groups of laborers. The fact that the capitalist is dominated by the pursuit of surplus value encourages the "petty pilferings of minutes" and "nibbling and cribbling at meal-times," to which Marx calls attention in chapter ten; likewise, piece wages offer individual capitalists endless opportunities to commit "frauds" upon their workers (*Capital*, 1:352, 694). Nonetheless, the prohibition and punishment of these individual frauds presuppose the structural fraud—the wage relation as such—of which they are the predictable consequences.

This "mystery of wages," because it makes the actual relation invisible, and indeed "presents to the eye the precise opposite of this relation," is the source of "all of the juridical notions of the laborers as well as the capitalists, all of the mystifications of capitalist production, all its liberal illusions, all of the apologetic evasions of vulgar economics."[122] Wages, because they seem to pay for labor, seem to originate in capital, a portion of which must be set aside to support the laborers. Hence the providential doctrine according to which only the progressive accumulation of capital can make possible an ever-mounting demand for labor and the high wages consequent to this demand. Hence, also, the fatalistic doctrine that the fund out of which wages are paid is inelastic. If wages are instead the price of labor power, as Marx maintains, then it is easier to argue that the workers produce their own wages before they produce the surplus product that is the material basis of all profits, interest, and rent. Rather than capital paying for labor, labor produces capital. What seems to emerge from capital's pocket—the wages of labor—was first extracted by capital from the laborers.

Antaeus: The Accumulation of Misery

Part seven, on the capitalist process of accumulation, is, as he says plainly in letters, Marx's response to Malthus. Malthus was one of the great polarizing figures of the nineteenth century. His *Essay on the Principle of Population* (1798) had outraged both sentimental defenders of the old system of patriarchal poor relief and populist radicals. It had also put great strain on the liberal optimism of certain Whigs. In place of the natural harmony of interests, Malthus had insisted on a natural conflict between the interests of the propertied—especially the owners of land—and the interests of the poor and propertyless, who might find no place at nature's feast.[123] Indeed, if there is anything at all to the "Ricardian socialism" label, which has been subjected to so much criticism,[124] it is

---

[122] *Capital*, 1:680; *MEGA*, II.6:502; *MEGA*, II.7:466.

[123] The passage on nature's feast is found only in the second edition of 1803; it excited the greatest denunciations of Malthus, and it is unsurprising that the author withdrew it again from later editions.

[124] The name originates in H. S. Foxwell's long introduction to Anton Menger's work, and in his belief that the ideas of these British writers, while "ignored by the leaders of English thought, . . . remained germinating in the minds of Marx and Engels; destined . . . to develope into that social democracy which is to-day the religion of large masses of the continental working class" (Foxwell's "Introduction," Menger, *The Right to the Whole Produce of Labour*, lxixx). Foxwell's student, Esther Lowenthal, published the first study of this supposed "English school" of socialism (*The Ricardian Socialists* [1911]). Both the grouping and the label stuck (see Claeys, *Machinery, Money, and the Millennium*, xxii–xxvi).

not any positive influence of Ricardian value theory[125] but the fact that in the popular politics of the period, Ricardo was the dean of liberal political economy *and* the embracer of Malthusian pessimism.[126] In his 1815 "Essay on the influence of a low price of corn on the profits of stock, etc.," he had incorporated Malthus's naturalistic justification of differential rents into his theory of profit and wages. Ricardo also advocated the abolition of the Poor Laws, on the authority of Malthus's arguments.[127] The picture Ricardo painted was one in which the wages of labor could never exceed, on average and at best, the cost of subsistence; the profits on capital would tend to decline as population increased; and the rent on landed property would ever enrich the proprietors at the expense of the workers and capitalists.

This picture, more than the labor theory of value, was critical for the development of popular political economy. It was not a picture painted only by Ricardo; its likeness was conjured by the economic downturns and bread riots after the Napoleonic Wars, by the debates over the Poor Laws and the Corn Laws, and by any number of tracts and penny papers. Many cooperativists and radicals—joined by more than a few Whigs and Tories—accepted that this picture truly depicted aspects of the present reality in Britain, but they denied that there was anything necessary or eternal about this situation.[128] The harmony of interests might be reestablished somehow. What united the socialist tendency of response was the conviction that a harmony of interests among the working classes might become a harmony of interests uniting the whole social body, provided that landed property and capital were, in some manner, reformed.

But, of course, the manner of this reform was itself the subject of much disputation. While everyone in the popular camp agreed that the rent

---

[125] Contra Marx himself (e.g., *The Poverty of Philosophy*, MECW, 6:138). See Claeys, *Machinery, Money, and the Millennium*, chap. 1; as well as the sources cited by Hollander, "The Post-Ricardian Dissension," 373n9.

[126] At least, this is how he was widely perceived. Samuel Hollander, most prominently, has argued that this was a misreading of Ricardo ("The Post-Ricardian Dissension"). (Of course, Hollander thinks that pretty much everyone has misread Ricardo.)

[127] On Ricardo's political interventions, see Milgate and Stimson, *Ricardian Politics*. On the old Poor Laws, see the classic revisionism of Blaug, "The Myth of the Old Poor Law and the Making of the New," and the (limited) pushback from Taylor, "The Mythology of the Old Poor Law," and McCloskey, "New Perspectives on the Old Poor Law." The political aspect of the Poor Laws debates is ably outlined by Harrison, *Robert Owen and the Owenites in Britain and America*, 11–25.

[128] As Milgate and Stimson note, "class conflict was integral to the Ricardian model of the economy, and . . . this was being deployed by the likes of Hodgskin to mandate a thoroughgoing restructuring of society" (*Ricardian Politics*, 9–10). Again, cf. Hollander "The Post-Ricardian Dissension."

was too damn high, and that the ones who made the stuff of wealth were unable to enjoy the wealth they created, it was unclear how things might be made better, or even different. The workers' movements that formed the beginnings of socialism divided along two axes when it came to the matter of how wealth might be produced so as to address the social question and the plight of the poor producer. In the first instance, early socialists and working-class radicals divided over the new techniques of manufacture and mechanical production. Machinery and manufacture undermined the standing of "manual industry," and thereby destroyed the basis of the independence and virtue of the artisan and peasant.[129] But they also promised to destroy the Malthusian counsel of misery for the poor by multiplying the productive power of the population. This cleavage was crosscut with another, over the value of isolated versus communal production. Some viewed the community of labor as the guarantee of justice and solidarity among workers, while others saw in it a sop for the lazy and a fetter upon freedom.

One gauge of Robert Owen's importance for the history of British socialism is that he seems to have settled both of these disputes. Overcoming his early horror at the effects of manufacturing and machine production, he embraced the industrial revolution as marking "a boundary never before reached in the history of man," the point at which humanity "passed the region of poverty arising from necessity, and entered into those of permanent abundance."[130] He was also, from his first forays into proposals for poor relief, a steadfast advocate of common property and cooperative production. In his conjoining of cooperative communism with industrial technology, Owen seems to be the decisive beginning point of the transformation of workers' radicalism in Britain away from agrarian primitivism and toward the socialism "of Marx and most varieties of twentieth-century Marxism insofar as 'modernization' and 'development' have been among their central goals."[131]

The story told by Marx himself in part seven is importantly different, however. Marx affirms the general impression of many socialists that Malthus's population doctrine had been taken over by the mainstream of political economy; he says of the "absurd" doctrine that "the movement of capital depended simply on the movement of the population" that it is "the dogma of the economists."[132] However, he drives a wedge between

---

[129] Claeys, *Machinery, Money, and the Millennium*, 28–30.

[130] *New Harmony Gazette* 3:9 (December 5, 1827), 65; cited by Claeys (*Machinery, Money, and the Millennium*, 53), whose discussion of this history has been my primary authority throughout this section.

[131] Claeys, *Machinery, Money, and the Millennium*, 50.

[132] *Capital*, 1:790; *MEGA*, II.6:581; *MEGA*, II.7:560.

Malthusian fatalism, on the one hand, and a different sort of pessimism, which he associates with Ricardo (and John Barton, Ricardo's source in this matter),[133] and which he wants to affirm for himself. According to this view, "the demand for labor depends on the increase of circulating and not of fixed capital,"[134] and fixed capital has a historical tendency to grow out of all proportion with circulating capital; hence, capital accumulates faster than the demand for labor. The growth of wealth does not automatically imply the improvement of the workers' lot.[135]

Moreover, as we have seen, there were important voices in the socialist camp who, however much horror they experienced at Malthus's image of nature's feast, still counseled workers to restrain their efforts to increase wages and consumption (Lassalle), or to police their own propagation through birth control (numerous British Owenites) or voluntary celibacy (Proudhon). In part seven, Marx sets himself against all those—economists and socialists alike—who worry about wages being insufficient to meet the physical needs of the laboring class, however numerous it may become. If wages are insufficient for this, then the obvious solution is for laborers to organize themselves to demand and enforce the value of their labor power.[136]

Marx's worry, instead, is about the insufficiency of wages to meet the *social* needs of the laboring class. It is the relative wage, the portion of social wealth that wages command, that draws his attention. And he credits Ricardo with making this focus on relative or social wealth possible, claiming that until Ricardo defined wages as a portion of the total value product of society, "wages had always been regarded as something simple and consequently the worker was considered an animal." In Ricardo's formulation, however, the worker "is considered in his social relationships." The conclusion, crucial for Marx's account of accumulation, is that "the position of the classes to one another depends more

---

[133] Marx augmented his discussion of Barton in the French edition (*Capital*, 1:783–84n13; *MEGA*, II.7:554–55). On the controversy resulting from Barton's argument and Ricardo's acceptance thereof, see Berg, *The Machinery Question*, chaps. 4–5.

[134] Barton, cited by Marx, *Capital*, 1:783–84n13; *MEGA*, II.6:575n79; *MEGA*, II.7:554–55; see also Berg, *The Machinery Question*, 105.

[135] Note that Malthus was far more *optimistic* than Barton and Ricardo about the effects of mechanization. He denied the possibility of technological unemployment (see Berg, *The Machinery Question*, 107–8).

[136] As he put it in his debate with Weston, the failure to organize for such demands would leave the proletariat "degraded to one level mass of broken wretches past salvation," since "the necessity of debating their price with the capitalist is inherent to their condition of having to sell themselves as commodities. By cowardly giving way in their everyday conflict with capital, they would certainly disqualify themselves for the initiating of any larger movement" (*Value, Price, and Profit, MECW*, 20:148).

on relative wages than on the absolute amount of wages."[137] Although he had clearly proclaimed in 1848 that the modern laborer "sinks ever deeper beneath the circumstances of his own class," Marx's position in *Capital* is that, "in proportion as capital accumulates, the situation of the worker, *be his payment high or low*, must grow worse."[138] It is the comparison between wealth and poverty that makes poverty into human misery; "if the extremes of poverty have not lessened, they have increased, because the extremes of wealth have."[139] We are social animals, and it is our sociality, and hence our humanity, that is put out of view when an increase in real wages is conflated with an improvement in the well-being of the working class.

Capital's promise of general human wealth is false, then, not because our capacity to feel need always outruns our wealth. This diagnosis would amount to Proudhon's fear that human nature is, "like the Hercules of old," "beset" by an "animality," by "infernal legions" of passions that "seems ever ready to devour" it.[140] That fear presents a dilemma: either one embraces untrammeled economic growth, racing with the wind, as it were, or one mortifies the flesh. Rather, the promise is false because the form of that wealth, capital, requires for its reproduction and accumulation a disposable human material in perpetual excess of its demand for labor power, a surplus population that must remain dependent upon capital and hence responsive to its beck and call during periods of

---

[137] *MECW*, 32:54; *MEGA*, II.3.3:1042. Immediately prior to his consideration of accumulation, Marx makes this thesis the centerpiece of his chapter on "National Differences in Wages." Marx argues here that high wages in developed nations are often *cheaper* for capital than are the low wages of less developed areas. This is because the rate of exploitation is so much higher where labor productivity and intensity have been ramped up by industrialization. The argument of this chapter is hard to grasp in the present, since the outsourcing of jobs to areas of the Global South with lower labor costs features so prominently in recent indictments of capitalism.

[138] *Manifesto*, *Political Writings*, 1:78; *MEW*, 4:473; *Capital*, 1:799; my emphasis; *MEGA*, II.6:588; *MEGA*, II.7:568. Heinrich claims, on this basis, that "what Marx criticizes is not a specific distribution of goods or income, but the 'miserable' working and living conditions [of the proletariat], in a comprehensive sense" (*Introduction to the Three Volumes of Karl Marx's* Capital, 129). This is, it seems to me, too simplistic. It would be more accurate to say that Marx criticizes *both* a distribution of wealth and the miserable working and living conditions that accompany and reproduce that distribution. Vast inequality of wealth is, according to Marx, one of the essential conditions of capitalist production, and is constantly reproduced by capitalist production. It is not the absolute quantity of wealth possessed by those at the bottom, but this necessity of a large relative disparity that he attacks in part seven. Lapides covers the historical debate over absolute and relative immiseration (*Marx's Wage Theory in Historical Perspective*, chap. 12).

[139] *Capital*, 1:806; *MEGA*, II.6:593; *MEGA*, II.7:574.

[140] *System*, 1:434; *OC*, 1:371.

expansion.[141] Marx argues that so long as the laboring class produces the means of its life in the form of capital, capital will in turn produce a reserve army of de-mobbed and precarious laborers, necessary for the functioning of the labor market, "whose misery stands in inverse relation to its torment of labor."[142]

We saw in the previous chapter that Proudhon had followed the Saint-Simonians in locating the exploitation of the workers in landed property, claiming that "the land," gives authority, the power to exploit, "an ever renewed force whenever the popular Hercules has overthrown the giant."[143] The giant in question, of course, is Antaeus. Proudhon's proposal, then, is that the popular Hercules must, like the mythical one, prevent the giant from touching the earth, and thereby slay it. Marx, on the contrary, argues that the ground supporting and empowering the modern Antaeus is the labor market. It is the capitalist producer "who extracts unpaid labor directly from the workers and fixes it in commodities," and who is, therefore, both "the first appropriator" of surplus value, and "the representative of all those who will share the booty with him."[144] The technologically dynamic production process dominated by this capitalist producer becomes more and more capital intensive and more and more productive, and this fact, "that the means of production and the productivity of labor increase more rapidly than the productive population expresses itself, . . . under capitalism, by the reversal, that the

---

[141] Mike Davis's *Planet of Slums* attempts to follow up on Marx's discussion of the relative surplus population; or, at least, it is read as such by, e.g., Aaron Benanav, "The Brutal Facts: Too Few Jobs for Too Many People." As well, Selma James has argued that, if "the Third World is the most massive repository of this industrial reserve army," then "the second most massive is the kitchen in the metropolis" (*Sex, Race, and Class*, 99). It is worth noting, however, that, regardless of what has happened in the intervening century and a half, Marx was primarily indicating by "the industrial reserve army" those who have already been drawn into capitalist production in one form or another, not those who have yet to be employed by capital. This is not to say that there is an incompatibility between Marx's concepts and their utilization by Davis, James, and others, but only a divergence of focus. The analyses of Davis and James are open to a misunderstanding, however, to which Marx offers a corrective. The reserves of surplus labor in the Third World and in the metropolitan kitchens are not survivals of precapitalist modes of production, awaiting absorption by capital. Rather, they are the product of the capitalist mode of production itself. Even if some new industrial revolution were to absorb those populations, the tendency of that new industrial revolution would be, via the rising organic composition of capital, to throw off an even greater mass of workers. My thanks to Alex Gourevitch for pressing me on this point, and to Ken Kawashima, who has stressed the centrality of the relative surplus population to Marx's conception of the working class.

[142] *Capital*, 1:798; *MEGA*, II.6:587; *MEGA*, II.7:567.

[143] *General Idea*, 195; *OC*, 2:258.

[144] *Capital*, 1:709–10; *MEGA*, II.6:522; *MEGA*, II.7:487–88.

population of laborers instead increases more rapidly than capital's need for valorization."[145]

We have seen how Marx argues that the capitalist mode of production betrays its promise of wealth and leisure by its subordination of the worker to an organization of work that cannot but be despotic. But this was not the only promise made on behalf of capitalism. Outside the factory, the rise of capitalism was supposed—including, at times, by Marx himself—to break down the particularities that divide the proletariat from itself, to strip them of every national, racial, and gendered characteristic, leaving the merely human. The picture painted by *Capital*, however is, if not exactly bleaker—after all, the reduction to mere humanity was also supposed by the Marx of the *Manifesto* to be the absolute immiseration of that humanity—at least more variegated and equivocal. If "the first result of the capitalist application of machinery" is to introduce women and children into the labor market, and if "the fact that the collective working group is composed of individuals of both sexes and all ages must under the appropriate conditions turn into a source of humane development," the transformation of everyone into employable labor power is also the differential pricing of those labor powers, and the use of the cheaper labor powers to "break the resistance" of the dearer ones.[146] "A new and international division of labor springs up" in the place of the de-composed local division of labor, and with this new division of labor comes new divisions of interest.[147]

Rather than simply producing a "contemporary, and final, realization of universality,"[148] the transformation of production creates a process of *universal differentiation*. Women are no longer confined to domestic production, but they become the means by which wages are driven down. Hence, "paradoxically, industrialization does not eliminate characteristics of embodiment classified by the age as 'natural,' . . . Instead, it

---

[145] *Capital*, 1:798; *MEGA*, II.6:587; *MEGA*, II.7:567. As others have noted, Marx clarifies this argument in the French edition (Endnotes and Benanav, "Misery and Debt"). There he claims that "the higher the organic composition of capital, the more rapidly must accumulation proceed to maintain employment, 'but this more rapid progress itself becomes the source of new technical changes which further reduce the relative demand for labour.' This is more than just a feature of specific highly concentrated industries. As accumulation proceeds, a growing 'superabundance' of goods lowers the rate of profit and heightens competition across lines, compelling all capitalists to 'economise on labour.' Productivity gains are thus 'concentrated under this great pressure; they are incorporated in technical changes which revolutionise the composition of capital in all branches surrounding the great spheres of production'" (quotations of Marx are from *MEGA*, II.7:552–54).

[146] *Capital*, 1:517, 621, 526; *MEGA*, II.6:384, 468, 391; *MEGA*, II.7:337, 426, 344–45.

[147] *Capital*, 1:579–80; *MEGA*, II.6:434–35; *MEGA*, II.7:390.

[148] Avineri, *The Social and Political Thought of Karl Marx*, 59.

enhances their importance."[149] Something similar can be said about racial and national differences. Especially with regard to the Irish Question, Marx became increasingly attuned during the 1860s to "the interplay between capitalist class interests and the use of anti-Irish racism to divide the working class."[150]

For Marx, these twin effects—objective domination in the factory, universal differentiation in the labor market—are consequent on the forms of social mediation proper to capitalism. It is because "the intermediary between the independent labors in society is the purchase and sale of their products, while the connection between the various partial operations in a workshop is mediated through the sale of the labor powers of several workers to one capitalist, who applies it as collective labor power," that the humanization promised by capitalist development turns out to be such a fraud.[151] The exchange of commodities stands between producers. The capitalist stands between the workers. Hence, what appears to be universal association, in the one case, and direct cooperation, in the other, turn out to be the opposite of what the socialist would hope for.

Conclusion

Marx's extensive investigation of the capitalist mode of production and accumulation (parts four through seven) comprises a rewriting of Dante's passage through the Malebolge, and the ambiguities and ambivalences of Marx's treatment are indicative of his conviction that capitalism is guilty of fraud. The development of the collective forces of production does not redound to the laborers' benefit, but functions as a means of subjecting them to despotic command within the factory. This also renders the direct producers ever more dependent upon capital, destroying as it does their independent capacity to make goods. This is partly a matter of the de-skilling of labor, partly a matter of the greater efficiency of industrial processes, requiring massive outlays of capital, and partly a matter of the wage form itself, since workers can only eat by first producing capital, and then buying food from capital. Moreover, the form of wages makes the laborers' slavery seem like freedom, and their exploitation disappear

---

[149] Wendling, *Karl Marx on Technology and Alienation*, 168.

[150] Bakan, "Marxism and Antiracism: Rethinking the Politics of Difference," 249. On Marx's approach to Ireland, see Anderson, *Marx at the Margins*, chap. 4. The recent essay by Rodden is marred by his unsupported (and incorrect) conviction that Marx viewed nationalism generally "as a reactionary force and a major obstacle to socialist revolution," and that, therefore, his approach to Ireland was a major anomaly ("'The Lever Must Be Applied in Ireland': Marx, Engels, and the Irish Question," 611).

[151] *Capital*, 1:475–76; *MEGA*, II.6:350–51; *MEGA*, II.7:304.

behind the apparent benevolence of the "job creators" who advance the capital to employ them. Finally, the accumulation of wealth in this form requires and fuels the production of a massive dependent population, in excess of the demand for labor power. This relative surplus population is the field of social impoverishment that expands in time with the fortification of social wealth as capital.[152]

The inescapable reference in all of this to a dynamic unfolding in time highlights the difficulty of discussing these parts of Marx's book, aside from their sheer bulk. Parts one through three are concerned with getting the critical theory of capitalism right. They take up the task of challenging political economy on the terrain of its ideality, and they take other socialists to task for failing to appreciate its ideal of competitive markets and fair exchanges. There are dynamics at work in these parts of Marx's work, but they are recurrent or cyclical dynamics. Commodities are bought and sold. Money is lent and repaid. Labor power is purchased and used, expended and reproduced. The same things happen again and again, so the task is to get these discrete cycles right, to identify and elaborate their inner mechanisms and to explain their social consequences. Beginning with part four, however, Marx opens the question of capitalism's historical trajectory, its tendencies and development. This is where things get messy.

In the face of this difficulty, I have emphasized what I take to be underappreciated aspects of Marx's account of capitalism's historical trajectory. Instead of reiterating the old story about how capitalism develops the productive powers to the point where conflict over scarce material wealth is passé, I have drawn attention to the absence of this story in *Capital*, and to Marx's indications that the most important material condition of communism is the subjectively felt need for a new form of cooperative production. This—a rational motive to cooperate—is what (as Proudhon noted) peasants and artisans lack, and what (as Proudhon missed) capitalist industrialization is producing. Beyond the factory gates, the accumulation of capital leads, in Marx's story, not so much to the absolute impoverishment of a humanity stripped bare—proletarians with nothing left to lose but their chains—as to a world in which the specters of un- and underemployment, precariousness, and obsolescence, divide the proletariat against itself in innumerable ways, and in which social impoverishment—being cut off from social wealth—is the rule.

Near the crescendo of his account of this social impoverishment, Marx refers to the "consolidated surplus population" as the "Lazarus-layers of the laboring class."[153] The reference has attracted some attention, but

---

[152] Hence, "to be wageless is not necessarily to be outside of the capitalist wage relation" (James, *Sex, Race, and Class*, 104–5).

[153] *Capital*, 1:798; MEGA, II.6:587; MEGA, II.7:567.

little analysis. This is a shame, since I think it contains one of Marx's most important prognoses of capitalist development.

The parable of Lazarus and the rich man was a natural touchstone for socialists and populists in the nineteenth century. The tale is told (Luke 16):

> [19] There was a rich man who was dressed in purple and fine linen and who feasted sumptuously every day. [20] And at his gate lay a poor man named Lazarus, covered with sores, [21] who longed to satisfy his hunger with what fell from the rich man's table; even the dogs came and licked his sores. [22] The poor man died and was carried away by angels to Abraham's bosom. The rich man also died and was buried. [23] In Hades, where he was being tormented, he looked up and saw Abraham far away with Lazarus by his side. [24] He called out, "Father Abraham, have mercy on me, and send Lazarus to dip the tip of his finger in water and cool my tongue; for I am in agony in these flames." [25] But Abraham said, "Child, remember that during your lifetime you received your good things, and Lazarus in like manner evil things; but now he is comforted here and you are in agony. [26] Besides all this, between you and us a great chasm has been fixed, so that those who might want to pass from here to you cannot do so, and no one can cross from there to us." [27] He said, "Then, father, I beg you to send him [Lazarus] to my father's house— [28] for I have five brothers—that he may warn them, so that they will not also come to this place of torment." [29] Abraham replied, "They have Moses and the prophets; let them listen to them." [30] He said, "No, father Abraham; but if someone goes to them from the dead, they will repent." [31] He said to him, "If they do not listen to Moses and the prophets, neither will they be convinced even if someone rises from the dead."

In 1851, a French anarchist and socialist by the name of Joseph Dejacques was banished from Bonapartist France for publishing a book of poems, *Les Lazaréennes: Fables et poésies sociales*. The untitled prelude to Dejacques's book set the parable from Luke in a Malthusian context:

> Lazarus is the poor, anonymous existence,
> The sufferer who knocks at the threshold of opulence,
> The famished who demands a place at the feast
> Where the rich sit, selfish and haughty.
> Lazarus is the specter waving its shroud,
>   The great disinherited
> Who rises from the depths of his cold misery
>   And cries: Equality![154]

There is no indication that Marx knew of Dejacques, but he was well acquainted with another commentary that mobilized the parable to attack

---

[154] *Les Lazaréennes: Fables et Poésies Sociales*, 5.

a contemporary form of wealth, Luther's *Sermon auf das Evangelion von dem reichen Mann und armen Lazaro* (1523). Marx was certainly thinking of the gospel when he composed part seven, which contains not only the reference to the Lazarus layers but also the claim that accumulation is "Moses and the prophets" as far as the capitalist is concerned.[155]

Hewing to the gospel more closely than did Dejacques, Marx does not focus on the demand Lazarus makes on the rich man, but vice versa. It is capital that asks the Lazarus layer to quench its thirst for accumulation, and to rise from the dead to save it in its hour of need. Capital is dead labor, but so, too, in a different sense, are the unemployed. Capital can only animate itself in times of growth by calling back to living labor those labor powers that it had earlier dismissed, either because of a crisis, or because wages had risen to the point where technical innovation and layoffs were called for. Marx takes Abraham's lines, reminding capital that, if his past accumulation (his Moses and the prophets) is not sufficient, then neither will raising up Lazarus from the dead be any good. Like Master Adam—the counterfeiter in the tenth pouch of the Malebolge, Dante's iteration of the rich man in Hell—the capitalists, in their agonies, "crave a drop of water" (1.30:63). But nothing can slake their thirst for surplus labor, for capital is its own Hell. This damnation of capital, not the salvation of the world, is certain.

---

[155] *Capital*, 1:742; *MEGA*, II.6:545; *MEGA*, II.7:517. This passage in Luke is the only biblical source for that particular phrase. Marx's citation also comes only a couple pages after he had quoted from Luther's invocation of Geryon, Cacus, and Antaeus. In the draft manuscript of *Theories of Surplus Value*, Marx's discussions of and excerpts from these two texts by Luther are back to back (*MECW*, 32:532–40).

CHAPTER 6

Cocytus: Treachery and the Necessity of Expropriation

Now Cain, which means "possession," is the founder of the earthly city, and his son, in whose name that city was founded, is called Enoch, which means "dedication." This indicates that this city has its beginning and end on earth, where there is no hope for anything beyond what can be seen in this world.

—Augustine of Hippo, *The City of God*, XV.17 (426)

Cain, the proprietor, according to *Genesis*, conquered the earth with his *lance*, surrounded it with *stakes*, made it onto property, and killed *Abel*—the *poor*, the *proletarian*—son like him of *Adam*—the *man*—but of an inferior caste, of a servile condition. These etymologies are informative: they say more in their naiveté than all the commentaries.

—Proudhon, *System of Economic Contradictions*, II.XI.iv (1846)

. . . the path to hell is easy:
black Dis's door is open night and day:
but to retrace your steps, and go out to the air above,
that is work, that is the task.

—Virgil, *Aeneid* VI

Controversy about Marx's arguments in the first twenty-five chapters of *Capital* centers on the most abstract and theoretical parts of the text. The value theory in chapter one has given rise to an immense literature, while the accounts of exchange and money in chapters two and three are largely ignored. In chapters four through nine, the technical details of surplus-value production and the exploitation of labor are minutely dissected, and the general theory of the labor process is an object of perennial interest. Meanwhile, the history of struggles over the length of the working day, in chapter ten, is acknowledged but not much analyzed or argued over. Parts four through seven are rarely commented upon at all, and are certainly not hotbeds of controversy. Part eight, however, disrupts this pattern in an important way.

The concluding eight chapters of *Capital*,[1] on "primitive accumulation,"[2] have bequeathed to us a field of historiography that is, every now and again, the site of great tournaments and battles between opposed factions, where political lines and philosophies of history seem to fall back for tactical support each upon the other. These debates—on the transition from feudalism to capitalism,[3] on the very notion of a transition,[4] on the possibility or impossibility of identifying an origin (for capitalism or

[1] There is a fairly widespread and persistent confusion about this chapter breakdown, confusion sown by the fact that all German editions of *Capital* retain the twenty-five-chapter structure of the second edition, while the English translations have followed the French edition in dividing the book into thirty-three chapters. Because Marx wrote *Capital* in German, an incorrect assumption has taken hold that the twenty-five-chapter plan is Marx's, while the thirty-three-chapter plan is due to Engels's editorial hand after Marx's death. Thus, for example, Geert Reuten claims that Engels "broke up the German Part Seven into two parts: Part Seven encompassing the systematic chapters . . . and Part Eight the historical chapters" ("The Inner Mechanism of the Accumulation of Capital," 275; compare Rodriguez-Braun, "Capital's Last Chapter," 307n1). Even where the origin of the thirty-three-chapter plan is properly identified, it may still be suggested that, "to make Part Eight, Engels, following Marx's *suggestions*, broke up the single chapter into several chapters" (Taylor and Bellofiore, "Marx's 'Capital' I, the Constitution of Capital: General Introduction," 15n20; my emphasis). One source for this myth of Engels's redivision of the book must be the translator's note—itself inexplicable—on page 110 of the Penguin edition. Claims such as these are made in support of the thesis that Marx's project in *Capital* is fundamentally incomplete, and that its apparent completion is a retrospective imposition, first by Engels, and then by the exponents of so-called traditional Marxism. However, that volume one of *Capital* was a finished literary product of Marx's hand in no way impeaches the view that the Marxist theory of capitalism requires ongoing reconstruction and amendment. These are simply two different issues.

[2] It has become somewhat customary to point out that "primitive" is a questionable translation of Marx's *Ursprünglich*, and that "original accumulation" would be a more appropriate rendering (e.g., Perelman, *Invention of Capitalism*, 2, 24). This overlooks the fact that "primitive accumulation" is both a perfectly admissible translation of Marx's German and finds its warrant in the French edition's *l'accumulation primitive*.

[3] There have been three major debates on the transition from feudalism to capitalism. First, there was the debate over the question of "feudal remnants" within the Third International in the 1920s. This was followed by the Sweezy-Dobb debate, which, in the late 1940s and early 1950s, recapitulated in a more academic scene much of the earlier debate (collected in Hilton, *Transition from Feudalism*). Finally, the Brenner debate of the 1970s and '80s restaged the controversy in the context of political questions of "Third-Worldism" and "the development of underdevelopment" (collected in Aston, *The Brenner Debate*; Brenner summarizes his position in "The Social Basis of Economic Development"; other important contributions include Wallerstein, *The Capitalist World-Economy*, chaps. 1, 8; Anderson, *Passages from Antiquity to Feudalism*; Anderson, *Lineages of the Absolutist State*). The first debate is discussed by Gavin Walker, *The Sublime Perversion of Capital*, chap. 2. The latter two debates are ably summarized by Holton (*The Transition from Feudalism to Capitalism*, chap. 3).

[4] The signal text here is Étienne Balibar's contribution to *Reading* Capital (Althusser et al., *Lire "Le Capital*," 520–68).

for anything else)[5]—have left indelible marks on the intellectual history of the twentieth century. However, they have done little to clarify what Marx was up to in the chapters that have inspired them.

In particular, they have sidestepped almost completely the problem posed by what Fredric Jameson has called the two climaxes of *Capital*.[6] What Jameson christens the *heroic climax* is the (in)famous conclusion of the penultimate chapter thirty-two, where, by "the negation of the negation," "the expropriators are expropriated."[7] By contrast, there is also, according to Jameson, a *comic or idyllic climax*, in the final chapter thirty-three. Here, instead of an epic confrontation and expropriation, the workers simply escape from capitalism, sloughing off its definitive social relations of production on the frontier of settler colonies, where cheap or free land allows them to work for themselves rather than for the would-be capitalists who provided for their transportation.[8]

That these two endings of *Capital* are also identified by Jameson with two potential ends of capitalism is both unsurprising and the heart of the problem. The conflicts fought out on the terrain of historiography and periodization are actually political conflicts. What is at stake in the discussion of the transition to capitalism are political strategies for effecting the transition out of capitalism. But, because they appeal either to the facts or to the logic of history, they simultaneously disavow their own political content and obscure the political content of Marx's text. Rather than reading "the chapters on 'primitive accumulation' in *Capital*" as setting out "Marx's theory of history,"[9] therefore, I read them as Marx's attempt to conclude his argument against Proudhonism and similar forms of moralism within socialism. This returns these chapters to the political ground from which they arose.

Read as an intervention into the socialist politics of Marx's day, part eight has a twofold purpose. First, it is supposed to warrant Marx's conviction that there is a sharp break between the feudal world and the capitalist world. Despite the appearance that Marx is here giving back to socialism the account of plunder that he had taken away from it in his explanation of capitalist exploitation, the tale of plunder told by part eight is quite different from the tale told by the Saint-Simonians, Owenites, and

---

[5] Almost the entirety of French "poststructuralism" might be included here, and Althusser's influence is decisive. On Althusser's relationship with Derrida, see Smith "Jacques Derrida, 'Crypto-Communist?'" On his influence more generally, see Montag, *Althusser and His Contemporaries: Philosophy's Perpetual War.*

[6] *Representing "Capital,"* 88–91.

[7] *Capital,* 1:929; *MEGA,* II.6:683; *MEGA,* II.7:679.

[8] *Capital,* 1:932–33; *MEGA,* II.6:685; *MEGA,* II.7:681. The language of two climaxes is Jameson's own, but the sense that *Capital* ends twice is fairly widespread.

[9] Uchida, "Marx's Theory of History Reappraised," 39.

Proudhonians. As Marx says, "it is far too easy to be 'liberal' at the expense of the Middle Ages."[10] Feudal property relations were relations of double-sided obligation, of service and paternalism. But, in England, the Wars of the Roses demolished the cultural bulwarks of feudal paternalism, and the lords and kings of England and Scotland set about betraying their obligations by appropriating the land for themselves. The material conditions of capitalism—accumulated private property in the means of production on one side, a mass of people with no direct access to means of subsistence on the other—were first created by the betrayal of the old order by those at its head. The dynamics of that old order gave them the power and the motive to do so. It is in this sense that feudalism gave rise to the material conditions of capitalism.[11]

Second, Marx's account of the creation of the preconditions of capitalism is supposed to foreclose the working-class separatism of the cooperative and mutualist movements, a separatism that imagines that workers can build a new world with their own hands by running away from capital, by setting up their own colonies and workshops, or by homesteading

---

[10]Marx, *Capital*, 1:878n3; *MEGA*, II.6:647n192. In the French edition, this note was elevated to the main text; *MEGA*, II.7:635.

[11]My reading of *Capital*, both here and in the previous chapter, diverges sharply from G. A. Cohen's. According to Cohen's construal of historical materialism, the underlying trajectory of human history is the expansion of the natural power of humanity. That is, despite all local and temporary setbacks, there is a tendency for the forces of production to *develop*. Historical materialism is *scientific* because it maintains that the historical development of the productive forces explains the form taken by the dominant relations of production, that is, by the economic structure of society. Economic structures that allow or encourage the development of natural power win out over those economic structures that hamper this development. In other words, social or economic power is *functional* for natural power, and takes the form that is compatible with the current level of development of the latter. Except, that is, when it is not and does not. For it is also true that, as Cohen puts it, "production relations are capable of fettering, that is, restricting the use and development of the productive forces" (*Karl Marx's Theory of History*, 41). During any period of time when fettering is occurring, "dysfunctional relations persist" (ibid., 161). Cohen generally ignores this dysfunctional state of affairs (but see his "Forces and Relations of Production," 16–17). It seems, however, to pose a significant difficulty for his construal of historical materialism, since, during periods of fettering, the relations of production are *not* explained by their functionality for the forces of production on hand, since they are dysfunctional given those forces. Hence, during periods of fettering, the perseverance of the economic structure, if it is to be explained at all, must be explained by something other than the material powers, as these are defined by Cohen. Once you admit that fettering occurs, you must also admit that while fettering is occurring—and hence during revolutionary periods—the status of the class struggle is irreducible to the level of development of the forces of production, and so other forces, other powers, must enter into the explanation. Marx's account in *Capital* does not encounter this impasse because he is, in practice, much less abstemious regarding which forces and motives can play an explanatory role.

in the colonies of the mother country.[12] Built into this desire for separation is a faith in the powers of relatively small-scale production to secure self-subsistence and independence for workers, and a concomitant faith that virtue, conviction, and hard work are sufficient to establish the colonies, associations, and communities out of which the new world will grow. In the final three chapters of *Capital*, Marx tries to undermine this faith and this imagination by arguing that the growth of the capitalist mode of production generates incentives for expansive state action that no small-scale or decentralized escape plan can overcome. The pursuit of economic growth—of national wealth in the novel sense articulated by classical political economy—comes, through the processes of primitive accumulation, to dominate "the concentrated and organized force [*Gewalt*] of society," the state.[13] Because the state comes to have a fundamental interest in economic growth, it will predictably, Marx argues, act so as to outflank or overrun any flight from capital on the part of the working class. The internal dynamics of the capitalist wage-labor system may be sufficient to secure the reproduction of the dependency of laborers on capital, but these economic forces also produce, by their very nature, a political supplement, the willingness of the state to intervene on the side of accumulated wealth wherever, as in the colonies, workers gain access, *en masse*, to a route of exodus from wage labor. Capital has usurped the state.

This second point is crucial for understanding the division between Marx's communism and the varieties of socialism he opposed. The republican heritage expressed itself within socialism in the widespread longing to reestablish conditions of independence for the workers. This desire for independence expressed itself in different forms. For populist radicals like Thomas Hodgskin, it meant that each family ought to be able to produce by itself the goods that would sustain it, either directly or by commanding a fair exchange from other families. For Owenites like William Thompson, it meant that workers had to combine in large numbers, forming autarchic and self-sustaining cooperative communities. For mutualists like Proudhon, it meant that each worker ought to be absolutely free to join or leave any association with other workers, and that each ought to be guaranteed the credit necessary to undertake any freely chosen endeavor. For social radicals like Bronterre O'Brien, it meant the nationalization of land and credit, with something like a basic income guarantee and the right of anyone to "cultivate land on his own account."[14] As varied

---

[12]I take the concept of "working class separatism" from Paul Thomas, who has very clearly indicated its roots and rationale in Proudhon's thought, as well as its intimate relationship to Proudhon's moralism (*Karl Marx and the Anarchists*, 179–84).

[13]Marx, *Capital*, 1:915; *MEGA*, II.6:674; *MEGA*, II.7:668.

[14]*Human Slavery*, 102.

as these schemes are, they all spring from the intention to reform society so as to universalize the independence that alone protects against slavery and domination, but which has hitherto been the exclusive province of the propertied. Hence, also, they all rest on the assumption that the problem to be overcome is not the form of property as such, but "the principle of its accumulation,"[15] the unjust manner in which it has been acquired. That is, the independence of the individual or the cooperative community requires that capital be restored to its real source, to the labor that has created it, and this restoration can only proceed from labor itself.

To Marx, the assumptions underlying this conjunction of republicanism and working-class separatism are profoundly confused. Marx proposed, instead, *a republic without independence*. The development and advance of the capitalist regime, he argues, eradicates every condition of independence. It makes each laborer dependent upon untold others. It destroys the skills necessary for independent production and propagates a taste for the good things that can come only from cooperative labor on a massive scale. It also empowers a form of social organization—the state—that can, and is interested to, act intentionally to thwart independence. In these conditions, Marx denies that workers can recover—individually or cooperatively—the independence of the yeomanry, the bulwark of the old-style republic. Instead, any future freedom will have to be the fruit of mutual dependency. Moreover, capital is nothing but the usurpation of labor. The working class can no more create its own capital than "the capitalist class of a given country, taken as a whole" can "defraud itself."[16] The desire that labor, and labor alone—"self-exertion, Social Co-operation and saving," in the indicative litany of the cooperator William King[17]—might be the source of capital is merely the repetition of the political economists' "nursery tale" of primitive accumulation.[18] By seeking a new beginning, the separatists replicate the founding gesture of capital, the fantasy that there is some part of the world that can be appropriated ex novo, without expropriating another. Their fantasy of independence is wholly internal to the Hell they seek to escape.

A positive articulation of Marx's republicanism without independence—his communism—will have to wait until the concluding chapter. This chapter is concerned to establish part eight's contribution to Marx's political theory of capitalism. It will do so by first reconstructing Marx's account of the origins of the modern proletariat and of the capitalist class, thereby

---

[15] Robert Owen, as quoted by Claeys, *Citizens and Saints*, 191.

[16] Marx, *Capital*, 1:266; *MEGA*, II.6:180; *MEGA*, II.7:132.

[17] From the *Christian Socialist* 2, no. 50 (October 11, 1851): 226–27; quoted by Claeys, *Citizens and Saints*, 263.

[18] Marx, *Capital*, 1:874; *MEGA*, II.6:644; *MEGA*, II.7:632.

harmonizing Marx's story about primitive accumulation with his understanding of capitalist exploitation. It will next turn to Marx's argument
against separatism and petty production. As in the previous chapter, the
material powers of the capitalist mode of production will show themselves
to be at least as passional and motivational as they are "technical." What
matters for Marx is that, just as the mass of workers are losing the ability
and desire to produce goods in an isolated or artisanal fashion, so financial,
military, and administrative institutions have been born possessing the ability and the desire to forcibly destroy independent production wherever it
continues in existence or springs up. Finally, in the light of these arguments,
this chapter will reconsider the place of chapter thirty-three in *Capital*. This
has been controversial, with numerous scholars arguing that the chapter
is out of place, in one way or another, as a conclusion to the work. I will
argue, however, that Marx's conclusion is appropriate in a very precise
manner, in that it reveals the real way out of the "vicious circle" of the
movement of capital.[19] The working class cannot exit capitalism via the
mirage of separation, but only through a confrontation with the necessity
of expropriation.

Primitive Accumulation as a Problem

Although part eight is supposed to examine the origin of capital, the
same can be said of each of the major sections of *Capital*. In the opening
chapters, "the circulation of commodities" is shown to be "the starting-
point of capital," and "all new capital enters the scene . . . in the form
of money."[20] In part three, Marx argues that, in order that money might
be transformed into capital, labor power must be exploited in the production process. This exploitation of labor power is hence the origin
of capital considered as surplus value. But, then, as parts four through
seven demonstrate, "capitalist production only really begins" where the
capitalist simultaneously commands a large number of laborers.[21] Hence,
capital's origins are traced and retraced in each of the major sections of
Marx's work. Nor is it enough to say that the origin revealed in the tale of
primitive accumulation is the *historical* origin; Marx says the same about
monetary wealth, exploitable labor power, and large-scale production.[22]
To be precise, then, Marx's account of primitive accumulation must be
read as a story about how these various "origins" of capital came into

---

[19] *Capital*, 1:873; *MEGA*, II.6:644; *MEGA*, II.7:631.
[20] *Capital*, 1:247; *MEGA*, II.6:165; *MEGA*, II.7:117.
[21] *Capital*, 1:439; *MEGA*, II.6:319; *MEGA*, II.7:276.
[22] *Capital*, 1:247, 273, 439; *MEGA*, II.6:165, 184, 319; *MEGA*, II.7:117, 136–37, 276.

being, as the "prehistory of capital." That is, it is meant to answer the question: What processes created hoards of monetary wealth and a broad market for the circulation of commodities, coincident with a large pool of available wage labor and the possibility of employing it in large-scale production? Only where all of these exist together can capital get off the ground as a mode of producing wealth.

Although the capitalist regime itself, according to Marx, normally produces all of these conditions, responsibility for the original instauration of these conditions cannot go to capital.[23] There are only two ways out of the "vicious circle." One can argue that the conditions of capital originate in the labor and thrift of the capitalist—which slowly build up a stock of tradable goods—combined with the preference for present enjoyment found in everyone else.[24] Or else one can argue, as Marx does, that "the knights of industry" benefited from conditions created by others, "exploiting events not of their own making,"[25] acts of spoliation, fraud, pillage, and usurpation. Taking this second path poses a problem, however, since it seems to throw Marx back upon the Saint-Simonian account of exploitation that he had repudiated in part three of *Capital*. In this section, I argue that this appearance is misleading, that Marx is actually here underscoring his disagreement with the Saint-Simonian narrative, but that this issue is, nonetheless, the key to appreciating how Marx presents primitive accumulation in *Capital*.

Saint-Simonian Recidivism?

If one is attentive to Marx's borrowings of language from earlier socialist schools, it cannot but strike one that Saint-Simonian language crops up at

---

[23] Very much to the contrary of those like Harry Cleaver, who claims that part eight "shows us how capital originally imposed the commodity-form of the class relation" (*Reading "Capital" Politically*, 85). Similarly, Antonio Negri claims that "in the period of primitive accumulation, . . . capital enveloped and constricted pre-existing labour forms" ("Twenty Theses on Marx: Interpretation of the Class Situation Today," 165). It is one thing to treat capital as an agent, another thing entirely to make it capable of self-creation. David Harvey, too, claims that part eight details "the historical origins of capitalism as *it* freed up labor-power as a commodity and displaced an earlier mode of production" (*A Companion to Marx's Capital*, 291; my emphasis). This way of talking, though it has precedent in Marx's manuscripts and notebooks, leads to utter confusion.

[24] The updated version of this origin story is the thought experiment about voluntary capitalist relations found in nearly every consideration of exploitation from an analytical point of view. Marx's note that "labour, before the existence of capital, can only realize itself in forms such as craft labour, petty agriculture, etc., in short, all forms which can*not stockpile*, or only sparingly," applies only to independent labor (*Grundrisse*, 506n; *MEGA*, II.1.2:409n). This is also the only form conceived by these thought experiments.

[25] *Capital*, 1:875; *MEGA*, II.6:645; *MEGA*, II.7:633.

precisely this juncture. Marx says of the rise of the "industrial capitalists, these new potentates," that it

> presents itself as the result of a victorious struggle both against seignio-rial power, with its revolting prerogatives, and against the regime of the guilds, with the fetters it placed on the free development of production and the free exploitation of man by man. But the knights of industry only supplanted the knights of the sword by exploiting events not of their own making. They have succeeded by means as vile as those that served the Roman freedman to become the master of his *patronus*.[26]

Alongside the contrast between the new industrials and the old "knights of the sword," a staple of Saint-Simonian history, this is the only place in *Capital* where Marx uses the phrase, "the exploitation of man by man." That he makes these borrowings at just the point where he begins to discuss the origins of modern private property in the forcible seizure of common lands and the violent expropriation of both the small propri-etors of Britain and the native peoples of Africa and the Americas might seem to undo the contrast between his own account of capitalist exploita-tion and the account of exploitation Proudhon took over from the Saint-Simonians. On that account, remember, the power to exploit the laborer is rooted in the monopoly of landed property, which was historically the fruit of conquest. The proprietor, enjoying the ill-gotten gains of a violent history, extorts a portion of the product from the poor laborer. By tracing the primitive accumulation of capital back to acts of forceful and fraudulent expropriation, Marx seems to be erasing his divergence from that account, thereby undermining his own argument that capitalist exploitation is not reducible to extortion or theft.

Indeed, this seems to be the lesson drawn, however reluctantly, by much of the reception of part eight. Michael Perelman, in his study of the history of primitive accumulation in the writings of the political economists, claims that, while "Marx's depiction of primitive accumula-tion conveyed an overriding sense of the unfairness of that altogether brutal experience," nonetheless, "this portrayal stood in contradiction to the main thrust of *Capital*. After all, Marx's primary message was that the seemingly fair and objective rule of capital necessarily leads to exploitation."[27] Since "Marx did not want his readers to conclude that the ills of society resulted from unjust actions that were unrelated to the essence of a market society," Perelman argues, Marx "denigrated" his

---

[26] *Capital*, 1:875; *MEGA*, II.6:645; *MEGA*, II.7:633.
[27] *Invention of Capitalism*, 29–30.

own treatment of primitive accumulation and downplayed "the continuing influence" of violent expropriation.[28]

This is also the conclusion reached by Silvia Federici, who takes Marx
to task both for trying to redeem the violence of primitive accumulation
by means of the communist future it eventually makes possible, and for
downplaying the ongoing cycles of primitive accumulation that, she argues, accompany capitalism at every step of its development. She writes:

> Though Marx was acutely aware of the murderous character of capitalist
> development . . . there can be no doubt that he viewed it as a necessary step
> in the process of human liberation. . . . He also assumed that the violence
> that had presided over the earliest phases of capitalist expansion would
> recede with the maturing of capitalist relations, when the exploitation and
> disciplining of labor would be accomplished mostly through the workings
> of economic laws. . . . In this, he was deeply mistaken.[29]

Jason Read is less categorical, but is clearly exercised by the same concerns. "Marx," he claims, "is somewhat ambiguous with respect to the
closure of primitive accumulation and its relation to the mode of production it engenders. At times, Marx appears to argue that primitive accumulation and the overt violence it involves disappear in the day-to-day
relations of exploitation; while at other times it appears that the violent
lawmaking power of primitive accumulation is merely privatized and
brought indoors in the factory."[30] For all of these readers, Marx's account
of primitive accumulation—according to which capital comes into the
world "sweating blood and mud from every pore"[31]—is so compelling
that the blood and mud gum up the supposedly clean workings of Marx's
account of exploitation.[32] Primitive accumulation cannot be hived off

[28] Ibid., 27, 30. Perelman's account has been repeated by David Harvey, who claims
that part eight "goes against the central presumption of the rest of" *Capital*, the immanent
criticism of political economy (*A Companion to Marx's Capital*, 289; Perelman is cited on
p. 293).

[29] Federici, *Caliban and the Witch*, 12.

[30] *Micro-Politics of Capital*, 28–29.

[31] Adopting the French text (*Capital*, 1:926; *MEGA*, II.6:680; *MEGA*, II.7:677).

[32] A similar intuition, but from the other side of the political/theoretical coin, is evinced
by the efforts of proponents of value-form theory to dismiss part eight as a purely historical
digression from the systematic presentation of capital that ends in chapter twenty-five (e.g.,
Arthur, "Capital in General and Marx's 'Capital'"; Arthur, *The New Dialectic and Marx's
Capital*, 75; Arthur and White, "Debate: Chris Arthur and James White on History, Logic,
and Expanded Reproduction in Capital," 130; Heinrich, *Introduction to the Three Volumes
of Karl Marx's Capital*, 32; Murray, "Reply to Geert Reuten," 161; Shortall, *The Incomplete Marx*, 178, 296; Smith, *The Logic of Marx's Capital*, 133–35). For these writers,
Marx's internal critical development of the logic of capital must be saved in its theoretical
purity from the confusion wrought by historical intrusions.

from the daily operations of capitalist accumulation, which in fact only perpetuate primitive accumulation.

But this has the effect of undermining Marx's theorization of the specificity of capitalist exploitation and accumulation. This can be seen very clearly in Federici's work, where Marx's periodization is thrown overboard in favor of a litany of resistance that encompasses everything from "the search by the medieval proletariat for a concrete alternative to feudal relations and its resistance to the growing money-economy" to Nigerian opposition to World Bank mandated structural adjustments.[33] Such a story of continuity between feudalism and capitalism is exactly what one would expect from a Proudhonist or Saint-Simonian account. Three options confront us, then. Either my reconstruction of Marx's exploitation theory is wrong, and he is more Saint-Simonian than I have allowed; or Marx contradicts himself, falling into a Saint-Simonian position at the end of *Capital* despite himself; or, finally, the Saint-Simonian reading of primitive accumulation is missing something. I will argue for the third option. Rather than relapsing into Saint-Simonianism, Marx's account of primitive accumulation underscores his criticisms of that school of history and is really directed at British working-class radicals, steeped in another tradition of historiography altogether. However, as we will see, this does not dissolve the tensions here, but only heightens them.

Marx's Radical History

Closer attention to the specific claims being made by Marx in chapters twenty-six through thirty-one significantly complicates the impression that he is reverting to a Saint-Simonian schema. His language in chapter twenty-six echoes Saint-Simonianism, but largely for the sake of overturning the Saint-Simonian historiography. Most patently, Marx inverts the historical tendency of exploitation, claiming not that the feudal order was more exploitative than the capitalist one, but the reverse: the guild regime placed "fetters" on "the free exploitation of man by man." This ironic reversal of Saint-Simonianism forecasts a striking appreciation of late feudalism that characterizes the early chapters of part eight, a sort of rapprochement between Marx and a popular republican historiography that valorized the ancient constitution and the lost independence of the peasant producer. This surprising rapprochement can only be explained by being situated within the rhetorical arc of part eight as a whole.

The Saint-Simonians understood feudalism to be a regime of force, eventually overthrown by the peaceful rise of the industrials; feudal remnants linger within the modern world, however, in the form of the state

[33] Federici, *Caliban and the Witch*, 32, 9.

and private property. This is the narrative taken over and exaggerated by Proudhon. While the Saint-Simonians recognized that Christianity and chivalry had, at least for a time, dedicated both the church and the nobility to "the defense of the weak,"[34] Proudhon reduced these institutions to expressions of the principle of authority and attributed their reputation as "the protector of the weak" to "intimate, invincible superstition."[35] Thus, on Proudhon's telling, there is a simple continuity between feudalism and capitalism—both are based on force and authority—and a linear measure of progress in the displacement of force and authority by justice and free contracts. The illegitimacy of capitalist profits springs directly from the force inherent in them, embedded in the history of the property held, and apparent in the state's enforcement of that holding.

On Marx's telling, however, this radically misconstrues matters. "The old order of things" embodied both "industrial hierarchy" *and* "guarantees of existence"; the producers may have been "bound to the soil, or . . . vassals to another person,"[36] but they also had direct access to "their own means of production." Like the bourgeois providentialists, socialists find it "too easy to be 'liberal' at the expense of the Middle Ages."[37] This "old order of things" fell apart, giving rise to "the constitutive elements" of the "capitalist economic order," not because of the attraction exerted by the moral gravity of the capitalist economic order, nor because capital is a *causa sui*, but because the old order was betrayed by those who seemed to benefit most from it, the lords of the land.[38] The institutional weakness of the feudal order in Britain, its susceptibility to a sort of abuse from above that destabilized the whole system, was revealed by a series of fortuitously connected events, beginning with the Wars of the Roses.[39]

The story Marx tells is, in the main, both highly compressed and rather ambiguous.[40] This may be why it is so often glossed over or mischarac-

---

[34] *Doctrine of St-Simon*, 18; *Doctrine de Saint-Simon*, 96.

[35] *Property Is Theft!*, 561; *OC*, 2:183.

[36] Marx's German is "*leibeigen oder hörig*"—literally *enthralled or belonging to*—but he dropped the reference to ownership of persons in the French edition, which refers only to being "*inféodé*" (*MEGA*, II.6:645; *MEGA*, II.7:633).

[37] See note 7 above.

[38] *Capital*, 1:875; *MEGA*, II.6:647; *MEGA*, II.7:635.

[39] Marx refers to "the great feudal wars" by this name in the French translation. The name itself originated only in Walter Scott's *Anne of Geierstein, or the Lady of the Mist* (1829). Marx was a great admirer of Scott (Prawer, *Karl Marx and World Literature*, 386). It is reasonable to surmise, therefore, that he picked up the name—and, perhaps, some of his sense of the underlying conflicts—from Scott.

[40] It has been rightly noted that "Marx's comments on social change in general and the transition to capitalism in particular are far from unitary or unambiguous" (Holton, *The Transition from Feudalism to Capitalism*, 64). That this is true not only of Marx's works considered as a whole but even of *Capital* considered in isolation is indicated by the fact

terized. My attempt to recount it here will strive to leave indeterminate what Marx does not clearly state. (Of course, there can be no question here of ascertaining what really happened, or of judging the correctness of Marx's historical account; I want merely to get a clear picture of what Marx says in *Capital*.) The feudal constitution, he claims, is premised on the "division of the soil among the greatest possible number of liegemen," for feudal power was essentially direct power over persons, existing as relations of dependency and fidelity. Their network of dependents and subdependents was the substance of the lords' power, but it also constrained their actions. Retaining and augmenting their retinues entailed responsibility and expense, and the services and taxes provided by vassals required that they have their own bases in the land, their own sources of security and livelihood. Hence, feudal power, as it had developed by the fifteenth century in Britain, protected a form of "popular wealth" that "excluded capitalist wealth."[41]

However, the Wars of the Roses decimated "the old nobility," and the newer generations of the aristocracy, locked "in open war with the king and Parliament," found that they had more use for money than they did for vassals and subvassals.[42] The market for wool in Flanders provided a ready means of getting money, but selling large quantities of wool on the Flemish market required turning out the peasantry and transforming the patchwork of small farms into massive demesnes operated exclusively as sheep pastures. The royal house, too, as the central state pulled away from the nobility, dismissed the mass of its retainers. In combination, these evictions created the first modern proletariat, a population of people with no claim to land or other ready means of subsistence.[43] At

---

that Holten himself claims *both* that part eight explains the transition from feudalism to capitalism "in terms of internal contradictions between productive forces and social relations, resolved through class conflict," *and—only a few pages later—*that Marx "makes no serious attempt" in part eight to explain the process of transition "by reference to the development of the productive forces" (ibid., 68, 72).

[41] *Capital*, 1:878; *MEGA*, II.6:647; *MEGA*, II.7:635. As sketchy as Marx's account here may be, it seems to presage, at least in this regard, the revisionism of K. B. McFarlane, which emphasized reciprocity and "good lordship" in late medieval Britain. It is also reminiscent of Tocqueville.

[42] Or, to duly recognize the fact that monetary payments had by this time largely supplanted direct labor services, they had need of more money than could be provided by tributes levied from vassals and subvassals.

[43] Contrary to Harvey's claims, Marx does not argue that the creation of the proletariat was due to "the way in which money power began to be exercised within and over the feudal order (e.g., by merchant capital and usury)," whereby "money dissolves the traditional community" (*A Companion to Marx's Capital*, 294). This is another version of the self-development story. As Marx says in the *Grundrisse*, "the mere presence of monetary wealth, and even the achievement of a kind of supremacy on its part, is in no way sufficient for this dissolution into capital to happen. Or else ancient Rome, Byzantium, etc., would

the same time, they also concentrated large swaths of land in the hands of a few lords. These two polar consequences, which Marx calls the "prelude" to the capitalist revolution, had as their attendant social condition the abolition of the ties that bound lord and tenant. Of course this meant that villenage was abolished, but it also meant "the abolition of the property of the agricultural laborer in the soil" and the demotion of the remaining peasantry to the status of "a servile rabble dependent upon the arbitrary will of the landlords."[44] That is, the destruction of the older system of land tenure was not the destruction of the lords' domination, but the destruction of the peasants' security, their bulwark against the lords' domination.

This story sounds less like twentieth-century historical materialism—and less like Saint-Simonianism—than like early nineteenth-century Radical history. It seems designed to hearken back to the 1820s, when pre-Owenite Radicals still agitated for a restitution and reform of the British constitution, deploying an updated version of "the Norman yoke" to explain the present misery of the laborer.[45] Indeed, Marx's litany of primitive accumulation in chapter twenty-seven—"the spoliation of the Church's goods, the fraudulent sale of the domains of the state, the pillage of communal lands, the transformation by usurpation and terrorism of feudal or patrimonial property into modern private property, the war on cottages"[46]—seems like the repetition of a commonplace when read next to, say, Cobbett's *Rural Rides* (1830). The Reformation, the Restoration, the Glorious Revolution: these are the watershed moments in the decline and fall of the British working class, its fall "from its golden age to its iron age."[47] This is old wine Marx is serving from a new bottle.[48]

have ended their history with free labour and capital, or rather begun a new history" (*Grundrisse*, 506; *MEGA*, II.1.2:408–9). And this despite the fact that, as Rodney Hilton has noted, Marx's view of merchant capital's role in the transition deflated between the writing of the *Grundrisse* and the writing of *Capital* (*Transition from Feudalism*, 23n15).

[44] Marx, *Capital*, 1:878, 882–83n9, 886; *MEGA*, II.6:648, 650–51n197, 653; *MEGA*, II.7:635, 64n11, 643.

[45] William Stafford has noticed this proximity between Marx's account of primitive accumulation and "the venerable conquest theory of the origins of exploitation" deployed by British radicals from Bentham and Godwin to Hall, Thompson, and Hodgskin. He has also noticed that this theory is distinct from Marx's account of exploitation within capitalist production (*Socialism, Radicalism, and Nostalgia*, 243–44).

[46] *Capital*, 1:895; *MEGA*, II.6:660; *MEGA*, II.7:651.

[47] *Capital*, 1:879; *MEGA*, II.6:648; *MEGA*, II.7:637.

[48] It seems to me that this otherwise odd reversion to British Radicalism must be explained politically by the resurgence of popular republicanism in the form of the Reform League. The Reform movement was led to a significant extent by members of the IWMA's General Council, especially George Howell, George Odger, Benjamin Lucraft, and Henry Cremer. It took up only the suffrage plank of the Charter movement, but it brought back into play many of those who had been involved in Bronterre O'Brien's National Reform

That this wine is a British Radical vintage rather than of a French variety certainly changes its character, but it does not solve our original problem. Indeed, it seems to compound it. If the transition from feudalism to capitalism is not a movement in the direction of substituting peaceful industry for military violence, this merely underscores the tensions between Marx's account of primitive accumulation and his account of capitalist exploitation. If the violent expropriation of the many by the few is precisely what makes the transition to capitalist production possible, how can Marx's exploitation theory be right? The use of force Marx documents in part eight is not the impersonal compulsion of market dependency, the force of circumstances, or the structural violence of capital's forcing of labor power, for which no one can be held responsible. Nor does it consist in the sorts of abuses that he drew attention to at several points in parts three through seven, abuses called forth by the capitalist mode of production but contrary to its basic norm of the exchange of equivalents among free persons. Rather, the cruelties of primitive accumulation are acts of massive violence and theft carried out by identifiable persons—individual or corporate—who might be held responsible. After all, these acts are supposed to precede and bring about the impersonal domination that renders moderns unfit to be held responsible for their social life. To make matters worse, Marx seems to have saddled himself with a nostalgia for a bygone era of independent petty production that is hardly compatible with his own obvious preference for large-scale cooperative production. Proudhon seems to be having his revenge, for Marx, in the first few chapters of part eight, seems to have undermined all the fortifications he built in parts three through seven against moralistic socialism's derivation of capital from force and fraud.

Treachery and the Birth of the Capitalist Order

In order to make sense of this, it must first be noted that the republican story of decline Marx rehearsed in chapters twenty-six and twenty-seven is, in its original, a story not just about war, looting, and theft, but about the treachery of the powerful. Those entrusted with the welfare of the community, in one way or another, betray that trust. This was the lesson of the Radicals' attack on Old Corruption. Cobbett, for example, never doubted that landlords and peers were always to be part of the British constitution; what roused his ire was the fact that those "country gentlemen" that commanded the greater part of both Parliament and the agricultural produce were "the MOST BASE of all the creatures that God

---

League twenty years earlier (and the new organization's name clearly implied continuity with the earlier struggles).

ever suffered to disgrace the human shape."[49] It is not that some have more power and prestige than others; that is merely natural.[50] The fatal malady is that the powerful and prestigious lack virtue or worth, and the constitution lacks the sort of transparency and publicity that would prevent the vicious from using power and prestige to enrich themselves by despoiling everyone and everything they ought to protect.[51]

Marx's story hits many of the same notes. By means of the Reformation, the Crown allowed itself to give away church lands "to rapacious royal favorites."[52] The Restoration Parliament, by "an act of usurpation," abolished their own feudal obligations and transformed their title to the land from a feudal one into a title of private property. The Glorious Revolution set off "a truly colossal squandering of the public treasure," as Crown lands were "given away, sold at ridiculous prices, or even annexed to private estates by direct seizure."[53] The Bills for Enclosure of the Commons realized a Parliamentary form of robbery.[54] This culminates in the tale of the Duchess of Sutherland and the other clan chiefs of the Highlanders, who, between 1750 and 1860, transformed the entirety of the clan lands, to which they had only a "nominal right," into their own private property, and expelled their clansmen.[55] In every case, Marx is interested not simply in the violence of expropriation but in a betrayal of the fidelity that bound upper and lower.

In Marx, however, this betrayal has two features it lacked in Cobbett's telling. The first arises from Marx's understanding of the logic of certain social roles. As he puts it in a footnote early in *Capital*, "this man is a king only because other men consider themselves his subjects and act as such. They imagine, however, that they are subjects because he is king."[56] The particular qualities of a person have no bearing, Marx is claiming, on their being a king. Kingship has its being outside the person of the king, in the comportment and actions of those who relate to the king as subjects. Kingship is constituted by these social relations of subjection, and this claim can be extended to cover other forms of rule. This approach is antithetical to Cobbett's basic belief that some people are born to be

---

[49] *Rural Rides*, 310.

[50] Stafford, *Socialism, Radicalism, and Nostalgia*, 261–66.

[51] Calhoun, *Roots of Radicalism*, 150.

[52] Marx, *Capital*, 1:881; *MEGA*, II.6:650; *MEGA*, II.7:638–39; compare, e.g., Cobbett, *Rural Rides*, 473.

[53] *Capital*, 1:883–84; *MEGA*, II.6:652; *MEGA*, II.7:641.

[54] *Capital*, 1:885; *MEGA*, II.6:652–53; *MEGA*, II.7:642.

[55] *Capital*, 1:890–95; *MEGA*, II.6:656–60; *MEGA*, II.7:646–51.

[56] *Capital*, 1:149n22; *MEGA*, II.6:89n21; *MEGA*, II.7:40n20. In the German text (though this is erased in the French), Marx makes clear that he is thinking in terms of what Hegel calls *definition by reflection* [*Reflexionbestimmung*].

lords and others are born to be laborers, and that, consequently, the point of political reform is to put everyone into their proper places in the order of things. This is relevant for the narrative of feudal decline because it entails that in Marx's version, but not in Cobbett's, the lords' systematic and accumulative betrayal of the relations of fidelity is tantamount to the abolition of the old order. In this sense, the feudal order created the material conditions of its destruction in that it gave rise to the means and the motives by which the lords dismantled feudal tenures and thereby abolished their own personal power for the sake of monetary wealth and private property, and the new forms of social power that came with these. This was *revolution*, not decay and corruption. The "old oak of the British Constitution" cannot be put right again by any reform, because it was cut down, chopped up, and sold off.[57] Something new has been planted in its stead.

Marx's second addition is prefigured in the odd final line of his invocation of Saint-Simonianism, where he claims that the industrial capitalists "have succeeded by means as vile as those that served the Roman freedman to become the master of his *patronus*." The analogy is obscure but very specific. Under Roman law, manumission did not sever all relations between master and slave, but it transformed the relationship into one of patron and client. The manumitted slave had customary duties toward

---

[57] This is congruent with Marx's stated judgment of Cobbett, from an 1853 article for the *Tribune*: "William Cobbett was the most able representative, or, rather, the creator of old English Radicalism. . . . He watched step for step the encroachments of political centralization on local self-government, and denounced it as an infringement on the privileges and liberties of the English subject. He did not understand its being the necessary result of industrial centralization. He proclaimed all the political demands which have afterward been combined in the national charter; yet with him they were rather the political charter of the petty industrial middle class than of the industrial proletarian. . . . If William Cobbett was thus, on one hand, an anticipated modern Chartist, he was, on the other hand, and much more, an inveterate John Bull. He was at once the most conservative and the most destructive man of Great Britain—the purest incarnation of Old England and the most audacious initiator of Young England. He dated the decline of England from the period of the Reformation, and the ulterior prostration of the English people from the so-called glorious Revolution of 1688. With him, therefore, revolution was not innovation, but restoration; not the creation of a new age, but the rehabilitation of the 'good old times.' What he did not see, was that the epoch of the pretended decline of the English people coincided exactly with the beginning ascendancy of the middle class, with the development of modern commerce and industry, and that, at the same pace as the latter grew up, the material situation of the people declined, and local self-government disappeared before political centralization. . . . He did not see the modern *bourgeoisie*, but only that fraction of the aristocracy which held the hereditary monopoly of office, and which sanctioned by law all the changes necessitated by the new wants and pretensions of the middle class. He saw the machine, but not the hidden motive power. . . . As a writer he has not been surpassed" ("Layard's Motion—Struggle over the Ten Hours' Bill"; *MEGA*, I.12:222–23).

his or her patron, and the former master was bound to protect and benefit his or her client. Freedmen could, although hemmed in by some social and political barriers, become quite wealthy and powerful. They could certainly own slaves. But for a freedman to become the master of his or her patron and former master! This would entail a fundamental betrayal of the client-patron relationship, and can only be compared, in Roman society, to a child murdering his or her own parents.[58] The patron has, quite literally, given civil life to the freedman by the act of manumission. To turn around and enslave him or her, to take away his or her civil life, would be unimaginable.[59]

By this analogy, Marx certainly highlights the treachery involved in primitive accumulation, but he also does something unexpected. He casts the nascent capitalist class as the beneficiaries of the lords' acts, and hence as owing honor and gratitude to the lords for their abolition of feudal power. Simultaneously, Marx also makes the capitalists out as the usurpers of the lords' status. That is, the treachery of the lords may have destroyed the feudal order in pursuit of money and private property, but the rise of capitalism has submitted these lords of the land to the rule of the capitalists, on whom the former are now as dependent as their vassals ever were. This is because, "whatever the proportion of surplus value which the capitalist entrepreneur retains for himself, or transmits to others [e.g., landlords], he is the one who in the first place appropriates it in its entirety and he alone converts it into capital."[60] Hence, it seems that there are actually *two* betrayals in Marx's narrative. The lords betrayed the people and thereby abolished feudalism and created the modern proletariat; this is Marx's development of Cobbett's history. But then the rising capitalists, emancipated by the abolition of feudalism, seized dominion over the landlords whose actions had freed them.

---

[58] A prominent example, which may have been in Marx's mind, comes from Tacitus's *Annals*, and makes the analogy patent. Nero, plotting against his mother, Agrippina, was spurred on by a freedman, Anicetus, who swore that he would personally oversee the murder. "Hearing him, Nero cried that this was the first day of his reign—and the magnificent gift came from a former slave!" (14.7) Literal matricide is made possible by and consecrates the reversal of a patron-client relationship, and the figurative, if not literal, enslavement of the emperor, who as tyrant, is a slave of slaves.

[59] For details about Roman manumission and patronage, I have relied on Henrik Mouritsen's recent monograph *The Freedman in the Roman World*; see especially chapters 3 and 4. Thanks to Patchen Markell for calling my attention to this work.

[60] Marx, *Capital*, 1:710; *MEGA*, II.6:522; *MEGA*, II.7:488. See also Marx's citation of Thomas Hodgskin in chapter thirty-one: "The capitalist may now be said to be the first owner of all the wealth of the community" (*Capital*, 1:914; *MEGA*, II.6:673; *MEGA*, II.7:667–68; quoting from Hodgskin, *The Natural and Artificial Right of Property Contrasted*, 98).

This second betrayal and usurpation has no parallel in either Saint-Simonian or Radical history, and it resolves one of the puzzles faced above. Despite the prevalence of this reading, the story told by chapters twenty-six through thirty is not one of capitalists originally amassing capital via plunder, and then switching over to the exploitation of labor power once they had monopolized the means of production. Rather, it is the story of landlords amassing land through plunder, thereby creating at the same time the modern proletariat, and of capitalists cropping up in between these two classes and rising to dominate both of them through the exploitation of the newly available labor power. Primitive accumulation "incorporated the soil into capital,"[61] not by making the capitalist the owner of the soil, but by making the owner of the soil, the landlord, dependent, for the cultivation or other utilization of the soil, upon the mediation provided by the capitalist. The direct producer no longer has direct possession of the soil, and the direct possessor of the soil no longer has direct access to labor. What has been torn asunder must be reunited in some way. And this is where the capitalist comes in, stepping in between the owner of the land and the worker of the land. The capitalists' new power stems not from a monopoly born of conquest and plunder but from the lucky fact that they are neither the monopolists nor the plundered.

This reading is supported by Marx's account, in chapters twenty-nine and thirty, of the rise of the capitalist farmer. Marx begins chapter twenty-nine by highlighting the fact that the story so far told has left unanswered the question: "where did the capitalists originally spring from?" Marx's answer is that they originate from those serfs and free peasants who were lucky enough to escape expropriation, and who were so situated as to benefit from the enclosures of common lands and the expropriation of their neighbors.[62] It is among the descendants of the bailiffs, sharecroppers, and lucky yeomanry that Marx finds the first industrial capitalists.[63] They were able to expand the field of production by utilizing the old commons for pasturage, and thereby manuring larger plots, and by employing larger gangs of farmhands in cooperative labor.[64] The produce of this increased production was for market, not for personal consumption, and the market has itself been massively augmented by "the annihilation of the domestic industry of the countryside" that went hand in hand with the expropriation of the mass of the peasantry.[65]

[61] Marx, *Capital*, 1:895; *MEGA*, II.6:660; *MEGA*, II.7:651.

[62] *Capital*, 1:905–6; *MEGA*, II.6:667–68; *MEGA*, II.7:660.

[63] As he says in a note at the beginning of chapter thirty-one, "in the strict sense, the farmer is just as much an industrial capitalist as the manufacturer" (*Capital*, 1:914n1; *MEGA*, II.6:673n238; *MEGA*, II.7:667n58).

[64] *Capital*, 1:906, 908; *MEGA*, II.6:668, 670; *MEGA*, II.7:660–61, 663.

[65] *Capital*, 1:911; *MEGA*, II.6:672; *MEGA*, II.7:665.

This finds further confirmation in what Marx wrote elsewhere. As early as the manuscripts on "the German ideology," Marx and Engels had criticized the German "True Socialists" for seeing "'the extremes of *our* society' in the opposition of rentiers and proletarians," an opposition "belabored by all moralists since time immemorial," and "resurrected" by writers like Cobbett and Saint-Simon.[66] As late as his criticisms of the Gotha Programme, Marx pointed out that, "in England, the capitalist generally does not even own the land and soil on which his factory stands,"[67] a fact that is crucial for indicating the duality of the modern ruling class, composed of the landowners and the capitalists.[68] Nonetheless, it is capital that is dominant. Marx took over the Malthusian-Ricardian theory of rent just to this extent, that modern rent is mediated by the market. But he criticized Malthus and Ricardo for thinking of the differential between parcels of land solely in terms of the natural fertility of the soil, rather than recognizing that industrialization and cooperative labor, coeval with modern rent, made rent differentials dependent upon differential employments of the land, and on the development and distribution of the forces of production. In this way, the landlords, far from being in a purely privileged position from which to dictate terms to the capitalists, are dependent, in the rent they can charge, upon the capitalists' development of industry.

Landlords do exact, on top of this differential rent, an absolute rent, by virtue of the fact that they, as a class, monopolize a nonreproducible resource, but the relative size of this absolute rent will vary dramatically with changes in production and trade, and there is no reason for landlords to rest assured of any price-setting power they enjoy.[69] As Marx puts it at one point in volume three, "Even though landed property can drive the price of agricultural products above their price of production, it does not depend on this, but rather on the general state of the market,

---

[66] *MECW*, 5:464; *MEGA*, I.5:447–48.

[67] *Political Writings*, 3:343; *MEGA*, I.25:11.

[68] Marx's statement, in this context, that "the monopoly of land ownership" is "the basis of the monopoly of capital" may appear to contradict my thesis, but does not. As I have argued above, according to Marx, only where the land has been consolidated into private property in the hands of a few are the mass of people reduced to propertylessness, and only where the land is thereby separated from the mass of people can the capitalist, owning the means of labor and renting the land, arise. As a necessary concomitant of mass expropriation, and a necessary condition for capitalist intermediation, the monopoly in landed property is a basis for capitalism without being constitutive of capital.

[69] The best recent treatment of Marx's understanding of absolute rent is found in Ramirez, "Marx's Theory of Ground Rent." This analysis, in my opinion, goes beyond those of Economakis, "On Absolute Rent: Theoretical Remarks on Marx's Analysis"; and Bryan, "'Natural' and 'Improved' Land in Marx's Theory of Rent." The basic contours of Marx's writings on rent are well delineated by many commentators.

how far market price rises above the price of production."[70] Or, in the simplified, more political form in which he puts the point in *The Civil War in France*, in modern society, "with its two poles of capital and wage slavery," "the landlord is now but the sleeping partner of the capitalist."[71]

The main consequence of this reconstruction is that Marx's account of primitive accumulation does not undermine his account of capitalist exploitation, for the simple reason that capitalists neither *carried out* the original expropriation of the producers nor *inherited* the monopoly power of the landed proprietors who did carry it out.[72] Insofar as the landlords "filch" an absolute rent, they stand opposed to capitalists, not behind them. Ricardo argued that "corn is not high because a rent is paid, but rent is paid because corn is high."[73] Analogously, Marx argues that exploitation is not high because rent is paid, but rent is paid because exploitation is high. There is a top to skim off because the capitalist exploitation of labor power produces a fund of surplus value sufficient to feed even the rentiers. The capitalists' ability and compulsion to exploit labor power comes from their situation in between the expropriated masses and the few landed proprietors. It is from this position of relative freedom—vis-à-vis the old constraints of vassalage and the guilds—that they and their strange gods were able to subjugate not only the poor laborers but also their old lords, who had delivered capital from its bondage only to become its bondsmen.[74]

The point of Marx's account of primitive accumulation is not that capital has its origin in acts of violence and theft, but that capital has its origin in the opportunistic exploitation of the new forms of freedom created by acts of violence and theft. Violence and theft cannot give rise to capital directly. There must be a displacement from the acts of violence and theft to the process of capitalizing upon the conditions thereby created. Part and parcel of capital's treachery is that it requires others to create its conditions of existence. As we will now see, this dynamic is also crucial for Marx's understanding of capitalism's imbrication with European colonialism, and for the practical lesson of part eight, how the laboring classes might overcome capital and establish a new mode of production.

---

[70] *Capital,* 3:898; *MEGA,* II.15:741.

[71] *Political Writings,* 3:212.

[72] Balibar makes this point well when he notes that "the history of the separation of the labourer from the means of production does not give us money-capital," and neither does "the history of money-capital" provide us with a history of "the 'free' labourer" (*Reading Capital,* 280–81).

[73] *The Principles of Political Economy and Taxation,* 38.

[74] Marx calls the colonial system the "strange God" of the European powers in the early period of capitalism (*Capital,* 1:918; *MEGA,* II.6:677; *MEGA,* II.7:671).

Negating the Negation

We have wriggled out of one of the knots. Marx does not relapse into Saint-Simonianism at the end of *Capital*, and he does not undermine his own account of capitalist exploitation by stressing the violent processes of primitive accumulation, for the simple reason that capital always arises at one remove from the processes of expropriation that are necessary for the creation of a class of propertyless laborers. Someone else always does capital's dirty work for it; capital merely *capitalizes* on the processes of expropriation carried out by others. But another knot remains. Marx has spent five chapters painting a romantic picture of the liberty proper to petty production, of the freedom and dignity of the yeomanry, of the absence of "any great social distance" between masters and artisans.[75] He quotes approvingly the younger Mirabeau's claim that the old system of small domestic industry, combined with petty agriculture, is "the only free" mode of manufacturing, and attributes to "popular intuition" this insight into the stakes of the dissolution of the old system.[76] Despite his divergences from Cobbett, Marx sounds throughout like a Radical republican of the old stamp, not a communist. In chapter thirty-two, however, Marx pivots dramatically, declaring that to continue in the old manner of independent petty production "would be, as Pequeur says judiciously, 'to decree mediocrity for all.'"[77] Rather than reestablishing independence, Marx advocates embracing the world of all-round dependency created by capitalism. How is the reader supposed to square the romantic Radicalism of Marx's historical narrative with the progressivism of his revolutionary counsel?

This sudden shift in Marx's argument is the prelude to one of the most infamous lines in all of *Capital*, the claim that capitalism has negated the "private property that is only the corollary of independent and individual labor," but that "capitalist production itself engenders its own negation, . . . the negation of the negation." It is by means of this negation of the negation that Marx means to close the door on the old republicanism of independent producers and to insist instead on the need for a system of "individual property, based on the acquisitions of the capitalist era, on cooperation among free laborers and the common possession of all the means of production, including the soil."[78] And yet this too seems to contradict what has come before. In chapter twenty-six, Marx had held up

[75] *Capital*, 1:900; *MEGA*, II.6:664; *MEGA*, II.7:655.
[76] *Capital*, 1:909–10; *MEGA*, II.6:670–71; *MEGA*, II.7:664.
[77] *Capital*, 1:928; *MEGA*, II.6:681; *MEGA*, II.7:678.
[78] *Capital*, 1:929; *MEGA*, II.6:683; *MEGA*, II.7:679. This rendering of Marx's claim combines the French and second German editions.

for scorn "the stoical peace of mind" of those defenders of the enclosures who had argued that they were necessary in order to produce "more labor," or else to establish "the due proportion between arable land and pasture."[79] These arguments defend the processes of primitive accumulation, not in themselves, but by reference to their consequences. They suggest that however ugly the expropriation of "the little farmers" may have been, it is retrospectively justified by the economic transformation it ushered in. But is this not what Marx himself does in chapter thirty-two? Does he not, as Federici puts it, believe that the capitalism unleashed by primitive accumulation "disposed of small-scale property, and that it increased (to a degree unmatched by any other economic system) the productive capacity of labor, thus creating the material conditions for the liberation of humanity from scarcity and necessity"?[80] Marx seems to be embracing the providentialism he criticizes among the defenders of capitalism.

In order to make sense of Marx's sudden change of course, I think it is important to read the last three chapters of *Capital* as a unit concerned above all else with identifying the alliance that has been forged between the state and capital. It is the brute fact of this alliance—actually, as we will see, the dependency of the state upon the accumulation of capital—and his sense of its importance, that explains Marx's about-face on independent production and his sudden concern with "the wheel of history."[81] Having mobilized the indignation inherent in the Radical narrative about the betrayal of freedom by corruption, Marx tries to channel that indignation against the state, urging a confrontation with and conquest of state power. For, so long as "the concentrated and organized force of society" stands on the side of capital, its interventions will tend to reestablish the material conditions of capitalism wherever these begin to disintegrate.[82]

A Hegelian Crutch?

Marx's pivot in chapter thirty-two has always attracted an outsized share of critical attention. One of the earliest reviews of *Capital*, by the German socialist and anti-Semite Eugen Dühring, was generally appreciative of Marx's treatment of primitive accumulation. When Dühring expanded on

---

[79] *Capital*, 1:888–89; *MEGA*, II.6:655; *MEGA*, II.7:645.

[80] *Caliban and the Witch*, 12. Maguire enshrined this interpretation at the heart of his attempt to lay out Marx's mature political theory, claiming that, according to Marx, "capitalism is born out of fraud and violence, and when it has 'done its job' it eventually succumbs to the proletariat" (*Marx's Theory of Politics*, 140).

[81] *Capital*, 1:930n2; *MEGA*, II.6:683n252; *MEGA*, II.7:679–80n76.

[82] *Capital*, 1:915; *MEGA*, II.6:674; *MEGA*, II.7:668.

his views a couple years later, however, he changed his mind.[83] "This historical sketch is not good and not reliable," he wrote, "but it is still, relatively, the best in Marx's book. It would have been somewhat less wrong had it not been helped along by a learned, not even yet dialectical crutch, namely, the Hegelian negation of negation, which must here, for lack of better and clearer means, perform the midwifery through which the future will be released from the bosom of the past."[84] Engels responded with a long chapter in his *Herrn Eugen Dührings Umwälzung der Wissenschaft* (1878), wherein he denied that Marx was relying upon the negation of the negation to work any historical magic, denied that Dühring understood the negation of the negation, and asserted that the negation of the negation was in fact a universal law of natural processes as well as a fundamental form of thought for understanding those processes. The *Anti-Dühring* being much more widely read than *Capital*,[85] Engels's exposition has tended to set the terms for the reception of Marx's own text.[86]

On Engels's reconstruction, the negation of the negation is ubiquitous, but at the price of being fairly meaningless. Any figure that can be found in every biological and every geological process, in every meteorological cycle, in every chemical reaction, and in every algebraic and geometric proof, is not going to have much specificity and is not going to reveal very much about the phenomena within which it is discovered.[87] And, in a way, this indeterminacy does seem appropriate to an explication of Marx's text. The use of the formula in chapter thirty-two seems to say little other than this: the overthrow of capitalism will destroy the forces that have destroyed petty production, without thereby reestablishing petty production. Calling this "the negation of the negation" seems merely to dress up in Hegelian phraseology a claim that neither relies upon nor illustrates Hegelian logic.[88]

---

[83] Given my recounting above, this change of mind seems appropriate. Dühring, like Proudhon, thought capitalism to be another instantiation of force in history.

[84] Engels softened this passage considerably when he quoted it in his book against Dühring.

[85] Carver, *Marx and Engels*, chap. 5.

[86] Even readers as wary of Engels as Kevin Anderson tend to reproduce Engels's understanding of the negation of the negation. Anderson claims that Marx's "recourse to Hegelian language at this juncture was . . . a methodological indication informing the reader that his overall presentation of capitalist production and its eventual collapse was grounded in Hegelian dialectics. . . . Dialectics fit into *Capital*, he seemed to say, not because he had imposed it on reality, but because reality was itself dialectical" (*Marx at the Margins*, 227).

[87] A fact that Engels admits, allowing that "it is obvious that I do not say anything concerning the *particular* process of development of, for example, a grain of barley from germination to the death of the fruit-bearing plant, if I say it is a negation of the negation" (*MECW*, 25:131; *MEGA*, I.27:336).

[88] I have made such an argument in print, though I now think my treatment was both too simplistic and, in part, mistaken ("The Reconstitution of Marxism's Production Paradigm: The Cases of Benjamin, Althusser, and Marx," 434–38).

However, there is a short analysis in the *Grundrisse* that puts things in a new light. There, in the midst of his consideration of the "money nonsense" of Bray, Gray, and Proudhon,[89] he claims that the market price corresponds to the labor value of a commodity, "never by means of an equation with real value as if the latter were a third party, but rather by means of constant non-equation of itself (as Hegel would say, not by way of abstract identity, but by constant negation of the negation, i.e. of itself as negation of real value)."[90] As discussed in chapter 3, Marx denies that divergences between price and value hide any systematic shifting of value away from laborers and toward money owners. Rather, these divergences are the dynamic mechanism by which price expresses value. This dynamic equation is what Marx identifies in the *Grundrisse* as the negation of the negation. What is striking is that this dynamic mechanism is entirely internal to the workings of the market. The labor theory of value, by which Proudhon and the Owenites wanted to indict the market with injustice, is actually, on Marx's understanding, realized only by the market itself, which embodies the competitive pressures by which labor is disciplined and regulated. Capitalism is not the negation of the principle "only labor creates value," but the negation of its negation—that is, its dynamic realization.

In chapter thirty-two, Marx starts with a premise akin to the labor theory of value—namely, the labor theory of property, "the property founded on the personal labor of its possessor."[91] And he deploys the same Hegelian figure. And yet, he ends up someplace radically different. Instead of claiming that capitalism is the dynamic realization of the labor theory of property, he declares that it is the simple negation of this principle, and that only communism—a system of "individual property, based on the acquisitions of the capitalist era, on cooperation among free laborers and the common possession of all the means of production, including the soil"[92]—would be the dynamic realization of it.

Moreover, as Christopher Arthur has noted,[93] Marx makes the actual analogue of the *Grundrisse* claim earlier in *Capital*, where, as in the *Grundrisse*, the conclusion seems to be the opposite of the one reached in chapter thirty-two. Reviewing the argument of the whole book in chapter twenty-four, Marx points out that "originally the right of property seemed to us to be grounded in a man's own labor," but that further investigation has shown that "property turns out to be the right, on the

---

[89] The phrase comes from Marx's letter to Friedrich Adolph Sorge, September 1, 1870; *MECW*, 44:57–58.

[90] *Grundrisse*, 137; *MEGA*, II.1.1:72.

[91] *Capital*, 1:927; *MEGA*, II.6:681; *MEGA*, II.7:677.

[92] *Capital*, 1:929; *MEGA*, II.6:683; *MEGA*, II.7:679.

[93] "Negation of the Negation in Marx's *Capital*."

part of the capitalist, to appropriate the unpaid labor of others." This passage from appearance to reality, however, shows us that "however much this [capitalist] mode of enriching oneself may seem to fly in the face of the primordial laws of commodity production, it results nevertheless, not from the violation of these laws but, on the contrary, from their application."[94] Here, the dynamic realization of the labor theory of property is, Marx claims, the right of capital to exploit labor power. Capitalism is, therefore, not the simple negation of the labor theory of property, but the negation of the negation, the actual existence, in process, of the labor theory of property.[95] Although he does not use the Hegelian phrase here, the form of the claim mirrors that of the *Grundrisse* passage and arrives at a conclusion opposite to the one drawn later in *Capital*.

I do not think that Marx is contradicting himself, because I think Engels revealed something, however unintentionally, when he rendered the negation of the negation as a completely indeterminate law of everything. In truth, "the negation of the negation" does not do any argumentative work. Its appearance in one context cannot contradict its appearance in another, any more than the use of the word "revolution" to describe capital's transformation of the production process can contradict the use of the same word to describe the overthrow of capital. There is a sense in which the labor theory of property is realized by capitalist production, for each worker receives, on average, the value equivalent of whatever he or she sells, and thus retains, after exchange, the magnitude of property with which he or she entered into exchange, property that could only originate in past labor.[96] But there is another sense in which the labor theory of property would only be realized in communism, for only there would the produce of labor be disposed of by the producers, collectively.[97] In both of these cases, the realization "in one sense" of the labor

---

[94] *Capital*, 1:730; *MEGA*, II.6:538; *MEGA*, II.7:507.

[95] Arthur argues, on the basis of this earlier passage, that we ought to reinterpret chapter thirty-two as indicating not a dialectic of history but a logical dialectic internal to capitalism; "This interpretation abandons the historical perspective with its problematic of causal genesis in favor of a structural problematic requiring an account of 'genesis' in logical terms" ("Negation of the Negation in Marx's *Capital*," 53). Arthur's suggestion is too clever by half. It must discard as figurative all of the historical language that Marx uses throughout chapter thirty-two.

[96] Presented in this way, Marx's argument in chapter twenty-four clearly echoes Hegel's argument in §77 of his *Philosophy of Right*. Hegel writes: "Since in the real contract each party retains the same property with which it enters the contract and which it at the same time surrenders, what thus remains identical throughout as the property that is in itself in the contract is . . . the value" (*The Philosophy of Right*, 68).

[97] This is reminiscent of William Thompson's argument, that the right of the producer to the produce could only be realized by cooperative production and collective property.

theory of property can be characterized as the negation of the negation of that theory, but this christening does not reveal any new information about the sense in which the theory is realized. "The negation of the negation" is not a crutch for Marx, since it does not help him move from one spot to another, however illegitimately. Rather than a Hegelian crutch, it is merely a Hegelian crotchet.

Tantae molis erat . . .

The indeterminacy of "the negation of the negation" indicates, I think, its essentially rhetorical function in chapter thirty-two. What matters for Marx is that the social republican attraction to dignified liberty be separated from the petty production and communitarianism that has seemed to shelter it, and become attached instead to a vision of cooperative, large-scale industry, coordinated on a national and international scale. In "the negation of the negation," he condenses this transformation in popular culture into a formula of historical inevitability. But in the text surrounding this formula he argues that the concentration and organization of property brought about by the rise of capitalism has coincided with and motivated a parallel concentration and organization of the state as an agent capable of and interested in securing the conditions for capitalist accumulation. This rise of the modern state is the obstacle that the working class must surmount to win its emancipation. Confronting the reality of this obstacle, and the demands it places on working-class organization and tactics, is Marx's challenge in the final three chapters of *Capital*. It is this argument, and not the Hegelian catchphrase, that ought to draw our attention.

There has been a massive literature devoted to Marx's account of the state in general and the modern, bourgeois state in particular. The better representatives of this literature distinguish between two models of the state in the work of Marx and Engels.[98] The first, and most commonly associated with "the Marxist theory of the state," figures the state as an instrument of class domination. The second model figures the state as a parasite, striving for or achieving a sort of independence vis-à-vis society. As opposed to the state as a mere instrument of the ruling class, the parasite state is "autonomous, its own master."[99] However, as is generally recognized, neither Marx nor Engels ever treat the state as truly independent of society. As Marx writes in his late notebooks on ethnology, "the

---

[98] Hunt, *The Political Ideas of Marx and Engels*, vol. 2, chaps. 2–3; Sanderson, "Marx and Engels on the State"; Sanderson, *Interpretation of the Political Ideas of Marx and Engels*, chap. 4.

[99] Hunt, *The Political Ideas of Marx and Engels*, 2:4.

seeming supreme independent existence of the state is itself only seeming and . . . it is in all its forms an excrescence of society."[100]

What I find in part eight of *Capital* is a third model of the state that amalgamates the instrumental and parasitic: the state as *dependent agent of capital*. The state is parasitic upon the accumulation of capital (in a manner I will discuss below), and this secures both its relative independence from the actually existing class of capitalists—"the concrete existence [*Dasein*] of capital as capital"—and a very imperfect instrumental relation to capital as such.[101] The state under capital is self-activating but subservient, a servile and corrupt henchman rather than an autonomous existence. This relationship between the state and capital is crucial for understanding what Marx calls "systematic primitive accumulation,"[102] and one manifestation of which is E. G Wakefield's proposal for "systematic colonization," with which Marx closes *Capital*.

The "industrial regime of independent petty producers, laboring on their own account," is neither integral to the feudal world, per se, nor a full-fledged epoch of its own. "It only prospers, it only deploys all of its energy, and comes into its integral and classical form, where the laborer is the free proprietor of conditions of labor that he himself sets to work, the peasant of the soil he cultivates, the artisan of the tools he handles, as a virtuoso handles his instrument." In England, these conditions only obtained between the disappearance of serfdom in "the last part of the fourteenth century" and the clearing of the estates, beginning in the fifteenth and sixteenth centuries.[103] Petty production could only flourish in this interregnum. Crucially, its very flourishing gave leave and motive to the landlords to destroy it by clearing the estates; in Marx's words, it provoked "the forces and the passions" that were "the material agents of its dissolution."[104]

As Robert Brenner has pointed out, where peasants possessed their means of production individually, rather than as a community, the lords are more likely to evict their tenants, either as an unintended effect of collectively imposed taxes, or as a rational strategy for maintaining or increasing their incomes.[105] A plethora of petty producers, scattered over

---

[100] Quoted in ibid., 2:25.

[101] Marx, *Grundrisse*, 464; *MEGA*, II.1.2:372.

[102] Marx, *Capital*, 1:915; *MEGA*, II.6:674; *MEGA*, II.7:668.

[103] *Capital*, 1:927, 877; *MEGA*, II.6:681, 646; *MEGA*, II.7:678, 634.

[104] *Capital*, 1:928; *MEGA*, II.6:681; *MEGA*, II.7:678. Again, I find myself in agreement with Balibar, who argues that the transition from the feudal mode of production to the capitalist mode of production must pass through a transitional mode of production, one that does not secure the conditions of its own reproduction (*Reading* Capital, 273–308).

[105] "The Social Basis of Economic Development," 53. Brenner's criticisms of commercialization models of the transition to capitalism are quite powerful, especially as they have

the countryside, may indeed provide a rich seedbed for the development of "manual ability, engineering skill, and free individuality," but their very independence and individual skill will also preclude "cooperation on a large scale, the subdivision of the job in the workshop and in the field, mechanization, the knowledgeable domination by man over nature, the free development of the social powers of labor, concert and unity of purpose, the means and the effort of collective activity."[106] These incapacities leave them helpless in the face of the lords' predations.

They offer no more resistance to "the concentrated and organized force of society," the state. But it is the state that has served as the agency of "all" the methods of systematic primitive accumulation, "without exception."[107] Under the colonial regimes, the states of Europe plundered the rest of the world, stealing means of production and labor power on a massive scale. They thereby "gave a great boost to navigation and commerce." Also, "the treasures directly extorted outside Europe by the forced labor of indigenous peoples reduced to slavery, by embezzlement, pillage, and murder flowed back to the mother-country in order to function as capital there." Colonial expeditions and commercial wars were financed by sovereign debt, the selling of public bonds. This system of state finance gave rise to a market for speculators, to national banks, and to a system of taxation that "contains within itself the germ of automatic progression." This system of taxation, together with protectionist tariffs, ruined the remnants of the peasantry and artisan class.[108] Against these state-led initiatives abroad and at home, the independent producers are impotent.

---

been articulated by his ally, Ellen Meiksins Wood. Wood, however, in the course of defending the thesis that capitalism emerged from the English countryside, casts "variable rents responsive to market imperatives" as the primary mechanism of capitalization, and the "improving landlord" as the agent who installed this mechanism (*The Origin of Capitalism*, 102, 114). Whether this thesis is historically true or not I cannot say, but it is not Marx's claim in *Capital*, nor is it compatible with this. Attacking the myth of the progressive bourgeoisie installing capitalism from below, Wood subscribes, instead, to the notion that capitalism was imposed from above, by existing elites. As she writes, it was "advanced by the landlords' powers against the peasants' claims to customary rights" (ibid., 118). Thus, the process of primitive accumulation indicates, for Wood, "the unchallenged victory of the landed class at the heart of agrarian capitalism" (ibid., 127). This is an updated version of the Saint-Simonian thesis, not Marx's. According to Marx, the landlords' victory was pyrrhic, and capitalism could only be imposed after it had emerged unintentionally. An account of early agrarian capitalism in Britain that is much closer to Marx's own is provided by McNally, *Against the Market*, 7–30.

[106] *Capital*, 1:927; *MEGA*, II.6:681; *MEGA*, II.7:677–78. Remember Marx's disparagement of the French peasantry as incapable of any unity of purpose, "like potatoes in a sack" (*Eighteenth Brumaire*, *Political Writings*, 2:239; *MEGA*, I.11:180).

[107] *Capital*, 1:915; *MEGA*, II.6:674; *MEGA*, II.7:668.

[108] *Capital*, 1:916–22; *MEGA*, II.6:675–78; *MEGA*, II.7:669–74.

This is not to say, of course, that they were passive in the face of these processes. Far from it. As Craig Calhoun has argued, "the members of declining craft communities" were both motivated and well-positioned to powerfully resist the advent of industrial capitalism; unlike the nascent class of factory operatives, they found in the new order no "place, potential material gains, [or] reasonably satisfying fallback positions if they did not get as much as they sought in their struggles."[109] And, contrary to the picture sometimes painted by Marx, petty producers were not atomistically isolated families, incapable of concerted action; they were integrated in "traditional communities" that were "important bases of radical mobilization." Nonetheless, as Calhoun himself admits, these mobilizations tended to fall apart whenever they extended "much beyond the range of direct, person-to-person communal ties."[110] In short, they were not in the same league as the powers they sought to resist, which were organized at the national and international level and were capable of employing to great effect the impersonal bond of monetary payment.

This is the crucial context for Marx's pivot, and for his invocation of Hegel. The "first negation" of the independent petty producer is the constitution of an agency or agencies powerful enough and interested in destroying petty production. On the one hand, this constitution is achieved by the development of capitalist large industry, which, as we saw in the previous chapter, very effectively erodes the know-how and the other material bases of petty production. On the other hand, it is achieved by the growth of the modern state, which is bound to the fortunes of capital, and which carries out the systematic policies of primitive accumulation that "abridge the transitional phases" from the feudal economic order to the capitalist one. This first negation—"carried out with a pitiless vandalism, spurred on by the most infamous motives, the passions most sordid and most hateful in their pettiness," forces and passions the society of petty producers "represses"[111]—was, perversely, provoked and made possible by the independence and "dwarf" scale of the producers' property, which made easy pickings for the lords and the state.

The negation of these newly constituted agencies of industrial capital and the modern state can only be the constitution of a new agency, powerful enough and interested to destroy both capitalist industry and the modern state. This "negation of the negation" cannot, Marx is arguing, be carried out by independent producers. To think otherwise is to think that the rise of the modern world was just a roll of the dice, a fluke, which might turn out differently were the experiment repeated. There is

---

[109] *Roots of Radicalism*, 31.
[110] Ibid., 98.
[111] *Capital*, 1:928; *MEGA*, II.6:681; *MEGA*, II.7:678.

no credibly conceivable agency, argues Marx, both powerful enough to challenge the state and capitalist industry and interested in creating and sustaining petty production. Against this option, Marx presses his claim that the increasing concentration of capitalist wealth, the progressive de-skilling and collectivization of labor, and the relative immiseration of the class of laborers dependent upon wages all conspire to make that class and only that class, which has been "disciplined, united, and organized by the very mechanism of capitalist production," capable of overthrowing capitalism for the sake of instituting "social property" in the means of production.[112] "The masses," unable to satisfy their needs except through cooperative, industrialized labor, have the means, via their "revolutionary combination," to expropriate "a few usurpers."[113] This coincidence of motive and means constitutes the material conditions necessary for overcoming capitalism.

The Exit from Capital

How the state came to have a corporate interest in the accumulation of capital is not a question that Marx explicitly asks or seeks to answer. He does, however, note some of the mechanisms by which this interest is preserved and recreated. The relationship between tax revenues and public indebtedness is one such mechanism. The state's ability to act, in a postfeudal world, is fundamentally dependent upon its ability to back up its threats and promises with money, which pays the salaries of its agents and buys the weapons and other implements with which those agents enact the state's sovereign will, no matter what the procedures of

---

[112] Compare Marx's comments on the machinery question before the General Council of the IWMA on July 28, 1868: "One of the great results of machinery is organized labour which must bear fruit sooner or later . . . machinery leads on one hand to associated organized labour, on the other to the disintegration of all formerly existing social and family relations" (*The General Council of the First International, 1866–1868: Minutes*, 229–34). At a subsequent meeting, on August 11, 1868, Marx summed up the outcome of the debate with the resolution: "that on the one side machinery has proved a most powerful instrument of despotism and extortion in the hands of the capitalist class; that on the other side the development of machinery creates the material conditions necessary for the superseding of the wages-system by a truly social system of production" (ibid., 241). The next topic for debate was the question of the reduction of working hours, which Marx brought back to the same considerations, arguing that reducing the length of the working day "had the effect of introducing more machinery, and made production on a small scale more and more impossible, which, however, was necessary to arrive at social production" (ibid., 244). The impossibility of small-scale production and the self-organization of the laborers in the face of overwork and mechanization are the negative and positive material conditions of social production.

[113] *Capital*, 1:929–30; *MEGA*, II.6:683; *MEGA*, II.7:679.

that will's formation.[114] The acquisition by the state of the money with which it acts is, however, essentially dependent upon the process of the accumulation of capital. This is true whether one looks to tax revenues or to public borrowing, and whether the government is "despotic, consti-tutional, or republican."[115] As Michael Heinrich has summed up Marx's conclusion, "the material foundation of the state is thus directly con-nected to the accumulation of capital; no government can get past this dependency."[116] This dependency is not passivity; hence, the state is not simply an instrument of the bourgeois class. Servants may anticipate the orders of their master, or try to stay on the master's good side while doing as little as possible, or try to play one master off against another. Servi-tude is a situation calling for strategic and opportunistic action, not for passivity. Where capital accumulation seems threatened, therefore, the state can be expected to act for the sake of securing those conditions, however irrational or superstitious the strategy it may follow.

Marx's account of systematic primitive accumulation is, therefore, im-portantly divergent from the liberal critique of conquest and usurpation, a critique largely replicated by moralistic socialists. Nineteenth-century liberals had ready-to-hand an analysis and condemnation of the imperial tendencies of the state.[117] *Doux commerce* made it possible for people to obtain their desires without war and plunder, and thereby rendered all offensive war obsolete.[118] Conquest can only establish itself as the policy of a nation either due to a sort of delusion about the capacity of military power or under the direction of a usurper, like Napoleon, who must make war in order to maintain his rule. Everything about conquest and usurpa-tion suggest anachronism, the futile effort to deny the reality of a world united by commerce. Thus, echoing Montesquieu, Benjamin Constant ar-gued that "not only does commerce emancipate individuals; by creating credit it also makes authority itself dependent." This is because, "in order to obtain the favors of wealth one must serve it; it is wealth which is

---

[114]This is not the only condition that must be satisfied, for the state also needs to culti-vate the perception of legitimacy, which raises the issue of ideology, patriotism, etc. None-theless, the extent to which agents of the state will carry out their mandates simply because they are paid to do so should not be underestimated. Legitimation and patriotic fervor are, often enough, simply side effects of sending the checks out on time.

[115]*Capital*, 1:919; *MEGA*, II.7:671. This is part of along passage added by Marx to the French edition.

[116]*Introduction to the Three Volumes of Karl Marx's* Capital, 212.

[117]The liberal debates about conquest and imperialism have been the subject of much recent work. For important contributions to the debate, see Mehta, *Liberalism and Empire*, and Pitts, *A Turn to Empire*.

[118]See, for example, the first two chapters of Constant's *The Spirit of Conquest and Usurpation*, as well as his lecture on "The Liberty of the Ancients Compared with That of the Moderns" (*Political Writings*, 51–55, 313–15).

bound to prevail."[119] An analogous condemnation of all militarism—and even all politics as such—was a powerful current in both French and British socialism, whether in the form of the Saint-Simonian distinction between military and industrial organization, or in the Owenite insistence that the social system would inevitably replace the unsocial system.[120]

Marx argues, against the grain of this critique of conquest in the name of society, that usurpation and conquest are the inevitable consequence of the dependence of the authority of the state upon wealth as capital. Insofar as the state is dependent upon and constrained by the accumulation of capital, capital has usurped the state power. The state will act as an "agent" of capital.[121] As capital's agent, the state does capital's dirty work, executing and enforcing the expropriations that capital cannot itself carry out. Hence, Marx's sarcastic invocation of "*doux commerce*" to characterize, immediately thereafter, the "treachery, bribery, massacre, and meanness" of Dutch colonial administration in Celebes, Java, and Malacca.[122] Far from being counterproductive anachronisms in an era of peaceful commerce, the methods of systematic primitive accumulation are the predictable outcome of the state's having "entered into the service of the makers of surplus-value."[123] Where the state can, by conquest and plunder, create conditions that can be capitalized, it can be expected to do so. If the liberal ideals behind the *doux commerce* thesis are thereby betrayed, this betrayal is utterly unsurprising.

For Marx, this conclusion has major repercussions for the strategy of working-class emancipation. These repercussions reveal themselves, of all places, in the British settler colonies, to which Marx turns in the final

[119] Constant, *Political Writings*, 141.

[120] *Doctrine of St-Simon*; Proudhon, *OC*, vol. 2; Thompson, *Inquiry*; see Claeys, *Citizens and Saints*, 49–62, for commentary on the Owenite distinction.

[121] In the French edition, *agent* replaces the German *Potenz* in Marx's famous claim that "Force is the midwife of every old society which is pregnant with a new one. It is itself an economic power" (Marx, *Capital*, 1:916; *MEGA*, II.7:669). The French reads: "*La Force est un agent économique.*" The "force" in question is *l'État*. Only in this one context does Marx's text capitalize *la Force*.

[122] *Capital*, 1:916; *MEGA*, II.6:675; *MEGA*, II.7:669. There is no evidence that Marx knew Constant's treatise on conquest and usurpation, but it is striking the extent to which Marx here echoes Constant's description of usurpation, which requires so much "treachery, violence, and perjury," and that must "put all the guilty passions as if in a hothouse, so that they may ripen faster" (Constant, *Political Writings*, 89). According to Marx, systematic primitive accumulation employs "the power of the state . . . to hasten, as in a hothouse [*treibhausmäßig*], the transformation process of the feudal into the capitalist mode of production" (*Capital*, 1:915; *MEGA*, II.6:652). The metaphor is missing from the French edition (*MEGA*, II.7:641).

[123] *Capital*, 1:922; *MEGA*, II.6:678; *MEGA*, II.7:674. The Fowkes translation translates Marx back into the socialist vernacular he was trying to escape by rendering *Plusmacher* as "profit-mongers"; the French edition has *faiseurs de plus-value*.

chapter. Chapter thirty-one had considered the outward face of colonialism, its decimation and expropriation of indigenous peoples. Chapter thirty-three considers its inward face, the opening it seems to provide for working-class settlers, and the lengths to which the mother country, dependent upon capital accumulation, will go to shut down that opening. The declaration that a colonized land is terra nullius, and the introduction of settlers into this "empty" frontier, seems to establish in reality the Lockean fiction of a world given to all in common and appropriated to each by labor alone. This realization of the working-class dream, in which land is there to be had for anyone intrepid enough to take it and hard working enough to develop it, is, for so long as it lasts, an insuperable barrier to the expansion of capital into the colonies. As E. G. Wakefield discovered in Australia, machinery and money are unable to command labor—that is, to act as capital—where "the bulk of the soil is still public property, and every settler on it can therefore turn part of it into his private property and his individual means of production, without thereby preventing later settlers from performing the same operation."[124] In such a setting, "where every one who so pleases can easily obtain a piece of land for himself, not only is labor very dear, as respects the laborer's share of the product, but the difficulty is to obtain combined labor at any price."[125]

Marx summarizes the roadblock faced by capital in the colonies:

> Today's wage-laborer is tomorrow's independent peasant or artisan, working for himself. He vanishes from the labor-market—but not into the workhouse. This constant transformation of wage-laborers into independent producers, who work for themselves instead of for capital, and enrich themselves instead of the capitalist gentlemen, reacts in its turn very adversely on the conditions of the labor-market. Not only does the degree of exploitation of the wage-laborer remain indecently low. The wage-laborer also loses, along with the relation of dependence, the feeling of dependence on the abstemious capitalist.[126]

The only way to remedy this "anti-capitalist cancer of the colonies,"[127] according to Wakefield, is for the government of the mother country to step in. By setting an artificially high price on the land at the frontier, and by using the money generated from the sale of this land to import new laboring settlers, the government can ensure the conditions of capital

---

[124] *Capital*, 1:934; *MEGA*, II.6:687; *MEGA*, II.7:683.
[125] Wakefield, *England and America*, 1:247; cited by Marx, *Capital*, 1:935; *MEGA*, II.6:687; *MEGA*, II.7:683.
[126] *Capital*, 1:936; *MEGA*, II.6:688; *MEGA*, II.7:685.
[127] *Capital*, 1:938; *MEGA*, II.6:690; *MEGA*, II.7:687.

accumulation even in the face of terra nullius. This is Wakefield's plan for "systematic colonization," a plan which was, for a time, taken up as policy by the British government.[128]

Wakefield's plan is important for two reasons. First, it tells against the strategy of worker separatism. The state's interest in capital accumulation implies that, wherever worker colonies or other efforts to escape from wage labor might actually endanger capital, worker separatists will confront not only the difficulties inherent in the organization of a new moral world but also governmental policies backed by force of arms. Emigration will only be allowed if the emigrants reproduce in a new land the social relations of the old. Hence, the story of Wakefield's discovery is an allegory about the necessity of political action to overcome capitalism. From the founding of the IWMA onward, Marx's great wish was to rouse the labor movement once again to political organization and action. If the IWMA were to "succeed in re-electrifying the political movement of the English working class," he wrote to Engels, this "will already have done more for the European working class, without making any fuss, than was possible in any other way."[129] From his inaugural address to his conflicts with Bakunin, Marx incessantly promoted within the IWMA the view that laborers should organize themselves by and for the sake of intervening in politics at the level of the state. This was one of the reasons he did not pick a fight with the followers of Bronterre O'Brien, despite their monetary quackery: they were steadfast proponents of political action.[130] The ending of *Capital* is one more piece of this advocacy. Without openly calling for a revolutionary movement to seize and overthrow the bourgeois state, Marx nonetheless builds a case for the necessity of some such confrontation.[131]

---

[128] See the excellent dissertation by Onur Ulas Ince, "Colonial Capitalism and the Dilemmas of Liberalism," chap. 4.

[129] Marx to Engels, May 1, 1865; *MECW*, 42:150.

[130] See Marx's letter to Friedrich Bolte, November 23, 1871; *MECW*, 44:251–52.

[131] Maximillian Rubel, in his edition of Marx's works, transposed chapters thirty-two and thirty-three, so as to make *Capital* end with the expropriation of the expropriators (Marx, *Œuvres: Économie*). He did so because he was convinced that chapter thirty-two was the real end of the book, and that Marx had "deliberately reversed the last two chapters" in order to hide its revolutionary conclusion from the German censors (ibid., 1:541, 1705–9; Rubel and Manale, *Marx without Myth*, 226). He was not the first to hit on this notion, either. Achille Loria, the Italian economist, had proposed the same thesis as early as 1902 (*Karl Marx*, 65; see Rodriguez-Braun, "Capital's Last Chapter"). Neither Rubel nor Loria had any positive evidence upon which to base their speculations. Rubel, at least, was driven to this speculation by his incredulity that Marx's final words would be "a historical chapter that ended and concluded the work with the defeat of the proletariat" (Marx, *Œuvres: Économie*, 1:1706). Rubel neglects to note that a historical defeat holds political lessons, too.

Second, in Wakefield Marx thinks he has found an invaluable treasure, a political economist who openly declares that political economy can only gain a foothold on the social terrain, as a science and as a form of government, where the direct producer has been expropriated. In chapter one, Marx declared that "the categories of bourgeois economics . . . are forms of thought which are socially valid, and therefore objective, for the relations of production belonging to this historical mode of social production, i.e., commodity production."[132] He argued in chapter six that capital "arises only when the owner of the means of production and subsistence finds the free laborer available, on the market, as the seller of his own labor-power," and that "it is only from this moment that the commodity form of the products of labor becomes universal."[133] Now, in closing, he has found a political economist who admits that, in order to find free laborers available, on the market, those laborers must be deprived of the ability to appropriate the earth to themselves as means of production and subsistence. In short, the categories of political economy require primitive accumulation as a necessary condition of their social validity. Political economy is the science of capital and rests on the same presuppositions as capital. It will betray its highest ideals—private property and labor as a title thereto—in service of its real master.

This claim, if true, is devastating, not only for political economy, in its aspiration to reveal the principles of wealth and social action as such, but also for socialists like Proudhon, for whom political economy, however rudimentary and one sided in its current state, must be reconciled with socialism in order to give rise to a true science of society. In the encounter with Wakefield, political economy reveals itself as its own opposite, a science of expropriation for the sake of property. No reconciliation is possible between this science and the movement of the laboring classes to emancipate themselves. It is the science of their subjection. And this is why Marx has to end *Capital* with Wakefield. Wakefield brings to a close the descent into the Hell of political economy. He declares, without meaning to, that the laborers need have nothing more to do with this.

CONCLUSION

Looking back over the ground this chapter has covered, we can discern the contours of Marx's conceit in part eight. The history of capitalism's creation is a history of treachery. The elements of capitalism were set

[132] *Capital*, 1:169; *MEGA*, II.6:106–7; *MEGA*, II.7:57.
[133] *Capital*, 1:274, including n. 4; *MEGA*, II.6:186, including n. 41; *MEGA*, II.7:138, including n. 41.

free by the betrayal of the feudal order by its lords, by their infidelity to the very bonds of trust that created their social power. The beneficiaries of this betrayal, the nascent class of capitalist farmers, turned around and enslaved their patrons, subjecting the landlords to the domination of the market. The state, transformed by these revolutions into a corrupt servant of economic growth, acts at every turn so as to keep the mass of its subjects—whose commonwealth it is supposed to be—poor and desperate, and to use its organized forces to carry out a policy of conquest, plunder, and colonization. Finally, political economy, the science of capitalist wealth and property, betrays its ideals: the wealth, property, and commerce it extolls and secures is, as Wakefield admits in the colonies, based in "the expropriation of the laborer," the source of that wealth, property, and commerce.[134] Capital can only exist and engross itself so long as the laborers who form it can be continuously degraded and rendered insecure in their existence. By its very nature, capital must eternally betray its creator.

This narrative of treachery, whatever partial precedent it has in the histories of the old Radicals, finds its most fitting illustrations in the depths of Dante's Hell, where those who betray special relationships meet their end. Cocytus, the frozen wasteland at the bottom of the world, entombs the treacherous in ice. The ice itself is hardened by the freezing winds fanned up by the beating of Satan's wings. The lord of the underworld towers over the pit, his three mouths gnawing on the three sinners whose acts of treason most closely resemble his own: Brutus and Cassius, who betrayed their earthly lord, Caesar, and Judas, who betrayed the Son of Man. Perhaps the most brilliant turn in Dante's portrayal of Cocytus is its denouement. In order to exit from Hell, Virgil guides the pilgrim right up to Satan's side, grabs hold of the beast's fur, and climbs down his flank, through a gap in the ice, into a cavern below the mountain of Purgatory. Dante must embrace and grapple bodily with Satan, the founder of all wrong, in order to get out of his realm. And, when he emerges, he finds Satan's feet sticking *up* from the floor of the cave.

The explanation for this reversal is simple. Satan is, in fact, in the very center of the earth. When they passed the midpoint, Virgil and Dante ceased to descend, and began to ascend. But the Aristotelian cosmology according to which the center is the limit of all downward motion is, in Dante, combined with an allegorical metaphysics according to which the journey toward God follows an ever-ascending path. Thus, the pilgrim's ascent does not begin when he transverses the center. Even when he's climbing down, in fact he's climbing up. The descent into the Inferno was an upside-down ascent through an upside-down realm ruled by an

---

[134] *Capital*, 1:940; *MEGA*, II.6:691; *MEGA*, II.7:689.

upside-down king, a fact that is only revealed by the pilgrim's emergence, right side up, in the cave. As John Freccero explains:

> The pilgrim is travelling upwards, even during his descent into hell, for true "up" in the cosmos is "down" to us; this is the literal justification of the moral truth which Augustine expressed with the exhortation: "Descend, so that you may ascend." In the spiritual life, one must descend in humility before one can begin the ascent to truth, and in the physical world, according to both Dante and Aristotle, one must travel downward with respect to our hemisphere in order to rise. The analogy between the mind's journey to God and the pilgrim's journey to the Empyrean is in this respect, as so often, perfectly exact. Furthermore, the Aristotelian convention helps explain why Satan, imbedded in the center of the earth, should have fallen down from the southern part of the heavens, and why he should appear right-side up in this world, of which he is prince.[135]

Thus, the passage through and out of Cocytus is a revelation. The upside-downness of the Earthly City is made manifest, its ideals and deities are shown for what they are, and the pilgrim is released from their grip in order to begin his life anew.

Something analogous has transpired over the course of Marx's confrontation with primitive accumulation. Of course, Marx has indicated from near the beginning that we were traveling through an inverted realm, one where, for example, a table "stands on its head, and evolves out of its wooden brain grotesque ideas."[136] Marx even stakes his claim to originality on having pointed out these inversions, for "that in appearance things are often presented in an inverted way is something fairly familiar to every science, apart from political economy."[137] But the inversion now, thanks to Wakefield's confession, seems to infect political economy in its entire breadth and depth. This science, which articulated the market as "the exclusive realm of freedom, equality, property, and Bentham,"[138] now recommends, explicitly and as a matter of policy, "the expropriation of the laborer,"[139] for the sake of securing the domination of capital. The political economists who "ask English landed proprietors, as God asked Cain about Abel, 'Where are your thousands of freeholders gone?'" are asked by Marx, in turn, "where do *you* come from, then? From the destruction of those freeholders. Why don't you go further, and ask where the independent weavers, spinners,

---

[135] "Dante's Pilgrim in a Gyre," 170–71.
[136] *Capital*, 1:163; *MEGA*, II.6:102; *MEGA*, II.7:53.
[137] *Capital*, 1:677; *MEGA*, II.6:500; *MEGA*, II.7:463.
[138] *Capital*, 1:280; *MEGA*, II.6:191; *MEGA*, II.7:143.
[139] *Capital*, 1:940; *MEGA*, II.6:691; *MEGA*, II.7:689.

and handicraftsmen have gone to?"[140] The English fratricide against the Irish—likened by Marx to the slaying of Remus by Romulus—is not an unfortunate affair, incidental or contrary to capitalist development, but a foundational moment, repeated by systematic colonization and the "Herod-like slaughter of innocents," the large-scale theft of children for the factories.[141]

There is a logic in this litany of crimes, or at least a rich network of associations. Dante's Satan presides over an Inferno created by his own betrayal of God, his father and creator, at the moment of his creation. The Earthly City was founded by Cain after he slew his virtuous brother, Abel.[142] Rome was founded by Romulus after he slew his brother, Remus.[143] All of these foundings are, as Horace said of the last one, presided over by "a cruel fate." Their origins are not confined to the past, and cannot be escaped or outgrown, but accompany the cities they originate right up to their end. Confronting the betrayal at the beginning forces the realization that the betrayal must be reiterated, that the forces by which the city is maintained in existence are equal to the force by which it was brought into existence to begin with.

G. A. Cohen has argued that Marx was committed to the claim that "socialism and social science are incompatible."[144] In socialism, as in all of the examples of "other forms of production" with which Marx concludes his consideration of commodity fetishism, "there is no need for labor and its products to assume a fantastic form different from their reality."[145] Hence, there is no need in any noncapitalist mode of production for an economic science to remove "the veil . . . from the countenance of the social life-process," for the social life process does not, except in capitalism, veil itself in the market exchange of the products of labor. What Cohen calls "the withering away of social science" under socialism is, for Marx, the inapplicability of political economy to any noncapitalist society. This inapplicability was denied by Proudhon, for whom "socialism is nothing but a profound criticism *and* an incessant development of political

---

[140] *Capital*, 1:913n8; *MEGA*, II.6:673n237. This note is elevated to the main text in the French edition *(MEGA*, II.7:666–67).

[141] *Capital*, 1:870, 922; *MEGA*, II.6:643, 678; *MEGA*, II.7:630, 674.

[142] One section of Cocytus is called Caina.

[143] Of course, there are multiple, incompatible versions of the foundation of Rome, but both Horace (in his Seventh Epode) and Augustine take as authoritative the account (recorded by Livy) according to which Romulus killed Remus after they disagreed about where to found their city. Romulus began to construct a wall around his preferred site, Remus jumped the wall to confront him, and Romulus slew him, saying "So perish every one that shall hereafter leap over my wall" (Livy, *History of Rome*, I.vi).

[144] *Karl Marx's Theory of History*, 396.

[145] *Capital*, 1:169–70; *MEGA*, II.6:107–8; *MEGA*, II.7:57–58.

economy."[146] And, although they did not state it as flatly, it was also denied by all those popular political economists in Britain who attempted to appropriate political economy as a science of the possible while changing its social perspective, who "believed in their various ways that it was both possible and desirable to utilize or harness the new science of economics directly in the service of the labor movement."[147] Marx alone wanted to lead the workers and socialists through political economy to the point where it reveals itself to rest upon the expropriation of the laborers. This revelation is supposed to free the workers' movement to turn away from the attempt to reconcile socialism and political economy, to extract the timeless model of social economy that the future order will most perfectly realize. Marx's mythic overcoming of political economy, embodied in Wakefield's confession, is also his theoretical overcoming of all these "scientific socialisms," and the precondition and premonition of the working classes' political overcoming of capital.

If Dante must confront Satan in order to escape his realm, then so must the laboring classes confront capital in order to escape the social Hell. Instead of trying to create their own capital, the laborers must realize that capital is wealth that betrays and turns against its creators. This—not a failure to work and save—is the original sin from which the laborers' condition springs. The feudal order could not survive the lords' plundering of the vassals and peasants, whose subjection depended upon their possession of land and tools. Capital, however, thrives on the separation of the laborers from the earth, the conditions of their labor. The capitalist mode of production, on the whole, reproduces that separation wherever it has been established. Wherever it has not yet been established, and wherever the normal course of reproduction is threatened, the servile and corrupt state—like an antirepublican Cassius and Brutus—can be expected to betray the commonwealth, its people, and all its "old idols" in an effort to forcibly establish the necessary separation. Capital's grip on the basis of the state's existence cannot be broken.[148] Meanwhile,

---

[146] OC, 1:76; emphasis added. As Gregory Claeys has documented, "social science" was originally an Owenite term of art ("'Individualism,' 'Socialism,' and 'Social Science': Further Notes on a Process of Conceptual Formation, 1800–1850"; the term was likely coined by William Thompson's *Inquiry*). A parallel development in France saw Fourier proclaiming the new science of the series, which would both reveal and institute the social order. One could say that the dream of a scientific socialism is as old as socialism itself. It is one of the greatest ironies in the history of socialism that the writer who came to be most firmly associated with the phrase was the most vociferous critic of the premises underlying the notion.

[147] Thomas, *Karl Marx and the Anarchists*, 230. As Thomas notes, his belief that "capitalism and political economy stand, or fall, together," also separated Marx from Rodbertus and Lassalle, the principle theorists of socialism in Germany. And, as Thomas also notes, the political stakes of this disagreement are profound.

[148] Dante's Cassius and Brutus are devoured feet first.

the political economists, like Judas, betray their proclaimed principles—labor and property—so that these might be crucified by the state. Capital is the true lord of their thoughts.[149] In their efforts to gain their freedom from capital, the laboring class can expect help neither from the state nor from political economy.

[149] Dante's Judas is devoured head first.

CHAPTER 7

Conclusion: Purgatory, or the Social Republic

The working class did not expect miracles from the Commune. They
have no ready-made utopias to introduce *par décret du peuple* . . . .
They have no ideal to realize, but to set free the elements of the
new society with which the old collapsing bourgeois society itself is
pregnant.
    —Marx, *The Civil War in France: Address of the General Council,*
      3rd ed. (1871)

To accomplish this act of universal emancipation is the historical mission of the modern proletariat.
    —Engels, *Herr Dühring's Revolution in Science* (1878)

All determination is negation and all negation is determination.
    —Marx, manuscript for *Capital,* vol. 2 (1863–65)

We have followed Marx as he has led us through the labyrinth of capital,
the social Hell. Let us pause to recollect the path we have trod, bringing
out as forcefully as possible Marx's appropriation of Dante's schema.

In its most readily apparent aspect, the society ruled by capital is a
commercial society, knit together by the interchange of commodities and
money. Kinetic and anarchic, this society subordinates each producer to
the hard discipline of the market, the blind forces of the social process.
This subjection provokes and renders futile the moralistic response of
those who urge us to exercise individual or collective self-control. Capital
is akratic, incapable of self-control, condemned to circulate eternally beyond the river Styx. The discipline of the market is an impersonal domination of each by the invisible and unchallengeable desires and choices
of innumerable others. This impersonal domination is possible, however,
only because most goods are produced as commodities, and most goods
are produced as commodities only where most people have to sell their
labor power to the owners of the means of production for a wage. Hence,
Marx led us into the workshop, where the agents of capital seize hold of
the laborers' bodies and make them work as much as possible. This limit-
less desire for surplus labor provokes the laborers' insistence on a natural

working day. Capital is unnatural, though, and violent in its demands, like the inhabitants of Dis. It can be checked only by a struggle, and by a coercive law, imposed from above.

Class struggle and coercive laws, however, only constrain capital to develop intensively. The command exercised by its representatives breaks down the workers' control of the labor process, masses them together in novel ways, strips their labor of any need for the exercise of their independent judgment, and yokes them to a social and mechanical machine that pumps ever more labor out of them. This development of the capitalist mode of production raises hopes of general opulence, liberal and just remuneration for labor, and universal society. But capital is a fraud, a counterfeiter of good things, a denizen of Malebolge. In its dominion over production, capital develops the powers of labor only in order to better enslave the laborers, negotiates a wage contract with the laborers only in order to disguise its despotic command over their labor, and produces ever greater wealth only in order to extend the social distance between the commanders of social labor and the mass of wretches dependent upon wages for life.

At bottom, this ensemble of social relations, and the Hell it occupies, must have been created, and must be secured and expanded, by a primitive accumulation of capital. Capital cannot perform this primitive accumulation itself, but it seizes upon whatever opportunity other agencies may create. Turning the tables on its landed patrons, who had separated the mass of the people from the land, capital conquered first the field of agriculture and then that of manufacturing. It has usurped and corrupted the power of the state, capitalizing upon every act of conquest, expropriation, and plunder committed by its mighty and brutal servant. The dream that workers might, individually or cooperatively, create their own capital, and thereby leave behind their wage slavery and domination by the capitalist class, is just that. Capital betrays—and must betray—its creators, and it rules this world insofar as it tempts others to similar acts of betrayal. It is the Satan of the social Hell, frozen eternally in Cocytus, the inescapable logic of its own emergence into the world.

Having seen how the "infernal machine" operates, and having been released thereby from the temptations of political economy, an obvious question presents itself to those who have followed Marx's guidance to this point: What now? And here we encounter a truism of Marxology, that Marx does not give us any detailed prescriptions for how a communist society might organize itself for day-to-day functioning and for the reproduction of its institutions. Marx does not tell us, in other words, what a postcapitalist society might look like.

This truism is often expressed as a complaint, and, as such, has been most fully and forcefully articulated by G. A. Cohen. According to Cohen,

Marx subscribed to an *obstetric doctrine* regarding politics. This obstetric doctrine is what lies behind Marx's derision of "writing recipes . . .
for the cook-shops of the future."[1] It is more fully elaborated in his 1859
preface to *A Contribution to the Critique of Political Economy*, where
Marx claims that,

> No social order ever perishes before all of the productive forces in it have
> developed; and new higher relations of production never appear before the
> material conditions of their existence have matured in the womb of the old
> society itself. Therefore, mankind always takes up such problems as it can
> solve; since, looking at the matter more closely, we will always find that
> the problem itself arises only when the material conditions of its solution
> already exist or are at least in the process of formation.[2]

Cohen argues that this obstetric doctrine is a deformed offspring of
Hegel, and that this congenital deformity "disfigured [Marx's] attempt at
science."[3] It underlay Marx's distinction between utopian and scientific
socialism, but it led Marx to mis-draw this distinction, to excise all "recipe writing" from science, and to thereby "foster a criminal inattention to
what one is trying to achieve, to the problem of socialist design."[4] In place
of the hard problems of specifying the ideals socialists hope to realize
and the institutions in which they hope to realize them, Marx's obstetric
conception of politics encouraged Marxists to suppose "that what Lenin
called the 'concrete analysis of a concrete situation' will disclose, trans-
parently, what your political intervention must be, so that you do not
expect and therefore do not face the uncertainties and hard choices with
which a responsible politics must contend."[5] Thus, for Cohen, Marx's
reluctance to write recipes for the cook shops of the future left the door
open for the horrors committed under the banner of socialism in the
twentieth century. That reluctance was based in an obstetric conception
of politics that positively encouraged those horrors.

On the basis of the reading of *Capital* offered in the previous four
chapters, I wish to contest Cohen's construal of the obstetric conception
of politics and his condemnation of it. By this route, I wish to challenge,
also, the truism Cohen expresses as a complaint. Marx is not so reluc-
tant as his reputation would suggest to offer a prescriptive account of
what communism ought to look like.[6] The terms in which he criticizes

[1] *Capital*, 1:99; *MEGA*, II.6:704; *MEGA*, II.7:694.
[2] *MECW*, 29:263; *MEGA*, II.2:101.
[3] *Egalitarian*, 57.
[4] Ibid., 77.
[5] Ibid., 76.
[6] See Ollman, "Marx's Vision of Communism: A Reconstruction," for a useful compendium
of Marx's statements about postcapitalist society. As will become clear, my interpretation of

capitalism reveal the principles according to which communist institutions would have to be, from his perspective, constructed and judged. Although Marx is widely read as a proponent of self-determination or autonomy, his diagnoses of capitalism's evils consistently point out forms of domination, not heteronomy. Hence, I read Marx as radicalizing the republican tradition for which freedom as non-domination is the highest virtue of institutions. Since Marx identifies novel forms of domination, his republic of labor looks unlike the republics advocated by others. However, it is supposed by Marx to be consistent with the federation of communist republics advocated by Robert Owen's later works. I argue, therefore, that Marx should be appreciated both as a radical republican and an (admittedly heterodox) Owenite communist.

MARX'S MIDWIFERY

Cohen's argument states clearly and argues explicitly for what many others have implied obscurely. For this reason, it is especially useful for confronting the basic assumptions according to which Marx's political theory has been received. Cohen's beginning point is his understanding of Marx's debt to Hegel. Hegel had claimed for philosophy the goal of complete comprehensibility. To achieve its goal, Hegel argued, philosophy cannot merely arrive at rationally demonstrable solutions to the problems that confront it. In order for these solutions to be really comprehensible, philosophy must demonstrate that "the answer resides within the question," or that "the solution develops out of the problem." Hegel's requirement of comprehensibility is also a good summation of his dialectical method: "The completion of the development of a (genuine) problem, and only that, provides its solution. Its solution is the consummation of the full development of the problem."[7]

Marx, according to Cohen, turned this thesis about the aim and procedure of philosophy into a political maxim. On this political construal, any genuine practical problem will find its solution in the full development of the problem itself. Applied to the practical problem with which Marx was most concerned, the problem of capitalism, this maxim becomes the conviction that "the solution-providing proletarian revolution is the outgrowth of the problem, of the contradictions of capitalism itself."[8] As

---

many of these statements diverges dramatically from Ollman's, and, unlike him, I will focus on Marx's position during the time in which he was writing and revising *Capital*. See also Hunt, *The Political Ideas of Marx and Engels*, vol. 2, chap. 7.

[7] Cohen, *Egalitarian*, 61–63.

[8] Ibid., 63.

the contradictions of capitalism develop, so too does the agency that will deliver us from capitalism. And this coevolution is not a lucky coincidence. The development of the contradictions just is the development of the salvific agency of the proletariat.

This conviction, in turn, is supposed to explain Marx's repudiation of utopian socialism and his appreciation of the original utopians, Fourier, Saint-Simon, and Owen.[9] Utopian socialists respond to the problem of modern capitalism by fleeing from it, in their imagining of alternative forms of society and in their practice of setting up secret societies and experimental colonies. They testify to the reality of the social problem. They emerge from a felt need to negate the present, and the audience they find for their imagined communities indicates the breadth of the dissatisfaction. Nonetheless, their negation of the present is an abstract one, since it identifies nothing in the world as it is that might lead to the new world. A truly scientific politics, by contrast, would trace the emergence of socialism from out of the social problem itself. Rather than trying to build a new society to imaginary specifications, it would seek only to help the present society give birth to the new one developing within it.

Without disputing either its presence in his writings or its centrality for Marx, I wish to flesh out Cohen's characterization of this obstetric conception of politics in such a way as to wrest it away from some of his criticisms of Marx's politics. I think Cohen misinterprets Marx's relationship to utopian socialism. Cohen claims that Marx affirms the vision of a better world contained in the writings of the utopians, and he quarrels with them only because they could not see that this better world was being brought about by the very capitalist world they criticized. While there is a sense in which this is true, it is not the sense identified by Cohen. The ends of socialism, insofar as these are common to Marx and the utopians, are not what Cohen takes them to be. Moreover, because he has misidentified these aims, Cohen cannot but fail to see the intimate connection between Marx's conception of these aims and the obstetric conception of politics. When the "content" of socialism is seen to be the universalization of republican freedom, a natural and unobjectionable connection emerges between socialism and Marx's midwifery.

The Ends of the Socialist Movement

Marx certainly conceived politics in obstetric terms. Although I have not emphasized it, or used Cohen's terms, my argument in this book supports Cohen's contention. Marx leads his readers into the Hell of political

---

[9]This connection has been pursued in greater length, and in explicit debt to Cohen, by David Leopold; see his "The Structure of Marx and Engels' Considered Account of Utopian Socialism"; also *The Young Karl Marx*, chap. 5.

economy in order to clarify the problems facing socialism, and hence the historic task of the proletariat. The study of political economy is necessary, not because political economy contains elements of the solution to the social problem, as Proudhon thought, but because political economy does *not* contain any such elements. Political economy articulates the problem facing the laboring classes, even if it does so unaware. Hence, Marx would agree with Cohen's interpretive claim that "all the socialist theorist has to do is to make the task facing the proletariat more explicit."[10]

However, Cohen also claims that the *content* of socialism remained essentially the same from the utopian socialists to Marx. Here, Cohen is self-consciously forwarding the tradition according to which Marxism has three sources and component parts, German philosophy, French socialism, and British political economy.[11] If French socialism is a source and component part of Marxism, then something of French socialism must be preserved in Marxism. According to Cohen, this remnant is the actual content of the desired transformation of the world. As Cohen puts it, these socialists propounded

> a vision of a better society, one lacking the manifest injustice and misery of capitalism; one, too, that was rational in its workings because planned, rather than market-driven and therefore anarchic and irrational, as was capitalism . . . The problem with the utopians was not that they were too optimistic in what they thought could be accomplished. . . . Rather, the socialists were utopian in the sense that they lacked a realistic conception of how socialism would come to be: they did not see that it was to be produced by social reality itself.[12]

Thus, the socialist vision of a better society is essentially constant. What is essential or basic to socialism is its commitment to the "principles" or "values" of community and equality.[13] "The problem" posed by capitalism, the genuine problem to be solved, "is to turn the world into a home for humanity by overcoming the scarcity in the relationship between humanity and nature which induces social division."[14] Marx did not transform or criticize this vision, says Cohen. He tried to show how capitalism

[10]*Egalitarian*, 63. Marx would, however, dispute the implication of Cohen's "all," that this is *less* than what the other socialists set out to do. Explicating the task facing the proletariat is, for Marx, akin to leading them through Hell, and is far more difficult than would be writing forty volumes of utopian fancy.

[11]Ibid., 47. Hence, his exemplars of utopian socialism are all French: Fourier, Saint-Simon, and Cabet.

[12]Ibid.

[13]*Currency of Egalitarian Justice*, chap. 10.

[14]Ibid., 49.

was producing the material conditions for the realization of this vision, including the agency that will bring it about.

There are places where Marx seems to support Cohen's reading. The most explicit of these is in Marx's first draft of *The Civil War in France*. Addressing those "patronizing friends of the working class" who denied that the Paris Commune had a socialist character since it did not "try to establish in Paris a *phalanstère* nor an *Icarie*," Marx writes that,

> All the socialist founders of sects belonged to a period in which the work-ing classes themselves were neither sufficiently trained and organized by the march of capitalist society itself to enter as historical agents upon the world's stage, nor were the material conditions of their emancipation suf-ficiently matured in the old world itself. . . . The utopian founders of sects, while in their criticism of present society clearly describing the goal of the social movement, . . . found neither in society itself the material conditions of its transformation, nor in the working class the organized power and the conscience of the movement. . . . From the moment the working men's class movement became real, the fantastic utopias evanesced, not because the working class had given up on the end aimed at by these utopians, but because they had found the real means to realize them, and in their place came a real insight into the historic conditions of the movement and a more and more gathering force of the militant organization of the working class. But the last two ends of the movement proclaimed by the utopians are the last two ends proclaimed by the Paris revolution and by the International. Only the means are different.[15]

This seems to say exactly what Cohen says. The final aims of socialism remained the same, from the time of the utopians, in the early decades of the century, right up through the Commune in 1871. Marx affirms those ends as the ends of the International.

But what are those ends? I have left out the crucial bit. The "last two ends of the movement proclaimed by the utopians" are "suppression of the wage system with all its economical conditions of class rule."

These ends are not Cohen's "vision of a better society." In order to see this, we need only recall the argument of this book, which provides all of the material we need to explicate the final ends of utopian socialism, insofar as these are affirmed by Marx. When Marx refers to the "suppres-sion of the wage system," he is referring to the abolition of wage labor, and hence of the exploitation of labor power by capital and of the re-serve army of the unemployed, which are its concomitants. This aspect of

---

[15] *Political Writings*, 3:262. The stilted syntax is Marx's; he wrote in English, and the draft contains many rough patches. Cohen cites this passage in an endnote; *Egalitarian*, 193–94n29.

capitalism was analyzed by Marx in parts three, six, and seven of *Capital*, and his arguments regarding it have been presented by me in chapters 4 and 5 herein. It encompasses the violence with which capital seizes the labor process, the fraudulence of the wage form, which makes this violence disappear behind the appearance of a free contract, and the accumulation of social misery that accompanies the dependency upon wages.

Marx's reference to "all its economical conditions of class rule" is more opaque. Luckily, Marx fleshes out this phrase in the final version of *The Civil War in France*, where he refers to the Commune as "essentially a working class government," and "the political form at last discovered under which to work out the economical emancipation of labor." Since "the political rule of the producer cannot coexist with the perpetuation of his social slavery," the Commune must, according to its nature, "serve as a lever for uprooting the economical foundations upon which rests the existence of classes, and therefore of class rule."[16] Here, and in the following paragraph, Marx seems to lay out what he means by the economical conditions of class rule that accompany the wage system. Again, there are three elements: the *political domination* of the workers effected by the state, the *objective domination* or despotism to which workers are subjected in production, and the *impersonal domination* experienced by all commodity producers. This side of capitalism is analyzed by Marx particularly in parts one, four, and eight of *Capital*, and by me in chapters 3, 5, and 6 of this book. Because this articulation of three modes of domination is not as immediately obvious in Marx's formulation, it is worth our while to spell matters out more fully.[17]

First, there is for Marx the bare but essential fact that the Commune was a working-class government. We saw in chapter 6 that, on Marx's account, the dependency of the state upon capital is an immense barrier to the emancipation of the working classes and a decisive refutation of the strategy of worker separatism. The first achievement of the Commune was to break the ties that bind the government to capital. It did this by three means: (1) Universal suffrage meant that the legislative, executive, and judicial functions were not literally representing only the wealthy. (2) By reducing all governmental salaries to match average laborers' wages, the conveyor belt connecting capital accumulation to governmental functioning via tax revenues was slackened; "cheap government" was a means

---

[16] *Political Writings*, 3:212.

[17] In what follows, I am laying out what I believe Marx took to be the decisive considerations. Whether Marx's reading of the Commune's actions is itself justified by the sources, whether the institutions of the Commune were in fact as he said they were, whether they would have achieved the aims he saw them working toward, and all other such questions, are here deliberately set aside. For a full treatment of Marx's attitudes toward the Commune, see Hunt, *The Political Ideas of Marx and Engels*, vol. 2, chaps. 4–5.

of liberating the state from its dependency upon capital. (3) By making all governmental functionaries electable and recallable, the Commune made it imperative that governmental action be readily justifiable to the majority of the governed, which meant the laboring classes themselves. By these means, Marx claims, the government would cease to express the general will of capital, and the state would no longer stand in the way of the laborers' self-emancipation.

Second, Marx read into the Communal decree turning some workshops over to be run by the laborers a declaration that the Commune "aimed at the expropriation of the expropriators." He branded this the institution of communism. Handing factories over to the laborers employed therein, to be run according to their collective wishes, is equivalent, in Marx's argument, to "transforming the means of production, land, and capital, now chiefly the means of enslaving and exploiting labor, into mere instruments of free and associated labor." This transformation would disrupt the objective domination within the workshop by making cooperative labor into something accomplished by the laborers themselves, rather than something imposed upon them by the capitalist. What and how each workshop produced would be up to the members to decide.

Finally, however, this self-government of freely associated laborers would be nothing but "a sham and a snare" if the various workshops continued to produce commodities for the market instead of coordinating their production with one another. On this point, Marx could not point to anything actually accomplished or declared by the Commune. Instead, he puts this condition into the subjunctive: "if united co-operative societies are to regulate national production upon common plan, thus taking it under their own control, and putting an end to the constant anarchy and periodical convulsions which are the fatality of capitalist production— what else, gentlemen, would it be but communism, 'possible' communism?" The abolition of the self-regulating market—and with it of the value form—was not on the agenda for the Commune, but without this abolition, the impersonal domination that is an "economical foundation" of capitalism as a system would remain in place. As we have seen in chapter 3, this was for Marx unworkable and unacceptable.

Thus, "the last two ends of the movement proclaimed by the utopians," which are also, according to Marx, "the last two ends proclaimed by the Paris revolution and by the International," are not Cohen's timeless basics of socialism, but two headings under which Marx inserts the content of his own critical analysis of capitalism, the way stations along his descent into the Hell of political economy. The earliest socialists did indeed wish to do away with wage labor and class domination, with all its economic foundations. However, as we have seen, Marx disagreed vehemently with most of these predecessors about what wage labor and class domination amounted to, how they worked, what social processes constituted and reconstituted them, and what would count as their abolition.

It is not the conceptual content of socialism that has remained the same, from Fourier and Saint-Simon down to Proudhon, Marx, and beyond. Rather, certain names and phrases—anarchy, money mystery, fetishism, capital, vampire, wage slavery, exploitation, despotism, and such—have remained in circulation, establishing the commonplaces of discourse, while the meaning of those names and phrases has been disputed, muddied, played with, corrupted, redefined, and contested. That Marx used the established phraseology of socialism is not in dispute. The question is: What did he do with it? How did his efforts at definition and disputation situate him vis-à-vis his predecessors and the socialist movement as a whole? The claim about continuity to which Cohen points us is Marx's attempt to embrace the history of French socialism, to appropriate the Commune to that history, to align both of those with the IWMA, and to give the whole motley ensemble a Marxian cast. It is an act of political speech, not Marx doing future scholars' work for them.[18]

Moreover, Marx's "last two ends," once they have been articulated, diverge in decisive ways from Cohen's basics of socialism. Cohen invokes the socialist vision of "a better society, . . . lacking the manifest injustice and misery of capitalism; . . . rational in its workings because planned, rather than . . . anarchic and irrational"; a society based on community and equality, which would "turn the world into a home for humanity by overcoming the scarcity in the relationship between humanity and nature which induces social division." The prominence of community or association is the only point where there seems to be a convergence between Marx and Cohen (even here, this appearance is misleading). They both, it is true, point out the anarchy of the present system's reliance on markets, but, rather than opposing this anarchy to the rationality of a planned economy, as Cohen does, Marx opposes it to the control exercised by free and associated laborers. Marx says nothing about overcoming scarcity; nor does he say that scarcity is the origin of social division. He speaks only of eliminating slavery and exploitation, which stem from the current form of wealth, not from scarcity. Indeed, Marx says nothing about the natural world; he is focused squarely on social relations. Neither, unsurprisingly, does he say anything about eliminating injustice or bringing about material equality. Between Cohen's socialism and Marx's communism, there seems to be barely any shared commonplaces.

---

[18] Thus, I also strenuously disagree with Hobsbawm's claim that "very nearly everything Marx and Engels said about the concrete shape of communist society is based on earlier utopian writings" ("Marx, Engels, and Pre-Marxian Socialism," 9). "Very nearly nothing" would be closer to the truth.

Neither is there any meaningfully common conceptual content. Looking at Marx's hymn to the Commune on its own terms, its overwhelming theme is *emancipation*, the winning of freedom for and by the laboring class. Its secondary theme is the *association* of laborers for the sake of winning and enjoying this freedom. Freedom and association: these are the principles of Marx's communism. Moreover, freedom and association have an intimate connection with Marx's obstetric approach to politics. Because Cohen's principles—equality and community—have no such connection to obstetric politics, he concludes that Marx's midwifery must have originated outside of Marx's commitment to socialism, and finds this source of alien contamination in Hegel. I want to show, instead, that Marx found in socialism and communism elements that were naturally harmonious with his Hegelian bent of mind and that seemed to cry out for an obstetric politics.

The Self-Emancipation of the Laboring Class

If socialism and communism name the emancipation and association of the laborers, and if emancipation and association are understood in a republican manner, then a commitment to socialism and communism practically entails a reticence to write recipes for the cook shops of the future. The precise institutional arrangements that will best suit any particular group of free and associated laborers will necessarily have to take into account the particularities of their situation, their common resources, their characters and histories and interrelations. The people best placed to know those particularities will be those free and associated laborers themselves. Anyone who presumes to say from afar how they ought to manage their common affairs might rightly expect to be told to mind their own business. The solutions to each association's problems will have to emerge out of the context of the problems themselves, and the institutions of freely associated people are their own affair, *provided that no one is dominated*. This proviso has bite, however, and so, as we will see, there are significant institutional prescriptions that are compatible with Marx's principled obstetrics, and that, contrary to Cohen's implication, Marx is unafraid to make.

That Marx thought the emancipation of the laboring class to be the primary goal of the socialist movement is quite clear from the record. Marx takes this goal so much for granted that he never feels the need to argue for it, but simply uses it as a criterion for deciding whether a text or author ought to be regarded as socialist at all. Thus, for example, he largely dismisses Saint-Simon from the socialist canon with the observation that the Frenchman only "speaks directly for the laboring class and declares their emancipation to be the goal of his efforts" in his final work, *Le nouveau chistianisme.*[19] His writings on behalf of the IWMA proclaim this aim repeatedly. It is, as the Rules of the Association declare, "the great end to which every political movement ought to be subordinate as a means." Those same rules declare that this aim "must be conquered by the working classes themselves."[20] My argument is that Marx's obstetric conception of politics falls out naturally from this conviction that socialism or communism amounts to the self-emancipation of the laboring class.

To see why this is the case, let us return to Cohen's objection to Marx's incipient Leninism. The epitome of the Marxian claim is that, so far as the self-emancipation of the laboring class is concerned, "what is to be done, and done *immediately* at any given, particular moment in the future, depends, of course, wholly and entirely on the actual historical circumstances in which action is to be taken." This sort of claim is said, by Marx's critics, to combine an "extraordinary optimism" with a "circumscribed role . . . for political action."[21] I think three responses blunt the force of this critical assessment and open the way to an appreciation of Marx's position.

First, Marx's reticence to specify a postrevolutionary program is, in many cases, a matter of perfectly understandable political caution. When Marx claims, in *Herr Vogt*, that "it was not a matter," in the run-up to 1848, "of putting some utopian system into effect, but of conscious participation in the historical process revolutionizing society before our very eyes,"[22] he is in the midst of defending himself against the accusation of being a conspiracy monger and agent provocateur. The same context is relevant to his claim that the revolutionary "can only be said to conspire against the status quo in the sense that steam and electricity conspire against it."[23] As I argued in chapter 2, Marx had to de-politicize his call for proletarian revolution in order to publish his writings, and he and his companions were repeatedly dogged by police spies and informers. That he did not think it prudent to lay out a "ten-point plan" for what the socialists would do should they come to power, at a time when there was not even a socialist party in existence, much less one in need of rallying its forces behind a program, is understandable, given that such things could attract police attention in every Continental nation.

[19] *Capital*, 3:740; *MEGA*, II.15:594.

[20] *Political Writings*, 3:82.

[21] Marx to Ferdinand Domela Nieuwenhuis, February 22, 1881; *MECW*, 46:66; see Leopold, "The Structure of Marx and Engels' Considered Account of Utopian Socialism," 463–64.

[22] *MECW*, 17:79; *MEGA*, I.18:107.

[23] *Revelations concerning the Communist Trial in Cologne*; *MECW*, 11:446; *MEGA*, I.11:414. This aspect of the context is neglected by those, including Claeys, who see Marx as inheriting "the anti-political assumptions" of earlier socialists (*Citizens and Saints*, 13).

Second, the claim that what is to be done in a particular set of circumstances cannot be determined except by an examination of those circumstances themselves is not at all exceptional, historically speaking. Indeed, it was part of the common sense of political theorists prior to the rise of early modern doctrines of natural jurisprudence and social contract. Aristotle criticized his forerunners for failing "to put forward an arrangement of a sort that would be easy for people to be persuaded about and to introduce out of their existing circumstances."[24] In order to supply what others had not, he had to collect accounts of the constitutions of 158 political communities in and around Greece, each of which comprised not merely the arrangements regarding the major offices but also the history of the political life of the community.[25] This use of history, location, and other circumstances as the starting point of situated political prescription dominated the subsequent history of theoretical treatments of political matters. This "situatedness" of theory was never taken to be a circumscription of political action, but precisely an allowance for it.

Third, and most centrally, the historical circumstances that most concerned Marx were the motives, capacities, and desires that might reasonably be ascribed to the mass of the laboring classes.[26] When he forecasts that, at "the moment a truly proletarian revolution breaks out, the conditions for its immediate initial (if certainly not idyllic) *modus operandi* will also be there,"[27] he is not subscribing to the magical thinking according to which the ascendant proletarians will find before them, not only all of the objective means they will need to construct socialism, but the instructions for how best to use them. He means, rather, that, if the proletarian party has managed to come into possession of the state power, then this will indicate that the workers have chosen to emancipate themselves. This makes a large difference.

Because Cohen—but not just Cohen—conceives the principles of socialism to be material and political equality and solidaristic or just community, he also conceives the material conditions of socialism to be certain objective factors. In particular, he thinks that realizing these principles requires an advanced technological basis that eliminates natural scarcity, at least so far as to allow everyone a reasonable modicum of real wealth. Without the technology to hold scarcity at bay with a minimum of physical labor, equality and community are both unlikely and unattractive (and unlikely in part because they are so unattractive). But the presence of such a technological basis, while necessary, is not sufficient

---

[24] *Pol.* 4.1, 1289a2–4.

[25] Moore, *Aristotle and Xenophon on Democracy and Oligarchy*, 143.

[26] This is the lesson of my rereading of "material conditions" in the previous two chapters.

[27] Marx to Ferdinand Domela Nieuwenhuis, February 22, 1881; *MECW*, 46:67.

for socialism. A set of subjective factors—widespread moral commitment to the principles of equality and community—are also necessary, and these are not provided either by the development of the technological base or by the causes of the development of the technological base. They require articulate arguments—a defense of justice and equality, education, and proselytization.

Marx's midwifery seems wrongheaded from this perspective, since it seems to imply the absurd belief that the existence of the technological, objective conditions of socialism will, by itself, guarantee that the subjective conditions—broad and resilient moral commitment to equality and community—will also be present, at least among the proletariat. This is why Leopold accuses Marx of unreasonable optimism and of problematically circumscribing the role for political action. Marx seems unreasonably optimistic because he thinks that the capitalist development of the means of production, and the consequent struggles between the capitalist and laboring classes, will, of itself, make it the case that the broad swath of humanity is committed to socialist principles. He seems to have unreasonably restricted the arena for political action because he thereby denies the need to articulate and defend socialist principles, adherence to which is identical to a subjective commitment to the socialist project.

I disagree with this reading on every point. The principled commitments of socialism, according to Marx, are not to equality and community, but to freedom—conceived as non-domination—and to the association that secures and expresses this freedom. The material conditions of socialism are not the objective factors of industrial technology identified by Cohen, but the proletariat's *felt need* for large-scale, cooperative production, coordinated on a national or global scale. This can only be a felt need when capitalist development has broken down the laborers' reserve of individual skills, so as to make their material interdependence obvious and robust, and when the power of the capitalist state has developed to the point where the futility of worker separatism has become equally obvious. Both of these developments have an objective, technological component. Industrial technology helps to realize the first condition; military and bureaucratic technology help to realize the second. But what makes these conditions *material to the foundation of socialism* is their apprehension by the laboring classes. The material conditions of socialism are the conditions that matter for its feasibility, and these are, for Marx, primarily the motivational—hence "subjective"—conditions of the mass of laborers. Insofar as these motivational conditions have objective, technological preconditions, the link between the two is not so problematic as in Cohen's construal. Cohen's subjective conditions are *moral* and other-regarding, whereas Marx's are *prudential*, and, while there is no reason to think that the level of industrial development has any straightforward repercussions for people's moral commitments, it would be very odd *not* to think that the level of industrial development has direct and specifiable repercussions for people's prudential strategies.[28]

This is not to say that Marx was not optimistic. He was quite optimistic about two matters related to the question at hand. And, about both of these matters, his optimism might well seem unwarranted. First, he was optimistic about the motivational force of the universal interest in freedom from domination. He thought, not unreasonably, that freedom is a "basic good," a good that anyone has good reason to desire no matter what other goods one desires.[29] He was optimistic, perhaps unreasonably so, that the mass of people were prudentially rational enough to realize this basic interest and to be motivated thereby to struggle to secure this basic interest. That is, he thought that, given the opportunity, people would fight for their freedom.[30]

Second, Marx was optimistic that the modern proletariat, given the opportunity, would not merely fight for its freedom but would, as Engels put it, "accomplish . . . universal emancipation" by creating a form of association in which all domination would be precluded. That is, he thought that the material conditions created by capitalism included all of the elements necessary to motivate the institution of a global republic, or global federation of republics. This universal republican system would go beyond any historical republic because it would not merely secure the political freedom of a local elite—more or less broad-based—but would expand freedom to cover the whole breadth and depth of social life. It would incorporate cooperative production, "associated labor plying its toil with a willing hand," whereby it would be proven that, "to bear fruit, the means of labor need not be monopolized as a means of dominion over, and of extortion against, the laboring man himself."[31] But, "to save the industrious masses, cooperative labor ought to be developed to national dimensions, and, consequently, to be fostered by national means."[32] This aspiration to organize production cooperatively on a national scale

---

[28] Mary Wollstonecraft famously asked, "how can a being be . . . virtuous, who is not free?" This insight, a staple of the republican tradition, is alien to Cohen's approach, which is perfectionist in the extreme, and asks everyone to put virtue ahead of freedom. In this sense, he is a true inheritor of the moralistic socialism that Marx combated.

[29] For an argument to this effect, see Pettit, *Republicanism*, 90–92.

[30] "Given the opportunity" is a significant qualification. This is why the developments of industry and the state matter. Atomized producers subject to personal domination and the consequent threat of organized violence, for example, are unlikely to fight for their freedom. Domination would not be such a persistent feature of human history were people predictably willing to fight for their freedom regardless of the consequences. Domination works because almost everyone almost always cares a great deal about the consequences.

[31] Marx, "Inaugural Address," *Political Writings*, 3:79–80.

[32] Ibid., 3:80.

requires the laborers' "fraternal concurrence," and this is impossible so long as the nations practice "a foreign policy in pursuit of criminal designs, playing upon national prejudices, and squandering in piratical wars the people's blood and treasure."[33] In short, the conditions under which alone the proletariat could win its own emancipation, even locally considered, seemed to Marx to imply a global struggle against all economic, political, and imperial domination and plunder. And he thought that the proletariat of western Europe was coming to grasp these implications, as well. The birth of the IWMA signaled to him that these implications were being drawn by the activists within the laboring classes. His work within the IWMA was directed toward encouraging and cementing this development, and his argument in *Capital* was supposed to provide the theoretical basis for its permanence within the socialist and workers' movements.

This goal—universal self-emancipation of the laboring classes, secured and developed by universal republican government in all arenas of social life—militates against Marx setting himself up as legislator for this future state, proposing elaborate rules and institutions, decision-making procedures, or the like.[34] Marx thought the workers could—and would have to—work out the means by which they would liberate themselves, and that their achieved liberation would necessarily take the form of "the self-government of the producers."[35] It is reasonable to think that self-government achieved by self-emancipation cannot very well be the object of extensive prescriptive specification. Marx did not want to set himself up as dictator of the form proletarian self-government would take in particular circumstances. Nor did he want to introduce sectarian splits into the movement by "dictat[ing] or impos[ing] any doctrinary system whatever."[36] He thought that the proletariat was in the process of liberating itself, and that, in order to support and encourage "the actual elements of the class movement," he ought not try to "prescribe the course of the movement according to a certain doctrinaire recipe."[37]

Thus Marx had a principled and in no way specifically Hegelian reason for refraining from writing recipes for the cook shops of the future. He attributed to the proletariat an interest in and a desire for liberation

[33] Ibid., 3:81.

[34] Hence, the terms in which Marx understood the problem foreclosed any of the elaborate specifications that occupied so much of the literature of Owenism. Owenism may have been "closer to republicanism than most other early socialist schools," but it was also strongly influenced by radical puritanism and natural jurisprudence, both of which inclined more in the direction of uniform institutional design (Claeys, *Citizens and Saints*, 13, 23, chap. 3).

[35] *Civil War in France, Political Writings*, 3:210.

[36] "Instructions for Delegates to the Geneva Congress," *Political Writings*, 3:90.

[37] Marx to Johann von Schweitzer, October 13, 1868; *Political Writings*, 3:155. The negative examples Marx has in mind here are Proudhon and Lassalle.

from capitalist domination, and he thought that the effort to realize this interest and desire in response to capitalist industrial development would, on the basis of prudential considerations alone, swell to embrace all people and all spheres of social life. Such a liberation movement did not stand in need of a special moral education in the principles of socialism. It needed only to know the extent of the system of domination it was trying to overthrow, and the mechanisms by which this system operates. It needed to know, in other words, the extent of the problem that confronted it. When the problem was clear enough, and an opportunity to act presented itself, the laboring class's desire for liberation would be sufficient to produce the solution. Marx felt confirmed in this belief by the Paris Commune. The Commune fell to the French military but demonstrated to Marx's satisfaction that, given the opportunity, the laborers were perfectly capable of discovering "the political form" in which they could "work out" their "economical emancipation."[38]

THE SHAPE OF THINGS TO COME

My argument has so far proceeded on the premise that Marx conceives freedom as non-domination, a conception basically republican in heritage. Taking this premise for granted has allowed me to make reasonable sense of many of Marx's claims that otherwise seem unreasonable or even nonsensical. This result, in itself, is a strong point in favor of that premise. In order to further specify Marx's sense of what economic emancipation looks like, however, a more explicit argument for Marx's republicanism is in order. This argument will also shed further light on Marx's self-conceived relation to the utopian socialist tradition.

When Marx's relationship to utopian socialism is discussed, the triptych of Fourier, Saint-Simon, and Owen are usually treated as a unit.[39] In this, the secondary literature simply follows Marx's precedent.[40] Upon closer inspection, however, Marx did not treat these three "patriarchs of socialism" with equal regard, and his divergent opinions of them does much to reveal the outlines of Marx's assumptions about how an emancipated laboring class would associate for the purposes of preserving and enjoying their freedom. To put it baldly, Marx had a much higher esteem for Owen than he did for either Saint-Simon or Fourier. He thought the least of Saint-Simon, who generally wrote "mere encomiums of modern

---

[38] *Civil War in France, Political Writings*, 3:212.

[39] Leopold, "The Structure of Marx and Engels' Considered Account of Utopian Socialism"; Hobsbawm, "Marx, Engels, and Pre-Marxian Socialism."

[40] See, for example, *Political Writings*, 3:329; *MEGA*, I.24:107.

bourgeois society."[41] After the 1840s, Fourier receives almost no attention from Marx, who tended to find the Frenchman either "humorous" or "childishly naïve," but in neither case worth discussing.[42] Fourier's "great merit" was "to have stated that the ultimate object is the raising of the mode of production itself, not [that] of distribution, to a higher form."[43] And Marx uses some of Fourier's criticisms of contemporary labor as points of reference.[44] But none of this has much relevance for Marx's vision of free association. It is otherwise with his borrowings from and appreciation of Owen.

In Owen, Marx perceived an early and consistent advocacy on behalf of the emancipation of the proletariat. Hence, when he dismisses Saint-Simon for his allegiance to the bourgeoisie, Marx underscores the judgment with the exclamation, "What a difference compared with the contemporaneous writings of Owen!"[45] But it is a matter not only of the *what* but of the *how*. Owen understood that the emancipation of the proletariat would require large-scale cooperative production and the dissolution of the division between mental and manual labor. Thus, Marx appeals to Owen to support his own views twice in chapter fifteen of *Capital*, regarding "the education of the future" and the theoretical importance of the factory system.[46] He also refers to Owen favorably, as the father of cooperative production, in his inaugural address to the IWMA.[47]

That Marx would pay homage to Owen in the context of his activities with the IWMA is not surprising, given the stature of Owen within British working-class activist circles. More remarkably, Marx has nary a bad word for Owen in any of his published works, or even in his letters.[48] Even when he is criticizing Owenites for their monetary schemes, their fatalism about subsistence wages, and their opposition to the Chartist movement,[49] he does not besmirch Owen in any way. In his attacks on the advocates of labor money, to take a crucial instance, Marx makes sure to exempt Owen from his criticisms. The ground of this exemption is, as Marx puts it, that "Owen presupposes directly socialized labor, a form of

---

[41] *Capital*, 3:740; *MEGA*, II.15:594.

[42] *Capital*, 1:403; *MEGA*, II.6:292; *MEGA*, II.7:245; *Grundrisse*, 611; *MEGA*, II.1.2:499.

[43] *Grundrisse*, 712; *MEGA*, II.1.2:589; this judgment lays behind Marx's appropriation of Fourier's terminology at *Capital*, 1:506; *MEGA*, II.6:374; *MEGA*, II.7:328.

[44] See, for example, *Capital*, 1:553; *MEGA*, II.6:413; *MEGA*, II.7:366.

[45] *Capital*, 3:740; *MEGA*, II.15:595.

[46] *Capital*, 1:614, 635n46; *MEGA*, II.6:463, 475n322; *MEGA*, II.7:420, 437n334.

[47] *Political Writings*, 3:80.

[48] By way of contrast, Engels is occasionally quite disparaging of Owen, and generally leans more in the direction of Saint-Simon.

[49] See, e.g., *Manifesto*, *Political Writings*, 1:97; *MEW*, 4:492.

production diametrically opposed to the production of commodities."[50] In Marx's mind, as we have seen in chapter 5, directly socialized labor is just as diametrically opposed to collective labor under the command of the capitalist as it is to commodity production. Fleshing out Marx's appreciation for cooperative labor on a large scale and for Owen as a representative of this possibility makes visible the way in which Marx hopes to reappropriate the results of the capitalist mode of production, and the extent to which his vision of a communist mode of production is actually quite determinate.

In particular, it demonstrates that Marx's understanding of communism is opposed to both market socialism and the bureaucratic central planning of state socialism. Market socialism attempts to do away with the despotism of the capitalist in the workshop while leaving in place production for the market. State socialism attempts to eliminate the impersonal domination of the market while retaining "the *a priori* and planned regulation observed by the division of labor in the workshop."[51] For Marx, however, the despotism of the capitalist is a consequence of the fact that the capitalist stands under the impersonal domination of the market. Trying to get rid of the despotism of the factory while retaining the impersonal domination of the market could only ever succeed in turning workers into their own capitalists, laboring under the same objective domination as they do now. Trying to get rid of impersonal domination while retaining the form of the capitalist factory, on the other hand, would only subject the workers to the despotism of the central planning board. Both the social division of labor and the division of labor within the workshop have to be subjected to the deliberate control of the workers themselves. This is what "directly associated labor" means for Marx—production is coordinated beforehand by discussion and deliberation—and this is why Marx's republicanism found support in Owen's appeals for cooperative communities regulating all production.

Owenism as Republicanism

I recognize that, despite his own declamations in favor of the social republic, my attempt to paint Marx as a republican is controversial. Marx does not do many of the things we expect republicans to do. He does not go on and on about cultivating the virtue of citizens. The traditional republican effort to balance opposed factions or classes and to mix modes

---

[50] *Capital*, 1:188n1; *MEGA*, II.6:121–22n50; *MEGA*, II.7:72n49.
[51] *Capital*, 1:476; *MEGA*, II.6:350; *MEGA*, II.7:305–6.

of government, is decisively refused by Marx.[52] The dangers over which republicans have traditionally obsessed—mob rule, corruption, lawlessness, civil strife, imperial pretensions, and so on—do not seem to attract Marx's attention or concern; indeed, he seems to many to positively relish the prospect of a lawless and insurrectionary mob, bent on empire. If Marx is an heir to a certain republican tradition, it is generally thought to be the republicanism of the French Revolution, where republicanism means little more than opposition to both monarch and clergy, or a sort of egalitarian populism.

I, however, endorse MacGilvray's problem-centered definition of republicanism, according to which "republican thought centers around the problem of securing the practice of virtue through the control of arbitrary power."[53] I think Marx tackles this republican problem in a novel way. It is hard to deny—although it has certainly been denied many times—that Marx hoped the proletariat would overthrow capitalism because this mode of production constitutes a barrier to human flourishing, or to "the complete development" that ancient slavery at least made possible for a few.[54] This is enough to class him among those who are concerned to secure the practice of virtue. The real bone of contention is the means by which Marx envisions this practice being secured. Some have argued that Marx presupposes, naively, that this practice will be secured automatically by technologically advanced socialist production, or that superabundance will eliminate all barriers to human perfection.[55] Others have thought that, since only a thoroughgoing system

[52] See, for instance, his criticism of Bakunin's more traditionally republican concern to bring about "the political, economic, and social equalization of classes" ("Alleged Splits in the International," Political Writings, 3:277–81).

[53] The Invention of Market Freedom, 22.

[54] Marx, Capital, 1:533; MEGA, II.6:397; MEGA, II.7:350. That the young Marx was, to this degree, a perfectionist has been ably demonstrated most recently by Leopold, The Young Karl Marx, 184–86, 223–45. That the "Theses on Feuerbach"—in particular, the sixth thesis—does not represent a break with this early position has been convincingly shown by Geras, Marx and Human Nature, chap. 2. That the Marx of Capital retains this position, as well, is, it seems to me, demonstrated by the passage cited above. On the other hand, as I hope to have shown in chapter 3, the fact that Marx operated with a concept of human nature, and the fact that he wanted to secure to everyone the possibility of perfecting themselves, do not, as Geras and many others seem to think (e.g., ibid., 51–2), tell against the "anti-humanism" Althusser (rightly!) discerns in Marx's critique of political economy. The crucial matter is that Marx's antihumanism is explanatory and diagnostic. After all, there is no way to get from historically constant facts about human nature to historically local explanations of social structure and dynamics. Part of what Marx seeks to explain is the systematic absence of responsibility under capitalism. He tries to diagnose this as a symptom of thoroughgoing impersonal domination. Thus, theoretical antihumanism is a prerequisite for understanding why capitalism is a barrier to human development.

[55] Elster, Making Sense of Marx, 521–24.

of moral education could possibly put everyone on the path to some shared conception of human flourishing, Marx must have been in favor of a stultifying system of indoctrination.[56] Both of these interpretations are nonstarters.

Others, more generously, have been drawn to Marx's early discussions of alienated labor and have tried to work out an account according to which it is the nature of modern labor that undermines the pursuit of virtue.[57] This reading hinges, however, on understanding any limitation of human mastery as a barrier to the pursuit of human flourishing; "what is alienating" about the capitalist system is that "human beings cannot be masters, whether individually or collectively, of their own fate."[58] Hence, this reading attributes to Marx a notion of freedom as individual and collective self-mastery; freedom consists in "the subjection of one's self and its essential functions to one's own conscious, rational choice," where these functions include "the social conditions of human production," and all "social relations" as such.[59]

If this reading is correct, then Marx's problem is certainly not a republican one, since human freedom understood as self-mastery "requires not only that people should not be . . . subject to the arbitrary will of others; it requires also that the social relations in which they stand should be products of their own will."[60] This is the reading of Marx I would most like to displace.[61] While it does have some basis in Marx's texts, I think this basis is not as secure as it may seem at first glance.[62] Moreover, it is, substantially, as far-fetched as either the superabundance thesis or the

---

[56] Popper, *The Open Society and Its Enemies*, chap. 22.

[57] There is no doubt that Marx did think that modern labor was inimical to human flourishing. For a concise survey of some of the reasons he adduces for this in his earliest discussions of it, see Leopold, *The Young Karl Marx*, 229–34.

[58] Wood, *Karl Marx*, 49.

[59] Ibid., 51.

[60] Ibid., 51–52.

[61] Besides Wood, who is admirably explicit and clear about what he is up to, it can also be found in more gestural forms in others. See Ollman, *Alienation*, chap. 16; Brenkert, *Marx's Ethics of Freedom*, chap. 4; and, perhaps, Sayers, *Marxism and Human Nature*, 140.

[62] For instance, Wood claims to find an "explicit" avowal of freedom as self-mastery in *The Holy Family*, where Marx claims that "to be free 'in a materialist sense' is to be 'free not through the negative power of avoiding this and that, but through the positive might of making one's true individuality count'" (*Karl Marx*, 51; citing *MECW*, 4:131). But this passage comes from Marx's presentation of "propositions . . . found almost literally even in the oldest French materialists," which he thinks indicate the proto-communistic tendency of those writings. He does not affirm these propositions for himself—he writes, "This is not the place to assess them"—and they include theses, such as the circumstantial determination of human character, that Marx subjects to explicit criticism elsewhere. Hence, this passage cannot furnish any independent evidence that Marx views freedom as Wood does.

moral indoctrination thesis.[63] For Marx, there are, indeed, social relations that, by the manner in which they elude our individual and collective control, constitute barriers to the pursuit of virtue: the commodity-mediated relations of those dependent upon the market, and the relations of production that go along with these. However, once these relations are properly specified, and the manner in which they elude our control is spelled out, it turns out that they are barriers to the pursuit of virtue in the same way that being subject to the arbitrary will of an identifiable person is a barrier to the pursuit of virtue. Impersonal and objective domination are still forms of domination.

Given this weakness of the interpretation according to which Marx understands freedom as individual and collective self-mastery, I think that Marx's silence on many traditional republican themes does not reflect his lack of concern so much as it betrays the extent to which he took republican intuitions about freedom, public discussion, and virtue for granted. This does not depend upon reading everything into his silence, either. Looking at Marx's writings for the IWMA, for example, turns up a number of indications that he thought a republican interest in submitting governors to the scrutiny and countervailing powers of the governed to be so uncontroversial as not to need explicit defense.

There is, for example, his argument for direct rather than indirect taxation, which he prefers "because indirect taxes conceal from an individual what he is paying to the state, whereas a direct tax is undisguised, unsophisticated, and not to be misunderstood by the meanest capacity. Direct taxation prompts therefore every individual to control the governing powers while indirect taxation destroys all tendency to self-government."[64] In a similar vein is Marx's objection to the Gotha Programme's call for "elementary education by the state." Marx insists that "government and church should alike be excluded from all influence on the schools," but also avers that "specifying the means available to elementary schools, the qualifications of the teaching staff, the subjects to be taught, etc. by a general law, as is done in the United States, and having state inspectors to supervise the observance of these regulations,

---

[63] Are all social relations supposed to be amenable to control by the collective will of the people, including friendship, love, and parent-child relations? This is both infeasible and unappealing, and yet these are surely very significant social relations, ones that profoundly affect our well-being. They certainly can and should be free of domination, but how could they be only products of our own wills? Can anyone decide who to fall in love with? Certainly no one can choose their parents or their children.

[64] "Instructions for Delegates to the Geneva Congress," *Political Writings*, 3:92–93. This is a concrete instance in which Marx was happy to ape his Proudhonist opponents within the IWMA in the hopes of isolating them on the issues where their position decisively differed from his.

is something quite different from appointing the state as educator of the people!"[65] The distinction between state interference and legal regulation is an obvious distinction for Marx, and not one that calls for any particular elaboration.[66]

A final example will prepare the way for considering Marx's understanding of the role of producers' cooperatives in a postcapitalist society. In his discussion of the Paris Commune, and again in his notes on Bakunin's *Statism and Anarchy*, Marx compares elections to the hiring of employees. The Communal constitution, says Marx, would render universal suffrage as effective for the people of the communes as is the "individual suffrage" of "every other employer in the search of workmen and managers for his business." Likewise, in response to Bakunin's claim that, for Marxists, popular government means "the government of the people by a small number of leaders, chosen (elected) by the people," Marx insists that in a cooperative factory or a commune "the distribution of general functions has become a business matter, that gives no one domination."[67] Jon Elster accuses Marx of utopianism on this score, believing him to be claiming that a "purely technical division of labor" cannot give rise to domination.[68] As we have seen, however, Marx is very sensitive to the objective domination that can attend the division of labor in the workplace. Wherever that division, however objective, represents a plan imposed by "the powerful will of a being outside" the workers,[69] it will be despotic.

In fact, Marx's meaning comes out clearly when he claims that "if Mr. Bakunin only knew something of the position of a manager in a worker's cooperative factory, all his dreams of domination would go to the devil."[70] It is not that, contemplating the communist future, Marx suddenly forgets that business matters provide ample room for domination. Indeed, Marx's argument rests on the assumption that, without some sort of safeguard, the business matters of supervision and management will give rise to domination. His point is that an employer's power to hire

---

[65] "Critique of the Gotha Program," *Political Writings*, 3:357; *MEGA*, I.25:23–24. As Richard Hunt has documented, in fact, Marx and Engels's writings contain "almost uniform praise for the political forms of American democracy" (*The Political Ideas of Marx and Engels*, 2:88).

[66] Compare, also, Marx's "Instructions for Delegates to the Geneva Congress" (*Political Writings*, 3:88–89). For the rule of law as a corrective to domination, see Pettit, *Republicanism*.

[67] *Political Writings*, 3:210, 336; *MEW*, 18:635.

[68] *Making Sense of Marx*, 457–58; see also Ollman, "Marx's Vision of Communism: A Reconstruction."

[69] *Capital*, 1:450; *MEGA*, II.6:328; *MEGA*, II.7:284.

[70] *Political Writings*, 3:337; *MEW*, 18:635.

and fire an employee leaves scant opportunity for the *employee* to dominate the *employer*. Hence, if managers and other general functionaries are "hired" by, and can be "fired" by the workers for whom they perform managerial and accounting tasks, Marx thinks this will be an effective safeguard against the workers being dominated from above. There is a recognizably republican assumption at work here. This is why Marx calls cooperative production "the republican and beneficent system of *the association of free and equal producers*."[71] Cooperative production—which Marx consistently links to Owen's name—is, for Marx, republicanism in the realm of production.

Republicanism as Owenism

These republican strands in Marx's writings indicate that the assimilation of Marx to the tradition of socialists advocating technocratic command economies, or scientific central planning, can only proceed by means of falsification.[72] The very features that recommended cooperative production to Marx as a republican institution reveal, as well, that the commonplace according to which Marx imagined that communism would do away with all politics rests entirely on an equivocation. Cooperative production frees the laborer from domination within the workshop in part because it frees the collective worker from the impersonal domination of the market. Decisions about what is to be produced are the outcomes of deliberations within and among the various cooperatives. Therefore, decisions regarding production and the division of labor within the workshop are also subject to deliberative discussion among the associated workers. In short, Marx anticipated a communist economy managed by deliberation and debate. Critics conjure away this conclusion by conflating Marx's opposition to political domination with an opposition to political deliberation and debate.

According to his critics, "although Marx had various ends that he hoped, from time to time, to bring about by means of political action, he had no commitment to the process of political deliberation, negotiation, and compromise as modes by which human beings, in the future socialist (communist) order, will decide what arrangements they are going to support and what actions they are going to undertake in their lives together

---

[71] "Instructions for Delegates to the Geneva Congress," *Political Writings*, 3:90.

[72] See, e.g., Elliott, "Marx and Contemporary Models of Socialist Economy"; Miller, "Marx, Communism, and Markets"; O'Neill, "Markets, Socialism, and Information: A Reformulation of a Marxian Objection to the Market"; Arnold, "Marx, Central Planning, and Utopian Socialism"; Wolff, "Playthings of Alien Forces."

as human beings."[73] The bits from Marx that are cited in this connection are all the various places where he claims that the social republic, the Paris Commune, and other attempts at workers' self-government do or will shed their political character. The question is not raised as to whether by "political character" Marx meant to point out "the process of deliberation, negotiation, and compromise." Rather, it is simply assumed that Marx's forecast of an end to politics is based upon a "repugnance to the public realm" and a dismissal of "action, speech, and thought" as mere epiphenomena of "social interest,"[74] or upon an "absurd" belief that all disagreements about what is good policy will, under communism, vanish into "unanimous agreement rationally arrived at."[75]

This whole interpretation rests on word play. Marx did not think that the *political* state was one in which "a process of political deliberation and debate" determined "the course of action to be pursued."[76] Rather, he thought it one in which a dominant class exercised its domination under the cover of legal forms, or secured its conditions of existence by force of arms. "Political power, properly so called," he wrote, "is merely the organized power of one class for oppressing another."[77] Politics, for Marx, connotes organized class domination, not debate and deliberation, or disagreement.

Thus, when Marx calls the Paris Commune of 1871 "the political form of the social emancipation, of the liberation of labor," he means that "the Commune does not do away with class struggle, . . . but it affords the rational medium in which the class struggle can run through its different phases in the most rational and humane way."[78] Marx thinks that the coercion and domination of the bourgeoisie entailed by this process of struggle is justified, since "the war of the enslaved against their enslavers [is] the only justifiable war in history,"[79] but he does not deny that the struggle of the working class is an effort to dominate the bourgeoisie, for the simple reason that "the lords of land and the lords of labor will always use their political privileges for the defense and perpetuation of their economical monopolies."[80] The bourgeoisie will not

---

[73] Megill, *Karl Marx*, 58.

[74] Arendt, *The Human Condition*, 165, 33.

[75] Elster, *Making Sense of Marx*, 458.

[76] Megill, *Karl Marx*, 118.

[77] "Instructions for Delegates to the Geneva Congress," *Political Writings*, 1:87.

[78] *Civil War in France*, *Political Writings*, 3:253.

[79] Ibid., 3:229.

[80] "Inaugural Address," *Political Writings*, 3:80. At least when Harvey Mansfield claims that Marx's commitment to eliminating all forms of slavery "required the elimination of politics in the Aristotelian sense," he specifies that "politics in this sense necessarily establishes some form of rule," by which he means some people ordering other people around

give up their power without a fight, and so the proletariat must impose a new regime unilaterally. But the result of a working-class victory is supposed to be a situation in which class domination disappears. Marx hoped for an end to politics because politics meant, for him, one class exercising the power to dominate another, and he hoped for an end to class domination.

Debate, deliberation, and disagreement, by contrast, are aspects of *social* life in Marx's terminology.[81] This must be kept in mind when we read Marx extolling "social production controlled by social fore-thought, which forms the political economy of the working class."[82] Or when he calls the expropriation of the expropriators "the transformation of capitalist private property . . . into social property."[83] Or when he "imagine[s], for a change, a union [*Verein*] of free human beings, work-ing with communal means of production, and expending their many in-dividual labor-powers self-consciously as one social labor-power."[84] This is Marx considering a form of production in which the fetishism of the commodity, and hence impersonal domination, disappears.[85] It is widely read as Marx's presentiment of the communist future. What is not widely

---

("Marx on Aristotle," 351). That is, *politics* for Mansfield, as for Marx, necessarily implies *dominium*. But Mansfield, too, falls back on the old verities, declaring that, in Marx's vi-sion, "economic laws that cannot be repealed will replace the makeshift, compromise laws that men legislate politically according to their varying opinions of their varying needs" (ibid., 358). Of course, Mansfield is unable to tell us what any of these "economic laws" of communism might be.

[81] This is why Marx claims that "the human being is by nature, if not as Aristotle thought a political animal, at all events a social animal" (*Capital*, 1:444; *MEGA*, II.6:324; *MEGA*, II.7:279–80). In his note to this passage, Marx claims that what Aristotle really meant is that "the human being is by nature a *Stadtbürger*," a citizen of a free city (*Capital*, 1:444n7; *MEGA*, II.6:324n13; *MEGA*, II.7:280n15). Marx is agreeing with the basis of Aristotle's claim, that human beings have speech and make arguments; Aristotle thought that the free city was the ultimate natural expression of this power, while Marx did not. But they both would have agreed that class domination—"politics" in Marx's use of the word—is most certainly *not* a natural expression of this power.

[82] "Inaugural Adress," *Political Writings*, 3:79. This claim contrasts with the approach of, say, Elster, who asserts that "the frequent references in Marx's work to production ac-cording to a 'common plan' show that there will have to be [in socialism] a central agency for planning. It will have at least the task of providing public goods and of preventing cyclical fluctuations and other wasteful phenomena." He makes clear that he thinks there is a contrast to be drawn between this "agency" and "the producers." He does conclude, mercifully, that, "given Marx's massive emphasis on self-realization and autonomy, it is impossible to attribute to him the view that communism would be a society in which all productive decisions were taken from the centre" (*Making Sense of Marx*, 455).

[83] *Capital*, 1:929–30; *MEGA*, II.6:683; *MEGA*, II.7:679.

[84] *Capital*, 1:171; *MEGA*, II.6:109; *MEGA*, II.7:59.

[85] One of four, alongside that of a solitary Robinson Crusoe, that of a serf, and that of a peasant family.

noted is that it is certainly an allusion to Owen's factory at New Lanark, and to the cooperative experiments that sprung up in its wake.

When Marx claims, then, that "Owen presupposes directly socialized labor,"[86] he is claiming that Owen's notion of cooperative production is based in a form of social mediation that excludes all forms of domination.[87] There is no room for personal domination, since no one has the power to interfere with anyone else in an arbitrary manner. There is no room for impersonal domination, since members of the cooperative do not interact with one another as independent producers exchanging goods at market prices. There is no room for objective domination, since neither do individual cooperatives interact with one another as independent producers exchanging goods at market prices. The division of labor and mode of production within each cooperative is decided by the deliberations of the members. The relations among cooperatives are likewise matters for deliberation and decision by assemblies of delegates. In what Marx considered "a very important work of Owen's in which he gives a résumé of his entire doctrine,"[88] the old utopian had called for such cooperative "townships or republics" to unite in expanding circles of federation "until they shall extend over Europe, and afterwards to all other parts of the world, uniting all in one great republic."[89] Marx saw in the Paris Commune the confirmation that "a republic is only possible in France and Europe as a 'social republic,' that is a republic which disowns the capital and landowner class of the state machinery to supersede it by the Commune, that frankly avows 'social emancipation' as the great goal of the republic and guarantees thus that social transformation by the Communal organization."[90]

This Communal organization is, for Marx, the equivalent beyond the workplace of Owen's direct association of workers, an association

---

[86] *Capital*, 1:188n1; *MEGA*, II.6:121–22n50; *MEGA*, II.7:72n49.

[87] Whether this was actually Owen's conception of cooperation is beside the point. As I have already averred, Owen's thought was interlarded with all manner of influences beyond republicanism, and even his most republican moments were more perfectionist than Marx's most perfectionist moments. Among other real differences, Owen's little republics were to be gerontocracies, overseen by councils of elders. They are also presented by him as uniformly small and semirural communities. Marx always presupposed, on the other hand, the features that the Paris Commune itself manifested: representative democracy in an urban setting, with a large and diverse population. Marx, in his appreciation of Owen, simply discounted or ignored all of these very real divergences in favor of emphasizing the points of convergence: a republican conception of freedom enjoyed in cooperative, large-scale production.

[88] Marx to Engels, August 8, 1877; *MECW*, 45:263. Marx has been digging through his attic gathering works by and on the utopians in order that Engels might use them in the composition of the *Anti-Dühring*.

[89] *The Revolution in the Mind*, 119–22.

[90] *Civil War in France, Political Writings*, 3:259.

mediated by conversation and deliberation.[91] As opposed to the a posteriori mediation of production brought about by market exchange, or the a priori mediation of the command of capital, Marx saw in Owen's cooperatives the germ of a mode of production mediated a priori by discourse.[92] Cooperative production compels individual producers and consumers to justify their preferences and to make decisions in common about what and how to produce. These are the features that would recommend it to Marx. Trying to imagine a global system of interdependent cooperatives managing all production by nested communal deliberation certainly gives rise to all manner of questions and doubts about matters logistical and procedural.[93] They are, however, different questions and doubts than those arising at the prospect of a global and technocratic command economy, the means of a priori coordination that has generally been attributed to Marx.[94] If Marx's optimism about our ability to work out the institutional questions of free and cooperative self-government was misplaced, this does not impeach his diagnosis of our need for it.

[91] Marx was not the last to notice an affinity between conversation and communism. Antonio Gramsci, in a 1919 article cowritten with Palmiro Togliotti, claimed that "the concrete and complete solution of the problems of socialist living can only arise from communist practice: collective discussion" ("Workers' Democracy," *L'Ordino Nuovo*, June 21, 1919; *Antonio Gramsci Reader*, 82).

[92] This, I think, goes some distance toward obviating Bidet's concern that Marx, in his sketch of socialism in the "Critique of the Gotha Programme," lost sight of his criticism of the labor money schemes (*Exploring Marx's Capital*, 62–67).

[93] John Dunn has argued that such a global form of cooperation is undeliverable, but he also tends to conflate this judgment with the judgment that the Soviet and Chinese systems did not get us any closer to it, which is a rather different matter ("Unimagined Community").

[94] Elster thinks there cannot be noncoercive common decisions that avoid both markets and the impossible demand of consensus. Timely decision making in the context of deeply felt disagreement will demand some recourse to either markets or coercive force (*Making Sense of Marx*, 458). He may be right, but it is at least worthwhile noticing that there are actual trade-offs here. It is also crucial to notice that, if Marx is read through a republican lens, recourse to coercive enforcement of collective decisions is not, in itself, a problem. Being coerced into going along with decisions that arise out of a decent process of deliberation is not the same thing as being dominated; it may not be ideal, but it is not a political evil. Marx is not Proudhon; he did not think that consensus was the only way to avoid domination. This is a common stumbling block in the literature on Marx's political ideas. Even Hunt, the most careful student of Marx to write on these topics, fails to differentiate between coercion and domination (compare, for example, his statements in *The Political Ideas of Marx and Engels*, 2:4 and 92). Others, like Maguire, seem genuinely puzzled by Marx's inattention to the difficulty of achieving unanimity on all matters. "Perhaps," he surmises, Marx "feels that where I am overruled simply by a specific temporary majority of my peers after being heard by them, I am not oppressed" (*Marx's Theory of Politics*, 230). Perhaps!

Conclusion

What matters for my purposes in this book is not that the reader be attracted to Marx's vision of free association, or even that the reader be convinced by his diagnosis of the evils of capitalism. My goal is more modest. I have provided a reinterpretation of Marx's critique of political economy that connects that critique to republican intuitions about freedom from domination.[95] I have argued that Marx provides a novel articulation of those intuitions in response to the rise of capitalism, commerce, and industrial development. Marx sees in the modern world a panoply of new threats to freedom. He sees in the market a domain of impersonal domination in which decisions about production and consumption, decisions that impinge upon every producer or consumer via the price mechanism, are made in dispersed isolation, without there being any possibility of these decisions being challenged by those they affect, and without there being any need for reasoned justifications to be given. He sees in a society organized around production for the market, therefore, a society of individuals rendered systematically irresponsible for themselves and their actions.

In this context, in which economic laws confront the individual producer as an external source of compulsion, the employment of wage labor can only be a system of the forcible extraction of surplus labor, a system within which overwork can only be curtailed—and then only imperfectly and temporarily—by the imposition of legal regulations. Moreover, within this system of capitalist exploitation, the workshop itself is a sphere of personal despotism and objective domination. The capitalist, in his or her private domain, acts as a vector for market imperatives, which thereby become objectified in the apparatus of production itself. This objectification of market domination massively develops the productive powers of collective labor, but only in a form that reduces the individual laborer's options to mechanical obedience or sabotage. This domination of the laborer is papered over by the form of the wage, which makes it appear that the laborers are paid for their services to capital, rather than for the vitality they lose in the process. Moreover, the growth and concentration of productive power, because it is based in the market for labor power, requires the existence and growth of a

---

[95] My interpretation gains what force it has from situating Marx in the context of his struggles with the IWMA. Paying attention to what Marx's interlocutors and competitors were saying has the benefit of making his responses more intelligible. And what his responses gain in intelligibility they also, by and large, gain in persuasiveness. Whether these gains are enough to overcome all the old objections and concerns—not to mention the new ones my reinterpretation might raise—is a question for another occasion.

relative surplus population, dependent upon wages for life but excluded from regular employment.

This monstrous mode of production—which enslaves everyone and leaves most people the slaves of slaves—is ushered into existence, Marx argues, by the betrayal of the peasantry by the lords of the land, the betrayal of the lords of the land by the rising class of capitalist farmers, and the betrayal of the commonwealth by the state, corrupted by its dependency upon capitalist accumulation. Its continued existence depletes the earth and the laborers, who have no recourse left them except the path of organized confrontation with both the state and capital. Only the overthrow of both can bring freedom to the world, not in the form of individual independence—which is powerless against the social forces of state and capital and impossible for de-skilled factory laborers—but in the form of cooperative interdependence. And only a descent through political economy can so clarify the issues as to make this necessity into a project.

This argument—encapsulating the political theory of *Capital*—is presented by Marx in the form of a descent into the social Hell that capital has made, and the political economy that is its ideal counterpart and attempt at self-justification. Marx's appropriation of Dante's *Inferno* is motivated by a double aim. He seeks to rectify the moralizing socialist critique of capitalism by redirecting it away from individuals and toward the ensemble of modern social relations. Thus he recapitulates Dante's descent through the moral wrongs of incontinence, force, fraud, and treachery, showing at each step that it is capital, as a system of all-around domination, that is responsible for these sins, not the individuals dominated by capital. By this route, he also seeks to purge the workers' movement of its tendency to fall for one or another aspect of this modern social system, to be tempted by its promises and ideals, to think that what seems good in it might be had without all the ills to which that apparent good is connected. As a new Virgil, Marx tries to guide his readers along the internal connections binding exchange to exploitation, contracts to conquest, prices to poverty, development to despotism. His hope is that a pilgrim with many heads and many hands will follow him, a new collective Dante, whose poetry will constitute a new republic beyond the empire of capital.

Bibliography

WORKS BY MARX (AND BY MARX AND ENGELS)

Marx, Karl. *Capital: A Critique of Political Economy*. Vol. 1. Translated by Ben Fowkes. London: Penguin, 1976.

———. *Capital: A Critique of Political Economy*. Vol. 3. Translated by David Fernbach. New York: Vintage Books, 1981.

———. *Early Writings*. Edited by Quintin Hoare. New York: Vintage Books, 1975.

———. *Grundrisse: Foundations of the Critique of Political Economy*. New York: Vintage Books, 1973.

———. *Later Political Writings*. Edited by Terrell Carver. Cambridge: Cambridge University Press, 1996.

———. *Œuvres: Économie*. Vol. 1. Edited by Maximilien Rubel. 2 vols. Paris: Gallimard, 1968.

———. *Political Writings*. Edited by David Fernbach. 3 vols. London; New York: Verso, 2010.

Marx, Karl, and Friedrich Engels. *Karl Marx, Frederick Engels: Collected Works (MECW)*. 50 vols. New York; Moscow; London: International Publishers; Progress Publishers; Lawrence and Wishart, 1975–2005.

———. *Karl Marx-Friedrich Engels-Werke (MEW)*. 39 vols., plus *Ergänzungbanden*. Berlin: Dietz Verlag, 1957–68.

———. *Karl Marx-Friedrich Engels-Gesamtausgabe (MEGA)*. 114 projected vols., ongoing. Berlin: Dietz Verlag, 1975–98, and Akademie Verlag, 1998–.

———. *Karl Marx / Friedrich Engels Papers (IISG)*. International Institute of Social History, Amsterdam.

WORKS BY PROUDHON

Proudhon, Pierre-Joseph. *Correspondance de P.-J. Proudhon*. Vol. 13. Paris: A. Lacroix, 1875.

———. *General Idea of the Revolution in the Nineteenth Century*. Translated by John Beverley Robinson. London: Freedom Press, 1923.

———. *Oeuvres complètes de P.-J. Proudhon, nouvelle édition (OC)*. 15 vols. Paris: Marcel Rivière, 1923–59.

———. *Property Is Theft!: A Pierre-Joseph Proudhon Anthology*. Edited by Iain McKay. Edinburgh; Oakland, CA: AK Press, 2011.

———. *System of Economical Contradictions: Or, the Philosophy of Misery*. Vol. 1. The Evolution of Capitalism. New York: Arno Press, 1972.

———. *What Is Property?* Edited by Donald R. Kelley and Bonnie G. Smith. Cambridge Texts in the History of Political Thought. Cambridge: Cambridge University Press, 1994.

OTHER WORKS

Albritton, Robert. *Dialectics and Deconstruction in Political Economy.* Basingstoke: Palgrave, 2001.

Albritton, Robert, and John Simoulidis, eds. *New Dialectics and Political Economy.* Basingstoke: Palgrave Macmillan, 2003.

Alighieri, Dante. *The Divine Comedy.* Translated by Robert M. Durling. 3 vols. Oxford: Oxford University Press, 1996.

Althusser, Louis. *Lenin and Philosophy, and Other Essays.* Translated by Ben Brewster. New York: Monthly Review Press, 1972.

Althusser, Louis, and Etienne Balibar. *Reading* Capital. Translated by Ben Brewster. London: Verso, 2009.

Althusser, Louis, Étienne Balibar, Roger Establet, Pierre Macherey, and Jacques Rancière. *Lire* "Le Capital." Nouvelle édition revue. Paris: Presses Universitaires de France, 1996.

Anderson, Kevin B. *Marx at the Margins: On Nationalism, Ethnicity, and Non-Western Societies.* Chicago: University of Chicago Press, 2010.

———. "The 'Unknown' Marx's *Capital,* Volume I: The French Edition of 1872–75, 100 Years Later." *Review of Radical Political Economics* 15, no. 4 (1983): 71–80.

Anderson, Perry. *Lineages of the Absolutist State.* London: New Left Books, 1974.

———. *Passages from Antiquity to Feudalism.* London: New Left Books, 1974.

Anonymous, ed. *Pictures of the French: A Series of Literary and Graphic Delineations of French Character.* London: Thomas Tegg, 1841.

Arendt, Hannah. "Freedom and Politics." In *Freedom and Serfdom,* edited by A. Hunold, 191–217. Dordrecht: D. Reidel, 1961.

———. *The Human Condition.* 1st ed. Chicago: University of Chicago Press, 1958.

Arneson, Richard J. "What's Wrong with Exploitation?" *Ethics* 91, no. 2 (1981): 202–27.

Arnold, N. Scott. "Marx, Central Planning, and Utopian Socialism." *Social Philosophy and Policy* 6 (1989): 160–99.

Arthur, Christopher J. "Capital in General and Marx's 'Capital.'" In *The Culmination of Capital: Essays on Volume Three of Marx's* Capital, edited by Martha Campbell and Geert Reuten, 42–64. Basingstoke: Palgrave Macmillan, 2002.

———. *Dialectics of Labour: Marx and His Relation to Hegel.* Oxford: Blackwell, 1986.

———. "Engels as Interpreter of Marx's Economics." In *Engels Today: A Centenary Appreciation,* edited by Christopher J. Arthur. Basingstoke: Macmillan, 1996.

———. "Negation of the Negation in Marx's *Capital.*" *Rethinking Marxism* 6, no. 4 (1993): 49–65.

———. *The New Dialectic and Marx's* Capital. Historical Materialism Book Series. Leiden and Boston: Brill, 2002.

Arthur, Christopher J., and James White. "Debate: Chris Arthur and James White on History, Logic, and Expanded Reproduction in Capital." *Studies in Marxism* 8 (2001): 127–35.

Aston, T. H., ed. *The Brenner Debate*. Cambridge: Cambridge University Press, 1987.

Avineri, Shlomo. *The Social and Political Thought of Karl Marx*. Cambridge: Cambridge University Press, 1971.

Backhaus, Hans-Georg. *Marx und die Marxistische Orthodoxie*. Berlin: Edition Suhrkamp, 1980.

Bakan, Abigail B. "Marxism and Antiracism: Rethinking the Politics of Difference." *Rethinking Marxism* 20, no. 2 (2008): 238–56.

Balibar, Étienne. *The Philosophy of Marx*. London: Verso, 1995.

Bastiat, Frédéric. *Harmonies Économiques*. Brussels: Meline, Cans, 1850.

Bazard, Armand, Barthélemy Prosper Enfantin, and Emile Barrault. *Doctrine de Saint-Simon: Exposition, Première Année, 1828–1829*. 3rd ed. Paris: Bureau de l'Organisateur, 1831.

———. *The Doctrine of St-Simon: An Exposition; First Year, 1828–1829*. Edited by Georg G. Iggers. New York: Schocken Books, 1972.

Bell, John R. *Capitalism and the Dialectic: The Uno-Sekine Approach to Marxian Political Economy*. London: Pluto Press, 2009.

Benanav, Aaron. "The Brutal Facts: Too Few Jobs for Too Many People." CUNY Graduate Center, 2010.

Berg, Maxine. *The Machinery Question and the Making of Political Economy, 1815–1848*. Cambridge: Cambridge University Press, 1980.

Bernstein, Samuel. "Saint Simon's Philosophy of History." *Science and Society* 12, no. 1 (1948): 82–96.

Bessner, Daniel. "Zarte Hände: Terrorismus, Frauen und Emanzipation Im Werke von Karl Heinzen." In *Terrorismus und Geschlecht: Politische Gewalt in Europa Seit Dem 19. Jahrhundert*, edited by Christine Hikel and Sylvia Schraut, 61–78. Geschichte und Geschlecter 61. Fra: Campus Verlag, 2012.

Bessner, Daniel, and Michael Stauch. "Karl Heinzen and the Intellectual Origins of Modern Terror." *Terrorism and Political Violence* 22, no. 2 (2010): 143–76.

Bevir, Mark. "Republicanism, Socialism, and Democracy in Britain: The Origins of the Radical Left." *Journal of Social History* 34, no. 2 (2000): 351–68.

Bidet, Jacques. *Exploring Marx's* Capital: *Philosophical, Economic, and Political Dimensions*. Translated by David Fernbach. Historical Materialism Book Series. Leiden and Boston: Brill, 2009.

Biernacki, Richard. *The Fabrication of Labor: Germany and Britain, 1640–1914*. Berkeley: University of California Press, 1995.

Blanqui, Auguste. *Maintenant, Il Faut des Armes*. Edited by Dominique Le Nuz. Paris: La fabrique éditions, 2006.

Blaug, Mark. "The Myth of the Old Poor Law and the Making of the New." *Journal of Economic History* 23, no. 2 (1963): 151–84.

Bloch, Ernst. *The Principle of Hope*. 3 vols. Cambridge, MA: MIT Press, 1995.

Boer, Roland. *Criticism of Earth: On Marx, Engels and Theology*. Historical Materialism 35. Leiden and Boston: Brill, 2012.

Booth, Arthur John. *Saint-Simon and Saint-Simonism: A Chapter in the History of Socialism in France*. London: Longman, 1871.

Booth, William James. "Economies of Time: On the Idea of Time in Marx's Political Economy." *Political Theory* 19, no. 1 (1991): 7–27.

———. *Households: On the Moral Architecture of the Economy.* Ithaca, NY: Cornell University Press, 1993.

Bowen, Ralph H. "Review: L'Actualite de Proudhon; Colloque Des 24 et 25 Novembre 1965." *American Historical Review* 74, no. 2 (1968): 629–30.

Braunthal, Julius. *History of the International.* Westport, CT: Praeger, 1967.

Braverman, Harry. *Labor and Monopoly Capital: The Degredation of Work in the Twentieth Century.* New York and London: Monthly Review Press, 1974.

Bray, John Francis. *Labour's Wrongs and Labour's Remedy; or, The Age of Might and the Age of Right.* New York: A. M. Kelley, 1968.

Brenkert, George G. *Marx's Ethics of Freedom.* London: Routledge and Kegan Paul, 1983.

Brenner, Robert. "The Social Basis of Economic Development." In *Analytical Marxism,* edited by John E. Roemer, 23–53. Studies in Marxism and Social Theory. Cambridge; Paris: Cambridge University Press; Editions de la Maison des Sciences de l'Homme, 1986.

Bridenthal, Renate. "Karl Grün (1817–1887): A Neglected Socialist." Columbia University, 1961.

Brogan, D. W. *Proudhon.* London: Hamish Hamilton, 1934.

Bryan, Dick. "'Natural' and 'Improved' Land in Marx's Theory of Rent." *Land Economics* 66, no. 2 (1990): 176.

Calhoun, Craig J. *The Roots of Radicalism: Tradition, the Public Sphere, and Early Nineteenth-Century Social Movements.* Chicago: University of Chicago Press, 2012.

Callinicos, Alex. *Making History: Agency, Structure, and Change in Social Theory.* 2nd ed. Historical Materialism. Leiden: Brill, 2006.

———. "Marxism and Contemporary Political Thought." In *The Routledge Companion to Social and Political Philosophy,* edited by Gerald F. Gaus and Fred D'Agostino, 266–77. Routledge Philosophy Companions. New York: Routledge, 2013.

Carlyle, Thomas. *Critical and Miscellaneous Essays.* Vol. 15. Thomas Carlyle's Works. London: Chapman and Hall, 1887.

———. *Past and Present.* 2nd ed. London: Chapman and Hall, 1845.

Carver, Terrell. Marx and Engels: *The Intellectual Relationship.* Bloomington: Indiana University Press, 1983.

———. "Marx's Commodity Fetishism." *Inquiry* 18, no. 1 (1975): 39–63.

———. "Marx's Political Theory of Exploitation." In *Modern Theories of Exploitation,* edited by Andrew Reeve, 68–79. London: Sage Publications, 1987.

———. *The Postmodern Marx.* University Park: Pennsylvania State University Press, 1998.

Claeys, Gregory. *Citizens and Saints: Politics and Anti-Politics in Early British Socialism.* Cambridge: Cambridge University Press, 1989.

———. "'Individualism,' 'Socialism,' and 'Social Science': Further Notes on a Process of Conceptual Formation, 1800–1850." *Journal of the History of Ideas* 47, no. 1 (1986): 81–93.

———. *Machinery, Money and the Millennium: From Moral Economy to Socialism, 1815–60.* Cambridge: Polity, 1987.

———. "The Concept of 'Political Justice' in Godwin's *Political Justice*: A Reconsideration." *Political Theory* 11, no. 4 (1983): 565–84.

Cleaver, Harry. *Reading "Capital" Politically*. Leeds, Edinburgh, and San Francisco: Anti/Theses and AK Press, 2000.

Cobbett, William. *Rural Rides*. London: William Cobbett, 1830.

Cohen, G. A. "Forces and Relations of Production." In *Analytical Marxism*, 11–22. Studies in Marxism and Social Theory. Cambridge; Paris: Cambridge University Press; Editions de la Maison des Sciences de l'Homme, 1986.

———. *History, Labour, and Freedom: Themes from Marx*. Oxford: Clarendon Press, 1988.

———. *If You're an Egalitarian, How Come You're So Rich?* Gifford Lectures. Cambridge, MA: Harvard University Press, 2000.

———. *Karl Marx's Theory of History: A Defence*. Princeton, NJ: Princeton University Press, 2001.

———. *On the Currency of Egalitarian Justice, and Other Essays in Political Philosophy*. Edited by Michael Otsuka. Princeton, NJ: Princeton University Press, 2011.

———. "The Labor Theory of Value and the Concept of Exploitation." *Philosophy and Public Affairs* 8, no. 4 (1979): 338–60.

Cole, G.D.H. *Socialist Thought: Marxism and Anarchism, 1850–1890*. Vol. 2. 7 vols. A History of Socialist Thought. London: Macmillan, 1954.

———. *Socialist Thought: The Forerunners, 1789–1850*. Vol. 1. 7 vols. A History of Socialist Thought. London: Macmillan, 1953.

Collins, Henry, and Chimen Abramsky. *Karl Marx and the British Labour Movement: Years of the First International*. London: Macmillan, 1965.

Comstock, Courtney. "Meet the First Big Exec to Pay for 'Unintentionally Defrauding' during The Credit Crisis." *Business Insider*. July 30, 2010, sec. Finance. http://www.businessinsider.com/gary-crittenden-made-20-million -while-unintentionally-defrauding-citi-and-only-has-to-pay-100k-2010–7 #ixzz3GL4LtGAz.

Considérant, Victor. *Principes du Socialisme: Manifeste de La Démocratie au XIXᵉ Siècle*. 2nd ed. Paris: Librairie phalansterienne, 1847.

Constant, Benjamin. *Political Writings*. Translated by Biancamaria Fontana. Cambridge Texts in the History of Political Thought. Cambridge: Cambridge University Press, 1988.

Crowder, George. *Classical Anarchism: The Political Thought of Godwin, Proudhon, Bakunin, and Kropotkin*. New York: Clarendon Press, 1991.

Cunliffe, John, and Andrew Reeve. "Exploitation: The Original Saint-Simonian Account." *Capital and Class* 59 (1996): 61–80.

Dana, Charles A. "The Bank of the People." *Spirit of the Age* 1, no. 22 (1849): 342–43.

Davis, Mike. *Planet of Slums*. London and New York: Verso, 2006.

De Angelis, M. "Social Relations, Commodity-Fetishism, and Marx's Critique of Political Economy." *Review of Radical Political Economics* 28, no. 4 (1996): 1–29.

De Brunhoff, Suzanne. *Marx on Money*. Translated by Maurice J Goldbloom. New York: Urizon Books, 1976.

De Grazia, Margreta. "Teleology, Delay, and the 'Old Mole.'" *Shakespeare Quarterly* 50, no. 3 (1999): 251–67.

Dejacques, Joseph. *Les Lazaréennes: Fables et Poésies Sociales*. Paris: Chez l'auteur, 1851.

Depew, David J. "Aristotle's *De Anima* and Marx's *Theory of Man*." *Graduate Faculty Philosophy Journal* 8, no. 1 (1982): 133–87.

Derrida, Jacques. *Specters of Marx: The State of the Debt, the Work of Mourning, and the New International*. London: Routledge, 1994.

De Ste. Croix, G.E.M. *The Class Struggle in the Ancient Greek World: From the Archaic Age to the Arab Conquests*. Ithaca, NY: Cornell University Press, 1981.

Draper, Hal. *Karl Marx's Theory of Revolution*. Vol. 4. 4 vols. New York: Monthly Review Press, 1990.

Dunn, John. "Unimagined Community: The Deceptions of Socialist Internationalism." In *Rethinking Modern Political Theory: Essays 1979–83*, 103–18. Cambridge: Cambridge University Press, 1985.

Economakis, George E. "On Absolute Rent: Theoretical Remarks on Marx's Analysis." *Science and Society* 67, no. 3 (2003): 339–48.

Edmonds, Radcliffe G., III. *Myths of the Underworld Journey: Plato, Aristophanes, and the "Orphic" Gold Tablets*. Cambridge: Cambridge University Press, 2004.

Elliott, John E. "Marx and Contemporary Models of Socialist Economy." *History of Political Economy* 8, no. 2 (1976): 151–84.

Elson, Diane. "The Value Theory of Labour." In *Value: The Representation of Labour in Capitalism*. London: CSE Books, 1979.

———. *Value: The Representation of Labour in Capitalism*. London: CSE Books, 1979.

Elster, Jon. *Making Sense of Marx*. Cambridge: Cambridge University Press, 1985.

———. "Marxism, Functionalism, and Game Theory." In *Analytical Marxism*, edited by John E. Roemer, 202–20. Studies in Marxism and Social Theory. Cambridge; Paris: Cambridge University Press; Editions de la Maison des Sciences de l'Homme, 1986.

Endnotes, and Aaron Benanav. "Misery and Debt: On the Logic and History of Surplus Populations and Surplus Capital." *Endnotes* 2 (April 2010): n.p.

Enfantin, Barthélemy Prosper. "Considérations sur la Baisse Progressive du Loyer des Objets Mobilier et Immobilier, Article Iᵉʳ." *Le Producteur* 1 (1825): 241–53.

Euchner, Walter, and Alfred Schmidt, eds. *Kritik der politischen Ökonomie heute: 100 Jahre "Kapital."* Frankfurt am Main: Europäische Verlagsanstalt, 1968.

Faure, Alain, and Jacques Rancière, eds. *La Parole Ouvrière, 1830–1851*. Paris: Inédit 10/18, 1976.

Federici, Silvia. *Caliban and the Witch: Women, the Body, and Primitive Accumulation*. Autonomedia, 2004.

Felix, David. *Marx as Politician*. Carbondale: Southern Illinois University Press, 1983.

Fourier, Charles. *Cités Ouvrières: Extrait de La Phalange*. Paris: Librairie phalansterienne, 1849.

———. *Pièges et Charlatanisme des Deux Sectes Saint-Simon et Owen*. Paris: Bossange, 1831.

———. *The Theory of the Four Movements*. Edited by Gareth Stedman Jones and Ian Patterson. Cambridge: Cambridge University Press, 1996.

———. *Traité de L'association Domestique-Agricole ou Attraction Industrielle*. Paris and London: Bossange, Mongie, et Bossange, 1822.

Freccero, John. *Dante: The Poetics of Conversion*. Cambridge, MA: Harvard University Press, 1986.

———. "Dante's Pilgrim in a Gyre." *PMLA* 76, no. 3 (1961): 168–81.

Garnett, Ronald George. *Co-operation and the Owenite Socialist Communities in Britain, 1825–45*. Manchester: Manchester University Press, 1972.

Garver, Eugene. *Confronting Aristotle's Ethics: Ancient and Modern Morality*. Chicago: University of Chicago Press, 2006.

Geras, Norman. "Bringing Marx to Justice." *New Left Review* 195 (1992): 37–59.

———. "Essence and Appearance: Aspects of Fetishism in Marx's 'Capital.'" *New Left Review* 65 (1971): 69–85.

———. *Marx and Human Nature: Refutation of a Legend*. London: Verso, 1983.

Ghosh, Eric. "From Republican to Liberal Liberty." *History of Political Thought* 29, no. 1 (2008): 132–67.

Giddens, Anthony. *A Contemporary Critique of Historical Materialism*. London: Macmillan, 1981.

Gilbert, Alan. "Historical Theory and the Structure of Moral Argument in Marx." *Political Theory* 9, no. 2 (1981): 173–205.

———. *Marx's Politics: Communists and Citizens*. New Brunswick, NJ: Rutgers University Press, 1981.

Godels, Greg. "Marx, Engels, and the Idea of Exploitation." *Nature, Society, and Thought* 10, no. 4 (1997): 509–22.

Godwin, William. *Enquiry concerning Political Justice and Its Influence on Morals and Happiness: In Two Volumes*. London: G. G. and J. Robinson, 1796.

———. *The Enquirer: Reflections on Education, Manners, and Literature*. London, 1797.

Goodwin, Barbara. *Social Science and Utopia: Nineteenth Century Models of Social Harmony*. Brighton: Harvester Press, 1978.

Gould, Carol C. *Marx's Social Ontology: Individuality and Community in Marx's Theory of Social Reality*. Cambridge, MA: MIT Press, 1980.

Gourevitch, Alex. *From Slavery to the Cooperative Commonwealth: Labor and Republican Liberty in the Nineteenth Century*. Cambridge: Cambridge University Press, 2014.

———. "Labor Republicanism and the Transformation of Work." *Political Theory* 41, no. 4 (2013): 591–617.

Gramsci, Antonio. *The Antonio Gramsci Reader: Selected Writings, 1916–1935*. Edited by David Forgacs. New York: New York University Press, 2000.

Gray, John. *Lecture on Human Happiness; Being the First of a Series of Lectures on That Subject in Which Will Be Comprehended a General Review of the Causes of the Existing Evils of Society [and a Development of Means by Which They May Be Permanently and Effectually Removed. To Which Are Added the Preamble and Constitution of the Friendly Association for Mutual Interests, Located at Valley Forge]*. New York: A. M. Kelley, 1971.

————. *The Social System: A Treatise on the Principle of Exchange.* Clifton, NJ: A. M. Kelley, 1973.

Grossman, Henryk. *Marx, die Klassische Nationalökonomie und das Problem der Dynamik.* 2nd ed. Politische Ökonomie, Geschichte und Kritik. Frankfurt am Main: Europa Verlag, 1969.

Gurvitch, Georges, *Les fondateurs français de la sociologie contemporaine: Saint-Simon et P. J. Proudhon.* Paris: Centre de Documentation Universitaire, 1958.

Hare, R. M. *The Language of Morals.* Oxford: Clarendon Press, 1952.

Harries, Martin. *Scare Quotes from Shakespeare: Marx, Keynes, and the Language of Reenchantment.* Stanford, CA: Stanford University Press, 2000.

Harrison, J.F.C. *Robert Owen and the Owenites in Britain and America: The Quest for the New Moral World.* London: Routledge and Kegan Paul, 1969.

Harsin, Jill. *Barricades: The War of the Streets in Revolutionary Paris, 1830–1848.* Basingstoke and New York: Palgrave Macmillan, 2002.

Hart, David K. "Saint-Simon and the Role of the Elite." *Western Political Quarterly* 17, no. 3 (1964): 423–31.

Harvey, David. *A Companion to Marx's Capital.* London: Verso, 2010.

Hayek, Friedrich A. von. *The Constitution of Liberty.* Chicago: University of Chicago Press, 1978.

————. *The Road to Serfdom.* Chicago: University of Chicago Press, 1994.

————. "The Use of Knowledge in Society." *American Economic Review* 35, no. 4 (1945): 519–30.

Hegel, Georg Wilhelm Frierich. *The Philosophy of Right.* Translated by Alan White. The Focus Philosophical Library. Newburyport, MA: Focus Publishing; R. Pullins, 2002.

Heinrich, Michael. *An Introduction to the Three Volumes of Karl Marx's Capital.* Translated by Alexander Locascio. New York: Monthly Review Press, 2012.

Heller, Agnes. *The Theory of Need in Marx.* London: Allison and Busby, 1976.

Hilton, Rodney, ed. *The Transition from Feudalism to Capitalism.* Foundations of History Library. London: New Left Books, 1976.

Hirschman, Albert O. *The Passions and the Interests: Political Arguments for Capitalism before Its Triumph.* Princeton, NJ: Princeton University Press, 1977.

Hobsbawm, Eric J. "Marx, Engels, and Pre-Marxian Socialism." In *The History of Marxism, Volume One: Marxism in Marx's Day*, edited by Eric J. Hobsbawm, 1:1–28. Bloomington: Indiana University Press, 1982.

Hodgskin, Thomas. *Labour Defended against the Claims of Capital; or, The Unproductiveness of Capital Proved with Reference to the Present Combinations amongst Journeymen.* Reprints of Economic Classics. New York: A. M. Kelley, 1963.

————. *The Natural and Artificial Right of Property Contrasted.* Clifton, NJ: A. M. Kelley, 1973.

Hoffman, Robert Louis. *Revolutionary Justice: The Social and Political Theory of P.-J. Proudhon.* Urbana: University of Illinois Press, 1972.

Holbrook, Peter. *Shakespeare's Individualism.* Cambridge: Cambridge University Press, 2010.

Hollander, Samuel. "The Post-Ricardian Dissension: A Case-Study in Economics and Ideology." *Oxford Economic Papers* 32, no. 3 (1980): 370–410.

Holton, R. J. *The Transition from Feudalism to Capitalism*. Basingstoke: Macmillan, 1985.

Hont, Istvan, and Michael Ignatieff. "Needs and Justice in the Wealth of Nations: An Introductory Essay." In *Wealth and Virtue: The Shaping of Political Economy in the Scottish Enlightenment*, edited by Istvan Hont and Michael Ignatieff, 1–44. Cambridge: Cambridge University Press, 1983.

Howard, Michael Charles, and John Edward King. *The Political Economy of Marx*. 2nd ed. New York: New York University Press, 1988.

Hunt, Ian. *Analytical and Dialectical Marxism*. Avebury Series in Philosophy. Aldershot and Brookfield, VT: Avebury, 1993.

Hunt, Richard N. *The Political Ideas of Marx and Engels*. 2 vols. Pittsburgh: University of Pittsburgh Press, 1974 and 1984.

Iggers, Georg G. *The Cult of Authority: The Political Philosophy of the Saint-Simonians*. Leiden: M. Nijhoff, 1958.

Ince, Onur Ulas. "Colonial Capitalism and the Dilemmas of Liberalism: Locke, Burke, Wakefield, and the British Empire." PhD. diss., Cornell University, 2013.

Isaac, Jeffrey C. "The Lion's Skin of Politics: Marx on Republicanism." *Polity* 22, no. 3 (1990): 461–88.

IWMA (International Working Men's Association). *The General Council of the First International, 1866–1868: Minutes*. Moscow: Progress Publishers, 1964.

Jaffe, James A. "Commerce, Character, and Civil Society: Critiques of Capitalism during the Early Industrial Period." *European Legacy* 6, no. 2 (2001): 251–64.

James, Selma. *Sex, Race, and Class: The Perspective of Winning, a Selection of Writings 1952–2011*. Oakland, CA: PM Press, 2012.

Jameson, Fredric. *Representing "Capital": A Reading of Volume One*. New York: Verso, 2011.

Jevons, William Stanley. *Money and the Mechanism of Exchange*. New York: D. Appleton, 1876.

Jossa, Bruno. "Marx, Marxism, and the Cooperative Movement." *Cambridge Journal of Economics* 29, no. 1 (2005): 3–18.

Kapust, Daniel. "Skinner, Pettit, and Livy: The Conflict of the Orders and the Ambiguity of Republican Liberty." *History of Political Thought* 30, no. 3 (2010): 377–401.

Katz, Claudio. "The Socialist Polis: Antiquity and Socialism in Marx's Thought." *Review of Politics* 56, no. 2 (1994): 237–60.

Kellner, Douglas. "Marxism, Morality, and Ideology." Edited by Kai Nielsen and Steven C. Patten. *Canadian Journal of Philosophy* supplementary volume 7 (1981): 93–120.

Kent, Bonnie Dorrick. "Transitory Vice: Thomas Aquinas on Incontinence." *Journal of the History of Philosophy* 27, no. 2 (1989): 199–223.

King, J. E. (John Edward). "Utopian or Scientific?: A Reconsideration of the Ricardian Socialists." *History of Political Economy* 15 (1983): 345–73.

Knowles, Rob. *Political Economy from Below: Economic Thought in Communitarian Anarchism, 1840–1914*. New York: Routledge, 2004.

Krätke, Michael. "'Hier bricht das Manuskript ab.' (Engels): Hat Das Kapital einen Schluss?" Beitraege Zur Marx-Engels-Forschung, Neue Folge, 2001, 7–43.

Krause, Sharon. "Beyond Non-Domination: Agency, Inequality, and the Meaning of Freedom." *Philosophy and Social Criticism* 39, no. 2 (2013): 187–208.

Lapides, Kenneth. *Marx's Wage Theory in Historical Perspective*. Westport, CT: Praeger, 1998.

Lattek, Christine. *Revolutionary Refugees: German Socialism in Britain, 1840–1860*. Routledge Studies in Modern British History. London and New York: Routledge, 2006.

Lebowitz, Michael A. *Beyond "Capital": Marx's Political Economy of the Working Class*. 2nd ed. New York: Palgrave Macmillan, 2003.

———. *Following Marx: Method, Critique and Crisis*. Historical Materialism Book Series 20. Leiden and Boston: Brill, 2009.

Lechevalier, Jules. "What Can the Pope Do?" *Reasoner* 7, no. 14 (1849): 217–18.

Lenin, V. I. *Collected Works*. Edited by Robert Daglish. Translated by George Hanna. 4th ed. Vol. 19. Moscow: Progress Publishers, 1968.

———. *Collected Works*. Edited by Stewart Smith. Translated by Clemence Dutt. 4th ed. Vol. 38. Moscow: Progress Publishers, 1976.

Leopold, David. "The Structure of Marx and Engels' Considered Account of Utopian Socialism." *History of Political Thought* 26, no. 3 (2005): 433–66.

———. *The Young Karl Marx: German Philosophy, Modern Politics, and Human Flourishing*. Cambridge: Cambridge University Press, 2007.

Liebknecht, Wilhelm. *Karl Marx: Biographical Memoirs*. Translated by Ernest Untermann. Chicago: C. H. Kerr, 1901.

Llorente, Renzo. "Marx's Concept of 'Universal Class': A Rehabilitation." *Science and Society* 77, no. 4 (2013): 536–60.

Logar, Tea. "Exploitation as Wrongful Use: Beyond Taking Advantage of Vulnerabilities." *Acta Analytica* 25 (2010): 329–46.

Loria, Achille. *Karl Marx*. Translated by Eden Paul and Cedar Paul. London: Thomas Seltzer, 1920.

Loubère, Leo A. *Louis Blanc: His Life and His Contribution to the Rise of French Jacobin-Socialism*. Evanston, IL: Northwestern University Press, 1961.

Lowenthal, Esther. *The Ricardian Socialists*. Clifton, NJ: A. M. Kelley, 1972.

Löwy, Michael. *The Theory of Revolution in the Young Marx*. Historical Materialism Book Series. Chicago: Haymarket Books, 2005.

Lukács, György. *History and Class Consciousness: Studies in Marxist Dialectics*. Translated by Rodney Livingstone. London: Merlin Press, 1971.

MacGilvray, Eric. *The Invention of Market Freedom*. Cambridge and New York: Cambridge University Press, 2011.

Maddox, Graham. "The Limits of Neo-Roman Liberty." *History of Political Thought* 23, no. 3 (2002): 418–31.

Maguire, John M. *Marx's Theory of Politics*. Cambridge: Cambridge University Press, 1978.

Mansfield, Harvey C., Jr. "Marx on Aristotle." *Review of Metaphysics* 37 (1980): 351–67.

Markell, Patchen. "The Insufficiency of Non-Domination." *Political Theory* 36, no. 1 (2008): 9–36.

McCarney, Joseph. *Hegel on History*. Routledge Philosophy GuideBooks. London: Taylor and Francis, 2012.

McCloskey, Dierdre N. "New Perspectives on the Old Poor Law." *Explorations in Economic History* 10 (1973): 419–36.

McCormick, John P. "Machiavelli against Republicanism: On the Cambridge School's 'Guiccardian Moments.'" *Political Theory* 31, no. 5 (2003): 615–43.

McLellan, David. Introduction to *Marx's Grundrisse*. Basingstoke: Macmillan, 1980.

———. *Karl Marx: His Life and Thought*. New York: Harper Colophon Books, 1973.

McNally, David. *Against the Market: Political Economy, Market Socialism and the Marxist Critique*. London: Verso, 1993.

———. *Monsters of the Market: Zombies, Vampires, and Global Capitalism*. Chicago: Haymarket Books, 2012.

Meek, Ronald L. *Studies in the Labour Theory of Value*. Modern Reader Paperback. New York: Monthly Review Press, 1975.

Megill, Allan. *Karl Marx: The Burden of Reason (Why Marx Rejected Politics and the Market)*. Lanham, MD: Rowman and Littlefield, 2002.

Mehta, Uday Singh. *Liberalism and Empire: A Study in Nineteenth-Century British Liberal Thought*. Chicago: University of Chicago Press, 1999.

Meikle, S. *Essentialism in the Thought of Karl Marx*. London: Duckworth, 1985.

Menger, Anton. *The Right to the Whole Produce of Labour: The Origin and Development of the Theory of Labour's Claim to the Whole Product of Industry*. Translated by M. E. Tanner. London: Macmillan, 1899.

Menger, Carl. "On the Origins of Money." Translated by C. A. Foley. *Economic Journal* 2 (1892): 239–55.

Menuelle, Thierry. *Marx, Lecteur de Proudhon*. Vol. 1. Paris: École des hautes études en sciences sociales, 1993.

Milgate, Murray, and Shannon C. Stimson. *Ricardian Politics*. Princeton, NJ: Princeton University Press, 1991.

Miller, Clarence H. "Hercules and His Labors as Allegories of Christ and His Victory over Sin in Dante's Inferno." *Quaderni D'italianistica* 5, no. 1 (1985): 1–17.

Miller, David. "Marx, Communism and Markets." *Political Theory: An International Journal of Political Philosophy* 15 (1987): 182–204.

Miller, Richard W. "Aristotle and Marx: The Unity of Two Opposites." In *Proceedings of the American Political Science Association*. Ann Arbor: University of Michigan Press, 1978.

———. "Marx and Aristotle: A Kind of Consequentialism." In *Marx and Morality*, by Kai Nielsen and Steven C. Patten, 323–52. *Canadian Journal of Philosophy* supplementary volume. Guelph, ON: Canadian Association for Publishing in Philosophy, 1981.

Mohun, Simon. "Ideology, Markets and Money." *Cambridge Journal of Economics* 27, no. 3 (2003): 401–18.

Montag, Warren. *Althusser and His Contemporaries: Philosophy's Perpetual War*. Durham, NC: Duke University Press, 2013.

Montesquieu, C. S. *The Spirit of the Laws*. Edited by A. M. Cohler, B. Miller, and H. S. Stone. Cambridge: Cambridge University Press, 1989.

Moore, J. M., trans. *Aristotle and Xenophon on Democracy and Oligarchy*. 2nd ed. Berkeley: University of California Press, 1986.

Mouritsen, Henrik. *The Freedman in the Roman World*. Cambridge: Cambridge University Press, 2011.

Murray, Patrick. *Marx's Theory of Scientific Knowledge*. Amherst, NY: Prometheus Books, 1990.

———. "Reply to Geert Reuten." *Historical Materialism* 10, no. 1 (2002): 155–76.

Negri, Antonio. "Twenty Theses on Marx: Interpretation of the Class Situation Today." Translated by Michael Hardt. In *Marxism beyond Marxism*, edited by Saree Makdisi, Cesare Casarino, and Rebecca E. Karl, 149–80. New York: Routledge, 1996.

Neocleous, Mark. "The Political Economy of the Dead: Marx's Vampires." *History of Political Thought* 24, no. 4 (2003): 668–84.

Noland, Aaron. "History and Humanity: The Proudhonian Vision." In *The Uses of History: Essays in Intellectual and Social History*, edited by Hayden V. White, 59–105. Detroit: Wayne State University Press, 1968.

———. "Proudhon's Sociology of War." *American Journal of Economics and Sociology* 29, no. 3 (1970): 289–304.

Norman, Richard, and Sean Sayers. *Hegel, Marx, and Dialectic: A Debate*. Brighton; Atlantic Highlands, NJ: Harvester Press; Humanities Press, 1980.

North, Douglass C. *Structure and Change in Economic History*. New York: W. W. Norton, 1981.

O'Brien, James Bronterre. *The Rise, Progress and Phases of Human Slavery: How It Came into the World and How It Shall Be Made to Go Out*. London: William Reeves and Martin James Boon, 1885.

O'Kane, Chris. "Fetishism and Social Domination in Marx, Lukács, Adorno, and Lefebvre." PhD diss., University of Sussex, 2013.

Ollman, Bertell. "Marx's Vision of Communism: A Reconstruction." *Critique* 8, no. 1 (1977): 4–41.

O'Neill, John. "Markets, Socialism and Information: A Reformulation of a Marxian Objection to the Market." *Social Philosophy and Policy* 6 (1989): 200–210.

Owen, Robert. *A New View of Society and Other Writings*. Edited by Gregory Claeys. London: Penguin, 1991.

———. *The Revolution in the Mind and Practice of the Human Race; or, The Coming Change from Irrationality to Rationality*. London: Effingham Wilson, 1849.

Panichas, George E. "Vampires, Werewolves, and Economic Exploitation." *Social Theory and Practice* 7, no. 2 (1981): 223–42.

Perelman, Michael. *The Invention of Capitalism: Classical Political Economy and the Secret History of Primitive Accumulation*. Durham, NC: Duke University Press, 2000.

Pettit, Philip. "Akrasia, Collective and Individual." In *Weakness of Will and Practical Irrationality*, edited by Sarah Stroud and Christine Tappolet, 68–96. Oxford: Oxford University Press, 2003.

———. *The Common Mind: An Essay on Psychology, Sociology and Politics*. Oxford: Oxford University Press, 2004.

———. "Discourse Theory and Republican Freedom." In *Republicanism: History, Theory, and Practice*, edited by Daniel M. Weinstock and Christian Nadeau, 72–95. London: Frank Cass, 2004.

———. "Freedom in the Market." *Politics, Philosophy, and Economics* 5 (2006): 131–49.

———. *Republicanism: A Theory of Freedom and Government.* Oxford and New York: Clarendon Press, 1997.

———. *A Theory of Freedom: From the Psychology to the Politics of Agency.* Cambridge: Polity, 2001.

Philip, Bruce. "Marxism, Neoclassical Economics and the Length of the Working Day." *Review of Political Economy* 13, no. 1 (2001): 27–39.

Pike, J. *From Aristotle to Marx: Aristotelianism in Marxist Social Ontology.* Aldershot: Ashgate, 1999.

Pilbeam, Pamela. *French Socialists before Marx.* Montreal and Kingston: McGill-Queen's University Press, 2000.

———. *Saint-Simonians in Nineteenth-Century France: From Free Love to Algeria.* Basingstoke and New York: Palgrave Macmillan, 2014.

Pitts, Jennifer. *A Turn to Empire: The Rise of Imperial Liberalism in Britain and France.* Princeton, NJ: Princeton University Press, 2009.

Plummer, Alfred. *Bronterre: A Political Biography of Bronterre O'Brien, 1804–1864.* London: Allen and Unwin, 1971.

Pocock, J.G.A. *The Machiavellian Moment: Florentine Political Thought and the Atlantic Republican Tradition.* Princeton, NJ: Princeton University Press, 1975.

Popper, Karl R. *The Open Society and Its Enemies.* New one-volume edition. Princeton, NJ: Princeton University Press, 2013.

Postone, Moishe. "Lukács and the Dialectical Critique of Capitalism." In *New Dialectics and Political Economy*, edited by R. Albritton and J. Simoulidis, 78–100. New York: Palgrave Macmillan, 2003.

———. *Time, Labor, and Social Domination: A Reinterpretation of Marx's Critical Theory.* Cambridge: Cambridge University Press, 1993.

Prawer, Siegbert Salomon. *Karl Marx and World Literature.* Oxford: Clarendon Press, 1976.

Prichard, Alex. *Justice, Order and Anarchy: The International Political Theory of Pierre-Joseph Proudhon.* London and New York: Routledge, 2013.

Prinz, Arthur M. "Background and Ulterior Motive of Marx's 'Preface' of 1859." *Journal of the History of Ideas* 30, no. 3 (1969): 437–50.

Puech, Jules L. "Le Proudhonisme dans l'Association Internationale des Travailleurs." F. Alcan, 1907.

Rabinbach, Anson. *The Human Motor: Energy, Fatigue, and the Origins of Modernity.* Berkeley: University of California Press, 1992.

Rae, John. "Ferdinand Lassalle and German Socialism." *Contemporary Review* 39, no. 6 (1881): 921–43.

Rambaud, Alfred. *Histoire de La Civilization Contemporaine en France.* Paris: Colin, 1888.

Ramirez, Miguel D. "Marx's Theory of Ground Rent: A Critical Assessment." *Contributions to Political Economy* 28, no. 1 (2009): 71–91.

Rancière, Jacques. *The Nights of Labor: The Workers' Dream in Nineteenth-Century France.* Translated by John Drury. Philadelphia: Temple University Press, 1989.

Read, Jason. *The Micro-Politics of Capital: Marx and the Prehistory of the Present*. Albany: State University of New York Press, 2003.

Reeve, Andrew. "Thomas Hodgskin and John Bray: Free Exchange and Equal Exchange." In *Modern Theories of Exploitation*, edited by Andrew Reeve, 30–52. London: Sage, 1987.

Reiff, Mark R. *Exploitation and Economic Justice in the Liberal Capitalist State*. Oxford: Oxford University Press, 2013.

Reuten, Geert. "The Inner Mechanism of the Accumulation of Capital: The Acceleration Triple, a Methodological Appraisal of Part Seven of Marx's 'Capital' I." In *The Constitution of Capital: Essays on Volume I of Marx's "Capital,"* edited by Riccardo Bellofiore and Nicola Taylor, 274–98. Basingstoke: Palgrave Macmillan, 2004.

———. "The Interconnection of Systematic Dialectics and Historical Materialism." *Historical Materialism* 7, no. 1 (2000): 137–65.

Ricardo, David. *The Principles of Political Economy and Taxation*. Everyman's Library. London and New York: Dent, 1973.

Ripstein, Arthur. "Commodity Fetishism." *Canadian Journal of Philosophy* 17 (1987): 733–48.

Roberts, William Clare. "Marx Contra the Democrats: The Force of the Eighteenth Brumaire." *Strategies: Journal of Theory, Culture and Politics* 16, no. 1 (2003): 51–64.

———. "The Reconstitution of Marxism's Production Paradigm: The Cases of Benjamin, Althusser, and Marx." *Philosophical Forum* 41, no. 4 (2010): 413–40.

Rockwell, Llewellyn H., Jr. *The Left, the Right, and the State*. Auburn, AL: Ludwig von Mises Institute, 2008.

Rodden, John. "'The Lever Must Be Applied in Ireland': Marx, Engels, and the Irish Question." *Review of Politics* 70, no. 4 (2008): 609–40.

Rodriguez-Braun, C. "*Capital's* Last Chapter." *History of Political Economy* 19, no. 2 (1987): 299–310.

Roemer, John E. "Exploitation, Class, and Property Relations." In *After Marx*, edited by Terence Ball and James Farr, 184–211. Cambridge: Cambridge University Press, 1984.

———. *A General Theory of Exploitation and Class*. Cambridge, MA: Harvard University Press, 1982.

———. "Should Marxists Be Interested in Exploitation?" In *Analytical Marxism*, edited by John E. Roemer, 260–82. Studies in Marxism and Social Theory. Cambridge; Paris: Cambridge University Press; Editions de la Maison des Sciences de l'Homme, 1986.

Roll, Erich. *A History of Economic Thought*. 2nd ed. London: Faber, 1954.

Rorty, Amélie Oksenberg. "The Social and Political Sources of Akrasia." *Ethics* 107, no. 4 (1997): 644–57.

Roth, Mike, and Michael Eldred. *Guide to Marx's "Capital."* London: CSE Books, 1978.

Rousseau, Jean-Jacques. *Emile*. Translated by Barbara Foxley. London: Everyman, 1993.

Rubel, Maximilien. *Rubel on Karl Marx: Five Essays*. Edited by Joseph O'Malley and Keith Algozin. Cambridge: Cambridge University Press, 1981.

Rubel, Maximilien, and Margaret Manale. *Marx without Myth: A Chronological Study of His Life and Work*. New York: Harper and Row, 1975.

Rudé, George F. E. *The Crowd in History: A Study of Popular Disturbances in France and England, 1730–1848*. New Dimensions in History: Essays in Comparative History. London: Wiley, 1964.

Russo, Vittorio. *Sussidi di Esegesi Dantesca*. Naples: Liguori, 1967.

Ryan, Alan. "Justice, Exploitation, and the End of Morality." In *Moral Philosophy and Contemporary Problems*, edited by J.D.G. Evans, 117–34. Royal Institute of Philosophy Lecture Series 22. Cambridge: Cambridge University Press, 1987.

Sanderson, John. *An Interpretation of the Political Ideas of Marx and Engels*. Monographs in Politics. London: Longmans, 1969.

———. "Marx and Engels on the State." *Western Political Quarterly* 16, no. 4 (1963): 946–55.

Schapiro, J. Salwyn. "Pierre Joseph Proudhon, Harbinger of Fascism." *American Historical Review* 50, no. 4 (1945): 714–37.

Schmidt, Klaus. *Andreas Gottschalk: Armenarzt und Pionier der Arbeiterbewegung, Jude und Protestant*. Cologne: Greven Verlag, 2002.

Schumpeter, Joseph A. "'The Communist Manifesto' in Sociology and Economics." *Journal of Political Economy* 47, no. 3 (1949): 199–212.

Schwartz, Nancy L. "Distinction between Public and Private Life: Marx on the Zoon Politikon." *Political Theory* 7, no. 2 (1979): 245–66.

Schweikart, David. "On the Exploitation of Cotton, Corn, and Labor." *Canadian Journal of Philosophy* supplementary volume 15 (1989): 281–97.

Sensat, J. "Exploitation." *Nous* 18, no. 1 (1984): 21–38.

Shakespeare, Rodney, and RT (Russia Today). "Global Finance Capitalism Is a Fraud," December 4, 2013. http://on.rt.com/ttmt6y.

Shortall, Felton C. *The Incomplete Marx*. Avebury Series in Philosophy. Aldershot and Brookfield, VT: Avebury, 1994.

Skinner, Quentin. "The Idea of Negative Liberty." In *Philosophy in History*, edited by Richard Rorty, J. B. Schneewind, and Quentin Skinner, 193–221. Cambridge: Cambridge University Press, 1984.

———. *Liberty before Liberalism*. Cambridge: Cambridge University Press, 1998.

Smith, Adam. *An Inquiry into the Nature and Causes of the Wealth of Nations*. Edited by Edwin Cannan. Chicago: University of Chicago Press, 1976.

Smith, Jason E. "Jacques Derrida, 'Crypto-Communist?'" In *Critical Companion to Contemporary Marxism*, edited by Jacques Bidet and Stathis Kouvelakis, 625–46. Historical Materialism Book Series. Leiden: Brill, 2005.

Smith, Tony. *The Logic of Marx's Capital: Replies to Hegelian Criticisms*. SUNY Series in the Philosophy of the Social Sciences. Albany: State University of New York Press, 1990.

Sohn-Rethel, A. *Intellectual and Manual Labour: A Critique of Epistemology*. Translated by M. Sohn-Rethel. London: Macmillan, 1978.

Sperber, Jonathan. *Karl Marx: A Nineteenth-Century Life*. New York: Liveright, 2013.

————. *Rhineland Radicals: The Democratic Movement and the Revolution of 1848–1849*. Princeton, NJ: Princeton University Press, 1993.

Springborg, Patricia. "Politics, Primordialism, and Orientalism: Marx, Aristotle, and the Myth of the Gemeinschaft." *American Political Science Review* 80, no. 1 (1986): 185–211.

Stafford, William. *Socialism, Radicalism, and Nostalgia: Social Criticism in Britain, 1775–1830*. Cambridge: Cambridge University Press, 1987.

Stallybrass, Peter. "'Well Grubbed, Old Mole': Marx, Hamlet, and the (Un)Fixing of Representation." *Cultural Studies* 12, no. 1 (1998): 3–14.

Stark, Werner. "Saint-Simon as a Realist." *Journal of Economic History* 3, no. 1 (1943): 42–55.

Stein, Hans. *Der Kölner Arbeiterverein, 1848–1849*. Berlin: Auvermann, 1972.

Stekloff, G. M. *History of the First International*. New York: Russell and Russell, 1968.

Strassmaier, James. "Karl Grün: The Confrontation with Marx, 1844–1848." PhD diss., Loyola University, 1969.

————. *Karl Grün und die Kommunistische Partei, 1845–1848*. Trier: Karl-Marx-Haus, 1973.

Tanner, R. "Marx's Theory of Commodity Fetishism as the Unstated Premise of What Is to Be Done?" *Rethinking Marxism* 13, no. 1 (2001): 57–68.

Tawney, R. H. *Religion and the Rise of Capitalism*. New Brunswick, NJ: Transaction Publishers, 1998.

Taylor, James Stephen. "The Mythology of the Old Poor Law." *Journal of Economic History* 29, no. 2 (1969): 292–97.

Taylor, Keith. *The Political Ideas of the Utopian Socialists*. London: Cass, 1982.

Taylor, Nicola, and Riccardo Bellofiore. "Marx's 'Capital' I, the Constitution of Capital: General Introduction." In *The Constitution of Capital: Essays on Volume I of Marx's "Capital,"* edited by Riccardo Bellofiore and Nicola Taylor, 1–34. Basingstoke: Palgrave Macmillan, 2004.

Thomas, Paul. *Karl Marx and the Anarchists*. London and Boston: Routledge and Kegan Paul, 1980.

Thompson, E. P. *The Making of the English Working Class*. London: Penguin, 1991.

————. "The Moral Economy of the English Crowd in the Eighteenth Century." *Past and Present* 50 (February 1971): 76–136.

Thompson, Noel W. *The Market and Its Critics: Socialist Political Economy in Nineteenth Century Britain*. London and New York: Routledge, 1988.

————. *The People's Science: The Popular Political Economy of Exploitation and Crisis 1816–34*. Cambridge: Cambridge University Press, 1984.

Thompson, William. *An Inquiry into the Principles of the Distribution of Wealth Most Conducive to Human Happiness Applied to the Newly Proposed System of Voluntary Equality of Wealth*. 2nd ed. London: Longman, 1850.

————. *Labour Rewarded: The Claims of Labour and Capital Conciliated; or, How to Secure to Labour the Whole Product of Its Exertion*. New York: A. M. Kelley, 1969.

Tiqqun. *Introduction to Civil War*. Translated by Alexander R. Galloway and Jason E. Smith. Intervention 4. Los Angeles: Semiotext(e), 2010.

Trox, Eckhard. *Karl Grün (1817–1887): Eine Biographie*. Lüdenscheid: Kultur-dezernat der Stadt Lüdenscheid, 1993.

Uchida, Hiroshi. "Marx's Theory of History Reappaised." In *Marx for the 21st Century*, edited by Hiroshi Uchida, 39–52. Routledge Frontiers of Political Economy. London: Taylor and Francis, 2004.

Van Donselaar, Gijs. *The Right to Exploit: Parasitism, Scarcity, Basic Income*. Oxford: Oxford University Press, 2009.

Van Gelderen, Martin, and Quentin Skinner. *Republicanism: A Shared European Heritage*. Vol. 1. Cambridge: Cambridge University Press, 2005.

Van Leeuwen, Arend T. *Critique of Earth*. Reprint. Cambridge: James Clarke, 2002.

Vandenberghe, Frédéric. *A Philosophical History of German Sociology*. London: Routledge, 2009.

Venturi, Franco. "Oriental Despotism." *Journal of the History of Ideas* 24, no. 1 (1963): 133–42.

Vincent, K. Steven. *Pierre-Joseph Proudhon and the Rise of French Republican Socialism*. Oxford: Oxford University Press, 1984.

Virno, P. "Natural-Historical Diagrams: The 'New Global Movement' and the Biological Invariant." In *The Italian Differences: Between Nihilism and Bio-politics*, edited by A. Toscano and L. Chiesa. Victoria, Australia: re.press, 2009.

Vrousalis, Nicholas. "Exploitation, Vulnerability, and Social Domination." *Philosophy and Public Affairs* 41, no. 2 (2013): 131–57.

Wade, Francis C. "On Violence." *Journal of Philosophy* 68, no. 12 (1971): 369–77.

Wakefield, E. G. *England and America: A Comparison of the Social and Political State of Both Nations*. Vol. 1. 2 vols. London: R. Bentley, 1833.

Walker, Gavin. *The Sublime Perversion of Capital: Marxist Theory and the Politics of History in Modern Japan*. Durham, NC: Duke University Press, 2016.

Wallerstein, Immanuel. *The Capitalist World-Economy*. Studies in Modern Capitalism. Cambridge; Paris: Cambridge University Press; Editions de la Maison des Sciences de l'Homme, 1979.

Walter, E. V. "Power and Violence." *American Political Science Review* 58, no. 2 (1964): 350–60.

Wayne, M. "Fetishism and Ideology: A Reply to Dimoulis and Milios." *Historical Materialism* 13, no. 3 (2005): 193.

Weeks, John. *Capital and Exploitation*. Princeton, NJ: Princeton University Press, 1981.

Weeks, Kathi. *The Problem with Work: Feminism, Marxism, Antiwork Politics, and Postwork Imaginaries*. Durham, NC: Duke University Press, 2011.

Wendling, Amy E. *Karl Marx on Technology and Alienation*. Basingstoke and New York: Palgrave Macmillan, 2009.

Wheen, Francis. *Karl Marx: A Life*. 1st American ed. New York: Norton, 2000.

Wilbrandt, Robert. *Karl Marx: Versuch Einer Würdigung*. Aus Natur und Geisteswelt. Leipzig and Berlin: B. G. Teubner, 1919.

Williams, Michael. *Value, Social Form, and the State*. Basingstoke: Macmillan, 1988.

Williams, Simon. "Haupt- und Staatsaktion." Edited by Dennis Kennedy. *The Oxford Encyclopedia of Theatre and Performance*. Oxford: Oxford University

Press, 2003. http://www.oxfordreference.com/10.1093/acref/9780198601746 .001.0001/acref-9780198601746-e-1724.

Wilson, H. T. *Marx's Critical/Dialectical Procedure*. London: Routledge, 1991.

Wolff, Jonathan. "Playthings of Alien Forces." *Cogito* 6, no. 1 (1992): 35–41.

Wolff, Robert Paul. "How to Read *Das Kapital*." *Massachusetts Review* 21 (1980): 739–65.

Wood, Allen W. *Karl Marx*. 2nd ed. Arguments of the Philosophers. New York: Routledge, 2004.

Wood, Ellen Meiksins. *The Origin of Capitalism: A Longer View*. 2nd ed. London and New York: Verso, 2002.

———. "Why It Matters." *London Review of Books* 30, no. 18 (2008): 3–6.

Young, Gary. "Doing Marx Justice." In *Marx*, 251–68. *Canadian Journal of Philosophy* supplementary volume 7. Guelph, ON: Canadian Association for Publishing in Philosophy, 1981.

Index